T0367546

An Old Man Thinking for the First Time

James Kalm Fitzgerald

Having lived a life generally never late to appointments or obligations, an old man would discover that he was almost late to life. Life only found through a narrow gate. Even a late comer can become an overcomer.

authorHOUSE®

AuthorHouse™
1663 Liberty Drive
Bloomington, IN 47403
www.authorhouse.com
Phone: 833-262-8899

Published by AuthorHouse 05/21/2024

ISBN: 979-8-8230-1754-1 (sc)
ISBN: 979-8-8230-1755-8 (hc)
ISBN: 979-8-8230-1756-5 (e)

Library of Congress Control Number: 2023921829

Print information available on the last page.

TABLE OF CONTENTS

About the Cover 1

Acknowledgments 5

Prologue 9

Chapter 1 15
What Made Me Seek Jordan Peterson 15
~ Note for Jordan ~ 16

Chapter 2 23
The Internet 23

Chapter 3 27
Six Decades of Sin 27

Chapter 4 33
The 62nd year Away in Babylon 33
~ Right and Wrong ~ 35

Chapter 5 39
American Thoughts Before I Knew 39
Prayer for the Lawmakers 43
~ Beware O Man ~ 43
~ America the What ? ~ 45

Chapter 6......49
Lake Christos......49
~ The 1st creek - 300 A.D. ~......52
~ The 2nd creek – 600 A.D. ~......54
~ The 3rd creek – 1500 A.D. ~......61
~ Cloudy Waters 90 A.D. - 2023 A.D. ~......62
~ Lake Christos Summary ~......64
~ Lake Christos ~......68

Chapter 7......71
Baptism......71
Seeds and Scales of an Old Man Thinking for the 1st Time......72
>>> 1955 – Seeds <<<......72
>>> Tangent - Paedo Baptism <<<......73
>>> 1967 - Seeds <<<......81
>>> 1972 – Seeds <<<......82
>>> 1975 - Seeds <<<......82
>>> 1972 to July 1979 - Seeds & Scales <<<......84
>>> 1980 – Seeds <<<......84
>>> 1987 - Seeds and Scales <<<......85
>>> 1989 – Seeds <<<......86
>>> 1995 – Seeds and Scales <<<......86
>>> 2006 – Seeds and Scales <<<......87
>>> 2015 – Seeds <<<......87
>>> 2016 – Seeds - Reshaping the Pot <<<......87
>>> 2017 – Seeds <<<......88
>>> 2018 – Seeds <<<......88
>>> 2019 – Spring Time <<<......89
>>> 2020 – Spring <<<......90
~ Tangent – Time ~......90
>>> 2020 – Seeds <<<......92
~ Proof of Grace ~......93
>>> March 2020 <<<......93
>>> December 2020 <<<......93
>>> 2021 – The Scales Are Falling <<<......95
>>> 2022 – February <<<......97
>>> 2022 – March through July <<<......97
>>> 2022 – July 10 – The Plunge <<<......99

>>> My proclamation <<<.......... 100
~ In conclusion at least for this part of the journey ~ 102
~ Cousin John ~ 103

Chapter 8 107
Post Baptism 107
~ Other Journeys to the Water ~ 109
>>> Interview with Heaven <<< 113
>>> Other First Baptisms I Witnessed <<< 124
>>> Interview with Mike <<< 129
~ He Can ~ 138
>>> Interview with Gary <<< 140
~ Providence ~ 141

Chapter 9 143
First Encounters of the Close Kind 143
~ The Barbers ~ 143
>>> Barber 1 <<< 143
>>> Barber 2 <<< 146
>>> Barber 3 <<< 148
>>> Summary of Barbers <<< 149
~ Coffee Shops ~ 149
>>> Coffee in Glendale <<< 149
>>> Coffee in Loveland Colorado <<< 152
>>> Coffee in North Phoenix <<< 154
>>> Coffee, Bible Study & Bibles <<< 155
>>> Coffee Shop Santa <<< 156
>>> Summary of Coffee Shops <<< 158
>>> Meeting at the Gate <<< 158
Summary 1st Encounters of the Close Kind 160

Chapter 10 163
The Right Line 163
~ The Right Line ~ 165
~ American Two Party System ~ 167
~ Progressivism ~ 177
~ Concerning woke-ism ~ 182
~ Summary of ism's ~ 185

The Starting Line of "The Right Line" 185
~ The Right Line Summary ~ The Individual, not the group...187
~ The Right Line ~..189

Chapter 11..191
Wrath..191
~ Real Time Gospel Tangent ~ 195
~ Back to wrath ~...197
~ World Realities Stir our Wrath ~.................................199
>>> The Family <<<..199
>>> The Children <<< 200
>>> The Women <<< 203
~ A Prayer for the Girls ~ 203
~ Another Prayer for the Girls ~ 205
>>> Men <<<... 207
>>> Society and Media <<< 209
>>> Society Waking-Up <<<..215
>>> Society Still Asleep <<< 217
~ Prayer for the Liars ~ 220
>>> The State of the Christian Church <<< 221
~ Summary of Wrath ~.. 222
>>> Idolatry <<<... 223
>>> False gods <<<.. 225
>>> The Lords Name <<< 226
>>> Sabbath <<<.. 226
>>> Honor Father & Mother <<<......................................233
>>> Murder <<<...239
>>> Adultery <<< 244
>>> Theft <<< 254
>>> Theft of the State <<<...257
>>> Theft in the individual <<<..270
>>> Tangent <<<..271
>>> Thou shall not covet <<< 275
Final Thought on Gods Wrath 280

Chapter 12 283
Judgment... 283
An Admiralty Allegory of Judgment 284

~ Judgment for Real ~ 287
~ Summary Thoughts on Judgment ~ 292
~ Example of a Righteous Judge ~ 296

Chapter 13 301
Hope 301
~ Hope for the Young ~ 305
~ Hope for Nations ~ 306
~ Hope for Governments ~
Especially USA 310
~ Hope for "We the People" ~ 324
~ Hope for the Church ~ 325
~ Allegory of the Fish ~ 327
~ Politics & the Church ~ 333
~ The Hope that is Easter ~ 341
~ The Scope of Hope ~ 345

Chapter 14 349
Is Science anything w/o God 349
~ Theorem of An Atheist ~ 350
>>> Postulation # 1 <<< 351
>>> Postulation # 2 <<< 352
>>> Postulation # 3 <<< 352
>>> Atheist Theorem Questions <<< 353
~ Theorem of a Christian ~ 354
~ Observations --- recorded history ~ 355
>>> Postulation # 1 <<<
Things tangible & intangible 356
~ Conclusions ~ Competing Theorems 358
~ Giants of Science & Origins ~ 361
~ Top Scientists of the 21st Century ~ 363
>>> Genetics <<< 366
~ Summary of Science ~ 366
~ God Makes a Scientist ~ 370

Chapter 15 373
Transcendence 373
~ Transcend ~ 382

Chapter 16 385
Just a Thought.. 385
~ Splitting Time ~.. 385
~ Smashing of a Toe ~.. 386
~ Affirmation of Horror ~.. 388
~ Words ~.. 390
~ Notice vs. Assignment ~.. 392
~ The Erosion of Trust ~.. 395
~ Two Industries of Malfeasance ~
U.S. Corp & Main Stream Media.. 399
~ The Exception to the Rule ~.. 401
~ Wasted Time ~.. 403
~ Appealing to Authority ~.. 405
~ Socially Constructed Idiots ~.. 409

Chapter 17.. 419
Close Calls & Redemption.. 419
~ Ford Hill & Mountain Lion ~.. 419
~ Navy Seal & the Helicopter Pilot ~.. 421

Chapter 18.. 425
Wrap it Up.. 425
The Old Man was Thinking.. 429
~ Thinking About Thought ~.. 430

Epilogue.. 433
~ The Gift ~.. 436

ABOUT THE COVER

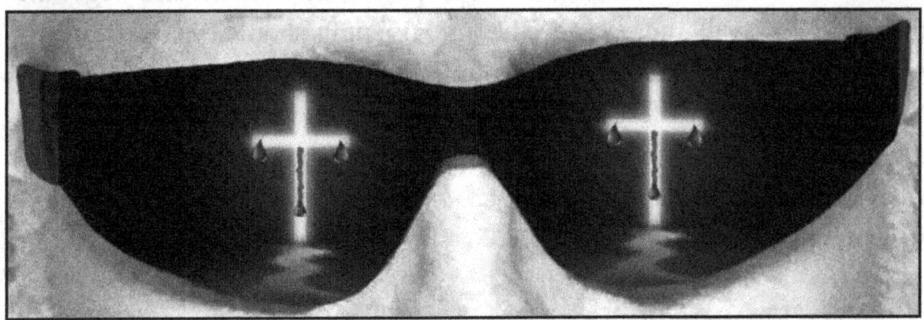

Something fair to say and proclaim is that as the graphic on the cover suggests, an old man is seeing the world and the way of things through a new set of lenses. It does accurately portray, and is a portrait of a truth. While the sunglasses with the Cross on the face of an old man explains at a glance what happened, and is happening to this old man, and that being that this world is now viewed with a sober, clear, introspective, logically considered view of what happened on that Cross.

> **superficial**: *presenting only an appearance without substance or significance*

Why it happened and what happened on the Cross and why for the first 62 years of my life I didn't see it can best be summarized by one of the definitions of "superficial" noted above. How could I have known?

How can one work through an algebraic equation without first understanding addition, subtraction, multiplication, and division. Then armed with those prerequisites working through the associative and distributive rules or laws that help the mind work through and see the answer in an algebraic equation. Basic math being foundational to algebra, which is foundational to calculus, which is foundational to higher and higher forms of mathematics. Each "discipline" of math being necessary to properly grasp and comprehend the "higher" forms. Those "disciplines" required "disciples" of math, or teachers, to show the truth of math. If one is interested in math study is required and discipleship is clearly helpful and most often required.

Reading, writing, and arithmetic and why the young need to be "discipled" in these "disciplines" to properly comprehend and negotiate the world is easy to understand. The fundamentals should be God, reading, writing, and arithmetic. Had my young life had God teachers in it, would things have been different? God only knows but what is reasonable is any and all I was exposed to as it concerns God, faith, and salvation was "superficial" that is, ***"presented only with an appearance without substance or significance."***

When I mastered any topic in school I had to work through the text, and often more than once. How then could I possibly comprehend fully the way of God without working through the text? I did not pick up the text until the 62nd year or 20% of the way into the 7th decade of my life. The previous statement a simple example of working through equations learned in math.

The text explains we are all at enmity with God. We don't think we are but we are. The why of that truth cannot be fully comprehended without working through the text? In like manner that I never would have been able to do an integral or a differential equation in calculus had I not first been taught addition as a 1st grader, I certainly could not understand the Cross and especially the resurrection had I not been taught the foundations of the Old Testament. But, in a twist of foundational learning I could not possibly comprehend the Old Testament until I first understood the New Testament. This truth took more than one pass through the text and many teachers.

That journey through the text, not once, but several times makes what students of the text refer to as the "scarlet thread" become a thing noticed after a time. With each journey through the valley of the text the scarlet thread becomes clearer and more obvious. Similar to the analogy of a city person walking through the woods and is oblivious to the signs that someone or something has passed where they now walk, but a tracker who has been discipled to know the signs and then studied the signs over and over sees clearly the way whom or what came before.

Sometimes an actual scarlet thread is referenced in the text and other times like a spider spins a web and leaves it in an inconspicuous corner or place, scarlet webs are left for the tracker; or reader; in inconspicuous places in the text that foreshadow the scarlet blood of Jesus on the Cross. One such scarlet web would be the scarlet web spun and left on the single and only door to the ark. Another would be the pitch used between the timbers of the ark to seal "in" salvation and seal "out" judgment for those "in" the ark. This scarlet web foreshadows the atoning blood of Jesus that seals "in" salvation for those that are "in" Christ; and seals "out" judgment for those "in" Christ.

Another would be scarlet webs left on both banks of the Red Sea, a single one-way route to safety and salvation. Perhaps the most awesome are the brightly colored scarlet webs left on the many characters in the Old Testament whose blood lineage was foretold to lead to the Messiah. On this side of the Cross the gospels and the epistles scribed from the Messiah's words make clear the scarlet threads left by those that had come before so that the trackers, i.e., the readers in our time can follow the path. Of course the end of all the scarlet thread tracking is the blood let by Jesus for anyone who would see Him and His scarlet blood and the why of that scarlet blood.

The "disciplines" or "doctrines" in the text of those teachers or "disciples" taught by the Son of God take time and study and I dare say confidently is the foundation for not only knowing God, Jesus, and the Holy Spirit, but also for comprehending "by grace alone," "through faith alone," "in Christ alone." It may take a reader, or "tracker," many walks along the pathway of the text to see clearly that Jesus is the "only way," "the narrow gate" that opens into the meadow of salvation. Jesus is the guide down that path. Perhaps the coolest thing gleaned is that the text is also foundational to comprehending everything and anything at all. That revelation may take a "tracker" many walks through the text.

The graphic makes a point; the scarlet blood of Jesus seen in the reflection in the lenses of the sunglasses is the point. In truth there are no magic glasses. Seeing the Cross and considering why the blood is a function of seeking, desiring, and a will to know the truth. I now see and think on the world through these new lenses so herein is some of the thinking I've done.

Author: James Kalm Fitzgerald

ACKNOWLEDGMENTS

1) The Word of God as explained in The Bible by 35 known and 5 +/- unknown authors.

2) Then it would have to start with Jordan Peterson, (explained in Chapter One. Then in no particular order truly great expositors of the "The Word" that have helped me revise my life from the road to perdition to the narrow gate:

Expositor	Ministry	Website
Jordan Peterson	Psychologist,Philosopher,Speaker	jordanbpeterson.com
John MacArthur	Grace to You	www.gty.org
R. C. Sproul	Ligonier Ministries	www.ligonier.org
Alistair Begg	Truth for Life	www.truthforlife.org
Ray Comfort	Living Waters	www.livingwaters.com
Gary Gerrard	Friend & Poet	NA
James White	Alpha & Omega	www.aomin.org
Jeff Durbin	Alpha & Omega	www.aomin.org
Jack Hibbs	Real Life w/Jack Hibbs	Jackhibbs.com
Frank Turek	Cross Examined	www.crossexamined.org
Voddie Baucham	Voddie Bauchman Ministries	www.voddiebaucham.org

Expositor	Ministry	Website
John Lennox	Professor Mathematics, apologist	www.johnlennox.org
Eric Metaxas	Author, Radio Host, Speaker	www.ericmetaxas.com
Lee Strobel	Author, Speaker	www.leestrobel.com
David Wood	Christian Apologist	www.acts17.net
Charles Spurgeon	Preacher	www.spurgeon.org
Arthur Pink	Author	www.godrules.net/library/pink
Jason Lisle	Astrophysicist, Author, Speaker	www.answersingenisis.org
Douglas Wilson	Pastor, theologian	www.dougwils.com
Robb Brunansky	Pastor - Desert Hills Bible Church	www.deserthillschurch.com
John Barnett	Preacher / Teacher	DTBM "Discover the Bible Ministries" on YouTube
Scott Gourley	Pastor – The Way Fellowship Church	www.thewayfc.net
Ken Hamm	Apologist	www.answersingenisis.org
Kent Hovind	Apologist	drdino.com: canceled on YouTube
Cliffe Knechtle	Preacher, apologist	givemeananswer.org; ask Cliffe on YouTube
Mike Winger	Preacher, apologist	biblethinker.org
Kerry Shahan	Friend, rancher, all around good guy!	NA
Andrew Rappaport	Preacher/Teacher	strivingforeternity.org
Anthony Silvestro	Apologist	strivingforeternity.org
Justin Peters	Preacher, apologist	justinpeters.org
Les Feldick	Teacher, rancher, farmer	lesfeldick.org/, YouTube – Les Feldick bible study
Noah Webster	Lexicographer	merriam-webster.com/
Todd Friel	Apologist, radio host	wretched.org

Expositor	Ministry	Website
Richard Spsrks	Graphics	N/A/
Harmony Sparks	Graphics	N/A

There are many more including atheists and many whom are sinners and/or advocates for the variety of sinners whom the scriptures say will not enter the Kingdom of Heaven. Reason suggests those above are overcomers.

I must also acknowledge my family for they listened to some of the words and were gracious.

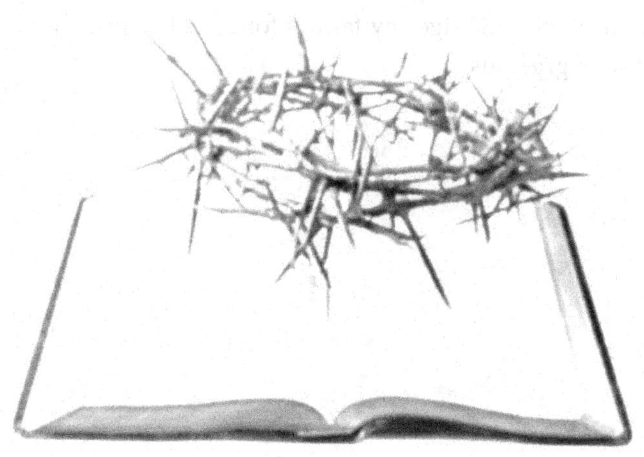

Knowledge can be true or false! Where did truth start?

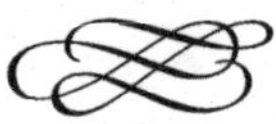

PROLOGUE

It seems certain men over the many years since Jesus did what he did and that being captured in the Christian Bible feel convicted to write their thoughts (commentaries) about the contents of those scriptures. Others write about their testimony of their particular journey to the foot of the Cross. Still others write about an apologetic, i.e., a defense of what is termed "the faith" in the Bible and most particularly what Jesus the Redeemer did for the world, and His message to the world, and His commands to those who desire a relationship with Him.

Within the true Christian community, the Bible uses many descriptors such as, the faithful, disciples, the bride of Christ, the elect, and others, and perhaps most commonly comprehended descriptor is "the church," or those that are convicted that Jesus Christ is who He said He was. Once one is so convicted he/she begins a journey. A reasonable word for this newly convicted person is a pilgrim, i.e., "one who journeys in foreign lands."

In varying degrees pilgrims want to search out this foreign territory. Some are happy to find a local church, as they should, and be comforted, consoled, and happy to be in fraternity with other believers. Others seem compelled, again in varying degrees, to know more. This spectrum of varying degrees ranges from simple prayer to seminary study of the rich history and doctrines contained in the Bible. The spectrum might look something like this:

1. hearing the "good news," i.e., The Gospel of Jesus The Redeemer
2. being deeply convicted of one's own sin
3. considering one's own plight: a) realizing there is a plight, b) realizing there are only two possibilities for said plight, c) reasoned

acceptance that there is a door, though narrow, through which you as a sinner may pass, d) prayer for help to know "The Way" through that narrow gate

4. becoming desirous of fellowship with others, then finding a church
5. being content that this is all there is, i.e., membership
6. discovering there are breakout groups:
    a. helpers to keep the corporate church (building, staff, etc.) going
    b. bible study groups,
    c. missionary works
        i. one on one, discipleship
        ii. local evangelizing,
        iii. foreign evangelizing
7. personal study - starting with reading the Bible (it only takes +/– 72 hours)
8. personal study – reading the thoughts and commentaries of those that in the past were convicted to know more and thankfully wrote it down for our consideration
9. personal study digital – (this is only a recent development because of the internet, 35 years +/-)
    a. watching and listening to old dead guys
        i. philosophers atheist
        ii. philosophers agnostic
        iii. philosophers Christian
        iv. theologians of the Christian faith
        v. theologians of other or false faiths
    b. Listening to current men inclined to pull out the richness of the Word.
    c. Preachers – true
    d. Preachers – false
    e. Theologians
    f. Scientists in any physical discipline (mathematics – John Lennox), (chemistry – James Tour), (cosmology - Jason Lisle), (geology – Kurt Wise); (physics, biology - Stephen Meyer); (biophysics - Michael Behe); (astrophysics - Jason Lisle and Hugh Ross); (archaeology – Douglas Petrovich); (genetics – Nathaniel Jeanson); and many more

g. Philosophy or metaphysical studies, i.e., that which cannot be measured or distilled in a laboratory – e.g., love, hate, empathy, existence, reason, conscientiousness, social, etc. - R.C. Sproul, Jordan Peterson, Doug Wilson

10. Personal study – university or seminary study (for a preview of the vastness of what can be learned nose around at www.gty.org – you will find an Academy, a University, and a Seminary – nose around through those respective web pages to realize there is so much to know. Check out other seminary websites also. The point is there is so much richness to learn and all for the glory of a Man who walked the earth in a way like no man before or after could have done. His impact changed the trajectory of mankind so much so that time itself was split.

The above is neither a chronological list nor a comprehensive list; it is only thoughts jotted down of how one might come to know "The Way." For example, my order was as follows:

✓ 9.a.ii, then 7, then 8 and 9, then 1, then 2, then 3, then 4, and continuing in 7,8, and 9, then 6.b, then 6.c.i

Sadly, some are born into 4, hear 1 but cannot articulate it, and never get to 2 and 3. It is this situation within "the church" as well as those without "the church" that brings one necessarily to realize that "The Great Commission" is a never ending proposition requiring the various talents of believers to consider what their talent may be and bring that talent to bare.

The varied possibilities of how one finds one's way to salvation could be a spectrum, however, not a linear or ordered spectrum. I find my path a chaotic spectrum, or put another way – an unusual pilgrimage. Too old to go to seminary, but young enough and blessed enough to live in this age of technology that the vast knowledge of great theologians of the past as well as many great theologians of the present are contained in a magic rectangle --- my phone.

It should be noted here that the above considerations do not have all of the necessary elements to be "born again." That phrase "born again" not being the point of this analysis, only one of the many nuggets to be encountered on the greatest pilgrimage. For a proper understanding of the phrase "born again" and many other rich and awesome treasures found within the text of scriptures, all that is required is to crack open the Bible.

There are four terms that the pilgrim may not hear for years and they are: regeneration, justification, sanctification, and glorification.

These words accurately describe the entire pilgrimage. These words will not be heard from the pulpit often yet they are most helpful. Perhaps the best book every written about this is "The Pilgrim's Progress" written by John Bunyan in 1681. That book captures what will happen to most every pilgrim if said pilgrim truly desires a quest to eternal life. Awesome read. Further, look the terms up on your phone (it will take 5 and on the outside 10 seconds). I would encourage pilgrims to use that device often to look up the definition of any and all words you may have heard or will hear on your pilgrimage but on reflection realize you have no clue what they mean. I should point out, however, I discovered a truth in this journey concerning the definitions of words found on the internet, and that is that those charged with, or more precisely the self-appointed guardians of online dictionaries now change the definitions of some words. Even the online Merriam-Webster, whom I would have considered a bastion guardian of Noah Webster's work, does distort the truth when it fits the new atheistic view of the world. An example will you will find later in this book. Most words with discernment are accurate, but if you stumble on a definition that causes you pause consider looking the word up in an older print of the dictionary. This revelation is a good reason not to throw out any old family dictionaries.

At some point on the journey the conscience for some may include discerning one's own skill set which can be utilized to share the "Good News" or "Gospel" of God. At that point the thought of talking to another about the Gospel often will cause anxiety not unlike when as a child your father says something to the effect, "son we need to have a talk". A child's mind most often will wonder what he did wrong and his stomach will turn over. At least that is how it was for me the first time I was confronted with a question that required a reasoned explanation to a question posed to me that the necessary answer was in that case the existence of God. I'll tell that story in Chapter 9 – First Encounters of the Close Kind; § The Barbers; § Barber 1.

One skill set available to all is one-on-one sharing of the gospel which has happened in the oddest of ways on my journey. More about that later. Another skill also available to all is writing. Few, however, statistically speaking, feel compelled and/or confident enough to give it a go. Speaking for myself, having no training in writing, lacking confidence, I nevertheless feel compelled to jot down my thoughts on my short journey (2 ½ years as of this key stroke). So here goes.....

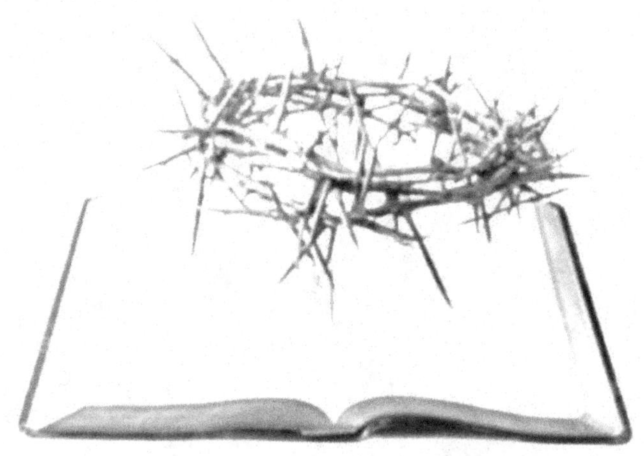

Knowledge cannot be found unless it is sought!

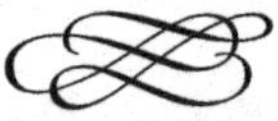

Chapter 1

WHAT MADE ME SEEK JORDAN PETERSON

First, it is reasonable to note that the "discovery" of the internet helped this pilgrim's progress to the foot of the Cross. A cyber journey as opposed to a physical journey, but a journey nonetheless. The word "discovery" is used purposefully as an acknowledgment that the internet is man pulling together many of the wondrous physical elements of God's created order to do a task. That task, while more complex, being no different than the discovery that physical elements shaped into a round disc will roll.

Second, if there is a pivotal moment that led me to truly understand what happened on that Cross it was when I stumbled upon Jordan Peterson on YouTube.

Four years ago before Jordan started his amazing surge to international stardom in the much needed realm of ideas, he popped up on YouTube speaking at a University of Toronto protest against a Canadian Bill C-16 that would outlaw certain speech and gave the Canadian government by legislation the power to compel only words they alone will decide may be uttered. Since Jordan spoke out against Bill C-16, the bill passed in June of 2017. Like the song said - "The Day the Music Died," that day in Canada is the day free speech died.

In January of 2022 reinforced by a new law, Bill C-4 goes a step further in outlawing freedom of specific speech that would relegate the Christian "great commission" to convert sinners as a crime against the state. It further tacitly states that the Christian Bible is a myth and therefore God is myth. So if God is a myth, then the Canadian government has by law decreed tacitly that Genesis 1:27 which states with specificity that God created male and female is a myth. Wow!!! It seems there is a new Titanic with demigods at the helm, a sick bay staffed by Victor Frankensteins, and the passengers hell bent on becoming a modern centaur, all heading for the iceberg, but in this case outlawing lifeboats.

Sorry, a tangent paragraph. Back to Jordan!

When I stumbled on Jordan I began listening to as much of Jordan as I could find. I picked up his book "12 Rules for Life" in the fall of 2018, read it, and continued following him. Jordan's lectures, debates, and interviews made me consider how great my ignorance was and that I make two major changes to my life.

The first change was to listen to someone smarter than me talk for at least one hour per day. When I started listening to Jordan's lecture series on the Bible the second change would be to read the Bible.

It took about one year to read the Bible the first time which was completed in approximately December of 2018. In the spring of 2019 as a supplement to reading the Bible Christian apologists started to pop up on YouTube which in turn lead me to the list of expositors listed in the acknowledgments. (Note, at that time apologist or apologetic is one of the many words embarrassingly I had to look up)

~ NOTE FOR JORDAN ~

You gave a talk for the group "How to Academy" on January 17, 2018 posted on YouTube. The topic was on your book "12 rules For Life." Your skill for articulating many and perhaps most of the "discovered," not "invented," social science categories and in a way that highly educated as well as any level below that level can hear your words, consider them, ruminate on those words, and discern that your articulations are, let's say, true. Statistical considerations of your success bear out that your spoken words - first, and your written words - second, are at minimum making both educated as well as uneducated and all Pareto distributions within the high and low of the category titled "educated," to consider there is a more reasoned way to consider life and specifically their life.

At approximately 50:20 to 58:48 minute mark and concerning Chapter Six you talk about Carl Panzram and the Columbine killers and their respective reasons for killing which they expressed both verbally and in writing. You give reasons for reading and listening to and accepting what they said, and further, believe what they said and not surmise that they were only bloviating about heinous acts. You made a case and rightfully note that when one hears such talk or reads such thoughts and recognizes that such words and speech are depraved; questions need to be raised both directly and or to others.

I'm struggling for a segue here..... You believe them, and because of your skills and training in psycho analysis, after the fact you are correct, i.e., after the heinous crimes, your analysis is spot on - they meant what they said. Now, the segue --- you believe them yet struggle with the writings of Moses. You describe the writings of Moses' as "archetypal stories," and I agree with that level of analysis and its utility to "discover" in a very cogent manner that which articulates, interestingly enough, the mind of God. However and more importantly you "wrestle" with God and transcendence through his Son.

Your coining of a phrase "Maps of Meaning" and your book titled the same, and your many speeches that lay out your, let's call them, "discoveries" about the mind and writing what might be termed by any reasoned consideration a "factual" authoritative work. It is my reasoned opinion that your work and your mind will someday be considered by history on par with the likes of Albert Einstein in the field of physics, or Stephen Meyer in the field of geophysics, or Michael Behe in biology, or James Tour in chemistry, or Kurt Wise in geology, or John Lennox in mathematics, etc. In your field you have synthesized the works of Jung, Solzhenitsyn, Marx, a myriad of postmodern authors, as well as the works of many of the great philosophical and theological thinkers into a brew of words that can be comprehended by the masses at a time in history when reading skills have waned, learning skills have waned, thinking has waned, and downstream of that, discernment has most certainly waned. In other words, well done, and bravo! As you are well aware many are thankful for you.

One way to consider your many interviews, panel discussions, lectures, Q & As, etc. is to equate those interactions with a game of chess or say a chess tournament. As an observer and I dare say most observers, you are the undisputed master. Many want to take you on singularly, (Sam Harris, Cathy Newman, Vice News), and sometimes ten against one. It doesn't seem to matter, though your opponents may make a cogent point or two, at the end of the match all of your pieces are still on the board, and all of their pawns have been, not so much sacrificed as slaughtered. The bishops have been defrocked, the castles knocked down, the knights bloodied, the king naked, and the queen bitch slapped. I hope that sounds funny, because that's how it sounded in my head.

It is most disturbing to not see academics in academy stand with you. Their cowardice and silence screams loudly to the world. They will not be missed at all. Similar to the movie "Run, Hide, Fight," Zoe will be remembered, the cowards will not. You Jordan will be remembered.

Back to meaning...... it seems there is enough evidence in all disciplines of science today as well as in the historical record, especially the New Testament writings backed up by extra biblical accounts. These accounts shy of being notarized are like affidavits and would hold up in a righteous court as reliable testimony to the single most important event in history, that being Jesus raised from the dead and that resurrection was for a very particular and specified reason. I know Jordan that you struggle with this, so much so that the consideration of which has made you weep on many an occasion.

You have also used stories like Pinocchio to articulate man's quest for meaning. This you certainly do brilliantly, so much so, that men and women who have not been privileged to study the great authors that shaped you, nevertheless can not only consider philosophy, perhaps for the first time, but can understand it. I am one of those. I can say before stumbling on you I had only heard the word philosophy. It is embarrassing to realize that it took till the 64th year of my life to comprehend my complete and total ignorance of the subject.

It is reasonable to at least consider that the Bible and unusual collection of authors that so strangely ended up as one literary work might be much more than "one" man's thoughts (like the many great singular authors that shaped your knowledge). It is at least reasonable to consider that the construct of the Bible had a different inspiration then that which inspired single authors. That seems to be the case, and if so, then that inspiration might just be God breathed or inspired or whatever term best articulates why so many authors ended up in one book that points in only one direction. Further, as you have stated many times, you recognize that if you live your life as if it (The Bible) is true then, with all of the discernment you have amassed and skills you have acquired to lay bare "truth," you know with certainty that things, all things including suffering, will go better if one lives one's life as if the Bible and especially the teachings of the New Testament are true.

Someone noticed and pointed out that the Old Testament is the New Testament concealed, and the New Testament is the Old Testament revealed. It makes perfect sense once the Bible is considered in its whole. The Old Testament did point to Jesus Christ and most importantly, and thankfully so, the New Testament writers testified to and captured all that Jesus did and that He is who He said He was and all that that reasonably and necessarily implies.

I was sad to hear of your aliment that took you away from your family and work and I know you know you were missed as well as.... and this should give you philosophical pause.... prayed for. Ruminate on that my friend. As your fans, including me, prayed for and awaited your return, it occurred to me that your absence and your ailment was very much akin to the night Jacob wrestled with God. You have been wrestling with God for many years and your ailment is Jacobs dislocated hip. Pray for God's blessing Jordan. How ironic it will be that when you seek God, He will help you, and in this instance will help you cross the Jordan, (yourself).

Podcasts in which you are a guest and those that you host are most certainly enjoyable as well as insightful. The most compelling thing to witness, however, are those moments where you get so close to the narrow gate, and fall emotionally spent outside the gate weeping. I understand as I have been there many times. It is an irony of sorts that it is you whom led me to the gate and for this I am quite literally eternally thankful. It took some time and God's Helper, i.e., the Grace of God that at a certain point in one's journey must be recognized as a "Spirit," and if that "Spirt" changes you with a bend towards righteousness how can that "Spirt" not be "Holy"? That "Spirt" did "in fact" capture me from a seed you dropped along the path of this sojourners transcendent journey. Thank you!!!

We may never meet, yet it strikes me how words, whether spoken or penned transcend time and space and that may mean that these words may someday reach you. I hope so. Even if we never meet I have a brotherly type affection for you. I guess you know why.

God bless Jordan,

Jim

P.S. I struggled with this note to Jordan for a week. On January 27, 2022 in the afternoon I finished the note at a Starbucks. When I packed up and headed for home I pulled up a YouTube to listen to during the drive. The one that popped up was Doug Wilson commenting on a Joe Rogan podcast of January 25th where Jordan Peterson was the guest. The link is http://youtu.be/

txBKDGGW6o . The last words Doug stated were these, "And I would say, as Jesus once said to his scribe many years ago, you are not far from the Kingdom." I wept for the next mile or so. If you read the above note to Jordan, then listen to the link, you will understand.

A few days later, January 29, 2022, a YouTube channel "JP - Pursuit of Meaning" posted a compilation of Jordan's talks concerning God. The link is https://youtu.be/x6_ESSfyiYE . I wept yet again.

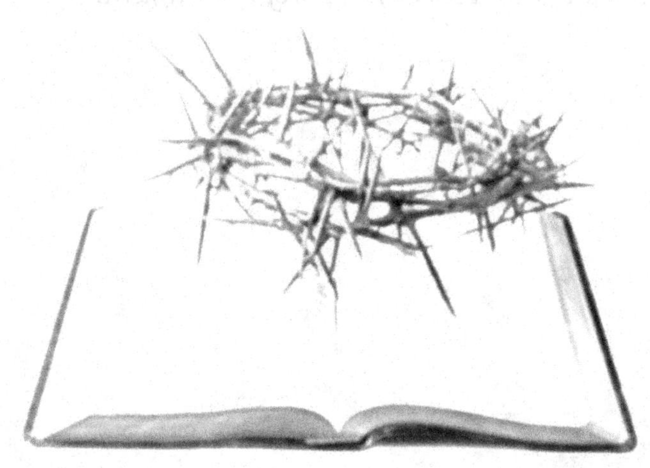

True and false knowledge

can be found in any technology!

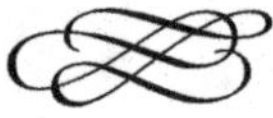

Chapter 2

THE INTERNET

I still remember when a friend; (*Jon Vaux from San Diego*); first told me about this thing that he thought had the potential to be big. It was 1990. He explained it generally and was correct that it would be big. Its history can now be found ironically on the internet, or World Wide Web. At the time it sounded interesting but like most people at that time we could not possibly have imagined much less know the implications of what was to be just 30 years in the future.

Like all other inventions ever conceived in the mind of man, it too had the potential to either 1) glorify God, or 2) not glorify God. For example the wheel. An ancient invention still used to this day to glorify God when it transports God's creation(s) in such a way that rightly takes dominion of the earth. When with righteous intent we walk, ride a beast, move about on wheels, through the air or through the water and we love God first, any and all places we might transport ourselves or any goods would only be to love one another and do that which praises God.

However, and sadly, much movement on the wheel does not glorify God. Transporting men and women for exploitation of any kind is evil. Transporting human beings to destabilize one area because those people have become hopeless because they have been exploited from whence they came does not glorify God. Those that conspire to do such things work for a different master. Another example is making and transporting anything that destroys the mind or body of God's children. There will be judgment. Be careful.

The internet moves information. Some of the information it moves glorifies God or I would not be typing these words right now. In other words, the technology created a circumstance that would send the seeds of God's word through wires, switches, modems and the air. Like a wheel transporting Bibles across Europe in the 1500s this 20th century invention transported seeds of God's word to me.

I was a fan of the sit com "Parks and Recreation." Ron Swanson, played by Nick Offerman, was an endearing character who was the boss of the department. He was the boss man in a government position and hated the intrusiveness of the government. He buried his gold in his back yard, was not a fan of technology as this too he considered intrusive. He was hysterical. In one episode his friends gave him an iPod with earphones and he acted like a puppy when it sees its own reflection. Dumbfounded, while staring at the iPod he asks, "How did they get all of those songs into such a small rectangle?" Anyway, I have since called my phone the magic rectangle.

In the 20th century moving Gods word went from wheels, boats, and planes, to air waves (radio and television), and in the last 10 years of that century the "World Wide Web." In the 1st 20 years of the 21st century the word of God would by factors unknown be available to most of the planet. I just looked it up…..Even though of the almost 8 billion people on the planet only 5 billion have internet access. That means 3 billion do not and reasonably require the wheel to transport God's word at least for now. Also, this does not mean that the 5 billion have accepted the "free gift," but it is reasonable that the majority have in all their clicks on the internet have read or heard the name of Jesus Christ.

In any event, a tap on my magic rectangle in 2016, a seed was providentially transported to me that changed my life forever.

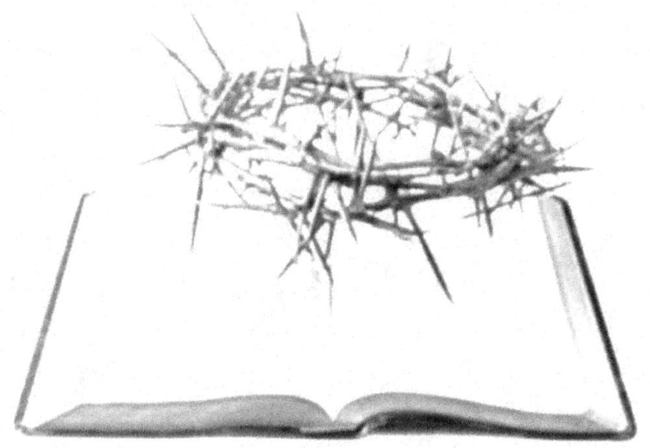

Undeserved Patience

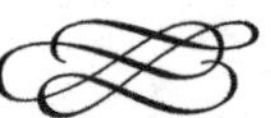

Chapter 3

SIX DECADES OF SIN

For sixty plus years I like most people thought I was a good person and if asked would answer in the affirmative. Thinking myself to be wise, I was "in fact" a fool. How easy it is to be a fool. I have been deceived a lot in my life, and have recognized deceit sometimes and side stepped a land mine or two. Now it seems with certainty I can claim the biggest deceiver was me. The words self-righteous are as clear as my own image as it reflects back at me in a mirror.

In the late 1980s I took my baby girl to visit my father's side of the family in Georgia northeast of Atlanta in some of the most beautiful rolling hills and forests. I remember visiting with a cousin whom was retired Air Force and had done or been attached to clandestine operations around the world. He passed away and what he did is still a mystery, at least to me. Anyway, one day he was working in his shop fixing a small engine and the conversation was on people being naturally good or evil. I was making the argument that the nature of man was naturally good while he argued the opposite.

I recall how vehemently each of us argued our positions. His position was shored up by all of the evil he had seen in other parts of the world and specifically that man and men can so easily kill each other. I on the other hand argued for the goodness of man thinking that generally we tend to do right. My examples were things such as "generally" we obey street markings and signage; we respect the boundaries of space like the walls that surround people's homes, companies, and institutions. My arguments I felt were reasonably statistical in that, although there are certainly those that break the norms, most conform to a civilized code. My cousin tried to explain that my perspective was narrowly viewed through the veil of freedom enjoyed especially in America, and also by most of the western thinking world and ironically by the power and might of the most powerful military and weaponry ever to be conceived in the mind of man and thankfully that might for the most part being rightly constrained.

As I now consider that conversation neither one of us was right. I was a man living in sin, generally trying to live rightly. He was a good man, I think perhaps tipped back the bottle a bit much, but generally trying to live rightly. I had heard and believed that Jesus was who he said he was and my cousin was Roman Catholic, yet neither one of us brought up the scriptures. I had never read nor considered at all much less with any discernment why the Son of God would say "There is no one good, no not one." Apparently my cousin didn't either for if we had our positions would have ended up in a reasoned conversation about the glory of God and why He came to save both of us.

My cousin passed away and I hope he found the narrow gate. If he did it certainly had nothing to do with this sinner and that is sad. I have a very large contingent of Romans in my extended family and I do not know them as I should. I have met many of them on four family reunions over the decades and love them all. I think all or certainly most of them consider themselves believers and wanting to live rightly. They are spread all over America and it would be nice to consider conversations about the best possible reunion available to all of us. I am hopeful some of them will read this pilgrim's thoughts and perhaps we can have a more blessed reunion!!!

Fast forward 35 years to the times we live in now and even if I did not understand "The Way of the Master" back then, it seems to me I would not have tried to argue as I did then. The depravity of the mind of man is so very prevalent and obviously so. Even though in my day to day life I personally don't smack into evil it is available to see everywhere in the world, right there at my fingertips via the World Wide Web.

Notice that as I start this chapter how easy it is to point to what the rest of the world is doing while the intent of the title of the chapter was intended to reflect on my "six decades of sin." How about that! As I reflect on my life from a "sin" perspective it isn't pretty. I could chronicle each decade and speak of some things done rightly, but the wrong things, the wrong thoughts would be too embarrassing. It's not really necessary as I dare say most anyone reading this would also be too embarrassed to confess not only the things they did or said, but also the thoughts and especially the thoughts they had that are shameful and certainly too embarrassing to say out loud. However, God knew and knows even now not only mine but yours too.

I'm not sure how this chapter is helpful, except to say that through the eyes of a 67 year old man who was not stricken down by Gods righteous judgment and reasonably should have been in any one of the six decades of sin I lived in, I would implore anyone to consider with a sober mind that we all are sinners and by God's grace and mercy alone there is forgiveness. Further, it is only what Jesus the Redeemer did, His bloody death, that provided a way for all of the hours, days, weeks, months, years, decades, centuries, and millennia of sin upon sin to be nailed with him to a Cross so that my decades of sin and yours too can be washed away.

It's a "free," let me say that again, "free" gift. It is 2023 and in America and reasonably the world over when the words "free gift" are uttered or offered by a sales gimmick or corporate enticement; (coupons, membership w/privileges, free enticements offered by government aka affirmative action, subsidizes, etc.); the words lose significance so much so that the consideration then of the "free gift" of eternal life is lost and goes in one ear and out the other without much thought. In other words it gets lost in all the multiplicities of all things offered "free." How then is the "free gift" of "salvation" supposed to compete with "buy one get one free" and other such enticements? If you have to think on that for more than 10 seconds and cannot see the difference then God help you.

A curious consideration about the enticements of corporate interests is that all of them have an expiration date. Coupons vary by various analyses of the product, greed, and the calendar. Memberships likewise are analyzed by product, greed, and the calendar. One thing they all have in common is that they all expire usually by a stipulated date and most certainly upon your expiration or death. Nothing more can be redeemed. Nothing more is offered. The "free gift" of salvation however is uniquely different in that this "free gift" can be redeemed after death in life. Ruminate on that!!!

I realize and so too do all that have accepted this "gift" and truly understand that "acceptance" of the "gift" of the crucified Jesus "freely offered" has to be "accepted" with the most sober considerations of the mind. If soberly, contritely, and with the meekness, that is to say, the obedience required when the "free gift" is accepted can be redeemed and gain one access into this place known as Heaven. A place where sin will not exist, a place where there is no suffering, only joy. This gift was bloody and so very horrific to be sure, and that fact is extremely hard to comprehend. I acknowledge that nary an attempt was made on my part to think on, much less comprehend, but now I understand why Christians wish for and desire that others and that means "you" please consider, ruminate, read the words of God in the Christian Bible, pray to God for understanding and that He send you the Helper He promised to send if you ask. Then repent for however many sins there are, and turn.

Decades, i.e., multiples of ten years! Most people, by the grace of God get a few of these in their lifetime. What to do with a decade? What to do with a decade if it can be grasped that a decade is a gift. If you are a parent you have probably been gifted with at least two decades plus or minus. When you hold your new baby you understand conscientiously or unconscientiously both "gift" and "love." You now move into future decades of responsibility and if considered soberly this too is understood to be a gift. Personally, I took my first six decades for granted with little or no attention to the gift. I offer this as a plea for any interested parties to stop a bit. Stop a bit to think on the gift of life generally and if you have made it through a decade or multiples of a decade, consider where that gift came from. Politeness in society when a gift is received is generally reciprocated with a thank you. The gift of your life and if you are fortunate enough to have had multiples of decades of life, a thank you in the form of a prayer to God whom gave to you that gift is in order.

This May 2023 I passed the 80% mark of my seventh decade which means first for the math impaired that I am now 68 years old. Second, I am closing quickly on the end of my seventh decade. Certainly there will not be seven more, or six more, or five more, or four more. One perhaps, two maybe, three highly unlikely. So what to do with possibly only two more? Since the first 7.2 decades were squandered as far as it concerns a proper relationship with God, whatever time may remain I hope to spend thinking with reverence for the gifts given and live with a greater sense that many souls are in trouble and perhaps I can help.

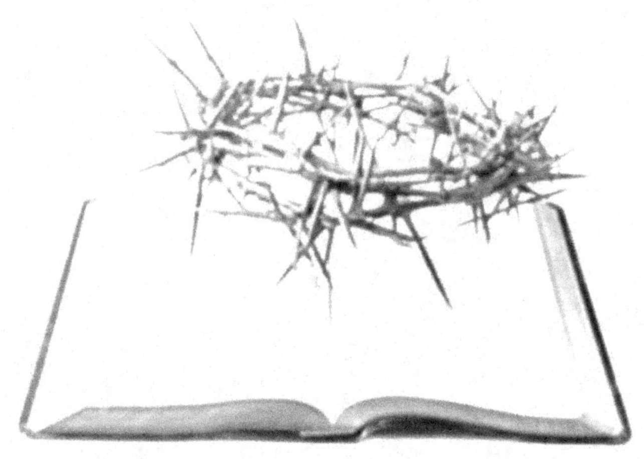

Jerusalem once set apart was judged!

America once set apart is being judged!

I should have known!

Chapter 4

THE 62ND YEAR AWAY IN BABYLON

As I reflect on this year my daughter had been married two years earlier which was a blessing. I was doing work as an independent property adjuster. I was conflicted about work, my marriage, life in general including the state of affairs in our country. My state of mind vacillated between anger, and being reasoned about life. If some men can be described as part of a group where "calmer heads prevail," well, I think most who know me would say I was in that group. However, I was not happy in my core, my soul.

As I look back now it seems a good analogy from the Old Testament is when the Jewish people were exiled to Babylon for a time, then returned home to start again. In my case, unbeknownst to me at the time He who makes, shapes, molds providence itself, or makes, shapes, molds the circumstance for all things, made it so I would be given the opportunity to go away for a season from a place, situation, and circumstance that did not allow for the scales of my iniquities to see the light. A friend asked that I build, or more precisely, manage the building of an office and other structures for his business. In this place far from home, the work that I did and the isolation in a small farm house in the country did in fact make for the re-tooling of my mind, my heart, and my very soul.

There wasn't much to do in that farm house. I do not watch much TV anyway so not having it wasn't troublesome; however, I did go purchase some DVD movies from Walmart to watch on my laptop. These didn't keep my attention so I spent a lot of time watching YouTube. It was here that more cerebral things started to show up. Then Jordan Peterson appeared.

What is interesting about AI and the algorithms that can and do direct traffic to your computer based on your browser history, if you search for porn if that's your thing, you'll get it non-stop. If you search for Philosophers, or philosophy it will show up. Matters of law, there it is. History of a particular period, there is more. Then, and here is the best, Christ and Christianity, so much you can't possibly get to all of it. While Christendom showing up all the time is awesome, sometimes the unsolicited things that keep showing up are really annoying. For example, while I was working up there I was looking for light fixtures to be mounted on poles for the project. I did find them, but for over a year, ads for outdoor light fixtures would be some of the first things I would see when I opened YouTube. Very annoying!

As I noted in Chapter One as I was stumbling around the internet one seemingly happenstance keystroke followed by another Jordan Peterson would get my attention and would change the direction of my life. At first and for several months his obvious command of words that deconstruct complex analogies of the way of man and in a way that the least articulate man can grasp grasped me. After listening to a few of his lectures I pledged privately to myself that I was going to spend at least one hour per day listening to someone smarter than me talk. I liked Stefan Molyneux a philosopher until he was banished from the various platforms. If you believe what is on the internet now you would think he is Hitler's right hand man. Nonsense! Anyway, he is not the point. Hearing words or reading words is all humanity has to consider what is good and what is evil or shades of all things between those bookends.

That time away from home had a perfect balance of work and isolation creating a way for the Potter to re-shape this pot. What started as one hour a day has changed greatly. Now I probably listen to an average of four hours per day to many disciplines of the created order. Biology, archaeology, history, cosmology, chemistry, geology, theology, soteriology, ontology, philosophy, and most of all, hermeneutics. And it seems most of my evenings I delight in listening to proper sermons or audio books about the "The Way."

I should note that things are not perfect, but now this non-perfection is better understood. Being a fallen child of God, understanding the why of a desire to seek the narrow gate, clears up the way of things. When a fog burns off in a valley and the sun rises in the day and you can see further down the valley, in a similar fashion when the scales, i.e., willful blindness begins to fall from your eyes that place that is further down the valley becomes very clear. It is at this point there is a new sense of what perfect is.

~ RIGHT AND WRONG ~

Oh God, my God, if you created for nothing,
Why then, oh why then is there an obvious something.
You needed us not, but yet here we are,
Each for a season, and each with one gift, and that is to reason.

With categories many, Your Glory to consider,
The why of it all, the way it should be,
After all that men think boils down to two things,
Do that which is right, or do that which is wrong.

Your will and Your wish that we be and stay strong,
To acknowledge our plight of the right and the wrong,
And once so acknowledged, we fall on our face,
To beg Your forgiveness and plead for Your Grace.

Now knowing it seems we tend to lean wrong,
Please Lord and what Lord and oh how can we see?
History, history a category made by the finger of God,
Your Word and the Truth you have left for us all.

You breathed and Your Word by the scribes it is known,
You entered Your world, to show clearly the right and the wrong.
You stayed for a time to share that God is the Father,
You are the Son, and the Spirit makes three that are One.

If we hear Your call and born again of the Spirit,
Your wrath will be clear, and we surely will fear it.
Wisdom takes hold so we will then know,
It's what You did on the Cross that will save us our souls.

Then you went to the grave that lasted three days,
And defeated death to show us the way.
Your goodness Your gift for the wrongness we made,
So we may join You if we follow The Way.

There's a place we can enter, through a gate that is narrow,
Without burdens to carry, no sorrows, no worries.
You came as a man, but Your Father gave You His Glory,
To heal not just the sick, oh my God, oh my Lord,
There's so much more to the story.

Try as any man might to try and do good,
To have a free will it seems was not understood.
It turns out it would be a curse, that did cause man to fall,
You knew it would be so, and we see it now too,
And that's why a Savior, you sent for us all.

Some will be grateful, a narrow gate they will find,
To that place known as Heaven where it is You we will find.
Some will not care, a wide gate to their peril,
The devil awaiting their master called Baal.

On this side of glory we pray for their souls,
But once it's all over the pit will be closed.
Oh man, oh woman use the reason God gave you,
To be right is not wrong, and to be wrong is not right,
Pray God for wisdom so wrong is clear folly,
And right is your choice that you may be in His Glory.

Amen
JKF 8-30-2022

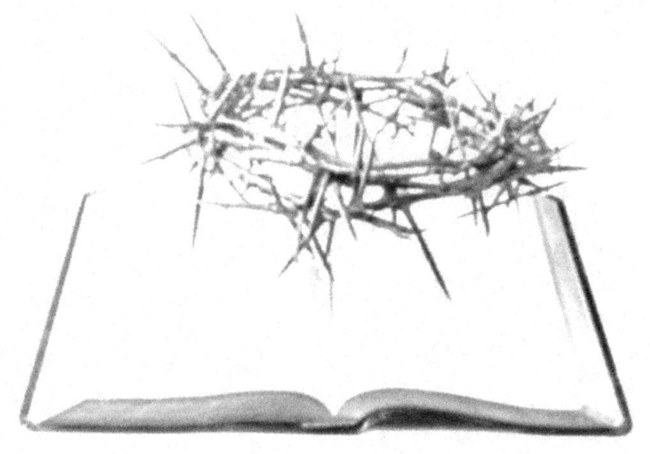

America in the beginning,

One Nation Under God!

2023 not so much!

Chapter 5
AMERICAN THOUGHTS BEFORE I KNEW

In about 2010 I had been thinking on and reading about Americas founding, corporations, law, etc. and how it seemingly is on a collision course with something other than that for which it was founded. Often times as I contemplate this or that I conjure up a picture board story to allegorically make sense of things. I remember exactly where I was when the following analysis popped into my head. I was traveling along I-40 near Holbrook Arizona.

I imagined standing in a great hall or gathering room. I thought about the New York Museum of Natural History with dark wood paneling as portrayed in the movie "Night at the Museum" with Ben Stiller. The viewer is staring at a wall with lots of windows looking into two rooms with 12 foot high ceilings. The one on the left is filled with the history of America and how it all went wrong. The room would be huge, for perspective say as big as a basketball arena or maybe two. The floor is wood and there are rows and rows of eight foot tall bookshelves with all of the approximately one million laws on the books as well as the de facto laws, or decrees not codified, also known as "color of law" that the people think are law and therefore follow as law. Around the perimeter are many stations with screens and headphones where the visitor can listen to the history, good and bad, about the founding and settling of this nation.

Now imagine the room to the right, same size also with a wood floor. In the middle which would be quite a distance viewed through the windows you would see a table with a book on the right, a few documents and a large book on the left with an easel behind it. As you stand outside your curiosity is peaked, but you cannot go in until you tour the room to the left.

You walk into the room on the left. The 1st thing you notice is the wall to ceiling glass curtain wall that separates the two rooms. In the hours you will spend in this room you cannot help and often notice the table in the middle of the room next door, and you wonder what's over there. Even with the wood floors what strikes you is the deafening silence as you walk around.

Hours are spent mostly watching and listening to the stations around the perimeter and as you do what went wrong starts to become clear and becomes heavy on your soul even if you don't review any of the documents in the massive room. The silence is real for all of the paper that absorbs the sound with all of the law that has so gradually changed what was by rational reasoned analysis the best possible condition ever created in all of human history in which all of mankind could thrive. But alas, that reason will be found in the room next door.

Imagine what you just did took all day. It was heavy as you reviewed a lot of ugly. Lots of death. Wars including Revolutionary, 1812, Spanish, Civil, WW1, WW2, Korea, Vietnam, Gulf, Afghanistan, etc. All of that blood, all the young men killing each other for the agendas of older men. Now throw in corruption of the individual, mobs, organized mobs, tribal mobs, every branch of government at local, state, and federal, as well as world and especially bankers. To be sure there were heroes, and many of them but they seem overshadowed by the carnage.

You need a break, dinner, a drink, conversation with a friend, and a good night's sleep. You try to sleep but it's hard for all that you just took in.

The next morning, refreshed a bit, you purchase your morning coffee and your curiosity gets you back to the museum for the room on the right. What could be on that table? You walk in and start across that wood floor noticing the intense echo of your footsteps which remind you of walking into an empty gymnasium when you were in high school, only this is louder. This arena size room seems at first like such a waste of time and space. Why this large massive room you think to yourself as that table would fit in a small room big enough for a pool table. Why this large arena?

As you walk you glance to the left and see through the window-wall the room and all of its contents that caused your mind to be so troubled and made sleep hard to find the night before. The very graphic film footage of things men can do to fellow man. The piles of dead bodies from the concentration camps in Germany; the retaliation of the Poles against the Germans after WW2; the Russian gulags and the Russian dead by starvation; the fire bombings of Dresden; napalm girl from the Viet Nam war; the Bataan death marches by the Japanese; the photos of Civil War men without limbs sawn off while conscience; the Marines without limbs in the 21st century wars from IED explosives; and on and on and on.

You wonder why is it that men, and especially men, after the multi-millions of dead bodies piled up in the 20th century has learned nothing.

You walk up to the table. The book on the right is the Christian Bible.

The documents in the middle include:

1. Declaration of Independence
2. Constitution for the united States of America
3. Preamble to the Bill of Rights
4. Bill of Rights.

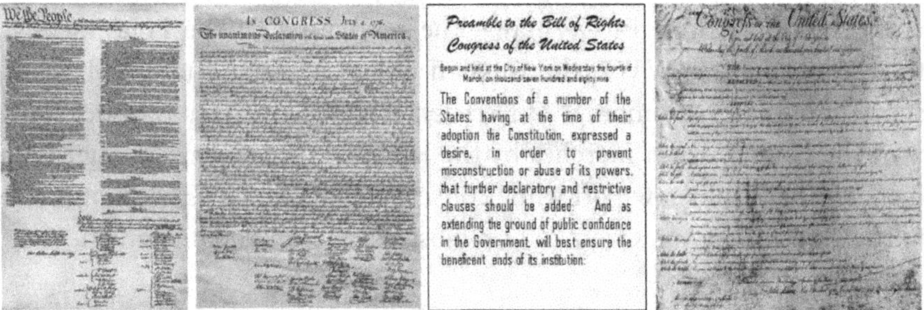
Preamble to the Bill of Rights
Congress of the United States
The Conventions of a number of the States, having at the time of their adoption the Constitution, expressed a desire, in order to prevent misconstruction or abuse of its powers, that further declaratory and restrictive clauses should be added: And as extending the ground of public confidence in the Government, will best ensure the beneficent ends of its institution.

The book on the left is a large thick book the title stamped on it is:

- New Laws

You open it noting that its pages are blank. On an easel just behind this book is a poster that says:

~~~ CAUTION ~~~

Beware to the man who writes any law in this book.
For if you do, what you write will take you down a path
That will cause the plight documented in the room next door.

PRAYER FOR THE LAWMAKERS

~ BEWARE O MAN ~

O man, O man, before you dare,
Consider greatly and with righteous care,
As what you write may cause much plight,
As history teaches and wisdom knows,
The Good Book only can shield from woes.

The people have ordained that you lead,
So never forget that Christ is King.
Kingdoms rise and empires fall,
For not adhering to God's law.

Beware beware O man O man,
The task at hand is so very large, and life itself is in your charge.
Tremble, pray and bend your knee,
And govern rightly for your God is watching thee.

Amen
JKF 9-1-2022

It all starts to make sense. The deafening quite in the room on the left is the stranglehold of tyranny choking the very life out of freedom. For contrast the echoes heard on the room on the right is freedom itself. The thoughts of the founders from the Puritans to the framers of the documents in the middle of the table are all men would need if men could govern themselves as outlined in the book on the right side of the table – The Christian Bible. Alas, sadly you know that it is reasonable that an additional
~~~

constraint or law or two will be necessary, and those constraints should constrain fictions more than men. Or maybe better yet have no fictions at all.

As I finish the considerations above it strikes me how at this time in history, i.e., 2023 there is much talk of a Great Reset. Ironically those that blather on about their ideas about this reset are using all of the corruption of the law in the room on the left, and continue to add even more restrictions to mankind's freedom including thought. This continued choking of liberty and freedom destines America to an early grave when compared to the empires of the past. For perspective the pagan Roman Empire lasted 1000 years; the switch to a Catholic Roman empire (or Byzantine) lasted another 1000 years; the British Empire lasted 400 years. America at a meager 246 years unless she repents and bends the knee to The Redeemer will fall. Even more ironically if there were to be a "Great Reset," the room on the right would be a much better reset point.

~ AMERICA THE WHAT ? ~

America the what, what did we do and what are we now?
If memory serves and history shows,
Intent was to be righteous, but we've lost that somehow.

It is obvious we are something, but what is not clear,
Once God and his law were the standard we cheered,
But now we are crumbling, the world it does sneer,
Our very existence is very unclear.

In God we trust, in 1776 was believed,
The only way that this nation would ever achieve.
Achieve what, - that's a good question you ask,
Freedom, yes freedom and that it never be thieved.

Moral law the foundation found in only one place,
Commandments from God, and surely by grace,
By the finger of God in stone they were left,
For all nations to follow if they would only embrace.

America did, and for a while she would flourish,
Knowing that the words of Jesus, is that which would nourish,
The soul of the nation and the people thereof,
If only, and only if, as the founders declared,
The states be united and only by God.

Now two centuries in the ship she does list,
Those at the helm steering straight for the rocks,
America as conceived may soon not exist.

Freedom and liberty and in God we do trust,
The right to be equal most certainly a must,
The right to live and let live, once protected by men,
Is now a thing canceled and only by whim.

America the what? What is it about?
It's as clear as the day; we are losing the light,
The torch of freedom that once shown so bright,
Is a flickering ember about to go out.

What was once greatness its foundations the truth,
America was built on and enjoyed once in her youth.
If the ole lady does not get down on her knees,
Repent for her sins, oblivion bound she is surely to see.

America the what? How did we get here?
Perhaps the answer a clue at the start,
The original document, a constitution with heart,
Made tacit a reference to Christ Jesus as Lord.

Section 7, sentence 2 states perfectly clear,
This document conceived, attested, and agreed,
In the "Year of our Lord," then known to be,
Without doubt, without question, a direct chain to the Cross.

A witness for sure the first president George,
A tradition he forged, to swear on the Bible,
A witness to all His Lord not to libel.

That tradition long gone, the state it seems captured,
Paving the way for the end and mishaps the rapture.
This nation once great, can be again,
If its people repent, and turn from their sin.
The church must step up, clean up her ranks,
Lead from the pulpit, praise God and give thanks.

Without anger or angst, and nothing but love,
Go out in the world and let everyone know,
The Lamb of God He did come and His blood it did flow,
If we repent and believe and with faith bend the knee,
America once blessed can once again be.

Amen
JKF 10-9-2022

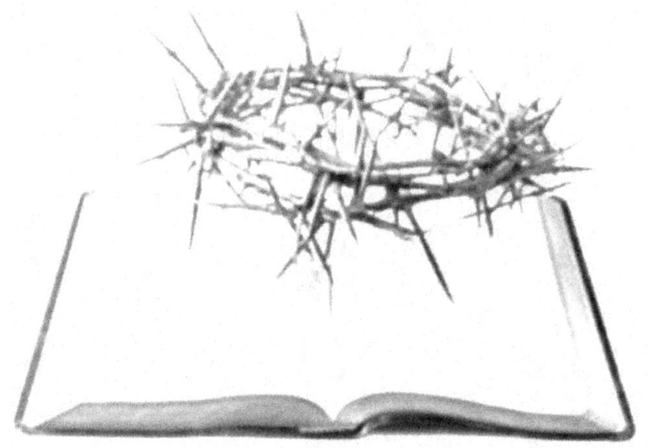

Thirst No More!

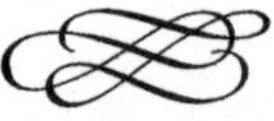

Chapter 6

LAKE CHRISTOS

In the first year of reading the Bible and listening to various history lessons about the early church, and by that specifically the early Christian Church as ordained in the New Testament, I was to run into a challenge of mind.

Having grown up with Catholic grandparents and Catholic mother as well as far as I knew all of my extended family on both my father and mothers side I never gave much thought or really any thought that there was a history. As I think on spheres of understanding it might breakdown something like this:

- 0 – 2 years, all within 5 feet of my existence, mostly mom and dad
- 2 – 5 years, all within the room I am in, all in my parents' house, hopefully brothers and sisters
- 5 – 10 years, all within the room plus yard, extending to school and school yard, some friends
- 10 – 15 years, extended to more friends, and exposure to those not considered close friends
- 15 – 18 years, mostly social with limited exposure to categories of other
- 18 – 22 years, mostly social with some expansion into categories of other

If in the first 20 years a youngster gets introduced to the past, i.e., history, it is reasonably certainty that less that ½ of 1 percent will be exposed to church history of any kind. My guess is purely conjecture. What's your guess?

As with most children my families Catholic leaning traditions is what guided any consideration of God at all much less the history of it all. It seems clear now; after the fact; that my reading along with the documented history I was studying made me run into the same wall of confusion Martin Luther ran into as he transcribed the Bible into German.

The Christian Bible reasonably has the early church centered right there around the very place that Jesus was crucified. The apostles and early disciples it seems to me started the great commission in the region near the Mt. of Olives and spread the Gospel all around the Mediterranean. So how then did HQ end up in Rome? It is fascinating and I recommend listening to various documentaries on the subject. If there is a nature of man that has elements we know as political, i.e., a body of men that governs the affairs of an institution, and knowing the nature of man seems to lean into a thing called pride, and downstream of that a thing called power, very boastful claims can be made by powerful men that can change the course of things. Therefore, it seems that politics played a big role in having Rome claimed by certain early players to be the capitol of Christendom. The leader(s) of this Roman church consider its beginnings with the apostle Peter, but that seems by all accounts I have thus far been exposed too, to be, how shall I say...shoe horned into history. It is fair to note here that although these powerful men would be in control of the early church for a millennia they did protect the Christian Bible. Providence? Yes, surly providence! The problem started when these men claimed for themselves titles that would require people to make idols of their claimed titles.

Then in the 1500s the structures of the claimed organization of what is now known as the Roman Catholic Church was challenged by a Roman Catholic monk and started what is still known as the Protestant Reformation. Armed with all of this information an allegorical picture began to take form in my mind.

In 2004 Mel Gibson released the movie "The Passion of the Christ." Jim Caviezel played the part of Jesus. My allegorical picture is the creation of what I call "Lake Christos." As the movie is nearing its end Jesus is on the Cross looking up as he says the words, "It is finished." Our Lord goes limp as He gives up the ghost. The camera angle moves up in the air looking down at the tops of the three crosses, the Roman soldiers, and woman gathered at the foot of the Cross. The camera angle is high enough to suggest it is in the clouds. Then a rain drop starts to fall and the camera follows it to earth. The camera angle switches to an elevation view looking up at Jesus crucified as the rain drop splashes near the foot of the Cross. The earth starts to quake, a storm is brewing, the soldiers feel the terror and want to flee, but not before one of them pierces our Lord in his side to be sure he is dead. Blood and water pour from His side. It is here that Lake Christos begins in my mind.

That raindrop from Heaven mixed with the blood and water from the Son of God would exponential grow into a great lake allegorically I call Lake Christos. It will take the lake 60 years to reach its high water mark. It is words; yes it is God breathed words to be sure that will fill the lake. The work of the twelve apostles that did the initial "Great Commission" work would be the pure water of the gospel that would fill Lake Christos. The lake reached high water when John finished the book of Revelation on the island of Patmos in approximately 90 A.D.

So, if the lake is the pure clean water of the New Testament, I struggled for a long time how to paint the allegorical picture of the Old Testament into my mind tapestry. Then it hit me! If an allegorical diver were to search the allegorical bottom of the lake he would find an allegorical well. The well is deep, say 1,450 years deep to the time when Genesis was penned. The Old Testament words in the well are also God breathed words that still to this day are spring waters that also keep Lake Christos full.

What fills the lake was documented very well and it seems was preserved and protected by God Himself no matter how many Kings, Emperors, potentates, presidents, government bodies of men and or woman, corporate entities, or individual depraved persons try to remove God from the mind of man. From the Caesars at the time of Christ, to Diocletian, to Hitler, Stalin, Mao, and now much of the US Corporation and oligarchs the world over doing their best to destroy God it has never succeeded nor can it. The Word is out! The lake cannot be drained.

The above explains the tapestry of Lake Christos. Now let me explain how the allegorical lake helped me get my head around the history of the Church.

Allegorically this lake is closer to heaven than any other lake since the water in it are Gods words and therefore it follows that they are the highest words in the world. Now since the great commission requires that this water reaches the rest of the world, little streams of the water flowed downstream to the nations of the world that were in a drought, so to speak.

~ THE 1ST CREEK - 300 A.D. ~

At the time of Christ the main power broker was Rome and so the water historically flowed that way first. For most of the first 300 years the Roman Empire tried to stop the flow of water and even tried to drain the lake completely. Those that carried the water from the lake were killed. Nevertheless the waters continued to flow. After a time the Caesars of Rome would give up trying to stop the flow and would declare that lake Christos is the only lake the empire could draw water from. Since Rome was the center of the empire or the Hollywood / D.C. of the day, and the nature of man gravitates towards that which is glitzy and or powerful it seems most reasonable that the early power brokers of the church would stay close to where the action is, which it seems they did.

Concerning Lake Christos water, rather than just drinking the lake water as it was, after a few hundred years, certain men started to add stuff to the water that was not in the lake. They would be successful in polluting the lake and the pure crystal clear water would be cloudy for a thousand years. During those first thousand years, perhaps the most egregious thing they did is make up the papacy, followed by the hierarchical structure of special men, they claim are alter Christos, or another Christ. The pope, of course is the boss "alter Christos," followed by lesser degrees of "other Christs." How did they acquire these titles….well they just said so.

And, if you are near the seats of power and influence, power and position so claimed can and did become the norm and still is to this day. It must be remembered that at that time the populace was largely ignorant, and to be clear not stupid, but unlearned. When people are raised in ignorance, they can be easily led or groomed and made to follow, especially by the use of guilt or fear or both. .

The other pollutants added to the pure water of Lake Christos were the Roman Catholic sacraments. They are listed here each with the comment "not in the lake." To be clear and forthright, all of the below are fallacious because each sacrament can only happen pursuant to the special men and their claimed alter Christos status. Once it is realized by drinking in the pure water of the lake for yourself, the claimed positions of the "special alter Christos men" is not in the lake, then all of the below sacraments fade away.

Sacraments claimed but not in the lake are:

1. Baptism of infants – not in the lake. (See chap. 7)
2. Confirmation – not in the lake.
3. Holy Communion per Roman prescriptions – not in the lake.
4. Confession – not in the lake.
5. Marriage per Roman prescriptions – not in the lake.
6. Holy orders – not in the lake.
7. Anointing of the sick – not in the lake

I recognize the sting of the above for Roman Catholics for I also was groomed into believing the above structures. However, after learning that it is a small percentage of people, 3% to 5%, who read the lake and consume its purity it becomes clear how and why so many are stuck in the mire of the polluted waters. It is my honest hope and prayer for my Roman Catholic friends and family to read the lake, ask questions, challenge mostly yourself, discern, search around for the many chemists that have worked and continue to work so very hard to clear away the pollution.

Beyond the above, other very strange and mystic things were also added to the lake that while seemly beautiful and innocent once honestly analyzed have become a muck or a quick sand which Roman Catholics get stuck in. To get out of this muck is very, very, very tough and can take years. Some of this muck includes:

A. Indulgences - not in the lake.

B. Mary as co-redeemer and co-mediator – not in the lake.
C. Purgatory – not in the lake.
D. The Mass – not in the lake.
E. Worship of idols – not in the lake.
F. The Rosary – not in the lake.
G. Sainthood – not in the lake.

Again, it is the claimed alter Christos status of "special men" and their self-perceived infallibility that gives any of the above consideration at all. Once it is realized that this "alter Christos" claim is not in the lake, all of the other claims will dissipate like the sun burning off the low lying fog of a misty morning.

Not only is there the lake for you to read yourself, there are many chemists that have held up various beakers of Lake Christos water to analyze. Read, or listen to the many chemists. I submit once you get started you will find it fascinating and most reasonably traumatic if you too have been stuck in the muck and mire. Once you pull your feet out of the muck, allegorically consider turning around on the shoreline of Lake Christos and stare out over the crystal clear water, take in its pure message of everlasting life, take a deep breath, close your eyes, look up, thank God, and then praise His Name. Now your journey begins! Welcome to the church.

~ THE 2ND CREEK – 600 A.D. ~

An unusual character rose to power in a most unusual time and started a most unusual religion known as Islam. His name was Mohammad. There is a trickle of water from the lake and that being "recognition" and a certain "respect" for the Torah, the Psalms, the four Gospels, and that Mary was a virgin and that Jesus born of a virgin was miraculous. However, "recognition" of these books could not be denied as these books or scriptures were well known at the time, i.e., he could not deny their existence nor the Word therein. In fact, it is reasonable Islam could not exist at all without that which it "recognizes" or borrows from. "Respect" I submit is a fallacious term to associate with Islam. The very definition of "respect" is:

> **respect:** *to feel or show deferential regard for, esteem or admire; to avoid interfering with or intruding upon; to avoid violating.*

Islam does not do any of those things especially the intruding upon, and violating part.

In fact its very mission is to intrude by force, and violate by death anyone who does not submit to the Islamic intrusions and violations of all that is the essence of the gospels. To be fair there are peaceful Muslims, but they will not speak out against those factions of Islam that call for complete subjugation of the world for fear of death.

While Roman Catholicism started with Lake Christos water and polluted it, Islam only recognizes Lake Christos, and made up its own Lake. Instead of sacraments, Islam's' lake has what it calls pillars. As noted above in the discussion of Roman Catholicism above each pillar noted below is followed by the note "not in the lake" meaning of course, not in Lake Christos. These pillars are as follows:

1. Confession of faith or Shahada – not in the lake.
2. Prayer of Salat – not in the lake.
3. Alms giving or Zakat – not in the lake.
4. The fast or Sawm – not in the lake.
5. Pilgrimage or Hajj – not in the lake.

Having given consideration to Islam and its history I recognize that Muslims are trapped much like Roman Catholics, with the difference that added to guilt is the added absolute fear of execution by the sword. Mostly by guilt followed by fear most Muslims would never consider a walk to the shores of Lake Christos. I would, however, note that the trip can be done privately on your magic rectangle, your phone. It should also be noted here that it is only 3% to 5% of Muslims that read their own book, the Quran. Those that do often memorize it in Arabic not understanding the very words they recite. Were the many millions of Muslims to read in the language they comprehend they would certainly see many things that would give them pause. Why?

All human beings have a God given trait called a conscience, Which is a place in the mind that is very much capable of using another God given trait called reason to sort out between two ideas or beliefs that when juxtaposed are conflicting. Many times and certainly this is true of the Gospels verses the Quran, the conflicting beliefs are going to fall into conflicting categories – true or false, moral or immoral, righteous or unrighteous, and ultimately good or evil. If my Muslim brother would sit quietly and alone and consider the claims of the Quran and the life of Mohammad in the Hadith and jot down those things that your conscience suggests are at least suspect, reasonably immoral, most certainly disturbing, and in many cases nonsensical. If the Hadith is read, the claims about the "blessed" nature of Mohammad will certainly cause the reader great pause.

It saddens me that a Muslim is very unlikely to venture to the shores of Lake Christos since the grooming starts early and most Muslims only understand their books by citations from clerics and very seldom read for themselves. Another cultural norm for Muslims is that group think and the peer pressure of the group does not allow for the time to be an individual and therefore think for and study for oneself. Pray for the truth. Ask yourself, if Christianity is the truth would I want to know.

The scriptures teach that God rains his blessings on the just and the unjust. It seems to me this very technology being used to type these words are a blessing from God from the skills of many craftsmen that perfected this modern day parchment and quill. One of God's gift to man is his reasoning capacity to categorize things and when useful for analysis of ideas laid side by side. The matrix below is such a tool. I wish to lay side by side the words in Lake Christos verses the words on the same subject in the Quran. The 3rd column is a brief comment hopefully to make the reader question or consider which is more reasonable. I pray your conscience and the reasoning power all God's children, both men and women, were gifted with makes you want to consider a ride in a boat on Lake Christos to fish for more truth.

Lake Christos	Lake Islam	Reasoned Consideration
Adam & Eve tended the garden and walked with God.	A rock fell from heaven so Adam takes it upon himself to build an altar.	For what purpose would Adam need a rock when he walked and talked with God??
Adam and Eve were the 1st people.	Adam and Eve were the 1st people	Hence we are all brothers and sisters. How then can anyone hate anyone else?
The seed of Noah & wife makes them parents of all mankind after the great flood.	The seed of Noah & wife makes them parents of all mankind after the great flood.	Hence we are all brothers and sisters. How then can anyone hate anyone else?
The sons of Noah – Shem, Ham, and Japheth had children whom would be cousins.	The sons of Noah – Shem, Ham, and Japheth had children whom would be cousins.	Hence we are all family by blood. How then can anyone hate anyone else?
Genesis 1:16 God made lights in the firmament of the heavens, with two great lights, the sun to rule the day, the moon to rule the night.	Suri 18, 86 The sun sets in a black muddy pool (hot water) and people live near this place. {Mohammad said Alexander the Great found the resting place} Hadith 4002, Mohammad states to friend the sun sets in a pool of warm water.	The Bible is not clear on the mechanics, but man through his quest for knowledge did figure the mechanics out. What Mohammad claimed was nonsensical even then. Please discern rightly what false means!!
The lake is silent on shooting stars.	Shooting stars are angels throwing missiles at devils trying to steal secrets from Allah	The Bible is silent….but Mohammad's claim sounds like the imagination of a four year old. Please discern!!
Ten Commandments – thou shall not bow down to any idol of anything whatsoever, and thou shall not bear false witness which would include lying to yourself.	Travel to Mecca, march around a black rock 7 times, kiss the black rock & claim it is not worship	To claim up is down when it is obviously up is self-deception followed by self-righteousness to deny it.
Mary conceived Jesus by the Spirit of God.	Mary conceived Jesus by the Spirit of God.	God is the divine half of the offspring, Jesus. Mary is the mankind half of the offspring, Jesus. Hence, God-Man

Lake Christos	Lake Islam	Reasoned Consideration
Jesus birth was miraculous.	Mohammad's birth was ordinary.	Which is closer to God????
Jesus life was righteous, peaceful, holy, and sinless. He taught love God, love your neighbor.	Mohammad's life was violent, murderous, condoned rape, adultery by legal sleight of hand, slavery and had sex with a child.	Which life is reasonably looked upon by God as good and therefore blessed, loving your neighbor or abusing and /or killing them???
Matt 18:6, Mark 9:42, Luke 17:2 ….whoever causes a little one to sin or stumble, it would be better for him if a millstone was hung around his neck, and he was thrown into the sea.	Suri 65, vs. 4 – If a man divorces a girl who does not have monthly menstrual cycle…. if a man wants to have sex with a prepubescent girl divorced by another he must wait 3 months before marrying her to have sex.	This more than any other consideration between the Christian Bible and the Quran / Hadith should cause great pause. Moral or immoral??? The answer to this should not take more than the blink of an eye.
Jesus was crucified.	God tricked everyone took Jesus, made Judas look like Jesus and crucified Judas.	Jesus foretold his death exactly as it happened. So Islam makes Jesus a liar.
The Torah, Psalms, and Gospels were all given by God (Allah)	The Torah, Psalms, and Gospels were corrupted. So God (Allah) sent Mohammad to correct with the perfectly preserved Quran.	If God was able to preserve His word in the Quran, why was God not able to preserve the Torah, Psalms, & Gospels?
Gospel - Free offer of salvation by faith is the gift of Jesus to all people. Faith in what? Read the Lake.	Shahada – Declare or die in this life by the sword of self-proclaimed superior men. Salvation by the sword???	Vengeance is Mine says God, not any mans. All men are commanded to love our neighbors and our enemies. ???
Jesus on purpose and with purpose died to forgive sin, defeated death, appeared to at least 500. Records of which have been recovered and are more numerous than any event ever.	The original recorded Quran's did not say the same things so some were burned. What is the truth is hotly contested even within Muslim communities.	Read, read, read. Pray for God to show you "The Way."

It is my honest hope and prayer for my Islamic friends to read the Quran lake in a language you understand, ask questions, challenge mostly yourself, discern, search around for the many chemists that have worked and continue to work so very hard to analyze the Islam lake water, shine a light on its beakers, and at the same time offer for your consideration the water in Lake Christos. Check out the book "Seeking Allah, Finding Jesus." A chemist extraordinaire! His journey took four years and started when his best friend David Wood and a Christian asked him what he believed, and then why he believed, and then finally this question, "If you are wrong, would you want to know it." I submit that is a question with the utmost of sincerity Christians the world over would ask their Muslim friends if they could. It doesn't get asked much especially in countries or neighborhoods that are predominantly Muslim as death is a likely consequence.

Throughout history men it seems can be easily rallied to various causes and be led to be extremely violent for whatever the claimed cause is. Any war ever fought is proof of this. The beginning of Islam is no different. Many men were rallied to violently conquer. Most such leaders that rally many men to war are forgotten. Mohammad is different. Different than any Cesar or general his legacy has lasted more than 1300 years where most others might last 100 years. It seems reasonable that this is because his followers started with violence and force, and that formula has worked and keeps Mohammad's memory alive for "only" that reason. I say this because by any reasoned standard of morality the life of Mohammad, especially viewed through the lens of Jesus, like Belshazzar, and the writing on the wall, or more precisely the writing in the water of Lake Christos, would find Mohammad wanting, and very much so.

Islam as a religion is large and grew by the power of the sword rather than by "Good News. Islam's' book; the Quran; while having some commonality with the Christian Bible it is certainly contradictory in the core tenant of salvation offered in the pure water of Lake Christos. By the time of Mohammad's demise after he was poisoned by a Jewish woman and suffered a long agonizing slow death there is no connection to Lake Christos, i.e., the creek was and still is a dry creek bed. Islam would be its own thing, its own lake and if it would have a name from a Christian perspective might be "Bad News" since there is no salvation freely offered and freely accepted, rather Islam salvation in their terms is by force, submit to the force or die, and works as prescribed by the force.

Islamic apologists, it seems, have perfected a lexicon of their own which I believe is accurately defined by "word salad." For example, if one is interested there are Islamic apologists available for anyone to see on YouTube. Very few will debate a Christian Apologist, but there are some that do and when they do the claims made about the virtuosity of Mohammad, the scientific claims made, the miracles claimed, the superiority of men over women, to name a few categories when exposed will at minimum cause the listener to wrinkle their forehead in confusion.

> **cobelligerent** - *a country fighting with another power against a common enemy*

Anti-Islamic apologists, including Christians, ex-Muslims, and some atheists do a good job of laying bare the fallaciousness of Islam. A curious example of a type of "cobelligerent" partnership would be David Wood (a Christian apologist) and Ridvan Aydemir (an ex-Muslim atheist apologist); who team up on YouTube to expose Islam for its faulty foundation, claims, and proclamations.

In that partnership David Wood, side by side, with an ex-Muslim atheist work together to dismantle Islam. Most of the apologetic work or debates with Islam seem to always pit the Bible and Jesus Christ against Mohammad and the Quran. The fruit of that unlikely cobelligerent partnership can be seen by the comments from Muslims the world over that have left Islam and becoming Christians just because of this unlikely partnership.

These apologists do a good job of bringing the clear waters of Lake Christos to those trapped in the Islamic "Bad News" lake. In fact, because of the new technology of the internet by their own admission the clerics in Islam recognize that they are losing their jihad in that they are finding it harder to recruit. Young and old Muslims alike are like Roman Catholics recognizing that they have been guilted into and stuck in the muck and mire that "in fact" started in the pure waters of Lake Christos but was greatly polluted. When the words of Islam are compared with the words in Lake Christos and the pollution settles out and "The Truth" of the gospel can be consumed, there will be a freedom not imagined unless…..!

If Mohammad and the claimed words received are so convincing why would it be necessary to put anyone to the sword? It seems the discerning mind will conclude that forced by threat of death to do anything at all is not a very convincing argument. If there is hell and damnation why hurry it along by the sword, it will come soon enough. Jesus offers a better way, and as it turns out he is very patient, he waited sixty four years for me to hear him call. He is waiting for you too.

God created you and all you see. That power certainly had the power to incarnate himself, which Muslims do acknowledge by the miraculous virgin birth of the Messiah. If you have a spirit, which you do, then Gods spirit is most certainly greater. That spirit is of God, the Son Jesus is of God, and then there is God. Hey, how about that, a reasoned explanation that God has three persons!

The best and reasonably the only way to find out is to come to Lake Christos and drink, consume, bathe the mind. It will be difficult especially because of the sword of Islam, but Jesus offers freedom through love and will save you if you seek Him. The water in Lake Christos is available for all of Islam to drink, and it's free. Please, on behalf of all Christians, welcome to Lake Christos, please come with us, and bathe your mind.

~ THE 3RD CREEK – 1500 A.D. ~

The waters would flow from Rome to Germany where a Catholic monk would analyze the Rome water and discover that it was polluted. This monks name was Martin. He was successful in sharing his analysis of the water and quickly set out to transport the clear water of the gospel to the rest of the world. Fortuitously or providentially because of a new invention called the printing press which in this allegory is an aqueduct to carry Lake Christos water. Martins re-discovery of the pure water with the pollution removed started a movement. People started to drink the water for themselves and not have it filtered through the vestments of the Roman bishops. People could see for themselves and protested, filtering the pollution out, and drinking in only the pure clear water of the lake. The people craved this water and desired to share it far and wide, how could they not?

The lake water itself says that men will try and pollute the water and sadly that continues to this day. Regardless, the lake is available for all that wish to go to its shores and bathe their minds in all of the words in the lake.

In essence Martin dammed up the creek that came from Rome and dug a new canal from Germany straight back to Lake Christos. Then by connecting aqueducts Lake Christos water would reach France, England, Switzerland, and then all of Europe, across a channel to The British Isles, and then cross the Atlantic ocean to reach the New World of the Americas. Along the way the aqueducts would find certain men that would further analyze the water and find beautiful truths to share. Most assuredly a benefit to mankind and most especially as the 2nd millennia A.D. nears its end.

~ CLOUDY WATERS 90 A.D. - 2023 A.D. ~

The pure water in Lake Christos is all captured in the Christian Bible in God breathed words and for 1,933 years, (2023-90=1,933) has been and still is available for all of mankind to drink from the crystal clear pure waters.

Because the nature of man is fallen it seems as described by Jesus the door is narrow and few will find it. Within what is called the Christian community it seems as also foretold by Jesus there would be many false teachers. So, what is the average, run of the mill, created in the image of God man or woman to do? With so much information in the world available to us, why can we not find it, sort it out, make sense of it, and so forth. The answer to the why is simple and complicated.

First what information are we talking about? I submit there are only two categories of information to consider, and they are 1) why are we here? And, 2) everything else. The Son of God tells us how to find the answer to the first category of information. In Matthew 7:7, Ask and it will be given to you, seek and you will find, knock and it will be opened to you (NKJV). There is only one book or one lake that has the answer and that makes it simple to find the answer to the first category of information.

The second category of information is complicated in that it encompasses "everything else" not in the lake or Bible. Fortunately, we were gifted with reason and over the span of time mankind has discerned that categories are useful to make sense of "everything else." There are so many categories of "everything else" that it is reasonably certain that no one will ever know much less comprehend all of the "everything else" categories. We naturally seem to specialize in and take interest in certain categories of "everything else" which is curious and fortunate in itself and naturally seems to organize mankind into social groups so that all may benefit by the interests of the individual.

Anyway, for the purpose of this old man thinking for the first time and for consideration of Lake Christos and the answers therein that are simple, I hope and I pray that you make the time to, as Christ said, 1) ask, 2) seek, and 3) knock.

When you do you will find the pure clean water in the middle of the lake, but like any lake there will be storms and near the shore mud may be stirred up and cloud the water. Why? The infallibility of man. In the scriptures early on as the apostles traveled about to spread the gospel and establish or plant churches where the saints (believers) could and necessarily should gather to "stay in the lake," or "stay in the word." Even then certain men would preach stuff that was not in the lake. Reason should tell you those that "knew best" were the apostles who were taught directly by Jesus. The apostles had to travel from town to town to correct the "cloudy waters." They clearly had the purest water from the source, that source being Jesus, the messiah, the Christ, the Son of God. Then as today, certain men would lead believers to their own coves preaching stuff that is not in the middle of the lake. The problem, then as now, the people tended to gravitate toward personalities, glitz, pomp, structure or tradition. If we would take a weekend or two to row out to the middle of Lake Christos, read and drink in the pure water for ourselves we would easily see the cloudy waters in the various cloudy coves.

Today there are many muddy coves and I suggest everyone should make a trip to the middle of Lake Christos. Note that the trip to the middle of the lake can only be done on a one man life raft or single person kayak. You have to see and drink as an individual, for we all will be judged individually.

Realistically it will take more than a weekend or two, but the entire lake can be read in 72 hours. The investment for you might just be that at glory you will not hear, "Depart from me, I never knew you." It should be noted that we are fortunate to live in a time that unlike in the days of Jesus, the teachers would have to travel days to spread the word. When errors were detected it might take weeks, months, and years for an apostle to travel and guide the error back to the lake. Today, you don't have to wait till the weekend or several weekends only to be disheartened to find out you ventured into a cloudy cove. The internet can take you on a boat ride to 10 different churches today, hear the messages, contrast those messages to what you yourself read. There are hundreds of proper gospel preaching churches in America, and hundreds that are in some very cloudy waters. If this old man could offer counsel or direction to good and proper teachers refer to the acknowledgments at the front of this book.

~ LAKE CHRISTOS SUMMARY ~

Certainly this allegory is different, however Lake Christos developed from biblical accounts as well as words used by Jesus. The use of blood, water, and also bread are allegorical "words" used by Jesus to explain why God incarnated Himself divinely and temporarily into this world. With consideration bread and water are very reasonable words since Jesus came from a metaphysical realm, i.e., a place beyond time and space, which to this day cannot be understood much less explained by the mind of man. The use of words man can understand, i.e., blood, bread and water may seem simple on the one hand, but most logically the same words are as complex as necessary since blood, bread and water are required for man's existence in this physical realm. So their use to explain how man can transcend to a metaphysical realm starts to make a little more sense as there are as yet no words in this realm that can state with a certainty anything in that realm except for the word "God."

Jesus used blood, bread and water in an allegorical sense in the following scriptures:

- **NKJV --- John 4: 13-14** -- 13 Jesus answered and said to her, *"Whoever drinks of this water will thirst again, 14 but whoever* *drinks of the water that I shall give him will never thirst. But the water that I shall give him will become in him a fountain of water springing up into everlasting life."*

- **NKJV --- John 6: 35** -- And Jesus said to them, *"I am the bread of life. He who comes to me shall never hunger, and he who believes in me shall never thirst."*
- **NKJV --- John 6:53-58** -- 53 And Jesus said to them, *"Most assuredly, I say to you, unless you eat the flesh of the Son of Man and drink His blood, you have no life in you. 54 Whoever eats My flesh and drinks My blood has eternal life, and I will raise him up at the last day. 55 For My flesh is food indeed, and My blood is drink indeed. 56 He who eats My flesh and drinks My blood abides in Me, and I in him. 57 As the living Father sent Me, and I live because of the Father, so he who feeds on Me will live because of Me. 58 This is the bread which came down from heaven—not as your fathers ate the manna, and are dead. He who eats this bread will live forever."*
- **NKJV --- John 6:60-63** -- 60 Therefore many of His disciples, when they heard this, said, *"This is a hard saying; who can understand it?" 61* When Jesus knew in Himself that His disciples complained about this, He said to them, *"Does this offend you? 62 What then if you should see the Son of Man* ***"ascend where He was before?"*** *63 It is the Spirit who gives life; the flesh profits nothing. The* ***"words"*** *that I speak to you are spirit, and they are life.*

Notice in these instances three life giving substances (blood, bread and or water) are used to explain a metaphysical place that is forever, or everlasting, or eternal. Simple on the one hand as we can understand this temporal existence, but mind boggling in that to comprehend forever is certainly complex. Also notice in John 6:62 (hi-lighted in grey above) Jesus with specificity says **"ascend where He was before."** Is that not a metaphysical place? Also, same sentence Jesus states with specificity that the **"words" are spirit**. Or, once again using words, (water, bread, and blood) known to man in this physical realm to explain a metaphysical realm.

If grace could be extended for my allegory, Lake Christos is filled with all of the God breathed words of God, through the Son, carried by the Holy

Spirit that I hope may be helpful for someone out there to make sense of the Bible, and also a way, albeit sophomoric, a simple way to see Church history.

It should be noted here that Lake Christos started with the crucifixion of Jesus the Redeemer. A bloody crucifixion, and although this entire lake allegory has a purpose that I hope is conveyed well, the blood of Christ as noted above is not allegorical. To be circumspect, if it is hard to comprehend blood, bread and water as a way to convey an eternal existence it is equally hard to comprehend why God the Father would be pleased to crush God the Son and so moved by the Holy Spirit of God to shed the very "real" blood of Jesus in such a horrific way to save sinners. This historical fact then requires a separation from the allegorical to the real.

The only way I can make any sense of it is to consider general revelation, i.e., the general nature of man. We know as mature men and women that a father or a mother would without hesitation jump between a lion, a bear, a rabid dog, or whatever threat if their baby or child was in eminent danger of death. We probably have seen or read of accounts where someone almost without thinking would jump into freezing water, flooding water, a burning fire, or whatever threat to save someone they don't know personally. What is that? What is that innate thing in the nature of man that would do such a thing? I think it is simple. We are created in the image of God. That should give us pause. If we have such a thing in our nature, that is to say, save a life, then surely God wants that all should have life and not only life but eternal life.

Jesus voluntarily, on purpose, and with purpose jumped in front of that threat and sacrificed Himself so that we might live. If you're asking what threat, the answer is death itself, yes death! The difference between the examples above is man's salvific act only lasts until the end of that saved persons temporal life on this planet. The salvific act of Jesus is eternal.

Although general revelation should make that easy to understand it isn't. It isn't until you consider it greatly, accept it, understand that His sacrifice was for you, that there is a right and a wrong way to live, and we all have a nature to live wrongly, repent for those wrong things, turn from those things, and live righteously. To do that is to have faith that Jesus

Christ is who he said he was and he shed His blood for you if you would simply believe.

It should also be noted that the right way to live is explicit, very explicit, in the pure waters of Lake Christos. I implore you, for your sake, read the lake, read every drop of water in the lake. In the very real sense that water sustains life for us now, to believe what the Son of God said and did sustains life forever. The Christian Bible is the water of everlasting life.

~ LAKE CHRISTOS ~

There is a lake with waters pure,
That to drink thereof, does have a cure,
For what you ask, I feel ok,
But please consider that's just today.

If today you walk through pastures green,
Tomorrow you may stumble into a great ravine.
It could be sorrow, it might be heartache,
It could be horror, or might be heartbreak.

It gets us all you're not immune,
To the way of life that will come to consume.
If not today, than on the morrow,
You can rest assured there will be sorrow.

We all have youth and while certainly fun,
When old age comes we know we'll soon be done.
Is that all there is, then what's it all for,
There must be more for this time under the sun.

You mentioned a lake that has a cure.
You cast that out there to be a lure,
I'm listening now, and want to be sure,
That I too may drink this water you say has a cure.

I have your attention, and for that I am glad,
But the lake is a metaphor, for words you already had.
Part of the words you had on your heart,
They were there for you early; they were there at the start.

For those that were missing your Creator did send,
His Son, the Good Shepard, to tell us this life's not the end.
He came with good news, for which you can be sure,
His life for ours is the trade and the cure.

The lake is called Christos, and it is filled with His words,
That heals all that is wrong from your head to your toes.
If you bathe in it daily, and drink till you're full,
You will find your salvation, the cure to all woes.

But enough of the prose, the metaphor made,
The message for all is His life that He gave.
Jesus His name, He died on a Cross, so that we see our sin,
And that we truly are lost.

The Bible to be sure are the words in the lake,
All that you are is all that's at stake,
Whether you read them or hear them,
Consider with haste, for there will be a time that it's too late.

God created man and knew he would fall,
Man did as expected so a correction He made,
God then left instructions, the law it is called,
But no one could do it, no, no one at all.

So He entered creation and did send His Son,
To forgive us our lot and all that we've done,
There was only one condition and only the one,
That we believe in Him and that He was God's Son.

If we would but do this, He promised a Helper,
To provide us with comfort and a permanent shelter.
It's as simple as that; He is a door if you will,
A gateway to Heaven where the waters are still.

Amen
JKF 9-6-2022

The truth will cause tears to baptize

the windows to the soul!

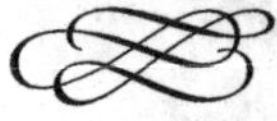

Chapter 7

BAPTISM

When first I considered writing this book it began with a list of topics or a prospective table of contents which included a chapter on baptism. At the time I was not a member of a church and only knew that it was a topic to think on. What happened turned out to be a real time journey to not only think on the topic but actually go through with the "ordinance of baptism." It seems in retrospect that this part of the journey happening while in the throes of writing this book seems to lay clear that things, all things encountered in this endeavor lead to a deeper understanding of God's grace and why the Cross and why the resurrection. Why Jesus left us with baptism, communion, gathering, prayer, and His words. Discovering these things and "thinking" on them turns out to be awesome. Awe being encountered often and I dare say daily.

This chapter then is a chronological accounting of thinking about the task, being compelled to move to the task, and then taking the plunge (ha-ha).

I had been attending Desert Hills Bible Church for a little over a year at this point and knew that I would be officially joining. The church has a process to join which very reasonably starts with an orientation to make it clear to those that want to land in, or find a biblical home, what they are getting into. By this time it was most clear to me that this was a proper home that would counsel me well. I filled out an application to join as well as a request to be baptized. The request for baptism doc turned out to be instrumental in that it caused me to consider with a magnanimous spirit how truly holy this sacrament is.

What follows then starts with witnessing 7 baptisms on February 13, 2022 and in particular the proclamation of a sister in Christ whose name is Heaven Dykhuizen. It was her testimony and proclamation of faith that gave me pause to consider that what might be proclaimed in front of the church, should be meaningful and hopefully inspire someone else to consider with the greatest of circumspection why this sacrament.

Taking Heaven's lead, I sat down to consider what it was in my journey that led me to the Jordan. So, I considered some specific landmarks, or "time-marks" in my life that I should have seen but did not. It didn't take long to consider a couple of Bible references for a title to the proclamation. The time-marks were seeds, why I did not see them were the scales on my eyes. Therefore, "*Seeds and Scales of an Old Man Thinking for the First Time*" seemed a good title for my proclamation and a good place to start.

So, I went back in time to think on the most obvious seeds that were there, but for scales could not be seen. It was a good exercise to write down particular events, some of which make no sense directly, others that make perfectly clear sense directly, but by the end explains with clarity how blind one can be. Retrospective consideration, or "Monday morning quarterbacking" and analysis of the game films points out the obvious missed opportunities. Just like an already played game, it cannot be replayed, but it can be a learning tool for self and most importantly for others..... (teammates and those on other teams).

SEEDS AND SCALES OF AN OLD MAN THINKING FOR THE 1ST TIME

>>> 1955 – SEEDS <<<

Born May 4th in Loveland Colorado to Richard and Mary Fitzgerald. Mother; deceased was in that category of clan called Irish-Catholic. My dad I do know was a believer, but for reasons unknown to me did not conform to the Roman Catholic doctrine. Both parents are deceased and I am sad at this point that I was not able to converse with them about the kingdom. I do not know if I was baptized as an infant. However, as I consider with reason that as a baby there was zero reasoning development at all to consider anything whatsoever how then might any infant mind be expected by ceremony alone to be conformed to Christ. In any event, 1955 is a landmark, but not significant to understanding.

>>> TANGENT - PAEDO BAPTISM <<<

I suppose this is as good a place as any to jot down thoughts about paedo or infant baptism. Note that my thoughts on the subject are, like this entire book, hatched in a mind that has only recently considered such things. On this topic I have listened to several debates and especially appreciated the kindness and love of neighbor that R.C. and Johnny Mac (R.C. Sproul and John MacArthur) showed each other as they discussed and defended their thoughts and considerations on this subject. I will not disclose their positions here, some of you know. Those that do not, I would direct you to their presentations at Ligonier Ministries. Your edification by many sources being my humble hope for you.

My thoughts center on the word ceremony. How did "ceremony" become such a part of the human experience? It seems reasonable to consider the 1st ceremony was the 7th day in which God rested. That "ceremony" being in recognition of that which He created (or accomplished) and noting that it was good. Taking God's lead and instruction the command that man and woman be joined as one, the ceremony of marriage was also instituted early on. It seems then if we have a nature like God; mankind easily took to the idea of recognition of good things and then having a ceremony. As parents we do it naturally to toddlers to ceremoniously recognize and reward them for the simplest of tasks. As children grow the utility of proper recognition and reward seems to come naturally. Why? I suppose because we, unlike any other living organism are created in the likeness and image of God. Ceremony, like other uniquely "human" natural characteristics is wholly distinct from the animal kingdom. Characteristics such as searching for meaning, considering meaning at all, creating structures and categories to make sense of meaning, etc. Elephants, pelicans, sea urchins, et al though reasonably very pleasing to God for His Glory do not possess the ability to reason, consider categories of reason, or recognize accomplishment and then have a ceremony.

So, considering through the lens of "general revelation" it seems man's nature innately conforms to God's nature in ceremony. When my daughter graduated from kindergarten there was an adorable ceremony complete with gown, cap with tassel, commencement music, and diploma. As a young father at the time I was proud as my daughter was asked to lead the procession holding a little American flag because she had been a good girl generally and scholastically gifted. However, it was not the children whom decided on the "ceremony." It was an "age old" tradition contrived by man reasonably and righteously following the lead of God to notice that a thing is good. My daughter had three more graduations, 8th grade, 12th grade, and 16th grade all too great fanfare, and each ceremony was good. Each ceremony commemorating a learned achievement.

The ceremony of paedo baptism, however, is not a ceremony of learned achievement for the baby. It might be, maybe, tangentially, possibly, be considered a "learned" achievement for the parents. Why?

In the movie, "A Few Good Men," Kevin Bacon plays "Captain Jack Ross," a JAG attorney, questioning a witness where in the Marine manual the procedure for "code reds" is found. The witness, Corporal Barnes, played by Noah Wyle, had to admit there is no such written word, code, ordinance, or instruction on "code reds." Since the defendants were claiming code reds as a defense and since "code reds" are not in any manual, in law they would be considered a fiction and therefore implying cannot be used as a defense.

However, Tom Cruise playing Lieutenant Daniel Kaffee, JAG attorney for the defense on cross examination of Corporal Barnes asks where in the manuals it states how to get to the mess hall. Corporal Barnes had to state that this was not in the manual. Kaffee feigning shock and surprise asks how then did he ever have a meal if it wasn't in the manual. Corporal Barnes stated he just followed the crowd at chow time.

This allegory illustrates how humans in many and perhaps most things just "follow the crowd at chow time." Discernment, interestingly enough, is a biblical instruction for God's people. So, in the movie it wasn't a bad thing to follow the crowd at chow time as that "following" led to sustenance. Even the "code reds" when not abused had utility to instruct and have a salvific effect of loving your neighbor as yourself. In that same courtroom scene Corporal Barnes stated that he had received a "code red" when he had forgotten to put resin on his hands, as trained, and his rifle slipped out of his hands on an assault drill because his palms got sweaty. That particular "code red" or "within the unit" discipline had utility to save. His unit through a blanket over his head and took turns punching him in the arm, which worked as a discipline as he noted in his testimony – he never dropped his rifle again. The use of the "code" got corrupted on another occasion when discernment from the top was corrupt because of an arrogant pride that infected the chain of command which ironically are very highly trained "sheep dogs." The sins compounded.

The commander, Colonel Nathan Jessup, played by Jack Nicholson had the sin of idolatry of position, idolatry of self, followed by the sin of bearing false witness, the sin of lying and using position to cover up the lye. King David in the Bible did a very similar thing that ended in the death of the husband of Bathsheba. King David ordered others to create the circumstance for the death of Bathsheba's husband. In like fashion the ordered code red created the circumstance for the death of a fellow marine. His next sin was using his position to cover it up and ordering his subordinates to sin. His junior officers some of whom were sycophants while others were cowards all compounded lie after lie making it worse and worse. In the end however there was judgment.

As Christians, we are supposed to be a unit, and our discipline comes from Christ. Like a good unit we are even instructed in the manual to hold each other accountable. Most unfortunately of the various branches (denominations) similar to the military branches, acquire an arrogance or pride concerning their branch. Ultimately, it will be adjudicated….. I pray God I do not hear the words, "Depart from Me, you workers of lawlessness." Matthew 7:23.

This is a good point to note that all, individually, not as a unit, will have such a judgment. So, use the discerning gift you have been given, read, read, read, discern. You're as intelligent as you need to be to figure this out. If you're struggling with which branch (military allegory) or denomination to consider study, study, study the branch brochures. Listen to Pastors, listen to other Pastors, and pray for guidance. As it turns out Jesus, the Christ, the Jewish Messiah, is called the Good Shepherd for a very good reason. Read the scriptures, you'll figure it out!!!

Back to baptism... From what I understand this particular (paedo baptism) chow line started about the same time as the (Roman Catholic) chow line approximately 300 years after the resurrection. At that time in history it was easier to goad the sheep, I mean crowd, as the leaders also forbade the sheep, I mean crowd, from reading the words. It was reasonably easier to do then as most of the populace could not read. Then in the 1500s the printing press was invented perhaps providentially at the same time as a Roman Catholic monk was transcribing the scriptures into German and noted that what he had been taught by his Roman Catholic teachers was "in fact" nowhere to be found in the manual. Also, and reasonably providentially, the first "manual" or book ever to be produced, published, and distributed to the sheep, I mean crowd, was the Christian Bible. Hummmm!!!......How about that!

Interestingly enough the "sheep" allegories in the Bible are useful, but only if one has some understanding of the nature of sheep. Today the masses have access to most all knowledge amassed for all of history literally at their fingertips, but know less and less and are being conditioned "or herded" to be content with being sheep and not using the God given gift of reason to read words that would let them open the sheep gate and walk out. For instance, the nature of sheep is a finger tap or mouse click away and then using the mind to see the obvious parallels to how people are so easily herded, yet, what are the odds that people will click that mouse or tap that screen to learn even about the nature of sheep?

A useful word to describe what happens when people follow the crowd at chow time is "tradition" or "custom." So concerning paedo baptism, it's not in the manual, i.e., the Bible, but like a "code red" in the above allegory it is a tradition that has made its way into the customs of some Christian churches. The question is then, is it a good or a bad tradition or somewhere in between?

Rather than "follow the crowd at chow time" for this particular ceremony, a modicum of acquired knowledge seems appropriate.

For the baby it is a no thing or "nothing" since the baby at this point in the new little life has achieved nothing in the way of knowledge, achievement, challenge or anything resembling wisdom. So why baptize a baby?

The best I can come up with is a ceremony of "welcoming." In other words if the adults had a mind to have a ceremony for this most joyous of arrivals to the family and discerning with understanding that such a ceremony is a good reason to celebrate a welcoming of God's newest. If that is a ceremony that can be joyous for such a welcoming committee (so to speak) great, but it seems to me that baby baptism has been conflated with being "born again" baptism which is rationally a conscience driven decision by the individual only when said individual has knowledge and per the scriptures is called. The danger seems to be when the adults think that the baby baptism ensures salvation and impart that notion to the child who grows up believing that. Further, at least in the Roman baptism dogma, the sprinkling of water on the baby is claimed to forgive the baby for a perceived sin the baby most certainly could not possibly have committed. The scriptures do say that sins of fathers will be "punished" or "visited" to the children to the 3rd and 4th generation. Certainly this "visit" does catch all, but really, during the first week or even the first year. First, note that it says "sins of the fathers," not "sins of the infants." Second, the "visit" and the "punishment" necessarily does start early on, say especially plus or minus two years of age. The brokenness curse shows up early, but at the same time the innate "blessing" of a natural "punishment" also seems to necessarily parallel the sin. In other words, the brokenness sin grows naturally with a little one, and the "punishment" or "corrective" discipline also "naturally" follows with the parents. If the discipline does not follow, well.... the world is full of what happens when God's corrections are not followed.

General revelation or more specifically, open your eyes while you hold a new born in your arms and try and make an argument that at this point, this very particular point, this infant has sinned. Yes, most certainly the sin of Adam will be "visited" on the new baby in due time, but with objective observation of the truth of a new baby, especially in your arms, certainly not that day. For more on this topic read the gospels and per the scriptures "discern."

The day I finished the above thoughts and over coffee I asked a friend his thoughts. My friends name is Jim, he is a Navy Seal. He was brought up Catholic, and is now Episcopalian, which he tells me is akin to Catholic light. (??) In any event, Jim suggested that paedo baptism is a baptism "into Christ." I had not heard that and had to ruminate on that. A couple of days later I met Jim again to run my thoughts by him. It seems to me that baptism "into" Christ, while seemingly a good explanation with obvious good intent, by retrospective analysis could be put in a category called "wishful thinking." Certainly, any Christian parent would have a wish that their newborn baby would grow to be a follower of Christ, but, that "wish" is different than the wishes of say a "last will and testament" which are considered in law as sacrosanct, i.e., beyond alteration, criticism, or interference. A wish in this sense can only be done by an adult with acquired knowledge. A baby clearly could never make a sacrosanct wish of any kind. So a better word might be hope.

The fallen part of man's nature will become very apparent to parents when the baby grows to around 2 years old. So the "hope" that a baby will conform to Christ will in short order become or understood to be "wishful thinking." Then what? Education, training, challenge, achievement, prayer, proper biblical instruction, and perhaps most importantly a loving mother and engaged father.

Paedo baptism then, while an obvious loving wish or better yet "hope" of a parent, cannot possibly have bearing on the baby's conforming to Christ. Old Testament examples are Eli, Samuel, and David. These examples are of righteous men whom had sons that surely their fatherly "wishful thinking" for them as babies would be for these babies to grow up in the ways of God. They did not. In other words, wishful thinking of even some of the most righteous of men does not ensure the righteousness of offspring. How many good Christian parents, all of whom would have hoped for their children to follow their lead and follow the ways of our Lord only to be greatly saddened when their children seem to have fallen away or taken another path altogether despite, and sometimes "in spite of" the righteous intent and hopefulness of parents.

I shared with Jim an allegory for consideration..... Jim was a Navy Seal. Jim was ceremoniously accepted into this elite group of warrior by training, acquired and specific knowledge, and challenge. Ironically, one of the specific skills trained into Jim was how to survive a total immersion baptism (of sorts). Seals are bound hands and feet and thrown into the water and learn how to survive, the Seals call it "drown proofing." Clearly it was the training that taught Jim how to stay alive. Jim has a son now who is a Marine. When Jim's son was born, Jim could no more baptize (drown proof) his baby boy into Navy Sealness than he could baptize him into Christ likeness. He might hope for his son to follow into his profession of Seal, and he might hope his son follow his lead into Christ, but that it seems is obviously and objectively for a future time and not subjectively by wishful thinking nor a custom made up by certain men that make claim to doctrine that is not in the manual.

Reason then might suggest that some comprehension and understanding of the ceremony of baptism is required or one should not go through with the ceremony. To forgo Seal training would be a fool's errand, fraudulent, endanger your team, not to mention it could get you killed. Likewise, to forgo a measure of understanding of what it means to be baptized into Christ likeness could also be a fool's errand, fraudulent, and endanger your team (the church), not to mention may leave you spiritually dead. There is much more to it than following the crowd at chow time or getting a participation ribbon without merit.

Some Seals, like all endeavors in life, will have those that excel, (like young Samuel). Such a man will generally rise to a rank of leader, but when in the conscription of their service all are held to account for the safety of their team and accountable to the team as proper Seals. Similarly, being baptized into the church, certain saints become leaders (elders) and are accountable for the safety (or souls) of their flock, and in like manner it is fellow saints that should keep their brothers and sisters (including elders) accountable to a certain type of character – that being the character of Christ.

Baptism then should be a good and a great ceremony to recognize a very specific and perhaps the pinnacle of achievement in one's journey in this temporal life. While my friend Jim's immersion in water as a specific lifesaving baptism of sorts that would and did keep him alive under some trying circumstances in the Vietnam War, his "drown proofing" was only a recognition of an acquired and specific salvific knowledge. Likewise, a baptism into the church of Christ is recognition of an acquired and specific salvific knowledge, that being the Son of God's already completed work on the Cross. To acquire this specific knowledge of noted completed work, read the gospels noting when you get there that Jesus made a statement for all who complete the training that "It is finished." Your training will only be complete when you truly understand this.

In the case of the Seal program a ceremony commemorates the completion of the training, this ceremony being ordained, as it were, by the Unit Commander. In the case of baptism into the church of Christ the origin of the ceremony was ordained by Christ himself who instructed the "Unit Commanders" we today call "Pastors" to perform the ordinance. It seems then reasonable to take very seriously why? Why do the ceremony? Read the manual!!!

As I go through this exercise of mind and discuss with friends, it dawns on me that discussions, writings, sermons, and canons have been instituted or not instituted on this issue since about 300 years after Christ walked the earth. All I can say with reasonably certainty is that I will be baptized at 67 years of age next month, or July 10, 2022 and after due consideration although late to the dance, it chokes me up a bit to think that I finally understand why.

It should be noted here that while my opinions are laid bare here I also very much appreciate and love the characters of two particular modern day theologians who are not Roman, but do perform paedo baptisms. One is recently deceased the other is in Idaho. They have been very fundamental to this pilgrim's journey. I have heard their positions. It seems to me though, that the very particular flocks in their charge will not be deceived into a mistaken belief that this "welcoming" ceremony gets the infant in the gate. Their flocks are very much guided into the "Cross" and all the trappings that make the words “It is finished” .....I’m struggling for a word here.... got it.... “pure gold.” The greatest gift!!

Sorry, tangents seem a likely continued occurrence in this book!!! Back to the seeds and scales timeline!

>>> 1967 - SEEDS <<<

An altar boy at 12 years of age would be soured by an unfairness and would have seeds of doubt cast concerning the church. I may have attended a Catholic school in 2nd grade, I’m not sure, but Mother enrolled all of her five children when I was in the 6th grade. It would be the last year. I don’t know why, perhaps it was financial. In any event, I would join the alter boy’s “Knights of the Alter” program which was a four year program from 5th through 8th grade. There was the ring the bells, hand the priest stuff part, and the scholastic part which was memorizing various Roman Catholic dogmas and doctrines. When ready we would recite a section to Sister Rose Marie who ran the program. Shorter sections would be scored with 2 points, while lengthy and more complicated ones would garner 5, 10, 15 or more points. Usually it was four years of memorizing, but it turns out I had a good memory for a kid and in that one year had acquired more points than anyone in the history of the school at that time. As I recall I only had maybe 2 more items to complete.

The ceremony part of the deal was receiving a “Knights of the Alter” pin. Each year of achievement would get you another pin all attached by a small chain. I did get two pins for 5th and 6th grade, but they would not give me the 7th and 8th grade pins. No reason was given, but to a 12 year old boy this seemed not right. As I consider the episode as an old man it seems the most plausible explanation is no one had ever done it before and the administrators did not know what to do. If they had said I not only needed the scholastic part, but the experience part also, I might have been able to grasp that. They didn’t have a reason. Reasons notwithstanding I thought it was “not fair.” Even though a 12 year old doesn’t understand the concept of justice an adolescent mind can and did grasp “unfair.” I know that this event was not traumatic or something I ever dwelled on or considered pivotal in why I did not have a passion for “The Way,” but it is curious that here I am recounting something that happened 55 years ago. In any event...scales!!!

In that same year a friendship would begin because of pee wee football....seeds!!!

>>> 1972 – SEEDS <<<

High school. The friendship that started because of football had two bonds. One for football and the other for rotten! If there was a record for rotten, we set the bar a little higher in those years. My friend was a quarterback and had an exceptional arm as well as mind for the game. I was a running back, small, fast, and could catch a pass reasonably well. In one game we had our Tom Brady / Julian Edleman moment. A long pass was thrown to the end zone. My friend got hit hard. I remember being surrounded by three maybe four guys. The ball was perfectly thrown to the only spot I had a chance to catch it, which I did and then was also hit hard by a swarm of defenders. When the dog pile cleared, and the referees signaled touchdown the fans cheered. Most every American football fan has witnessed many such moments year to year, but that one was ours.

I recount this as a seed moment though neither he nor I might say it was anything other than a scales period of our lives. The "hit hard" part and the "cheering" part are relevant as I look back on my friendship with this man.

>>> 1975 – SEEDS <<<

The one that threw the pass would join the Air Force and find himself on the other side of the globe during the Vietnam War. The one that caught the pass would start college and join the Air Force ROTC. Seemingly similar trajectories to this point, but..... The quarterback would find and understand the Cross in Okinawa. The particulars are his to tell, but from a friend's observations and recollections of those years part of his journey to the narrow gate is in no small measure because he became smitten with a beautiful girl. This girl at the time was a good Catholic girl of the type that right thinking parents would want their sons to fall in love with. At the time one would have wondered how she could be smitten with him because as I noted earlier we had set the bar pretty high in the rotten category. All these years later if you know both of them it is clear what she saw in my friend. "God only" knew that together they would in their little corner of the world would do, live, and be greatly blessed because their household would be governed by Christ.

A story I liked about their courtship was when she would fly to Okinawa for a visit. At the time my friend was drinking too much and often. When she arrived my friend was excited to take his soon to be bride to a party which involved drunkenness. She stated to him that, "If this is to be our life, please take me back to the airport."......he stopped drinking....how about that....my wayward friend may not have been able to fully articulate why at that time, but the righteousness of Christ was reaching him through at least in part this maiden. Whatever caused that change in direction in my friend's life, it is reasonable to use the phrase "hit hard." This hit happened only three years after the hit in the aforementioned football game. It seems both of them desired a future in righteousness and also a biblical marriage. She being Catholic, they went to a priest to learn about the sacrament. My friend was apprehensive when they were asked to sign a contract pledging that they would raise any children in the Roman Catholic Church. It seems my friend had discernment beyond his theological knowledge at the time. He was troubled enough to visit a Chaplin that took him to the scriptures. It did two things at that time: 1) convicted my friend about his own sin, and 2) made him want to rightly follow "The Way" and live with his new bride as one flesh in Christ.

Again, their particulars are theirs to tell, but as his friend and recounting what I remember, the above is what caught me as special. In any event the friend that threw the pass would be "hit hard" for Christ along with his new bride on the other side of the globe both baptized in the East China Sea in Okinawa during the Vietnam War. He and his lovely wife have lived a Christian life that has as of this moment has blessed them greatly to the third generation.

The running back that caught the pass and "hit hard" would spend the next 45 years with scales on his eyes. During my friend's time in Vietnam I would be in college and seems would be "hit hard" by the forces of the darker side of possibilities. No God, no church, no desire to turn. I can say though, that with each fleshly desire, opportunity and engagement, even now, I remember knowing at the time it was wrong. How the phrase, "written on your heart," at this very moment reaches across time and convicts me.

>>> 1972 TO JULY 1979 – SEEDS & SCALES <<<

These years I can recount as fundamental for acquired skills and knowledge (seeds) which were a blessing to me to navigate the physical / natural / material world. In other words, math and organization helped me greatly in the field of construction management. In a biblical revelation as noted in Matthew 5:45, "….it rains (a blessing) on the just and the unjust." Although I was living a very unjust life, acquired knowledge and skill was most definitely a blessing that can only be recognized as having come from the grace of God. As it turns out I would not recognize this until this moment (as I type these words).

>>> 1980 – SEEDS <<<

My 1st marriage. After a courtship of one year I was married to my first wife. She was and is a good and God fearing woman. My mother gave us a large beautiful home Bible, not just a seed, but the entire harvest. But for the scales on my eyes I might have read it. I did not. Had I read it, it is reasonable that I would have been a better son, brother, husband, father, friend, laborer, and neighbor. The lost opportunities to have reasoned conversations about the kingdom from that time until now are lost.

The seeds in this season were laughter, joy, being a couple whom enjoyed being a couple, friendships, family, very much enjoying the seasons commemorating those things. For example, New Year's and "Auld Lang Syne" whether we understand the lyrics or not that music moves us to consider the one your with and feel gratitude as well as friends and the hope of a bright tomorrow. Easter, even though not comprehended rightly, our families gathered. Birthdays were enjoyed with the gifts that we wanted to give. Veterans Day, considering albeit brief thankfulness to the vet that protected the shores of America whom at least for a season was "Under God." Thanksgiving, we enjoyed big meals with family and even if for a fleeting moment gave thanks to God for the blessings of the nation. Christmas we very much enjoyed though very much trapped in the secular, commercialized realm with only small spaces, if at all, spent on what should have been considered. That time when God was born into this world and walked among men should have had reverence and worship.

The scales in this season as I consider them are my complete misplaced acknowledgment of why all that was good about God's grace and the very blessings I enjoyed during those years. If, but for the scales on my eyes, I would have been on my knees and had I been on my knees.....well???

Providence. It can only be providence. It seems these words I write are not mine, and it seems and I pray are for someone else.

Although several years were to be spent in what was a "good" marriage, it would take a turn because of my sin.

>>> 1987 – SEEDS AND SCALES <<<

My daughter was born. Sadly, at the same time as what was and still is certainly one of the greatest blessings of my life to date, trouble was to be in my future. The seed part was witnessing the birth of my baby girl and knowing full well the glory of God. The scales part was the serpent tempting and me succumbing way to easily. Knowing full well the wrongness of things I chose the wide gate.

>>> 1989 – SEEDS <<<

My 1st wife loved me and knew I needed something and I dare say knew exactly what that was. Since we were not attending a church and could not be properly attended to by a pastor, all she had was at least the knowledge that the answers were in a Book. So, on Valentine's Day, and I suspect with much hope, she gave me a beautiful King James Bible personalized with my name on the cover, again not just a seed, but the entire harvest. But for the sin I was living in and the scales on my eyes I might have read it. I did not. The scales by this time were thick. It wouldn't be until Christmas 32 years later that I would thank her properly for this greatest of treasures.

>>> 1995 – SEEDS AND SCALES <<<

Having by this time been divorced 3 years and very much in despair I bought a study Bible for myself, and for a third time not just a seed, but the entire harvest. Most certainly my conscience was pierced enough to know that I needed help and very ironically knowing full well the answers were in this "Book." But for the scales on my eyes I did not pick it up for 22 years. Looking back it seems obvious I had discernment enough to know that God was the answer. Why? Why, oh God, so long!! As I consider this time and what transpired, God as the potter knew very well that this pot required more molding, shaping, breaking and then molding and shaping again.

It would be in this year that I met and started dating my now wife. Still not in or in any way associated with a church we began a new chapter together. It strikes me now that this chapter would be a season in which God "rained" (a blessing) on the just and the unjust. My now wife is a naturally beautiful and what all who know her would describe as kind and sweet. However, in retrospective analysis, we both were broken vessels to be reshaped over the ensuing years to be conformed to Christ likeness. We dated for eleven years.

>>> 2006 – SEEDS AND SCALES <<<

In December of this year I married for the second time. It would be another eleven years until I would know the "Way of the Master." However, God raining on the just and the unjust and showing His grace for all of the years with my new wife, I can now see the extreme blessings of the five-way relationship between my x-wife, her new husband, my daughter, my new wife and myself. All who had occasion to see all of us interact through this time, which includes to the present, would concur that our care for each other would be reasonably described as a one-in-a-million circumstance. Grace, most certainly grace!!!

>>> 2015 – SEEDS <<<

April 4th my daughter married raining blessings on the unjust. There was much excitement about my daughter being wed to a man whom I would consider to be man that would properly care for her. Even not having read the Bible I did set up a meeting with my daughter and a Baptist minister that I hoped would provide some guidance for consideration about the ceremony. My intent was on track; however, my life was in the "Potter crushing the pot" phase to begin a reshaping season. The wedding, though, was definitely a blessing for me. I was a father so completely full of joy for what that day was, is supposed to be, and it seems even now in my memories is in the top five of best days ever!!! What a day!

>>> 2016 – SEEDS – RESHAPING THE POT <<<

October, via YouTube Jordan Peterson, a professor of psychology in Toronto, Canada providentially appeared on my magic rectangle. He inspired me to listen to someone smarter than me talk for at least one hour per day. I was working for that childhood friend whom threw that pass all those years before building an office and other structures for him in Colorado. I lived in a small old farm house that my friend owned. I was alone so I spent many an evening listening to Jordan and others discuss various disciplines of science, philosophy, theology, and religions. I read his book "12 Rules for Life."

While there my friend had dropped seeds in that he invited me to go to his church, so did his daughter once. I went and it was awesome and I enjoyed it. Although I was starting to read I clearly hadn't got to Ephesians yet. I didn't go unless I was invited as I thought I was interfering somehow in my friend's family time. These scales seem so ridiculous now. It wasn't my friend's house; it was the Lord's house. As much as I enjoy throwing my friend under the bus, as friends do, and would like to even now for this infraction I can't do it.... This one is clearly on me....my scales. How easy it is to be deceived and be blinded with scales!!!

>>> 2017 – SEEDS <<<

This man, Jordan Peterson, whom I do not even know dropped a seed. Inspired by a Bible lecture series by Jordan in the 62nd year of my life I would pick up the greatest seed and read it. It took a year. The scales began to fall.

>>> 2018 – SEEDS <<<

About Christmas time I finished. Unbeknownst to anyone in this physical realm I did this alone, unbeknownst to anyone in this physical realm the scales started to fall from my eyes. Other seeds were providentially being dropped for me via the magic rectangle. I had never heard names like Baucham, Sproul, MacArthur, Begg, Washer, Spurgeon, Comfort, Pink, Luther, Calvin, Lewis, Turek, Hamm, Barnett, Tozer, Wood, Qureshi, Ryle, Moody, Feldick and many others, but here they were popping up on the magic rectangle. Hours were spent listening to these seed sowers. Prior to this all I had witnessed on any media platform was on TV and thought most of what I saw was nonsense. Hinn, Kraus, Copeland, Osteen, Myer, etc. It seems discernment may have been somewhat in play. The seeds now planted, begin to take root. However, there were scales yet to be removed.

>>> 2019 – SPRING TIME <<<

Privately in the 64th year of my life finding myself broken at the foot of the Cross, I repented and knew that changes were in order. So it began. My wife knew that I was spending a lot of time reading the Bible, but in the beginning I did not talk about nor share much - why - scales. I purchased "The Evidence Based Bible" by Ray Comfort and started again.

The 2nd time it took about 6 months. Gradually, patiently, not having a clue how to be a proper husband, I consciously desired for my wife to see a changed man. So, perhaps just making obvious that a Bible was around and that I was reading it was how things were to change a bit in our relationship.

It is odd to me that I felt and still feel awkward with this reshaping season with my wife. I can say with reasonable certainty that, at least, we both recognize that we are in the throes of a reshaping season. We seem to be at least equally yoked as we are tender with each other's fragile brokenness as God is reshaping us.

Also in this year I would share my new found faith with a rancher friend from New Mexico. He counseled me, and I knew he was correct, that I needed to be baptized. However, more scales needed to fall. As I think on my friendship with this man whom I met around 2010, he being a go to church on Sunday, Bible reading Christian cowboy shared with me that when we met he recognized by inquiry that although I was seeking truth and worked with him in pursuit of truth I was not saved. We have since discussed this situation. He being a friend for 9 years and my other childhood friend for 55 years, recognized that although I could be trusted with certain aspects of this temporary existence and stand by them locked arm in arm in pursuit of temporal righteous endeavors, they knew I could not be trusted with my own salvation.

The Bible refers to a certain caliber of men as "true" men. My friends while they were a light to me in the way they lived, it would only be the grace of God whom could lead me to the narrow gate. What strikes me now is how the 2nd greatest commandment as stated by Christ himself was rightly understood by these friends of mine. In other words, "Love your neighbor as yourself." I can see this clearly in these two men as they did not give up on me nor turn their back on me. Even though I know they had their doubts, they were and are thankful that I too can now lock arms with them in a brotherhood I could not possibly have understood until I read and heard the "Good News."

>>> 2020 – SPRING <<<

I started reading the Bible for a 3rd time. This time it took 3 months. I am an old man now and feel convicted to catch up. I started a 4th time. If I could give counsel now to anyone and especially the youth in the church and most especially without the church….time is fleeting. Notice that 65 plus years were just recounted and that time went by so fast and what might have been done to share the gospel is lost.

~ TANGENT – TIME ~

For some reason the reading of the Bible seems a daunting task. Overwhelming!! Why?? In my life, so much so, that although a task I knew as a young man should be, and need be done, the "Book of Books" was thrown into the storage closet of my mind where it collected dust for 62 years. With a mind that analyzes much of what I have done in my life with math… the Bible breaks down like this.

- plus or minus 780,000 words
- average reading speed for non-fiction is 238 wpm (words per minute)
- 780,000 / 238 = 3,277 minutes
- 3,277 minutes / 60 minutes / hour = 54 hours
- read 1 hour / day = 54 days to read the Bible

How about that….. That is 1 month and 3 weeks. Why then did it take me a year? Clearly I could not find 1 hour per day.

John Barnett of DTBM (Discover the Bible Ministries) has dialed in the "average" number to read the Bible at 72 hours. I can hear it already…… but this excuse, and but that excuse…. Dear God, help us... plus or minus 72 hours!

The 5th Harry Potter book is almost as long as the Bible and my daughter read that in a weekend. In fact in 1997 when the first of the series was published my daughter was 10 and in the 4th grade. She was first in line each year a new novel came out and finished each of them in 1 to 3 days tops. The point here is that if the imaginations of children can be so captivated by muggles, magic spells and complete nonsense then grown-ups should be able to focus a bit for the truth.

Women can find the time to read the Twilight series (about vampires no less) and I dare say all of them in less than 4 months. Men who read can get through a Tom Clancy novel in a couple of weeks. Why then, oh why, the most important words every to be written take so long, if we get to them at all?

If we could find 2 hours a day the Words of God, or as Jesus shared with the apostles, "give us this day our daily bread" that which feeds the mind could be ingested into the mind in a month.

Prayer for all, but most especially Christians:

> *Dear God in Heaven, please, please clear the stumbling stones from our minds so that we use the reasoning power you gave us to pick up Your Word and read. With the reasoning power you gifted to us we most certainly know that we can know Your Mind better, not completely, but most certainly better if we would but hear the Word and more specifically, all of them. Amen.*

Imagine, if you will, a marathon, a 26 mile race. Even if you are not a runner you have watched one either on TV or in person. In person is quite something. What is most striking even as spectators you will find yourself in awe watching not only the fastest, but the slowest cross that finish line. The most awe seems to be felt when those that are close to the point of complete physical failure, dig deep, and cross that line. I submit to you if you challenge yourself to dig deep with that kind of fortitude to read the

Bible, you may not have spectators in this realm, but it seems to me the angels will be clapping!!! I'm just saying. Also, worthy of note, reading in no way taxes the mind like running taxes the body. It's more akin to eating angel food cake. Think on that little allegory.

Back to the Seeds and Scales....

>>> 2020 – SEEDS <<<

In January of this year that childhood friend from Colorado that threw that pass all those years before came to Phoenix. Over coffee, early in the morning I announced to him that I was a Christian. My friend the quarterback, his name is Gary. I know that morning Gary was well pleased. Gary noted to me that through the years he had dropped seeds, but as sinners do even though not in any way offended I would change the subject, why? Scales! Even in a first class friendship a saved friend would like to rip the scales off a friends eyes, but that is objectively not how it works. The only "One" capable of removing the scales is the same "One" who has the authority to open the seven seals.

In any event, immediately, my friend would disciple me to do two things. One find a local church and two get baptized. I tease my friend that he is like a teenage girl given his proficiency in texting. It turns out he and I would converse greatly with the magic rectangle. Some of our back and forth was nonsense and proved to be fun for the decades old quid-pro-quo of exchanging insults. However, and more importantly, we had many exchanges concerning "The Way." Gary is very knowledgeable and well-read concerning "The Way" and also spent much time counseling, sharing, challenging, and mostly just being a true friend. As an example of my friends mind and his contemplation of what it means to know what happened on that Cross the following is one of his poems:

~ PROOF OF GRACE ~

O let me break this earthly chain,
That binds my heart with sorrows pain.
Lift me from these husks I crave,
To help me see beyond the grave.

Raise my sight above the dust,
Of flesh and pride and eyes of lust.
Help me know what waits in store,
And what it means to "sin no more."

Bind my heart with cords of strength,
And love that knows no depth or length.
Then seat me in thy holy place,
Where I shall live as "Proof of Grace."

Gary Michael Gerrard

>>> MARCH 2020 <<<

Covid and lock downs. I had been looking for a church although not with any particular zeal. I found three in my area on John MacArthur's seminary website, Desert Hills Bible Church being one of them, and had even driven by. In retrospect it is clear that scales in the form of procrastination, kept me from pulling the trigger. I did try one church, although lovely for whatever reason did not quite resonate with me.

>>> DECEMBER 2020 <<<

My friend, the quarterback, was tired of me not getting the playbook i.e., my procrastination. He had asked a member of his church in Colorado if he knew of a church in Phoenix – as it turns out was Desert Hills Bible Church. Providence? Gary flew down for a weekend; we went to coffee and for a good hike on Saturday. Sunday we attended Desert Hills.

Recently I asked Gary what it was that made him make that phone call because it seemed to me that there is a lesson there. During that first year since I told Gary that I was a Christian he was in fact elated, but knew that most of my acquired knowledge to date had come not only from the reading of the Bible, but also from listening to the many sources on YouTube. In his words he had a concern that YouTube not become my church. What he didn't know was finding a church was very much on my radar, what I didn't know is how procrastination was too much a part of my life.

What did Gary do for his friend? First, he was elated. Second, he was concerned. Third, knowing the requirement to disciple, but not perhaps the particulars of how in every instance, he pondered that concern into an action that did bear fruit. Here is how it happened:

Gary listened, and asked. He queried me about whom I had been listening to. When I told him John MacArthur was one of preachers I listened to Gary took the time to go and listen to some of John's sermons. Discerning that John MacArthur was solid, he wondered how he might help me find a local church in Phoenix that had a preacher of similar character and theology. Gary had suggested I try a particular church that was in fact solid Biblically speaking, but at the same time my friend new my character and that another venue might be preferred.

Gary then remembered that his Pastor's brother who himself is a Pastor in a neighboring city had gone to John MacArthur's seminary in California. Not having a particular plan, per se, one day Gary was at an event where his Pastor's brother was also in attendance. It was he who suggested Desert Hills. Then, Gary went to that website, listened to Pastor Rob Brunansky and discerned rightly that this was it. All that took about a year. If I analyze this game film, this friendship, and the obvious concern turned into action points directly to the forbearance of God. The take away lesson I suppose is if God's desire is that all be saved and He is patient with certain stray sheep, like me, and any of us, like Gary, can be helpful in any way to guide the sheep home, well, be patient.

After Gary and I attended Desert Hills he told me afterward if there might ever be occasion for him to have a home in Phoenix it would have to be near this church. Why would he say such a thing? He and I felt the same thing I dare say those that attend Desert Hills felt the 1st time they experienced this place. In a phrase, joy of the gospel! Having listened to hours and hours of theology and the beliefs of various denominations, studying the history of why the denominational splits, and most especially reading the Bible over and over, the why of what I heard on that first visit was at least enough to suggest a further look was warranted. A few visits later I learned that Desert Hills was one of many churches around the country that grew during the Covid crisis. Interesting! At the time I did not know the half of it, all I knew that day was this might be a home.

>>> 2021 – THE SCALES ARE FALLING <<<

Having been grafted into the tree, growth within the body of a church became painfully obvious. Being new to this thing called a church, I am delighted by Desert Hills. Pastor Rob, the associate Pastors, Bob at the mens' Bible study, Rich, John and Josh at the 10AM Sunday Bible Study, the home Bible studies at the Hubbards' are very much making this sojourner grow. What gets me the most, however, is the singing. I have heard gospel songs in my life certainly, but to be in this place, and hear the congregation raise the roof, as it were, I cannot sing. Why, it's the tears. When I hear lyrics such as, "when I fight I fight on my knees," and now knowing clearly what happened on that Cross, the lump in my throat and whatever that is in my conscience that causes tears to well up in my eyes???? I am hopeful to someday join in.

Also, in this year, my wife Jennifer watched her husband change. I didn't do it well and still don't, but she recognizes at least that I am trying to be a Christ follower. I can say with certainty that I need the grace of the "Master Potter" most especially in our marriage. I feel most blessed that we are doing this together and that this woman is by my side. She more than anyone knows my faults and that I have much work to do to be a better husband. I thank God for her and her kindness and her patience with me. I very much love her. Jennifer and I have had our problems and could easily have thrown in the towel. I am very thankful we did not. The potter and the clay analogies are most appropriate here. We both are being shaped by the potter into better vessels.

One thing I learned in this year about my wife is that as a young girl she was raised in a church environment and was involved in youth activities at the church. In college, she and others began a new season which involved new activities which take the time that new activities take and which could not be shared with the youth activities of the church. At that time there was also a changing of the guard at her church. They hired a woman pastor (a biblical problem in and of itself) whom it seems to me would have made a good warden in a correctional facility. Without a meeting or a phone call, Jennifer as well as other kids that grew up in this church received a letter that they were to be excommunicated. Ouch!! I cannot imagine. My wife as a mature woman weeps at the slightest hint of humanity in movies, so I most certainly can imagine the horror of being so rejected by an institution that she grew up in and loved. It seems clear we were equally yoked on a non-church trajectory for much of our time together.

Anyway, my wife worked hard, went to college and reasonably could have had better influences in her life. I met her when she was 26 and I was 40. Yeah, I know!!!!

At present my wife is the youngest of six siblings and has taken on the mantle of caring for her mother. Mother is 91 this year and is in need of care pretty much 24/7. My wife's name is Jennifer and I love her very much. She cannot always join me at church and in fact we trade off since one of us has to stay with her mother, however when we can we certainly prefer to go together. She, like me now has a desire to get this ship sailing in the "right" direction.

My daughter, Lea, also knows my faults and is aware that I am trying to do better. Trying to articulate Lea's influence on her dad is tough. As I think of the infant, toddler, grade schooler, pre-teen, teen, college girl, young adult, nurse, wife, and now mother of two granddaughters to me, it seems at least a chapter if not a whole book could be written to each of these seasons of her life and how great she has been to me. A blessing not deserved, but most certainly the most refreshing of springtime rains on an unjust man. My love for her is as a fathers should be.

>>> 2022 – FEBRUARY <<<

As noted at the beginning of this chapter it was the testimony of Heaven Dykhuizen that inspired me to take the time to consider with care why get baptized, why now?

>>> 2022 – MARCH THROUGH JULY <<<

Witnessing baptisms as well as being pestered, I mean descipled by Gary, I quit procrastinating and filled out an application to join the church and get baptized. The application process was very much needed and thought provoking. In 2021 I had attended three orientation classes, but... procrastination scales. Until this time it had been a consideration of mine to be baptized in a river in northern Colorado where I grew up. I had every intention of going that route, but once again providence it seems would play a role in steering this vessel into different waters. I told my friend about my intentions and he once again took the time to listen, then think on the circumstance, and then articulate in writing in a thoughtful and measured way why I should reconsider. He counseled me why being involved in a local church is part of the journey and is ordained in the scriptures. Further, that when ready, making proclamation in front of local church saints is necessary and like my Seal Team allegory earlier, these saints can and should hold me accountable to the team or saints.

Pastor Jason, one of the associate pastors, performs the baptisms. Pastor Jason reviewed my application and met with me and my wife to rightly see if I knew the why of it all. Going into this my preconceived idea was that this was a minor formality, but the application had two questions that gave me pause to be introspective and take seriously joining a church as well as be baptized.

<u>Question # 1</u> was: Why do you want to get baptized? Another good question? So I wrote:

> *Even before I was "broken against the rock" I often felt the need to. I suppose that is the mind, the conscience, the will, the soul knowing that there is something to transcend to. Now that I understand what Jesus*

did for me it seems most reasonable to consider my acknowledgment of the gift of the Holy Spirit having been extended freely to me. Therefore, it is my wish to partake in that ceremony prescribed and ordained by my Lord, Jesus. I shall do this in full public view for all to witness and hear me.... I accept Jesus the Christ as my redeemer. Thank you Jesus!!

Question # 2 was: Describe your life as an unbeliever? While this chapter captures much of that I wrote the following:

Christ summarized the commandments into two. Matthew 22:37 and Matthew 22:39. I did not nor could I have given the 2nd greatest commandment its due reverence as I did not give the first its proper place. In other words --- I am guilty of all.

Question #3 was: What is the gospel. When I read that I thought to myself, OK smart guy, swing away, let's see what you've got? The following is what I came up with:

***The Gospel of God is this**: That God entered into His creation by taking on the form and nature of that which He created in the beginning. God did this because men left to their own devices failed to understand the will of God. So God being righteous and just and being desirous that all of His children not have justice fairly applied for unrighteousness, sent His one and only begotten Son, miraculously conceived of a virgin into His creation. That His Son, known to us as Jesus, made known the truth about His Father, Himself, His Helper, heaven, hell, sin, condemnation to perdition and the only way to salvation leading to eternal life with God. That Jesus, did perform miracles to prove His authority and power, and although was believed by His followers, was reviled by those who should have known but for their pride and covetousness of their positions, did conspire to betray Him, have Him arrested, tried by a foreign court who could not find fault, but did nevertheless crucify Him.*

Jesus having prophesied about His own death and also making known to His chosen men called apostles, that He would rise from the dead in three days, did in fact leave the tomb and made Himself known and seen by His apostles as well as at least 500 more. After having made Himself known risen, He ascended into Heaven, this also being witnessed.

> *After death, but before ascension Jesus opened the eyes of the apostles to the Old Testament scriptures so they would clearly see that He was predicted throughout those ancient writings. Armed with this revealed knowledge they went on a great commission to share that God crucified His son to take on the sin of the world as well as mine, great as it is if I would but believe, which I do.*

Question # 4 was: Share your response to the gospel. Another good question? So I wrote:

> *And now that I believe and may have opportunity I shall share this gospel, how can I not. For if I am to love God with all my being, and am commanded to love my neighbor, and God desires that all be saved, how can I not have a mind to be a soldier for God and His Son Jesus and knowing the armor for this commission being the Helper promised by Jesus, i.e. "the Spirit of God." I acknowledge that this commission is simple once justified, but at the same time complex and unreachable for those whom will not see or hear. Nevertheless by the grace of God, I implore Your Helper be with me as I do what I may to spread "The Word."*

Pastor Jason asked that I prepare a proclamation and send it to him. We laughed afterward because I can be a bit wordy I had to cut it in half, not once, but twice.

>>> 2022 – JULY 10 – THE PLUNGE <<<

After all the preparation, thought, and counseling and for this pilgrim the word "finally" seems most appropriate. At 67 years of age, "finally" hearing the call of the Master three years prior I would and did take much comfort in obeying an ordinance of our Lord.

Note: everything below was written using what was written above in this chapter as an outline on the day of my baptism.

>>> MY PROCLAMATION <<<

First I would like to thank my wife for her patience with me. Please bear with me – this is a brief timeline of my journey to the Cross. I have titled it:

Seeds and 1Scales of An Old Man Thinking for the 1st Time.

1980 - Seeds. My 1st marriage. My mother gave us this Bible, not just a seed, but the entire harvest. But for the scales on my eyes I might have read it. I did not. Had I read it is reasonable that I would have been a better son, brother, husband, father, friend, laborer, and neighbor. Further, I would have been better in those capacities only had I known and comprehended the greatest commandment. The lost opportunities to have reasoned conversations about the kingdom from that time until now are lost.

1989 - Seeds. My 1st wife, who is here today, gave me this Bible, again not just a seed, but the entire harvest. But for the sin I was living in and the scales on my eyes I might have read it. I did not - scales. I would thank her 32 years later.

1995 – Seeds. Having been divorced 3 years, in despair, I bought this study Bible. But for the scales on my eyes I did not pick it up for 22 years.

2017 – Seeds. A Bible lecture series by Jordan Peterson in the 62nd year of my life would cause me to pick up the greatest seed and read it. It took a year. The scales began to fall.

2019 – Seeds. Springtime. About ¾ of the way through the Bible I found myself broken at the foot of the Cross. I repented and knew that changes had to be made.

2020 – Seeds. In January of this year a childhood friend from Colorado came to Phoenix. I announced to him I was a Christian.

My friends name is Gary and he is right over there →. I know Gary was well pleased. My friend would disciple me to do two things, find a local church and get baptized.

2020 - Seeds – In December my friend asked a member of his church if he knew of a church in Phoenix – as it turns out was this one. Providence? He flew down, and we came here. Gary told me afterward if there might ever be occasion for him to have a home here, it would have to be near this place. Why would he say such a thing? He and I felt the same thing I dare say all of you felt the 1st time you experienced this place. In a phrase, joy of the gospel!

2022 – I joined this church and requested that I be baptized. I met with Pastor Jason, which brings us to now. My friend Gary counseled me along with Pastor Jason about making proclamation in front of a local church. So, here I am, before you making this profession of faith. Therefore, pursuant to my understanding of the "Good News": *That God crucified His Son to take on the sin of the world as well as mine, great as it is if I would but believe, which I do.*

In conclusion, my scales like leaves in the fall lay at of the foot of the Cross, while my sin has been nailed to it. My name is James Kalm Fitzgerald and in the 67th year of my life, I express across these lips to you the church - I believe Jesus is Christ, and my Lord, and with all due reverence and humility I go now with understanding that this act of public baptism is my acknowledgment of Christ's already completed work on the Cross that imputed His righteousness to me.

Time passes quickly do it now, repent and believe!!!

Actually I was nervous and messed up a little, but that's it, that is essentially what I said. One thing I wanted to say, but had to be cut was the following:

~ IN CONCLUSION AT LEAST FOR THIS PART OF THE JOURNEY ~

Exactly 50 years ago my friend Gary threw a pass that I caught in the end zone in a high school football game and the crowd cheered and there was a brief moment of joy. 50 years later to the year, Gary would disciple his friend into the waters of baptism which for this story is an end zone of sorts. Like that touchdown half a century ago, the crowd cheered.

~ COUSIN JOHN ~

Come to the water John would beg of the crowd,
I have something to shout and I need to be loud.

Our God has been silent for 400 years,
While once through the prophets His voice we did hear,
We have transgressed & trespassed on His Word and His law,
Stiff necked and stubborn this all He foresaw.

His forbearance and patience it seems ran its course,
So He sent us His Son with miraculous force.
By the seed of the Spirit in the womb of a woman,
A Baby was born, the best possible omen.

I am His cousin, John is my name,
Called to hearken His coming, and boldly proclaim,
The Messiah the Savior, His time it is near,
The purpose salvation and for that we can cheer.

Listen please listen there are things I must do,
Although I am not worthy to lace up His shoe.
I've been called from the desert, to make way for His coming,
To do a most unusual thing and immerse you in water,

But before I do that you must acknowledge your sin,
Then repent and be willing to follow the Son,
The One that we've waited and waited and waited for years,
And now He'll be with us but not without tears.

This new thing introduced, baptism it's called,
Will be a new ceremony to those that are called,
Jesus my cousin will come and make clear
The truth and the life if we only but hear.

Why do I baptize, I'm not sure I know,
But in the desert my God said my Cousin will show.
To the best of my knowledge this side of the Cross,
It's for those in the future to acknowledge their lost.

They and you must consider contritely you're a sinner at heart,
Beg and plead for forgiveness and that you want a new start.
When this is done & accomplished & declared to the church,
Jesus is Lord to whom you "will" to surrender, at your new birth.

A ceremony if you're willing and compelled so to do,
An ordinance perhaps, following the lead of the Lord,
But only and only when you know with certainty sure,
That Jesus now is your Master, your Lord and your cure.

Now go to the water, and declare to the church,
Your gladness and happiness to start a new life,
Rejoice, you've been baptized, and now without strife,
Come join your new family, your brothers and sisters in Christ.

Amen
JKF - July 2022

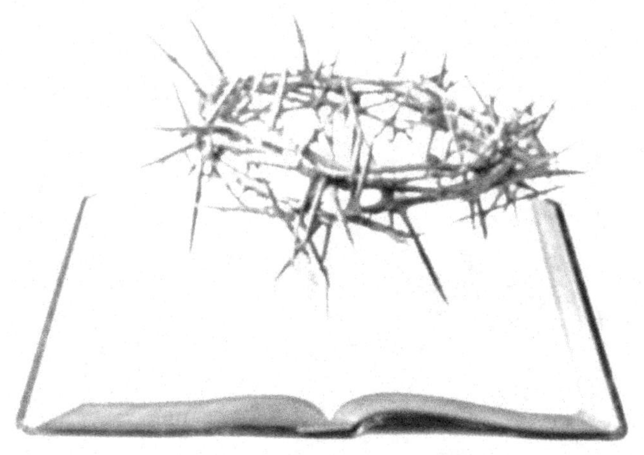

Washed in the Blood of the Lamb!

Now What?

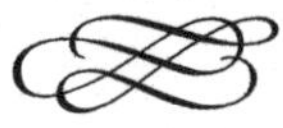

Chapter 8

POST BAPTISM

July 10, 2022 it happened. A few weeks after being baptized someone asked me how I feel. I thought that is a good question and might be a good chapter to include. My first reaction might be similar to when after one has a birthday and someone asks how it feels to be a year older. On the one hand, like the birthday, as time passes not much thought is given to "I'm a year older," nor is much thought given to "I am now baptized."

It is now February 2023 and 7 months later and perhaps a good time to revisit the question. In the Chapter titled "Baptism" a lot of time and thought went into the consideration of being baptized. It encompassed a lot of time, 67 years to be precise, and many people that one way or another influenced me, and the many circumstances in my journey that lead me to the water.

The timeline post baptism is shorter, 7 months to be exact, and not a lot of time to consider the changes, the circumstances, and people this side of that great day. Generally speaking, however, a certain anxiety was relieved. Being a natural procrastinator and having certainly procrastinated reading the Bible for 62 years, baptism was on my radar; however, not with any sense of urgency. After being broken at the foot of the Cross my sin of procrastination did not magically go away, clearly, for it took learning, reading, the discipleship of a friend, and time to find a church, and way too long to quit procrastinating baptism. What made me move my baptism to the front of the line of things to get done was when on February 13, 2022, I witnessed a member of the church, Heaven Dykhuizen, get baptized.

For whatever reason, I knew. Scratch that. The reason I was moved, was seeing Heaven being moved by the gospel of God to, like those that willingly walked into the Jordan when asked by John or others to "repent" and make way for the "Redeemer." Was that an ordinance? Perhaps, but in any event it cannot be denied that many sinners once convicted of their sin feel compelled to get baptized. After that day there was a sense that I too, needed to obey the calling in my mind. As I think on the time writing the chapter on baptism which took about a month there was a certain building up of anxiety that I get this done, for what if I were to die beforehand??? I cannot say if such anxiety is warranted, but it was there nevertheless. Anyway, it's moot, for I obeyed my conscience.

Post baptism then is staying the course. I choose to stay in the word, I choose to pray daily, I choose to and strive to be a better husband, father, grandfather, brother, uncle, friend, and neighbor. I choose to love the church, I choose to love those that are enemies of God, I choose to worship. An interesting reality as I write the word "choose" is that it is precise as an explanation for it is true that I "choose," but the "choosing" has no constraints, no chains, no guilt, no shame, etc. There is a liberty and a freedom to the "choosing." As I write this paragraph I am at a coffee shop in north Phoenix, the doors are wide open and there are trees outside with birds chirping away. That noise sounds like freedom and glory. For reasons hard to explain that chirping, the trees, the budding flowers on the trees, the bright blue sky, I do not take for granted anymore. Each day when I wake up I am a different kind of happy. I don't think on the "happy" as "choosing" so in that sense "choose" is the wrong word. Just as the outside world seems so colorful and majestic and easy to interact with and enjoy; likewise to stay in the Word, pray, go to church, hob nob with the saints are likewise enjoyable. I suppose it is exactly as Jesus said when He said:

> **NKJV --- Matthew 11:28-30** -- *28 Come to Me, all you who labor and are heavy laden, and I will give you rest. 29 Take My yoke upon you and learn from Me, for I am gentle and lowly in heart, and you will find rest for your souls. 30 For My yoke is easy and* <u>*My burden is light.*</u>"

That last part, ***"<u>My burden is light</u>"*** best explains the "choosing" and the "happy" I am struggling to convey. His burden, my sins, nailed to the

Cross finally comprehended, makes my "choosing" and my "happy" feel like liberty and freedom and most certainly "light."

~ OTHER JOURNEYS TO THE WATER ~

Part of my journey includes being a member of a church which is new. Like a kid going to school on the first day, what to expect, all the new people, none of whom you know is a bit daunting. It took a little time to get to know this new thing. I feel blessed in my particular experience that Desert Hills Bible Church in north Phoenix is where I landed. I did my best and am doing my best to get to know people and much appreciate the services, the singing, the expository preaching, and the break out classes and home groups. Since my time at Desert Hills there have been four services, the beginnings of which were set aside to baptize those called. I now consider those days to be my favorite.

I have noticed in this new journey that saints seem to be interested in how other saints came to know what happened on that Cross and then knowing or in some way feeling convicted to go to the Jordan. Desert Hills has two services and on baptism day with usually six to eight or nine baptisms. They split them up between the two services which is appropriate for the time it takes. Curiously, I find I want to see them all. I attend the first service and on baptism day I'll hang out to watch those baptized in the second service also. Why? It's the testimonies. Whether young or old to hear the way very broken people bare their souls and their brokenness and in such a variety of ways found themselves at the foot of the Cross gets me every time. By that I mean I choke up. In this I am not alone, for to glance around the church many an eye is moist.

Most feel that nervousness that comes with public speaking, nevertheless, they have thought about it, written it down, discussed it with an elder, and then stand the post, i.e., at the pulpit and spill their guts, so to speak. Nervous yes, shaking sometimes, tears and choking up often, compelled absolutely. When the testimonies are done they fold up their testimony walk over to the baptism pool where Pastor Jason awaits them. Pastor Jason holds them as he says the words,

"(Saints name here), on the professing of your faith in Jesus Christ as your Savior, I now baptize you in the name of the Father, and the Son, and the Holy Spirit!"

After Pastor Jason immerses the saint, the next thing to happen is most glorious; the newly baptized saint comes out of the water to a standing ovation from the congregation with shouts of joy and much applause. It truly is awesome!!! I cannot help to think that the angels in heaven are also cheering and applauding.

Further, as I consider this aftermath of applause and unbridled cheering something comes to my mind. This event, this ceremony, this thing that broken Christians are compelled to do, why? Just shy of two thousand years ago as the history book of history books recounts in Matthew 3:16 – 17, the baptism of baptisms:

> **NKJV --- Matthew 3:16 -- 16** *When He had been baptized, Jesus came up immediately from the water; and behold, the heavens were opened to Him, and He saw the Spirit of God descending like a dove and alighting upon Him.*

In baptisms two millennia later the Heavens do not literally open up as then, but the church opens up and the Spirit is most obvious as the cheering and applause land most graciously on the ears of the newly convicted saint.

It further strikes me that then as now this ceremony is a fulfillment of sorts and a proof of Matthew 3:12 and specifically the part where Jesus is gathering His wheat into the barn, and also this ceremony is Christ the Redeemer giving notice to all that will notice that the threshing floor is being cleared.

Further, if to God a day is as a thousand years and a thousand years is as a day, then per:

> **NKJV --- Matthew 3:17** -- *And suddenly a voice came from heaven, saying, "This is My beloved Son, in whom I am well pleased."*

Then, if in Gods time, i.e., the thousand years as a day, then it was just two days ago that the Heavens open and God declared His pleasure in

His Son. If this can be comprehended even minimally by our very limited capacities, then as new saints go to the water in the 21st century and they know why, then might it be reasonable that Jesus is smiling and God shares a moment with His Son and still thinks, "This is My Son in whom I Am well pleased."

Anyway, in order to add interest it occurred to me to bring others into this chapter starting with Heaven. I thought I would start by interviewing Heaven Dykhuizen and her husband for Heaven's testimony was the first time I had ever heard such a thing. May 27th, 2023 I met with Heaven and her husband Alex. But first here is:

Heaven's testimony

Hello, my name is Heaven Dykhuizen, my husband I and our three children have been attending Desert Hills since October 2019. I pushed the conviction of baptism aside for the last few years considering I have been baptized twice before. I am excited to share how the Lord has worked in regenerating my heart. As a child I grew up in nominal Christian home, at age eight I decided to get baptized, although I had little knowledge of the gospel and my true need for a Savior. I found assurance in my own self-righteousness being the good kid in school, compliments on my behavior and even in my own name at times. At age twelve my parents had an ugly divorce and stopped attending church altogether. Drugs, alcohol, and trauma were some of the things I began to see firsthand. A deep and bitter anger filled me with the hypocrisy that I witnessed in the adults in my life and a rue of bitterness began to form. Yet, the very hypocrisy I hated watching began manifesting itself in my own life. While I would have called myself a Christian and appear somewhat good on the outside, anger, bitterness, and self-righteousness entangled me. Later in my teen years bulimia began to rule my life. --- 16 years old a junior, a way of controlling, 7 or 8 years, until 1st pregnancy, HG caused a change of heart from thinking you were in control to realizing you were not. I suppressed so much of my hurts and my eating disorder anger focusing on the sins of others and minimizing my own sin. I believed that I was ultimately a good person and with good intentions telling myself God knew my heart without realizing my heart was unregenerated and desperately wicked. At seventeen I ran away from home and wanted a fresh start. I had knowledge that God existed and this is where I felt that my life had finally changed. It was in this season of life I was unknowingly introduced to the charismatic word of faith prosperity gospel. This false gospel was presented to me as God loved me and had a great plan for my life, never confronting my sin or need of repentance. I wanted everything the prosperity gospel promised me, health, wealth, and happiness. I made the decision to re-dedicate my life and was baptized again at age eighteen. I still had my mind on the things of the flesh and wanted and continued to think flippantly of sin often times justifying my own and thinking critically of worse sins. Over the next eight years I was living what I thought to be the Christian life. I believed I was zealous for God. Truthfully I had a zeal without knowledge. I was zealous for a God of my own choosing, a God that I had created in my own image not the God of the Bible. It was easy to serve a God like that because He suited all of my needs. The thing about deception is you do not know you are deceived until God removes the scales from your eyes. My husband and I began to have questions about the "word of faith" prosperity teachings and we were led to watch John MacArthur's "Strange Fire Conference." As I watched the conference the Lord began to open my blind eyes. He convicted us that we had been under false teaching and we knew we couldn't stay in that church any longer. This started a three year journey of discovering what is the truth. I was wrestling with difficult doctrines that were hard to understand and come to grips within my own knowledge. One day as I was pondering on the lives of disciples I thought to myself, there has to be more to the Christian life that just mediocre Christian living. There has to be more than just opening your Bible every once in a while and reading it. How is it that my sin is so great that Jesus had to die for it, and how am I living in reflection to that. There was nothing in me that was going to see the truth of Scripture. His Word says it's the Spirit that gives life and the flesh is no help at all. By the help of the Spirit I finally began to see the true and pure Gospel in a new light. I saw how hostile I was towards God and I was deeply humbled. His Word says for those that *are according to the flesh set their minds on the things of the flesh, and those who are according to the Spirit the things of the Spirit. For the mind set on the flesh is death, but the mind set on the Spirit is life and peace because the mind set on the flesh is hostile towards God, for it does not subject itself to the law of God for it is not even able to do so. And those who are in the flesh cannot please God. All my attempts to please Him in the flesh whether it was my good deeds, my self-righteousness, my good intentions and even my ignorant zeal were filthy rags before Him. It was only the perfect work of Christ that made me right with God. God began humbling me and reorienting the desires of my heart. I had finally tasted the goodness of God and longed for the pure spiritual milk. I started exhibiting a Godly sorrow over my sin and hungered for obedience. He was sanctifying me in His truth as Jesus said in His high priestly prayer, "sanctify them in Your truth, Your Word is truth." Today I am being baptized as a believer in Christ in obedience to Him, testifying to the redeeming saving work of God through His Son Jesus Christ.*

>>> INTERVIEW WITH HEAVEN <<<

Meeting with Heaven and her husband Alex confirms, I suppose, what should be no surprise at all that the sin in one's life cannot be summarized in a proclamation of one or two paragraphs. The "between the lines" story often is more tragic. Although Heaven summarized the truth quite well, the details would make for a novel or movie filled with at least some of the following sins.

Honor God	*Idolatry*	*Honor Parents*	*Adultery*	*False Witness*	*Covet*
anger	alcohol	rebellion	betrayal	lies / fibbing	coveting
arrogance	drugs	flight	adultery	deception	praise of men
boasting	idolatry of self	disobedience		denial	power
complaining	conceit			conspiracy	envy
cowardice	narcissism			hypocrisy	greed
evil thoughts	pride			treachery	
unrighteousness	foolishness			psycho-abuse	

And all of this while in churches led by wolves in sheep clothing.

As I consider the screenplay of Heavens life it would break down as follows:

1. ***Act 1*** – 0 to 8 years old. Through 3th grade
2. ***Act 2*** – 8 to 12 years old. 4th grade through 7th grade
3. ***Act 3*** – 12 to 17 years old. 8th grade through 12th grade
4. ***Act 4*** – 17 to 19 years old. 12th grade through marriage
5. ***Act 5*** – 19 to 26 years old. Young wife and mother
6. ***Act 6*** – 27 to 31 and ??? . Wife, mother, regenerated, sanctified

The above matrix lists 32 sins with an attempt to categorize them. I made the list by reading Heavens proclamation and listening at our interview. In ***Act 1*** it might be reasonably assumed that since Heaven at eight years old got baptized by her own volition that her home was reasonably stable. This stability included church with at least the knowledge of God and Jesus with enough impact that an eight year old desired to get baptized. In ***Act 1*** she learned to not only honor mom and dad, but elders as well as, and this, the most important part, the existence of God, His Son, and the Holy Spirit. As I stare at and consider the list only two sins pop out as a maybe, fibbing and perhaps the beginnings of pride in her name. It is hard to say what sins may have been in the household in ***Act 1***, but as the screenplay moves into ***Act 2*** which ends in her parents ugly divorce, many of the sins on the list were within the household, but reason dictates none of them can be attributed to Heaven. The circumstance, however, will certainly play a role in a slow boil of anger that would not have been there were in not for the sins of those that were charged to bring her up in the ways of the Lord.

Act 2 is four years long. At year three in this act when Heaven is eleven years old and in the sixth grade she and her younger sister would find drugs and drug paraphernalia in her parent's bedroom. Sixth graders in America in 2003 are not stupid. With all that children are exposed to mom's denial and feeble attempt to suggest it was an herbal thing were and insult to even an eleven year old intelligence. Problems between mom and dad were obvious in ***Act 2***, so much so that one day while Heaven was at a dance mom shows up with a packed car and moves her and her two sisters in with a grandmother. The writing on the wall, this family will be broken.

Time Tangent – I am not sure how far to go back in time, but at least one generation before Heavens parents, i.e., her grandparents. Forty to sixty years prior to this situation, the grandparents on both sides were cursed with the idol of alcohol, alcoholism and the many chains of sin some of which are in the above table. Living to party and not much else would have Heavens parents start their life together without God centered role models. Somehow before Heaven was born and her parents were starting their life together they found a church and wanted to break the curse. At the time, so much so were they hopeful to change that they named their first baby girl Heaven as a reminder that they had to change. Sadly, that alone would not be enough. They both fell right back into the pit. Not only alcohol, but drugs would be but some of the sins not easily shaken. ***End Time Tangent***

The reason mom packed up the kids and left is because dad was violent. Mom, knowing she was fleeing the situation and that it would end up in court she would have to detox so that drugs were not in her system for custody considerations. Over a year would be spent with grandma and ultimately mom, Heaven and her younger sisters would move in with a boyfriend. Both mom and dad are bitter. Mom blames dad for lacing the pot they smoked together with drugs. This would not be true, but is not uncommon that we as humans want to blame our sins on others, i.e., claim victimhood.

An ugly divorce ends ***Act 2***.

Act 3 is five years long. Heaven is 13, now a teenager in the eighth grade and mom has been questioned about her iniquities by Heaven and from a biblical perspective, but mom tells Heaven she should be grateful and that God knows her heart. Her mom is not wrong about that last part! Her dad sadly it seems spiraled out of control with alcohol and anger, so much so that visitation with his kids was by court order to be chaperoned. Dad got worse and visits stopped and Dad for 15 years would be plagued by alcohol and drugs, in and out of jail and prison, in and out of relationships, sleeping in abandoned houses, behind bushes and garbage cans. Sometimes months would go by sober, then one drink would begin another binge, drinking until his body gave out, or he ran out of money, or woke up in jail. Months and sometimes years Heaven would not see her dad although throughout her teenage years she would grieve for her dad. After all, daddies and their little girls is by the grace of God a thing, and cannot be easily dispensed with even through the direst of trials. Years later Heaven's dad on his own journey would be saved and broken at the foot of the Cross. Sadly mom to this day has not found her way back, her main idol being self and also the tag along idols that come with that.

In the second year of ***Act 3*** Heaven at fourteen in the 9th grade, and church already two years in the rear view mirror for the family, would begin a journey of rebellion. She would lapse greatly in her homework and found mom to be emotionally detached, blackmailing Heaven's emotions that she should be grateful for this new situation. Now with a broken family and forced to accept this new family even though it was foisted upon her and her sisters in a sneaky hidden hand of deception maneuver. It seems rather than a consideration of guidance that might have been provided by proper church elders; instead Heaven should just be grateful. Not an unusual story in America when 50% of marriages end in divorce leaving the kids scarred. The egos of the adults foregoing the Ten Commandments and foregoing God's intention for marriage leaving a wake of troubled youth.

At school, however, I suppose because of and in spite of her circumstance, as she stated in her proclamation Heaven still considered herself a Christian and "somewhat" good on the outside. I questioned her on this point, she said that at school she chose to side with underdogs and be polite to elders. In other words, a veneer of righteousness, while on the inside anger, depression, and hypocrisy had already taken root and were coming to the surface.

In the fourth year of ***Act 3*** Heaven, 16 years old, a junior in high school would begin a delusional escape into the world of bulimia. I asked why. Heaven said it was a "power" thing. It was something she alone had the "power" to do and control. This delusion would spill over into ***Act 4*** and ***Act 5*** lasting about 6 years. It would be hidden from everyone including her future husband for the first two years of ***Act 5*** which began with their marriage. More about that later.

Act 3 ends when Heaven is a senior in high school. At the end of the school year, Heaven now graduated is 17 ½ years old. The home front is unbearable so Heaven conspires with sympathetic relatives on her dad's side. The conspiracy would be that relatives in California would conspire with relatives in Arizona to meet halfway and drop Heaven off at the border. She is 17½ and technically a minor so this could have ended very badly for the grownups, and since Heaven was just shy of 18 no one pursued the potentially very ugly consequence of kidnapping across state lines, thank God. She ends up in Anthem, Arizona and was at least safe. Her mom was extremely upset and reasonably so, but time did its thing and things are better now.

Act 4 - Now in the home of an Aunt and Uncle in Arizona she would join them at their "charismatic," "prosperity," "word of faith" church and was happy for a time and feeling she was on her Way to know the Way. Unbeknownst to her she did not know what she did not know. Heaven did have a sense, after years away from the church that she wanted back in. That sense leads her to want to get baptized again. She did, but it wasn't in the Jordan and she would not know this for a dozen years.

Act 4 would be short lived, two years to be exact and ends in a most unusual way. Enter Alex, a member of the same church, handsome, 6' 6" tall, and a 210 pound basketball star on the state champion basketball team. Heaven and Alex would meet at a church function and soon after start dating and all would be well for a short season. The season would change when the topic of marriage surfaces.

Act 4 ends when Alex has his own trials. Alex a high school basketball star and now on a scholarship in college had suffered and would suffer concussions on the court. Then, on an ATV outing with some friends he would be in a tragic accident. He would get rear ended in a violent crash that would leave one of his friends dead and Alex with a severe concussion. This one would be the end of basketball and be so bad that memories of before that day are few. Back home Alex and Heaven are talking marriage.

A most curious second conspiracy in Heavens screenplay would be between Heaven's Aunt and Uncle and the charismatic, prosperity, word of faith church. In this case aunt, uncle, and church conspired to keep Heaven and Alex apart. It seems Heaven and Alex in this particular instance could not by their own "word of faith" "name and claim" their own destiny. The aunt, uncle and the church elders would break their own "theoretical" doctrines and conspire to "name and claim" Heaven and Alex's destinies for them.

So convicted were aunt, uncle, and church that Heaven was given an ultimatum, either break off this relationship or she could move out. Ouch! Why? In their opinion Heaven was damaged goods and not good enough for Alex. She moved out and was homeless. At this time Heaven was working for Alex's mom and riding a bike to work. She had saved $2,500 dollars to buy a car and was ripped off in Craigslist scam. Now she doesn't even have a car to sleep in. Thankfully enter Alex's parents whom are quite fond of Heaven. Alex at this time was away in New Mexico on a basketball scholarship so his Mom offered that Heaven stay with her family as well as help Heaven get a car. Another potential tragedy averted, i.e., a beautiful teenage girl it seems hungry for righteousness in her life being literally kicked to the curb for the self-righteous egos of theoretical Christians, and why, because she and Alex were falling in love. Ouch again!

In all of the turmoil of ***Act 4***, the providence of God would see to it that Heaven after a six year hiatus from the church would join her aunt and uncle at a church and feel as she noted in her proclamation a need to "rededicate" her life to Jesus and hence a second baptism. In a misguided church yes, part of her own "pilgrim's progress" most certainly. Providence in motion!

Act 5 will be seven years long and starts with a terminated basketball trajectory for Alex, and an as yet unforeseen reshaping season for him and his now bride. Back home now Alex and Heaven would wed, both wanting for their new life together to be in the way of the Lord. They start their life together and have trials and issues to deal with. They get through it and two years into ***Act 5*** they have their first child. It is at this point Heaven is God smacked with a pregnancy disorder called hyperemesis gravidarum, or (HG). It is here in ***Act 5*** that the delusion idol called bulimia and the self-delusion idol of her "power" to control it hit Heaven square in the ego. Faced with a very necessary consideration of her responsibility to be a mother she gave up, or, phrased Biblically Heaven would deny self, realizing most cognitively that God was in control and had the "power," and she did not. An in your face example of God reshaping one of his pots in a most sober way.

On the church front Heaven and Alex are still in the church and very much involved with a community of friends there.

Alex's parents would leave the church and end up at Phoenix Reformed Baptist Church led by Pastor Don Fry as the teaching pastor and James White at that time an attending elder. A few years later Alex and Heaven would question things about their church. Alex's dad would suggest that they watch John MacArthur's "Strange Fire" conference on YouTube.

It is now four years into ***Act 5.*** After seeing the "Strange Fire" conference and considering that they were being deceived, led by Alex whom discerned immediately and rightly that he and his bride were in a false church being led by wolves in sheep clothing. Alex pursuant to reason, respect, honor, and humility took the proper lead of a true man and took his bride to their church pastor to ask questions which could not be answered. Since some basic biblical doctrines could not be answered Alex informed the pastor they could not stay.

What to do now? Three years were spent wandering and wondering. Visiting a few churches while also watching many John MacArthur sermons on line, they found Desert Hills Bible Church on John MacArthur's seminary website. Thus ends ***Act 5***.

Act 6 begins in October of 2019, i.e., smack dab at the beginning of the "covid" debacle. This would begin a reshaping season for Heaven, i.e., the Master Potter reshaping one of His own. To be fare Alex is necessarily included in this reshaping for they are wed and therefore yoked together. Together and I suppose unknown to them at the time, this church would welcome them into what was at that time a modest church with plus or minus 300 souls. Over the next two years primarily because the "One Nation Under God" America the people thought they understood had been high jacked. The US Corporation, once bold and sensible, now weak and captured, used covid as an impetus for rule by despot using a bureaucrat(s), "theoretically" "science" itself, to declare the church as non-essential for its citizens. Desert Hills would grow fivefold because the shepherd of this church said no.

Heaven and Alex would now be in a proper church where the scriptures are expositorily preached for what the Word says. This would be quite a contrast from their prior church experience where emotions, feelings, and the tickling of the ears lead many souls falsely.

In Heavens case after four years of reshaping by the Master Potter, i.e., sitting in a proper church led by proper shepherds and opening up the Word and now reading and consuming the Word Heaven hears the call. The scriptures speak of milk and meat as an allegory to explain what Heaven noted early in her proclamation, i.e., a nominal Christian church which leaves its congregants with a nominal Christian faith. If one studies just a little about some of the various theoretical Christian churches like the ones Heaven was exposed to in her early life and contrasts what Heaven is now learning from good shepherds as well as consuming the Word herself, the milk and meat allegory becomes as clear as the darkness of night and the light in the day. One might even say she wasn't even getting milk, muddy water maybe!

In any event Heavens scales are falling and she now contemplates greatly her sin, the Cross, and that she missed the boat, so to speak. She is convicted that her first two baptisms were done under false pretenses and in that she is not wrong, she has discerned rightly. She was like many and perhaps most Christians following the crowd at chow time, as noted in Chapter 7.

Some might argue that a third baptism is not necessary, but they would not be seeing the Cross through Heavens eyes. Her cross, her burden, the "***Acts***" of her life played out to this point are solely and exclusively hers, but it seems were also the result of curses of at least two generations of unregenerate family. By the providence of God and by His grace the curse would be broken with Heaven. Had she grown up in a proper church and in a proper Christian home her eight year old baptism would be sufficient, but for Heaven's pilgrim's progress it feels tainted, she feels cheated.

For the first hour of our interview it was Heaven and I around the kitchen table. Alex was being dad with his kids in the back yard pool. Alex joined us, and the kids wanted to go in the front driveway to shoot some hoops, but dad in a gentle voice said no and states that the kids could watch a movie. What struck me about this simple occurrence was the clear and unambiguous "no" and the immediate follow up direction of what the children could do. The children without angst, complaining, or any strife whatsoever, were meek, that is to say, obedient to their dad. They ran along happy it seems. What ran through my mind was that Alex, from my perspective, that being old, is blessed as he knows his position as a Godly head of household.

It is here where I learn a bit about Alex and weave him into ***Act 4*** through ***Act 6*** above. Alex's journey was not the intent of this interview, but it cannot be helped to touch on it a little since Heaven for better or worse has hitched her wagon to Alex and vice versa. Are they equally yoked, dear God I hope so. Certainly they have the same trials and tribulations of any young family and have "overcome" much together. I asked Alex what the week looks like for his Christian family, i.e., what does the week look like Monday through Saturday. It was awesome to hear that they pray together and they study the Word with their children not every day, but often. I asked about invoking Christ's teachings in discipline. Alex chuckled as he has to get involved often as their children do as children do and Alex it seems has Jesus front and center as the head of household and conducts his dad responsibilities accordingly.

We are near the end of the interview. I asked Alex about something, I can't recall exactly, but it was something about when they first met. Alex explained that some things about even the beginning of their courtship he struggles to remember because of the accident. Timing is everything in a joke! In this case a decade is just right! I said to Heaven, "He's going to milk this memory thing." We all laughed, Alex most heartily. Another thing about Alex, he is a giant of a man. As I noted to him to see him around campus I would have thought he was a linebacker for the Denver Broncos. You see, Alex is no longer the skinny 6'- 6," 210 pound basketball player, he is 270 pounds and carries it like a linebacker in the NFL. I asked him what basketball would have been like had he weighed 270 backed then. Alex laughed and said, "Much easier!"

The interview is over, I pack up and thank them and here we are. My best attempt to read between the lines of the screenplay of Heavens life to now. Heaven and Alex are still in ***Act 6***. Surely they will have a circumstance, a trial, a tribulation that will be the end of ***Act 6*** and the start of ***Act 7.*** However, it is possible they will stay in ***Act 6*** until death do them part.

One thing seems certain though, Heaven is blessed with Alex and Alex is blessed with Heaven and their children are blessed that there mommy and daddy are overcomers. Like Job, Joseph, and Jonah they have overcome, further they understand completely the One whom "overcame" death and that they too may and will follow suit.

In a summary consideration for this interview, I hope it suggests to a young girl somewhere out there that although your life may likewise be in a season of stormy weather, you too can overcome. Recognize it for what it is, turn to Jesus, pick up His Word like Heaven did, repent, throw your burdens on the Cross and live anew. There are many lessons in the screenplay of Heavens life, but one for young girls and woman to ruminate on would be to find an Alex. A Godly man to lead wherever that may lead you and hopefully a family with the blessing of children and connected with a proper church.

Last night I could not sleep for thinking on Heavens parents and especially her mom. In the ***Time Tangent of Act 2*** we learn that Heavens parents name there first baby girl Heaven as a reminder for them to stay faithful to the word. It is reasonable to conclude that this thought came somewhere in the nine months before Heaven was born. This was and still can be a noble hope.

> **irony:** *1): incongruity between the actual result of a sequence of events and the normal or expected result; 2): an event or result marked by such incongruity.*
>
> **omen**: *an occurrence or phenomenon believed to portend a future event.*
>
> **portend**: *to give an omen or anticipatory sign of*

There is a great irony at play here. Heavens parents had a desire, a hope, although short lived that their first born baby girl would be an omen to portend the future event of their salvation. Here is the irony --- Heaven, intended to be a reminder, was in fact exactly that per her parents' wishes. In ***Act 3*** armed with the common sense God gave a 13 year old with the megaphone of her vocal cords did exactly as her parents wished. In ***Act 3*** and specifically as her mom is concerned and as her mom portended that Heaven be when conceived and for a short season thereafter, Heaven reminded her mom that her path was off track, that is to say crooked. Heaven asked questions and did what she could being a child at the time, but mom was and is still oblivious to the awesome original intent of the omen. Heaven the portended omen as it turns out, broke a generations old curse, but not without trials of her own. Residual trials and tribulations of the curse perhaps, but clearly Heaven has landed quite firmly at the foot of the Cross. That original intention is still there, that hope, that desire need only be dusted off and reconsidered.

This is perhaps strange flowing off of the fingertips of "An Old Man Thinking for the First Time," but I cannot not weigh in here. I write the below letter which happens to be for Heaven's mom but could be written to ten to twenty million other women and a like number of men whom are in a similar situation in America.

> *June 3, 2023*
> *Subject: An Impossible Situation*
> *Dear Heavens Mom,*
>
> *I don't know where you are in the screenplay of your life, but it strikes me that Heaven is still the omen you intended. Heaven is not the answer, Jesus is, but having met your daughter it is clear that she most certainly loves you and prays for you. Now you can be sure a few more souls will also pray that the scales fall away from your eyes, you see the Cross, see that all sin including yours was nailed to that Cross. Salvation then is a free gift; please seek your Lord, thee Lord, the same Lord you once had occasion to know. Jesus hasn't gone anywhere; He is still there if you seek him.*
>
> *This morning I listened to the sermon presented at Desert Hills Bible Church on May 28, 2023. The sermon can be found on YouTube and is titled,* ***"The Impossible Situation - Exodus 14 (Darren Dirkson)."*** *There are baptisms, prayers, and singing which are awesome and if you can I certainly would*

*encourage a listen. The sermon as I listened to it is apropos to me, your daughter, "**you**" and everyone. I plead and pray you might give it a listen. Fast forward to minute 45:20, Darren most certainly exposits the Words of God very well. The title, "The Impossible Situation" while correct on the one hand is not correct on the other. That is to say while our lives seem like "Impossible Situations" they in fact are not. I think you know what I mean.*

Very truly and most humbly yours,
An Old Man you don't know!

*PS. Ironically that baby girl "you portended" to be an "omen," if you are "**honest,**" has greatly exceeded any hope, desire, wish you may have had as a young mother. To be "**honest**" the mind necessarily must be quite and clear, and free from "**all**" earthly and fleshly distractions or vices. ("honest" Emphasis mine!)!*

Postscript 1 --- 6-25-2023, Heaven texted me to say that her dad was baptized this day. His testimony and proclamation of faith can be witnessed at: http://share.icloud.com/photos/052u0b16AZhLR6tMffBdp3fvw another compelling journey! I can only imagine how elated Heaven is for her dad.

>>> OTHER FIRST BAPTISMS I WITNESSED <<<

That same day I heard four other young women and a young man give testimonies and be baptized.

I just went back and listened to all of the testimonies from that day. They can be found on YouTube with a search for ***"Desert Hills Church Baptisms - February 2022."*** As I watched and listened again 15 months later I wept yet again. My memory refreshed, it was all of them that inspired me to think seriously about baptism. Those souls were the first souls I had ever heard do such a thing so it strikes me that they all were the inspiration for Chapter 7.

- There was Emma, a pre-teen young girl whom of her own volition told and asked her parents that she wanted to get baptized. She made a brief and clear profession that she knew the gospel. Her simple and bold profession made it clear she wanted to obey her conscience and declare before fellow saints her wish to be baptized. I met and talked with her father months later on a Worship Day. Her father's countenance made it clear how pleased he was with the maturity and understanding of his daughter.
- There was MaKayla, a young woman I guess to be in her mid-twenties who did not grow up in a Christian home, but did attend church on Sundays with her Aunt. She choked back her tears through her entire testimony obviously and sincerely aware of and repentant for her younger life replete with sin. Then three years prior she was made whole recognizing her sin and why Christ and why He did what He did, and that she needed Him. She expressed her thankfulness to have found a body of believers at Desert Hills, and ended with her honest hope to hear the words when she enters the gates of Heaven, "Well done my good and faithful servant."
- Madison, a most endearing little girl of nine years who recounted her hard times to know and believe in Christ. Then when she was four years old she came to know more about Christ and when she was eight years old she wanted to learn and know what baptism really is. She quoted John 3:16 and came to know she can't get to Heaven by herself. She reads her Bible every day and recounts that if she didn't come to know Christ she would not have grown up into the person she is today. She ended by letting the congregation know that she can pray and help others to know Jesus. Then she went to the Jordan. Adorable, outstanding and Amen.
- Jillian is married and was raised in a Christian home and first baptized at six years old. She made it known that when she was young she believed in Jesus, but as she grew up she would as a teenager in high school discover from her own actions as a bully she was truly a sinner. Not an epiphany in her case, but a realization over time that the "*evidence*" of her actions was that she was broken and that she needed the salvific work of Jesus. When she did see her sin she repented and turned. Now she looks back and can see "*evidence*" of the changes as she turned and felt compelled to profess her new life and be baptized with full knowledge.

- Isaac moved from California to Arizona on a football scholarship to Arizona Christian University (ACU). He spoke of living the sin of seeking comfort in food and being 380 pounds. Hating himself as a man and cutting people and family out of his life. Isaac did not share particulars, but it seems as though he found friends he refers to as family including Jeff, Rose, Kelly, and David as well as his fiancée Caitlin (now his betrothed). This blessing helping him to find Christ. This it seems a catalyst to lose 150 lbs. Isaac moved to tears as he expressed his appreciation and obvious love for his fiancé and this family and obvious tearful comfort in knowing Jesus. He noted a blessing of a job that allows him to share the gospel every day. Through his tears he expressed this thankfulness and then he went to the Jordan.

That day in February of 2022 being the first time I had seen such a thing I was moved and very much so. As I watched the video of that day on YouTube this morning the proclamations still emotionally moved me in the same way, but I also noticed something. The younger girls Emma and Madison did not weep as they spoke. It strikes me that perhaps they and their parents are in Desert Hills which when attended is so obviously not only a church, but a church where the Word is preached with no holding back on both the love and the wrath of God and why the flock needs to know. No compromise! I am not sure, but it seems likely that Emma and Madison have been raised in a church and not just any church. If these young girls get it, certainly it is not just one day a week at church that got them there. Discernment would indicate that they live in a scripturally based home where dad is truly the head of household and mom knows why it is she is blessed to be a mother. Since the scriptures call parents to raise their children in the ways of the Lord one might surmise that the confidence exuded by these young girls is "*evidence*" that they are blessed to be in such a home.

All of the others were in their 20s or 30s and while they knew "of God" and knew "of Jesus" they, like me and reasonably the larger percentage of "church goers":

A. Were not raised in a household where the family dynamic included the "Word of God," i.e., "Daily Bread" each and every day; prayer at each and every meal; Bible home study/ discussion, bedtime prayer; family prayer; etc., and all of this with dad as the head and mom as co-pilot and nurturer.

B. Were sent off to Rome to be educated and very early on became Romans.

C. And, most recently sent off to cyberspace and very early on indoctrinated that up is down, down is up, and truth is subjective, and narcissism is virtue. This of course being reinforced by the schools and universities of Rome.

And, perhaps the saddest revelation of all is the churches they may have attended were neither sound in their doctrine nor attentive to the wolves at the door and in many a case lead by a wolf.

What does this have to do with anything? The answer is everything! The answer in reverse order is the nations, America, the 50 states, the counties, the cities, schools, the neighborhoods, the families, the father, the mother, and the children since Christ called that all be descipled to know "The Way" have been let down by the church. This is not to make the church a scapegoat for the evidence of God's glory is everywhere and touches each of the five senses of everyone 24\7. Further, morality is written on the heart and obviously so, and it is the individual "alone" whom will be judged by God, but, and this is a question, can the Church do better?

nominal: *existing or being something in name or form only*

mere: *1) being nothing more than; 2) having no admixture, pure; 3) being nothing less than, absolute*

Christendom: *the part of the world in which Christianity prevails*

In any event, the Christian Church should be united in "Mere Christendom," but as the scriptures warned us, there are wolves in sheep clothing. It will always be thus, the evidence being proclamations like some of those above where it is adults that came later in life to know the Word and then compelled to "reconsider" baptism. What was it, what is it that would cause a person who has already been baptized to "reconsider"?

If one witnesses proclamations in which "reconsideration" of baptism has driven a saint back to the Jordan to be ceremoniously washed again, the answer might be varied.

1. Sin at long last being comprehended and so much so that the words, "I'm a good person," or, "people are generally good" is in an epiphany type of realization utterly *trite, hackneyed, tired, and stereotypically foolish*.
2. Following this realization embarrassment, not to the world, but inwardly to one's self before God whom you now know also knew of your foolishness.
3. When sin is comprehended then the wrath of God becomes real.
4. Recognition that a previous baptism was a show, a pomp and circumstance show to fit in, or as noted in the previous chapter, following the crowd at chow time.
5. Or, most reasonably all of the above.

As Heaven Dykhuizen noted in her proclamation she was raised in a nominal Christian home and by logical extension a nominal Christian Church, only to find when she ran away from home and landed in another church it to was not just nominal, but strayed far from the richness found in the Bible and was led by a wolf and his/her pack of idolaters of self.

The lesson I suppose for all of time will be as Christ said in the gospel of Matthew:

> **NKJV --- Matthew 18:2-3** -- *2 Then Jesus called a little child to Him, set him in the midst of them, 3 and said, "Assuredly, I say to you, unless you are converted and become as little children, you will by no means enter the kingdom of heaven."*

I suppose that is why the proclamations of Emma and Madison were and are worthy of note and much consideration for all!!

>>> INTERVIEW WITH MIKE <<<

Mike sometimes plays the drums at the church I attend and watching him is intriguing. Mike could in no ways be considered dull or monotonous as he plays the drums. Not only do his arms and hands control the sticks with obvious intent and passion, but his torso, his head, and especially his facial expressions are an inseparable part of the beat and rhythms he joyously adds to the worship of God by the excellent group of musicians and singers at Desert Hills Bible Church.

I first approached Mike after a Sunday service over a year ago when he happened to be sitting across the aisle from me. I introduced myself and commented to him that he plays the drums well, but could he not find a little joy in his craft. He laughed as did his wife. She noted that even when playing at home he cannot not be overcome by joy as he bangs away on his drums. I mentioned to him that he reminded me of Mick Fleetwood of the band Fleetwood Mac, which may not resonate with a younger crowd, but Mike knew exactly what I meant and that it was very much a compliment.

Many months later someone mentioned to me that Mike had quite the journey to the Cross. I recently asked if I could interview him with a particular interest in his baptism. He texted me an interview he did with a local podcaster, Louise Sedgwick, at *louisesedgwick.com/podcast.* His story from a spiraled out of control drug addict, to a saved born again Christian from the bowels of Joe Arpaio's tent city prison is very much worthy of consideration for the Kendrick Brothers.

Central New Jersey, middle class suburban upbringing, stable home, loving parents, except for one little transgression not unlike what is heard over and over about how it starts. Mike's sister a few years older than Mike found some pot that their mom hid under her mattress, so the two of them would smoke together. Mike loved it from the first moment and never stopped. Throughout his school years his nickname would be "Weed." This first encounter was 1980 and Mike was in the 5th grade and 11 years old. Two years later 1982, Mike is in the 7th grade and his folks split up, about two years after that in 1984 or 1985 in the 9th or 10th grade crack cocaine hits the streets.

Mike was a straight "A" student, thinking as did all of his dirt bike riding, music playing, weekend partying friends, that his intellect would keep him in control. By the time Mike was 18 or 19 he and his mom smoked together. At this time Mike and a group of his friends started down the crack cocaine path not thinking in any way there was a problem. Selling pot to feed his crack cocaine habit and a friend stealing money from his well to do black out drunken father, Mike was able to feed his habit, all the while thinking there was not a long term problem.

Mike would start to realize he had a problem when he could not "not" have crack cocaine on hand. In 1987 as a senior he and some friends wanted to go to "Six Flags." Mike could not go without just a bit of crack cocaine to get him through the trip. After a night of smoking crack and very high they thought they could drive, but…! They got pulled over, drugs found, leading to Mike's first arrest. It was at this point that Mike's intellect would meet his arrogance. His intellect questioned his arrogance and he realized he had done something irrational, that thinking he could be high, drive, as well as have crack cocaine in his car and all would be well. Now he knows he has a problem, but …. well you know, arrogance and addiction, a tough brew of temptation and sin.

That year Mike would enter the engineering program at Rutgers University thinking the safety of being in a studious environment would steer him away from the drug scene. While that thought, one would think is rational since institutions of higher learning should be structured in such a way that would be strictly disciplined to turn out model, God fearing citizens, they in fact do not. Rutgers started that way in 1766, but in 1945 it would be transferred from the headship of Christ as Lord God to the headship of the state of New Jersey. In 1952 after the state was at the helm for only seven years a fraternity that Mike would join started serving beer on tap 24/7 and the beer has not stopped flowing to this date. Not particularly conducive to Bible study, prayer meetings, or setting aside a day to worship God.

In any event, Mike washed out of engineering school in 18 months, got a job at an auto shop and would befriend another mechanic who was a crack cocaine addict and the two of them would work, spend time at the go-go bar, drink and stay hopped up on crack cocaine. His friend at 23 or

24 years old had a heart attack in the bathroom of the bar, the door had to be kicked in, and his friend almost died. This scared Mike enough that, as he says he "moderated" his usage for a while, but by this time he was an addict. He would stop the cocaine, but still drink and smoke pot. The dragon, however, could not be kept at bay, for Mike always came back to the cocaine thinking he could control it but finding each time he swirled deeper and deeper into its clutches.

Mike worked as a mechanic for about six years, each year distancing himself from a rational, normal world. Mike would distance himself from his family and old childhood friends because he did not want to have anyone tell him he had a problem. Shame certainly was the factor that made Mike distance himself although at the time he would have never conceded the point. Staying high kept shame at bay. Mike describes a time when he, in the rain, car on his lawn, was pushing an entertainment center onto the roof of his car to trade it for some cocaine. An old friend drove by; they locked eyes, but the friend drove away having given up on Mike.

Mike also played drums in a band and dabbled in sound work. After six years in what was reasonably a stable job, the crack and the influence of the party atmosphere of the band scene, Mike would quit his job. He would bounce from gig to gig and could not keep it together even when a friend tried to save him by taking him on the road to do some sound engineering work in other cities. He would get a job, lose it, get another lose it, stop paying his rent and power, and finally lose his housing. In 1995 working as a traveling sound engineer and falling off the cocaine wagon again, he got into a fight with his boss in Houston, Texas and was fired. Having nowhere to go he called his mom who was now living in Phoenix Arizona. She flew him to Phoenix and laid down the law. She demanded that he cut his hair, get a job, get his own place and get right.

It could only be love for his mom and her caring that made for a circumstance in which Mike would be free of the crack cocaine habit, at least for a time. He did continue to smoke pot, but otherwise he did as his mom requested. He would land a job with an in-house audio visual company at a five star resort in Scottsdale Arizona, and become an operations manager. That catalyst would provide a new place to live, a truck, a new dirt bike, and he would join a new band that was not in a party scene type of environment. All was well and lasted about four years.

One day coming back from a dirt bike track in Chandler Arizona Mike would see a drug deal going down on the side of the road. As he tells it his truck seemed to drive itself over to the dealer. He had a lot of money so he bought a lot of crack cocaine. All of the progress, all that he had amassed, his life on track and happy, all of it would be completely gone in three months.

Mike was smoking so much crack at the end of that three month period and could not stop. His four years clean would come to an end when he was smoking crack in the bathroom of the resort and could not come out when he was supposed to be doing a sound check for an event featuring former Dallas Cowboy quarterback Roger Staubach. The demon of crack addiction controlled him. His boss fired him.

Sometime in 2000 his mom would save him yet again. She put a roof over his head and put him to work in a commercial cleaning company she had with her sister. Somewhere during that time Mike discovered meth. He thought rather stupidly that it could keep him from crack cocaine since you could stay awake for days and in your mind think you are functioning normally. Not the case.

Doing this for a time Mike thinking he was fooling his mom. Could it have been the extreme weight loss from normally about 190 lbs. down to 130 been and indicator? Surely a rational mind might consider such a thing, but a mind on meth is anything but. Unbeknownst to Mike because his mind was delusional he was scaring his mom so much so that one day in the spring of 2002 he came home to find a moving truck in front of the house. Mike was to find out that his mom was moving away and would not tell him where. She said you are a danger to me, you are a danger to yourself, and you are a danger to everyone around you, and I'm not going to deal with it anymore. Mike was clueless.

It would be a short six months more for Mike in meth hell. Either he would be dead or……? Now on the street, bouncing from tweeker pad to tweeker pad. At one such stay at a tweeker pad he refused to leave a girls apartment. The cops came through a window, arrested Mike with possession, took him to jail, told him to come back to court which he did not do.

Then on September 5, 2002 in Phoenix, Arizona, a walking emaciated skeleton of a 6', 128 pound, homeless, no socks, no family, no friends, wearing a ratty old tee shirt, riding a ratty old bike, on his way to a Motel 6 down the road with a plan in his head on how he could stay high for a few days. All that was in front of Mike was death. He would find himself in a Circle K parking lot when a feeling, a voice, something not easily explained gripped him.

It was then that Mike would be confronted by a female officer in that Circle K parking lot. The officer locks eyes with Mike with the compassion of a mother and asks Mike if he is okay. Mike, for the first time in a long time heard the voice of another human that truly cared. That officer caught Mike at the very bottom of bottoms that a person can fall under the addictive influence of drugs. She said she needed to see his ID, not because she had probable cause, but because as she stated to Mike, "you are dying on your feet," which I submit comports with the 2nd greatest command of Jesus. Probably not in the police manuals for "service" but it clearly is in God's manual.

Mike gave into her compassion telling her he was not okay. She handcuffed Mike and told him, "you're gonna get better, we're gonna get you some help." What happen next can only be inferred as it is most unusual in today's generally "unjust" legal system. When at his hearing, I assume Mike's court appointed attorney instead of the normal plea bargaining that would have released Mike back to the streets suggested that Mike not be released, but rather be held to a higher level of accountability. The judge it seems was perplexed as this borders on unethical behavior for a lawyer, but it seems the "Holy Spirit" would lead the attorney to do a thing in a similar fashion as the cop, and that was for Mike to be put on a trajectory to the narrow gate whether the secular legal system liked it or not. The judge could have made issue of the lawyers unusual conduct, but it seems he also was to be moved by the Holy Spirit, like it or not, to do God's work and do the right thing in this instance and sentenced Mike to a "safe place" which meant 6 months in "Tent City." Look it up, it made national headlines for a time.

I would have surmised that the officer conferred with the attorney which might suggest not one, but two righteous persons caring for another by God's 2nd greatest commandment while dancing in a system that seldom does. Mike said that the officer did not confer with the attorney which makes it more unusual that the attorney was moved to do what she did. The judge, reasonably unwittingly, was a 3rd party co-conspirator to Mike's salvation even though the judge had no idea, even now. Even through corrupt systems God's providence can do what God does as He calls His sheep unto Himself.

In "Tent City" the 4th person that Mike would confront in jail was a fellow addict that also loved Mike per the 2nd greatest commandment though he might not have understood that at the time. The friend said when he saw Mike, "Hey, you made it."

Mike, "huh?"

Friend, "you're not dead, you made it."

Mike, "What are you talking about, this is jail."

Friend, "There's something going on, I think God might be real, I've been reading this Bible, I think God might be real, I feel different, I feel like there's hope." The friend suggested that Mike go to the church service and told him they have coffee and doughnuts. Mike, starving was first in line to the protestant church service. He walks in looking for the doughnut cart; the Pastor asks him what he is doing?

Mike said, "I heard there was coffee and doughnuts."

The pastor tilted his head back and laughed hysterically, said to Mike, "That's hilarious, sit down."

Mike recalls that through his delusional, out of focus state of mind that this pastor seemed intelligent, had a ring on his finger, and what Mike thought was most peculiar was also a volunteer. This man talked about hope, redemption, and recovery. Mike at least had the presence of mind to see that this man was genuine in what he believed as he talked about this Jesus character. After the service the Pastor pulled Mike aside and told him he had something better than coffee and doughnuts and gave him a Bible and told him to flip towards the back and read the gospel of John.

Mike did just that, and even though he was mentally and physically at the bottom he had the correct conclusion that what he read was true.

Reading, attending church, going to any and all classes available Mike was to be transformed. At a certain point in his six month stay Mike felt the need to reach out to his dad whom he had not seen or talked to in years. He calls collect from jail to his dad who answered within ½ a ring. His dad started to sob and said, "thank God, I thought you were dead." Mike recounts that he had never heard his dad cry so to hear his dad sob broke him in that he felt an inexplicable burden of shame. That same day, in jail, Mike goes to a church service feeling this extreme burden of shame and brokenness. Forty men were singing a song which included the words, "Holy Spirit Come." Mike was crushed under the weight of his sin and how he had hurt a lot of people and especially his mom and dad. Mike describes with undeniable clarity that the Holy Spirit took the wheel of his life that day.

To my way of thinking this is reasonably an affidavit of fact, that an emaciated drug addict can read the Word of God in only one of the gospels and conclude correctly it must be true. It can only be the Holy Spirit piercing the clouds of addiction including pot, alcohol, crack cocaine, and meth to come to the conclusion after one reading of the gospel of John that the Words were true. Such a turnaround doesn't make any sense at all by any natural analytic.

I did a little research to see what meth withdrawal normally looks like or phrased another way "a natural analytic." Naturally and normally a meth addict would go through the following acute symptoms when withdrawing from meth addiction:

> *Fatigue, Anxiety, Irritability, Lack of energy, Weight gain, Dehydration, Chills, Insomnia followed by hyper-somnia (sleeping too much), Dysphoria (low mood) could progress to clinical depression and suicidal thoughts, The inability to think clearly, Anhedonia (loss of ability to feel pleasure), Withdrawing from others, Drug cravings.*

Mike was detoxing for a couple of weeks or so, so some of the symptoms would reasonably be somewhat abated; however reason might suggest not that much. Mike did point out that some of these symptoms did not go completely away right away, but as he notes he in fact was changed in an instant through all of that fog. This side of the fog, Mike says with an undeniable sober conviction that it was the Holy Spirit that pierced that fog and saved him. In other words a "natural analytic" cannot account for such a transformation, and if this is so a metaphysical consideration by reason must not only be probable, but actual.

That was 21 years ago and Mike's journey to the Cross and beyond is inspirational and once again I would guide anyone interested to the podcast noted above. I don't think it is possible to put in the written word what one can hear in Mike's voice as he recounts such an encounter as he was hit hard by the Holy Spirit. When you hear it from Mike, through his tears, one can only hope for such a crushing and at the same time uplifting transcendental experience.

This is most certainly what the scriptures say about being "born again." Mike, by the fruit that one will notice, if only to see him play the drums, has been born again.

All of the above I transcribed in summary from the podcast and is a good introduction to Mike. I wanted to know about his journey from feeling the call of the Holy Spirit to the ordinance of baptism, so I called Mike. We met for coffee and here is the rest of the story:

Mike would become "sober" and be "born again" in Joe Arpaio's tent city jail in September of 2002. Mike was released from tent city jail in March of 2003 having to then move to a half-way house. While there his roommate Andy suggested he check out his church. In March of 2002 he would attend this church and be blown away by the worship music and knew he had found a new home. The church had a screen for announcements and to show the lyrics to the songs. The first announcement that captured Mike's attention was that there would be baptisms at the upcoming Easter service the following month.

Mike was all in; he wanted all of it, all that was offered. His baptism would be a short month away so Mike immediately sought counsel on what next to do. He went to the church office and met with a young man, Ryan. Wanting to understand that Mike knew what baptism was all about Ryan would have to listen to Mike recount his journey. As Mike tells it Ryan was speechless. Ryan being young had never encountered such a story nor known anyone from that kind of world. What Ryan was able to ascertain from Mike's words and tears was the obvious transformation and that Mike very clearly understood the "Good News" and that Jesus Christ is who He said He was and the Mike clearly had given over his all to Christ.

Just before the Easter baptism ceremony Mike knew he had to say something. Mike recounts that certain parts of his journey have had very unusual elements that can only be explained by understanding that the "Holy Spirit" truly does touch us. The day Mike was crushed in jail and submitted to the Lord was such a day. Within a few days of being broken at the foot of the Cross, in prison no less, Mike would sit down and in five minutes pen what he would say a few months later to the church just before he would walk to the Jordan. Here is what Mike penned and said:

~ HE CAN ~

I had an invitation to desperation,
But traded it in for a new salvation,
A revelation of contemplation,
That bore the seed of a new creation.

Can it really be true?
Have I seen a new and brighter star before my eyes?
It was born on a new day,
That showed me the true way to get the hurt out of my life.

He was a quiet man with an awesome plan,
To take a stand and He took my hand,
And He said, "I can."
So off I ran and for ever more I'm His greatest fan.

Now I know I've seen a new and brighter start before my eyes.
I was reborn on a new day,
That showed me the true way to get the love into my life.

Now I am a glistening soul,
Come up out of my hole, with a tale to be told,
Of a renewal of soul and regain of control.

And in sight of the whole picture I tell you.
I know you know you can hear me, and you can feel me too.

Because the brighter light burns in my eyes
Makes it easy to see that I wear no disguise, and I tell you no lies.
And brother and sisters --- He can do it for you too!

Michael Elia
Sept. 2002

From sure death as a drug addict to penning the above through the fog of detoxing it seems very clear that the Holy Spirit moves among men.

Since that time Mike has become part of the worship team at Desert Hills Bible Church utilizing his passion for drums that most certainly adds not only a beat to hear and follow, but joy one can see. He also spent 15 years going back into the jail system to work with inmates, although that came to a halt when covid hit. Just recently the jail system has opened up again for volunteers to work with inmates. Mike is now badged as a religious volunteer and will lead two church services on Thursday mornings.

The system requires that volunteers be sponsored and then badged to gain access to work with or minister to inmates. The sponsor now is Desert Hills Bible Church that has the requisite training that gives the state reasonable assurance that inmates are cared for per the 2nd greatest commandment. That may not have been the states intent, but the unintended consequence is the same? The scriptures call for saints to put on the armor of God so it seems an irony that the state issued "badge" is in a sense "armor" provided by the state!!! How about that, God's word cannot be stopped!

Twice a year Mike works at a camp for recovering drug addicts doing audio visual work and leads a church service on Sunday morning. As a new comer to the church it is an awesome curiosity to me that converts like to go fishing in the lakes they came out of. In other words, converted Christians that come out of various cultures or cults which includes the various cultures of dependence often seem compelled to help those from whence they came.

In summary it took Mike about 22 years from his first puff of pot as an 11 year old in the 5th grade to his last puff of meth as a 33 year old man to lose everything including his mom and dad and become a skeleton of a man incarcerated in the desert. However, it would be in the heat of that desert tent city jail that God would find one of his lost sheep.

It has now been 21 years and Mike is completely sober, a life saved, changed, and very much a Christian soldier.

It occurs to me that Mike's adolescent arrogance was the same in the 1980s and 1990s as adolescent arrogance has always been and still is today. How to reach the young? How indeed! Mike's story, a different journey and a tragic one at that, to know the name of Jesus and why He and only He can rescue should be, needs to be, must be taught to today's adolescent arrogant youth.

Mike has for various reasons ended up at Desert Hills Church and is yet another brother in Christ I am blessed to know and will get to know better if for no other reason than I wanted to know his story and he was gracious enough to share. Our paths very much different, but wow! I am glad I thought to introduce myself to Mike.

>>> INTERVIEW WITH GARY <<<

I talked about my good friend Gary in the last chapter and his influence on my baptism journey. I called Gary and asked that he think about his "post baptism" thoughts which for him were about 50 years ago. His first statement was, "that was a long time ago, I'm not sure I can remember that long ago." His next statement was, "as I think on your post baptism, the word loathing comes to mind." I didn't understand what he said so I asked, "What did you say?" He said "loathing." I laughed really hard. I asked Gary to think about it anyway, but if I don't hear back from Gary, this is enough.

I did talk about Gary in chapter 7 as he was fundamental to part of my journey. As noted there, if I consider Gary's post baptism journey he has been truly, truly blessed in many ways to the third generation. Gary and his wife Mary raised three God fearing children and now have nine God fearing grandchildren, so far so good, 50 years of blessings and counting. I am blessed that he is my friend.

~ PROVIDENCE ~

My lot in life, at least for a time,
Was the sin I chose not considering why,
It took a while I must confess,
Six decades long and four years more,
To find the way to Heavens door.

A journey long and full of strife,
Not with others as one might surmise,
But only me to my surprise.

With blinders on and hearing impaired,
I trudged through life without much care.
I knew of God and His Son,
But did not understand what He'd done.

A good friend of mine a life we/ll lived,
With a family strong in faith and deed,
His house blessed three generations now,
Since he found the Lord in the heat of war.

Since that time he prayed for me,
It took a while, but now look at me.
I know the Cross and what it means,
To accept the sacrifice imputed me.

The blinders off I now see clear,
The wrath of God and His enduring love.
Why the path he chose for me,
I know not why, but I hear the call He calls to me.

Amen
JKF 2-21-2020

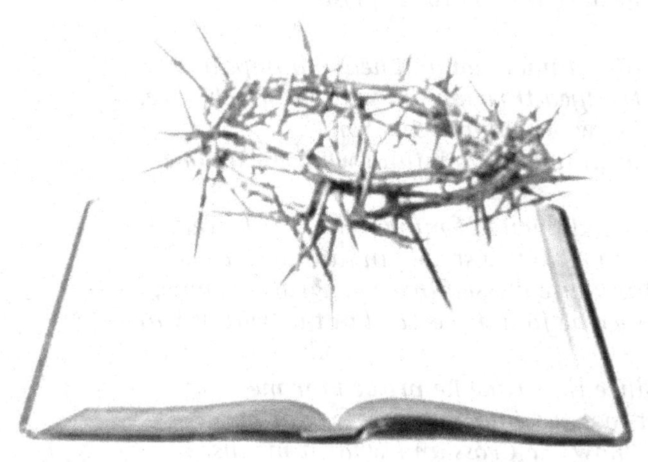

Take the Field Rookie!

Disciple the Nations!

Chapter 9

FIRST ENCOUNTERS OF THE CLOSE KIND

~ THE BARBERS ~

>>> BARBER 1 <<<

The great commission is a clear ordinance for Christians which I had known since I was a kid. Once convicted and accepting of my plight the consideration of evangelizing would be a long time coming. Procrastination, lack of knowledge, and fear I suppose the primary impediments to getting out there. In my case it seems as with my conviction of my sin and being broken at the foot of the Cross, the Holy Spirit would make a way and a time for this vessel to take the field.

In the summer of 2020 early in the morning I was at coffee shop at 16th & Bethany Home in Phoenix reading my Bible. This particular morning a handsome and fit black man with a neatly trimmed beard sat next to me. He was a barber making an appointment with someone for a haircut. When he was done I asked if by chance it was the barber shop in the adjacent strip mall as years before I used to get my hair cut there. He said it was, but now it is called Beardsmith & Barber. He handed me a card and that was that. I thanked him and suggested I might stop in.

About two or three weeks later I did. When I walked in early one morning there were two barbers working, his chair was available so I sat down. Probably because he recalled that when we met I was reading the Bible, he initiated a conversation by asking me a question relating to my reading, followed by a statement that he looks to the universe for guidance comfort, or something along those lines. I'll never forget the pang in my stomach.

When I was a teenager there were occasions when my father would say words to the effect, "son, we need to talk." When stated with a certain inflection or tone most every kid can recall the very real lump in the throat, the pang in the stomach, and or an increased heart rate. When the tone is heard it is generally because 1) you did something wrong, and 2) you deserve whatever may follow.

In the case of the barber I felt the same sort of pang, i.e., I knew I was in trouble. In this case not because of something I had done wrong, but I might be in trouble for something I might not do right, i.e., defend the faith. While in the process of learning and very much lacking in knowledge the pang in my gut was at minimum an indicator that it was time to take the field.

By this time there were two more customers sitting in the guest chairs, the other barber and his client and me and my barber, so six people and I'm up. The "Coach" sent me into the game and the "QB" was about to call a play where I would be handed the ball. Never having stepped foot on the gridiron or even suiting up, and in this case not even knowing the apologetic playbook. Down, set, hut, hut....

Here is what happened: When the barber made reference to calling on the universe as his spiritual source or consideration of inner something or other, what came out of my mouth amazes me even now. The barber was holding a comb and a pair of scissors, so I spewed out, "You might as well talk to that comb."

The barber said, "What do you mean?"

I replied, "That comb is material. All that is out there in that universe is material, rocks, ice and gases. It'll do you just as much good to talk to that comb."

Where did that come from??

The barber then asked me why I believed in God. I followed with a question, "Have you ever bought a house?" To which he replied he had.

I then asked him, "Would you have ever found that house had you not started looking for it?"

He said, "Of course not."

I cannot remember my exact words, but it went something like this. "If there is life after death, or a place called Heaven, is it not reasonable that it is a home."

To which the barber concurred.

I continued, "If it is a home is it not reasonable that like your house you are not going to find it unless you start looking for it." Once again the barber concurred and asked where he might start looking.

At this point I should point out that I was conscious that I had the attention of everyone in the room, all parties listening.

I continued, and asked if he knew about Jesus. He said that he did so I suggested a good place to start looking is the truth of the claim that Jesus defeated death, walked out of the tomb, and then rose from the dead. If he were to look into that and find evidence of its truth with reason that home awaits.

The barber then asked where he might start looking. I talked awhile about Lee Strobel and his research and journey and that he might start there with the book or better yet the movie "A Case for Christ." At this point the barber said, "Just a minute." He went and got a sticky note and wrote down my suggestion. I also referred him to Frank Turek, and J. Warner Wallace I think, which he also stopped and wrote on a sticky note. Of course, and most importantly he should start reading the Bible.

That was not all of the exchange and I cannot remember all of it, but I do remember I was answering questions for a least a half an hour all the while having captive five men all seemingly attentive. When the haircut was done and I was paying the bill, the barber surprised me with this statement, "I want to thank you."

I responded, "For what."

He said, "You are the first Christian that didn't say to me, you believe because you have faith."

I said, "You're welcome."

I left and walked back to the coffee shop smiling, feeling a type of good I'd never had the occasion to feel.

For the next few days the encounter made me think, "what was that?" Where did those words come from, I had never heard such an apologetic. Talk to your comb, have you ever bought a home? How? How indeed! Holy Spirit much?!!! Those analogies had never occurred to me until that strange and unlikely encounter. Further, how would I have known, or anyone else for that matter, that this man would have turned a "blind ear" had I said I believed because I have faith. I think on him once and awhile and pray a little prayer that he looks for that home.

I love sports allegories, football mostly, but baseball is also useful. In a baseball analogy I think on the encounter with the barber in this way. I am a minor league player. On that day I was called up to the Big Show, walked through the tunnel into a big league ballpark and got my first at bat. My first at bat clearly not a home run, but it is reasonable I hit the ball well enough to make it to first base. It is also reasonable that after that hit I was sent back down the minors for more practice.

>>> BARBER 2 <<<

I went back to that barber shop about 18 months later hoping to follow up only to find that the man no longer worked there. I did, however, have yet another encounter with another barber. This time my barber was a very large, loud, boisterous, extroverted man maybe 35 years old. I first asked for the aforementioned barber and that's when I was told that he had moved on. My barber was to be this large; and by that I mean NFL left tackle large; seemingly happy, extroverted, and ready to converse. My read would be that he would be the life of the party wherever he might happen to be. His other trait was that he cussed like a sailor, and he was wearing a crucifix.

When I first sat down I was disappointed that the other barber was not there and my hope to find out if he had started the search for the "big house." This let down, however, was replaced by a completely different opportunity with a completely different personality and yet another completely unexpected call by the "Coach" to take the field.

We made small talk, he taking the lead asking prying questions. When he asked what I did, and told him I was writing a book, the follow-up question is always about what. When I told him the title, why the title, and considering the world through new lenses, he was ready to espouse his Christian faith. He went on for a bit about being from Chicago, Irish and Catholic, growing up learning and becoming street smart, having to use his wit to survive, and all this intermixed with an expert like command of very colorful adjectives that I recognized all too well. Having, in the not so distant past, been an expositor of the very same colorful adjectives, I was now confronted with a new understanding. Putting in the armor of God I called him out.

I said something like, "I'm glad to hear you're a believer, but I'm calling you out brother, you need to put your faith where you mouth is." Having already established a friendly relationship I didn't feel any hesitancy to call him out and he did not take offense. To the contrary he apologized, agreed, and showed a sincerity that at least looked like he knew that he was caught with is mouth in the cookie jar, so to speak, and that he might ought a put those dirty cookies back.

Like my first venture with a barber, there were two more barbers with customers and one or two clients waiting. The big man's co-workers were giggling when their buddy was being called out by an old man, but they too listened to the next half an hour of a part Christian and a part political conversation.

Somehow the conversation turned to politics and he did have a better than average grasp of the real underlying problems with US Corp and that was a fun exchange also. I cannot remember everything, but he did clean up his language for the remainder of the haircut, so, a small victory. At the time I had recently finished Chapter 5 – "Thoughts on America"; and invited him over to the adjacent coffee shop to see that chapter. He took me up on it and came over after his next appointment.

I did not expect him to show so I was pleasantly surprised when he did show about 45 minutes later. He joined me for coffee and I read aloud all of Chapter 5. He expressed appreciation for the words and more importantly he expressed appreciation that I crossed his path. Pretty awesome! Too paint a clear picture, I am a small of stature white haired old man and here was a giant of man in his prime, with a foul mouth, but also having a Christian upbringing of some sort which he was not afraid to show the world as evidenced by the Cross around his neck…..but! Is this yet another example of the patience of God wanting His players to put on the armor the Bible talks about, and in His time and with His players; broken third string players; does make for an encounter on a most unlikely gridiron to send out onto the field this old player to take the ball and run headlong into this mountain of a man. The answer is most assuredly yes and if we analyze the game film it seems a little guy can knock a big guy on his butt, allegorically speaking. I hope I hit him hard enough!

Like the previous encounter at this same barber shop 18 months prior that day I went to sleep feeling that certain good feeling not often encountered.

>>> BARBER 3 <<<

On the other side of town on the occasion of yet another haircut I went to my normal barbershop to find that it had gone out of business because of Covid. Fortunately a new shop had recently opened about three doors down so I thought I would give them a try. This morning there was only one barber, a young man only recently graduated from barber school. On this morning I had no intention of talking at all for I was tired. I sat awkwardly for a bit and thought to engage this young man in some sort of conversation, not at all thinking about a topic, biblical or otherwise. When I came in he had been listening to something on his phone so I asked what he listened to when it's not particularly busy.

To my surprise he said sermons, biblical topics, etc. I asked his age, which as I recall was 19 or 20. So, here I was again, what now? As I now consider that day I was perhaps a third string QB signaling from the sidelines the QB on the field whom for this game was Voddie Baucham. This young man was in the game and that was and is awesome, however, some of his coaches I recognized as not particularly the best defenders of the faith. I did not consider challenging him on any point; all I did was let him know that one of my favorite sermons is Voddie Baucham, "The Rescuer." I gave him a brief overview and encouraged him to check it out. We had a nice exchange and that was that. I have been back there several times hoping to see him again, but too date have not. I am still hopeful that he listened to Voddie.

>>> SUMMARY OF BARBERS <<<

Barber shops it seems is a good place to have conversations that can lead to the sharing of the Word even if unexpected and you're a rookie.

~ COFFEE SHOPS ~

>>> COFFEE IN GLENDALE <<<

As you may have surmised this sojourner enjoys a cup of java and my favorite is a good latte. I visit many a coffee shop and most of this book was written while enjoying an early morning coffee and on some occasions an interaction that leads to an opportunity to buckle the belt, put on the breastplate, strap on the sword, pick up the shield, put on the helmet, take the field or for my favorite allegory, the gridiron. Properly girded with the gospel of peace on a flip card strapped to your wrist, like some quarterbacks, now available to plant your feet firm ready to vanquish the linebackers of lies, you wait.

Then when you least expect it the Coach sends you into the game. This encounter was my second. In a coffee shop in Glendale, Arizona at 59th and Olive, early one morning I was sitting on a bench seat reading my Bible. This is weird, but it cannot not be mentioned, I was just about to get started, had opened by Bible to the page marked by the ribbon. I glanced out the window and said a five second prayer something to the effect, "God if you want for me to talk to someone today, let it be." Just then a Mexican woman sat immediately to my right on the bench and a Mexican man directly to her right. It seemed clear they were a couple; more about that later.

The instant she sat down she looked at me and said, "I see you're reading the Bible."

To which I replied, "Yes, I try and read it every day."

She then asked, "Can I ask you a question?"

I said, "Of course."

Her next question was a shocker, she asked, "Am I going to hell?

I of course asked, "Clearly something is weighing heavy, why would you ask me such a thing?"

She said, "Because I killed my baby." She then went on to say. "When I was younger I aborted my baby, so am I going to hell."

It is here that as I think back on the encounter that the God of all, who most assuredly wanted this woman to hear Him for some reason, sent me. So here comes me, newly armored and most certainly with no playing time, the Coach sends me anyway. Girded and equipped enough to satisfy Him I am called to the field to vanquish some minions of the evil one. Without a seconds hesitation I put my hands on the open pages of my Bible and said, "Yes."

I followed with, "Paul the Apostle was a murderer by trade and God forgave him and made him one of the greatest expositors of the gospel, so if Jesus forgave Paul, His mercy can forgive you."

I then asked her if she was Catholic, which she affirmed. I then went on about the curious nature of her guilt given that she is a Catholic and had gone to confession many times and sits here asking an old man about her plight. I did the best I could to suggest politely that it is only the triune God that can forgive her sin, not a man. We talked, she asking questions, me doing my best to answer them all. This went on for an hour and the conversation I pray was fruitful for her.

To complete the encounter let me describe both her and her partner. She was an attractive woman I would guess to be forty plus or minus, and was well dressed. She had revealed in our conversations that she was a mother and had gone on to have more than one child although how many did not come up. Her partner was a handsome Mexican fellow with a handsome smile wearing matching gray sweat pants and long sleeved sweat shirt and a stocking cap. He had tattoos that could be seen on his neck. Through the first hour he sat quietly listening as he looked around her taking in my responses to her questions and always smiling.

So, about an hour in I thought to engage him so I said to him, "You look as though you have something on your mind or may have questions?"

I had assumed they were a couple, and they were. It turned out, however, she would learn about a past he had not shared with her too date. He also had been contemplating right and wrong a lot, but for different reasons. The next half an hour he shared his life. He also, I would guess to be forty plus or minus, but had spent half of his adult life in prison. He had been in a federal penitentiary four times. The woman did not know.

I surmised that is was gang related with all of the expected drug activities and other bad deeds. He was very open and shared some of his prior bad acts and it was clear he did not want to go back to prison. I asked if he was dressed to cover gang tats, he acknowledged that was in fact the case. I asked what he did to avoid the possibility of prison in the future. He said that number one he stays away from anyone from that world and two he spends a lot of time running and listening to music. He wanted something different, something better that was clear. Ah hay, an opening.

Once again I put my hands on the open pages of my Bible and suggested that his answers also are in this book. We talked for another half hour him asking a few questions and me doing my best to guide him into the Word as well as suggesting that they both find a reformed church and what that even means.

An hour and a half, a good conversation with two lost souls came to a close in yet another very unexpected way. She looked at her watch and said to her partner, "We need to go, it's time." She shared that they were on the way to check her into jail. Ouch! I don't know why, but ouch!

How the meeting ended was pretty cool. We stood up the woman hugged and thanked me, and the man, this ex-gang banger; this ex-con walked around her and gave me a big hug and thanked me.

Another good day, feeling I suppose the right word is blessed, perhaps honored, and most certainly joy of a kind new to me.

Another baseball analogy: Called up from the minors once again to the Big Show, once again I get an at bat, and this time maybe I got a double.

>>> COFFEE IN LOVELAND COLORADO <<<

Loveland, Colorado, 2021 summertime. I was at yet another coffee shop in north Loveland on a beautiful Colorado morning sitting outside reading my Bible. I went inside for a refill and as I came out an attractive young woman, Latin, slight build was getting out of her car right in front of the front doors. She went into the shop got her coffee came out, put her coffee in her car and noticed me reading this big book. She very curiously asked me what I was reading. I told her the Bible at which point she said she also likes to read and then reached into her car and pulled out a stack of books about eight high she had just purchased. I walked over for it seemed she wanted to know what I thought. Weird right! I'm glad she did for the first book was "The Secret." I told her interesting read, but it's a bunch of crap. The other books were in varying degrees a clear search for meaning in her life. She asked if we could talk, I said sure, she grabbed her coffee and she joined me at my table.

We talked for about an hour. I was to find out she was from Brazil, had left an abusive marriage as well as an overbearing Mormon church she felt very uncomfortable in. She pulled up stakes with her three children, a girl about sixteen and a boy about eight and a baby and ended up in Colorado. She was recently entangled with another man who said he loved her and she him. They were going to buy a home together she providing the 25K down payment from her savings. When she got cold feet about putting all of her savings into the deal and suggested they wait he dumped her. Broken hearted and further stressed about finishing up real estate school and finding a job. All of this history making clear why the pile of books.

Clearly desperate to ask a stranger, an old man to boot, for help, so here we go again, down, set, hut, hut…..!

We talked about the message of the biblical gospel vs. the missteps of the Book of Mormon and "The Secret" nonsense. I asked if she had found a church, she had not, so I suggested my friends church which I was going to attend the following Sunday. She said she would meet me there, so far so good. We chatted for another hour about salvation.

On Sunday she did meet me and I introduced her to my friend's daughter who has children about the same age. At church I gave her a Bible and we all sat together. After the service we visited as people do in the church parking lot and then went our separate ways. Shortly after that I had to travel back to Phoenix. I stayed in touch for a time hoping that the hand off to my friend's daughter would provide the spiritual grounding she was looking for when we met under the most unusual of circumstances. This coffee shop encounter sadly was not to be the season to help this lovely woman.

Today is Friday 2-24-23 as I finish this section so what better time to check on Miss K. I just called her. She was not able to make it in real estate and now cleans houses with a friend as well as caring for the elderly. She said her daughter is in Brazil, doing well and starting college, her son is now 13, and her little one is 6. We talked about the speed of time, and then I asked if she had ever found a church. She had not and said that she works on Sunday. I asked if she reads her Bible, to which she said that she prays and her Bible is right by her bedside. She said it's right there to make her feel guilty, to which I replied, no it's there for hope and encouraged her to read the book of John. She thanked me.

I told her about this book and that I was writing about my unusual encounters such as ours. She said that is awesome and thanked me. I then learned that she lives not too far from my friend's daughter and suggested she might have coffee or a meal. She thought that would be nice. I asked if she still had my phone number and my friends daughters number, which she said she did. I told her I would pray for her and asked her to pray for me, for which she was grateful. I told her I would call again and read to her this section which she once again thanked me.

Well, what to do with that? Can a kind word 1½ years later help this struggling soul? Can prayers help? The answer is yes, and yes. We'll see!

>>> COFFEE IN NORTH PHOENIX <<<

Everyone has a favorite coffee shop and mine is on west Bell road in north Phoenix and my 2nd is on west Greenway road also in north Phoenix. One morning at the Bell road location there was a line and I was behind a young man with an unusual look. I struck up a conversation there in line about nothing which we carried on for perhaps 3 or 4 minutes. He seemed relaxed and it struck me that he was going to stay and enjoy his beverage. I don't know why, because I've never done such a thing, but I asked he wanted to join me for a cup of coffee and a conversation. He bowed out saying he had to get home to his pet. No harm, no foul that was it.

About two or three months later I was sitting at a table in the same coffee shop reading the Bible and this young man having just picked up his beverage was heading out, but not before coming over to my table and asking if I remembered him. I said that I did. He then asked if I recalled asking him to enjoy a conversation and coffee. I said of course. He then asked if I was going to be awhile he would go run an errand and join me. I said, great.

When he returned he joined me and explained that when I had asked him to join me when we met in line it caught him off guard and he did not know how to handle it. He confessed that he was a bit introverted and did not want to be, and after dwelling on my request at some level he regretted it and questioned why he would reject an offer to just have a conversation. So when he saw me this day he ventured forth into the unknown world of visiting with an old man. Surprise, surprise! This time since I was in the middle of reading my Bible the conversation leaned into the gospel fairly quickly. He had questions which I did my best to answer and as I recall I used some of Ray Comforts tactics to move his mind. It was obvious he enjoyed conversing and was relieved and perhaps a little proud of himself for taking a risk to just visit with someone.

I haven't seen him since, nevertheless it was a good day!

>>> COFFEE, BIBLE STUDY & BIBLES <<<

Another adventure at the west Bell road location that wasn't me being put in front of someone to do the great commission, but a bunch of someone's were to be made to cross my path to edify me. One morning the owner came to my table and handed me a pocket sized Bible and said someone had left it and that I should have it. I said I can't take that; someone will surely come back and get it. The owner said no it would be alright. I told him I think I know who it belongs to. I had previously noticed that periodically a group of men would meet in a corner and talk church. I thought they were church elders meeting for church business. The following Wednesday they showed up again so I walked over to their meeting, excused myself, and told them I thought one of them had left it. They laughed.

Turns out it was a men's Bible study group that called themselves "Men at the Gate" that had been meeting for over 20 years. They were Gideons and one of the men, Wendell, has been distributing the small Gideon Bibles for years.

I said I see what you're doing here, you're leaving bread crumbs. We laughed, they invited me to join them and whenever I can I join them on Wednesday mornings. For a time we would all chip in a few bucks so we could rent the meeting room that was available for public meetings. Wendell had also asked the owner if he could leave a small stack of free Gideon New Testament Bibles in a convenient location for patrons. The whole arrangement was working perfectly, win, win! Then the owner went and threw a wrench in the works and told us to redirect the money for the meeting room and give it to Wendell to purchase more Bibles. Well, so far, in the last 18 months or so Wendell and this "coffee shop" have moved over 1,000 free Bibles.

>>> COFFEE SHOP SANTA <<<

I almost forgot about this one! In November of 2021 at my favorite coffee shop the proprietors approached me and asked if I might be interested in being Santa Claus for a day about a week before Christmas. Never having done such a thing, and generally not in my wheelhouse at all, I was taken aback by the request, but said yes nevertheless. As a Poppy to beautiful grand babies, in my case two little girls, and loving the enchantment of it all I suppose is what made me say yes. Or was it something else?

I've done it twice now in 2021 and 2022 and it was great fun. The photo ops with not only children, but also adults were the draw for the coffee shop and why I was there and that was great fun. The little ones asking me questions about the North Pole and reindeer, which was a challenge for they had to help me with their names. Fortunately I was able to dance effectively around that conundrum. I handed out Bible tracks to all the kids. The tracks were from Ray Comfort's ministry and included tiny comic book gospels, million dollar bills with Santa on the front and the gospel on the back, and the favorite with the kids, the shiny silver coin with the Ten Commandments on one side and the gospel on the other.

When there were no photos to be taken I walked around the shop, which seats about 110 people, and made a point that every customer received a million dollars. My approach varied a little, but generally I would walk up to a table, wait for them to stop talking, which they always did, look them in the eyes and ask if they had been good the previous year. Usually the response was yes, some hesitant, but always the exchange produced laughter. Then I would give them the gospel coin and/or the one million dollar bill with Santa on the front and would tell them on the back was a one way ticket Heaven, just follow the instructions. It was great fun and no one got mad not even once.

I have had several memorable encounters, but the following is one of my favorites. This last Christmas, 2022, I walked up to two gals visiting over their coffee clearly having girl fun. I walked up to their table, leaned on it with my white gloves and looked at them rather sternly and asked if they had been good this year. One of them leaned back in her chair, turning very red, to show me her tee shirt which read, "I can get you on that naughty list." Both of them giggling and I went to work.

I said, "Oh it's you!" Pause. Looking into her blushed face, holding back her snickering, her friend laughing, I continued, "I've been wanting to talk to you for years."

She replied while giggling, "You want me to tone it down a little?" while she gestured with her hands from high to a lower position.

I said, "No no, I want you to turn this ship completely around 180 degrees and head a different way, chart a new course." Her friend was laughing hysterically.

I slid a silver coin Bible track across the table, one to her and one to her friend, as I continued. "Read this at least once a week, turn this ship around and I want to see you back here next year, and I want a full report, understood!"

We had a laugh, it was unusual and fun and that was that. I hope she seeks me out next year!!

Between "2021" and "2022" three maybe four hundred Bible tracks were handed out.

>>> SUMMARY OF COFFEE SHOPS <<<

Coffee shops are better than barber shops since more coffee is needed than haircuts. However, both are excellent venues for commission work since conversation is generally part of the experience in both types of "shops."

>>> MEETING AT THE GATE <<<

Another unusual encounter was at my front gate one morning when two young girls came calling to solicit political help for a precinct in an area across town in need of representation. Intriguing already as they were probably about 20 or 21 years old. We talked a bit about their mission which I found very interesting because of their age and that they were dropped off from a pick-up load of other young people canvasing the neighborhoods, and in this case all apparently conservative and republican.

Not by any plan or expectation of mine the conversation was to end up at the gospel, both girls in tears. Here is what happened. Being curious about their mission and how they ended up being conservative especially in this day and age I asked how it was that they became conservative. They shared that they saw firsthand the corrupt hand of government when they had adopted a little baby girl whom was in the system because the father was abusive. "Oh," I said, "So you are lesbians?"

They replied, "Yes." I should note that their demeanor was timid about sharing this fact. Which after the fact I thought was refreshing as my only exposer to lesbians at all was seeing accounts on TV or YouTube in which the word militant best describes what I thought an encounter might look like.

To which I followed up with, "Tell me more, what happened?

They told a tale very sad indeed. They were married and wanted a baby and went through the system to become adoptive parents. Paper work done, a baby granted by the system that had been rescued from a bad situation which included a man with drug issues and was abusive to the baby. The mother wasn't brought up. So, they are happy raising a baby which they had fallen in love with and had been with them for a couple of years as I recall. Then the father, whom had been incarcerated for a time, got out and wanted the little girl back. They fought hard with attorneys to maintain custody, but lost that battle and the toddler was taken away.

Let me describe the girls. Both pretty, beautiful skin, one with reddish hair, the other light brown and curly hair, one white and the other black. As they recalled the story they started to tear up and pulled out their phone to show me photos. Pictures as they say are worth a thousand words, many photos of all of them, the little one with glasses and the most beautiful smile. Photo upon photo of big smiles, happiness and joy easily captured. I told them I understand the joy for I am a father and now a grandfather and pulled out photos of my grand babies. The three of us did the expected and natural oohs and aahs, they continuing to wipe away their tears.

So, here I am again, down set, hut, hut!!

We had already spent way too much time for the job they were sent to do and they had to get going for they were expected to meet their party soon. I told them that I was a new Christian and asked them if they were believers to which they said they were. I asked if they had read the Bible, which they had not. I closed our encounter telling them fairly quickly and in an empathetic tone that," It is easy to empathize with your plight, your tears are expected and understandable, your suffering clear, your anger at government understandable in that they would take a child from a loving environment and it seems put the baby right back in harm's way, not to mention ripping hearts in two, you for the baby and the baby for you. However, the answers to your suffering is in the gospels, so I encourage you both to pick up the Bible, read it and listen to some Voddie Baucham.

I don't remember if I told them about Voddie's "Rescuer" sermon, but I may have because I do that often.

As I consider the encounter, 1) wow!, 2) once again the lost being put in this old man's path, 3) how to proceed at all just flowed, outcome who can know, 4) we parted company with them thanking me, tears still in their eyes.

I almost forgot about this unusual meeting and I'm glad it popped back into my brain. I prayed a little prayer for them then and here goes another one. I hope they find the narrow gate.

SUMMARY 1ST ENCOUNTERS OF THE CLOSE KIND

These are a few of what I hope will be many more. I can attest that the gut wrenching fear that happened in my 1st encounter with the barber never happened again. In fact, I rather enjoy it when in the most unusual and unexpected ways I am called up to the "Big Show" and have no choice but to step up to the plate and swing away. In the baseball analogy, all Christians might consider that they too will be called up the "Big Show" and like it or not you'll have to step up to the plate and the pitcher is going to serve you up a pitch, which is a lost soul for which you will have to swing at. Like baseball you'll swing, sometimes striking out, sometimes hitting a foul, and sometimes getting on base. In my case I like to think I made a base hit, but in all of my at bats someone had to or will have to come after me to bat clean up, hopefully driving a soul to glory. It is not lost on me that the final clean-up batter in every case is a Ghost!

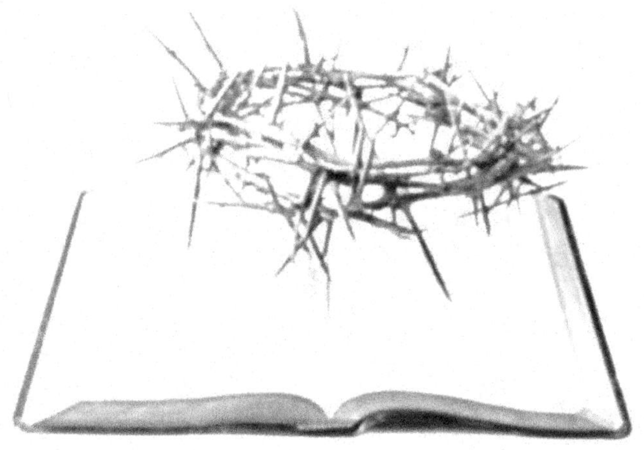

Left made Right!

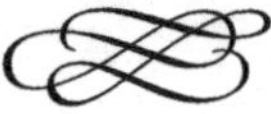

Chapter 10

THE RIGHT LINE

In 2005 I did some work in New Orleans after hurricane Katrina. When I first arrived there was no place to stay in New Orleans so I had to stay in a motel in Mobile Alabama. The drive was 2 hours each way which did not leave much daylight to work. In order to get the work done workers would sleep in their cars in a truck-stop one half-hour north of New Orleans, this required because New Orleans was locked down at dusk by the national guard. One day after a long day I made my way back to the truck stop. Usually the truck stop would be open 24 hours, but because of the hurricane it would only be open 8 hours a day for a time. There was a small convenience store not far from the truck stop so I walked there hoping to find something to eat. When I walked in there was a young Asian woman working the register to my left, a man talking on a cell phone in the back, and mostly empty shelves. On the right wall there was a small freezer case with ice cream bars so I grabbed a Blue Bunny bar and went to the register.

To make conversation I asked the attendant what her story was relating to the hurricane. She started to cry, but was appreciative to talk to anyone. She recounted that she lived near the ocean in the neighboring state of Mississippi and that her house and everything in it was completely wiped from the face of the earth. She said was tired and thankful that the owner of this store, who was the man in the back on the phone, gave her not only a job, but let her sleep on an air mattress in the little office behind the register. She was a conscientious employee and worked more hours than normal and might have liked some time off, but the owner couldn't get any of his other employees to work as they were being subsidized by the government and said they wouldn't be back at least for the time being.

What she said next would be what I think now is a providential moment for my journey. **She said she wanted to kill herself.** What I said next in retrospect could only be the Holy Spirit working through a most sinful man to help one of His children who certainly was in the valley of the shadow of death. My life thus far was constrained to the world of "true, plumb, and square" i.e., things relating to buildings, structures, math and the like. No training in social, no training in psychology, and certainly no training from a Biblical perspective.

What I said fell out of my mouth quickly. I said, "Wait a minute, let's talk about this." I drew a line on the counter with my finger about 12" long. I asked her how old she was and as I recall she stated she was 31. I drew a small circle approximately a third of the way down the line while telling her the line was a 100 years long and that she was reasonably going to live the greater length of that time.

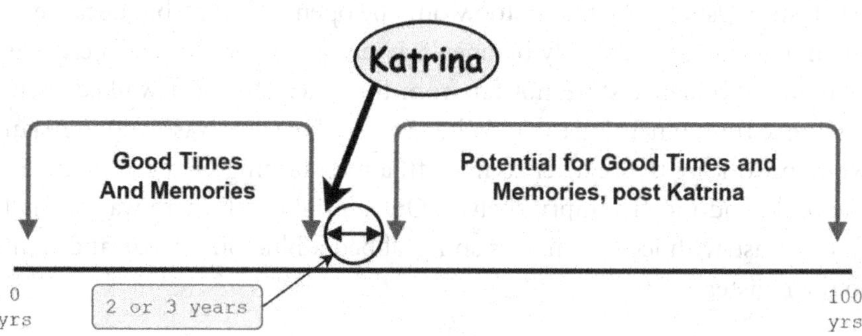

Then while gesturing towards the birth end of her line I asked her if before Katrina did she have any good memories, such as family, laughter, good times, and good friends. She replied, "Certainly." Then I drew a little circle at year 31 or the Katrina event and I told her the circle was about 2 maybe three years in diameter. I told her that Katrina was a major setback, a horrific, bile infested hiccup in her life, however, the hiccup will end. Then I traced the longer line to the 100 year end point and asked her if it is reasonable that there is time on that line to have more of what she had on the shorter end, i.e., before Katrina.

She had to and did acknowledge that answer was yes. We talked a bit more, doing my best to be compassionate. Her tears changed I think from a place of extreme sorrow to a different place perhaps with a spark of hope. Anyway, she thanked me as I left. I don't know what happened to her, but I think about her from time to time. She made me think a lot about the levels of suffering there are in the world.

~ THE RIGHT LINE ~

It was the recollection of the line drawn on a counter in 2005 as well as a background in construction scheduling that yet another allegorical picture began to take shape in my mind to make sense of things. Lines are used in many ways to make sense of things. Lines most generally are thought of in terms of "straight" with respect to mathematical analysis. Lines have been used to graphically represent units of time and by incorporating a scale, large segments of time can be considered by viewing a line on a piece of paper. "Straight" lines are also used classically to metaphorically refer to a right way. For example, "the straight and narrow path."

Perhaps one of the most profound uses of a line in an analogy was by C. S. Lewis when during his journey to the Cross and as an atheist he began to question his bent (ha-ha) presuppositions of why? He stated,

> "My argument against God was that the universe seemed so cruel and unjust. But how had I got this idea of just and unjust? *A man does not call a line crooked unless he has some idea of a straight line*. What was I comparing this universe with when I called it unjust?"

Unrelated to any of the above something else had always bothered me and that is the labeling of the political right and the political left. It never made sense to me that to be right, far right, ultra-right, etc. could be in any way considered unrighteous. Lines have been used to analyze the political left and right, but the categories put on the line seem to vary by the particular author doing the analysis. In other words, you can peruse through several websites that speak to the left and right and fairly quickly ascertain the political bent of the author. The left leaning will slant the analysis so that the right seems unrighteous and vice versa.

Also, when people use a line to analyze political right and left, the mind naturally puts the right on the right end of the line. It seems ironic that generally the right side is more righteous in its nature. That aside, when a line is used to analyze time, the beginning of the line is always on the left and the future time is on the right end of the line. It is these two paradigms that bothered me and were stumbling stones.

Beginning or Time Now → **Future Time**

But alas, my goofy mind toyed with an idea. What would happen if I reversed the time line to put the beginning on the right end of the line? It struck me that if I were to draw a timeline with the beginning of time on the right and the end of time, or at least the time being considered for analysis on the left, then what God created which was good would always be to the right and all of history would unfold to the left of that which was initially very good. By the time of Jesus and the Cross on the timeline anything to the left would be less right.

So, let's try it out for an analysis of the political right and left. The gist is a complete paradigm shift as follows:

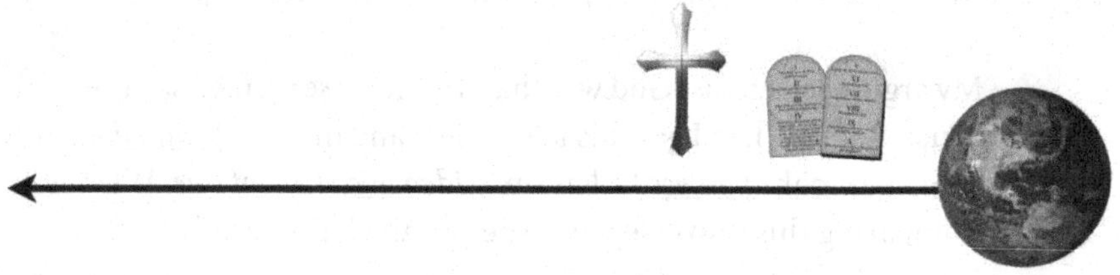

Now if we analyze anything, anything at all in the past, present or future and it does not comport with clearly moral and "righteous" superlatives on the right end of the line and especially as articulated and codified by the Son of God, then the political right and most particularly today's left (2023) will be found judged by the right end of "The Right Line."

Categories, individual concepts, ideas, ideologies, or individuals can be put on "The Right Line," so to speak, and be judged. It is likely that today the word "judged" will cause offense to some so if that is the case use the word analyzed. How to judge "rightly" as it turns out was explained by the author of the lake!!!

~ AMERICAN TWO PARTY SYSTEM ~

To see if it is helpful I toyed with a few examples. As an American and recognizing my good fortune to live here, but also knowing that this nation is in trouble perhaps the easiest thing to put on "The Right Line" as a trial run is the "Blue Jackass" and the "Red Elephant."

Not wanting to seem prejudiced when placing the donkey and the elephant on "The Right Line" I wondered who should be on the left and who should be on the right. So I thought to look up the seating charts and noted the arrangement in the chambers of "the Senate" and "the House of Representatives" when viewed from the gallery; which are "The People;" the democrats sit on the left and the republicans sit on the right. So following the seating arrangements of the "theoretical" "peoples representatives" I put the democrats (jackass) on the left and the republicans (elephant) on the right. So, placed on "The Right Line" might look something like this:

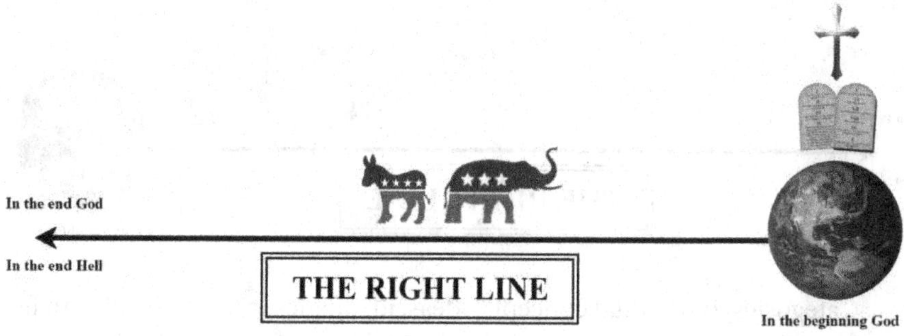

Whether it is providence, God only knows, but it is most certainly a great irony that the elephant it seems whether viewed through the gallery of the people or placed on the "The Right Line" is perhaps generally on the "right track," so to speak, or at least more right than the jackass.

To analyze with discernment both parties are so far left of the right end of "The Right Line" it's tragic. To get right to the bottom line and the essence of the complete failure of both parties in there violations of the very explicit moral code on the right end of "The Right Line," i.e., the Ten Commandments.

The Table below lists the moral law, i.e., the Ten Commandments which are the foundational highest laws of the land in America. It is that highest law; not the Constitution; which man and groups can and must be judged. In this analysis the groups to be analyzed and judged are the American Democrats and the American Republican parties.

#	*The Highest Law*		
1	Thou shall not have no other Gods before Me	Note 1, Note 2	Note 1, Note 2
2	You shall not make unto you any graven images to worship them	Note 3	Note 3
3	You shall not take the name of the Lord your God in vain	Note 4	Note 4
4	You shall remember the Sabbath and keep it holy	Note 5	Note 5
5	Honor your mother and father	Note 6	Note 6

#	The Highest Law		
6	You shall not murder	Note 7, Note 9	Note 8, Note 9
7	You shall not commit adultery	Note 10	Note 10
8	You shall not steal	Note 11, Note 12	Note 11, Note 12
9	You shall not bear false witness	Note 13, Note 14	Note 13, Note 14
10	You shall not covet anything that belongs to your neighbor	Note 15	Note 15

Note 1 – As a party there is no evidence of recognition of God, Jesus, or the Holy Spirit. No one acknowledges God or prays in a way the people would know about. When public speaking, no one begins, ends, or asks for the guidance of God. The best they seem to be able to muster is an occasional "Our prayers are with the ________" when there is a tragedy. It's not nothing, but when the glory of God is providential to their every breath, the invocation to prayer only in times of tragedy comes off as an insincere platitude. Repent and pray, don't just suggest you might....do it. For you are representatives of the kingdom of God and subordinate to your Lord and Master Jesus the Christ. Invoke his name!! Lead righteously.

Note 2 – What the people see are atheistic actions by the lawmakers. If there is an evil one, i.e., Satan, then what is being seen and done in D.C. obviously is what one would consider the devils will.

Note 3 – Concerning graven images. Washington D.C. very ironically is filled with pagan statues, images, and symbolism. A journey down that rabbit trail is disturbing and not a topic to be addressed here, although any man or woman who walks with God the Father, God the Son, and God the Holy Spirit need not fear to tread through pagan territory. Confess His name boldly and unashamedly so that the people can see. If you lead thus, America will most assuredly right itself and be blessed. If not.....well the trajectory we are on seems obvious.

Note 4 – As a matter of political self-preservation lawmakers are wise enough not to blaspheme the name of the Father, the Son, or the Holy Spirit in public by their spoken words. However, if you vote for a law that covets the labor of a man for the benefits to another man, and worse yet covet another man's God given rights and privileges and pass laws that steal that man's labor and or property, how is that not a direct taking of God the Father, God the Son, and the Spirit of the thrice Holy God in a contemptuous way for your vanity and your personal benefit? You were, in America, conscripted by the people to protect "all" that is righteous pursuant to the laws of God and very specifically enumerated on the right end of "The Right Line." Judge yourself!! If God is love and God is righteous and God is just, the lawmaker's very special and unique position per Gods law requires that they flee from all evil, vices, graft, and corruption. God is watching and your every move will be judged should you vote for anything that would violate the rights God gave to each and every man, woman, and conceived child of God pursuant to the right side of "The Right Line."

Note 5 – As a matter of public trust it would be nice if the people knew their government representatives attended a church. It certainly would not let the people know if the lawmaker was saved, but it would let the people know at minimum the lawmaker considered God at least once a week. Even for atheists it is reasonable that if lawmakers worship once a week there might be a bent towards righteousness. For a discerning mind having removed God from the public square was a big mistake.

Note 6 – The Constitution does not allow for a religious test, but it would be nice to know if our lawmakers did honor their mothers and fathers. Those that honor their mother certainly could not vote for anything that could take away motherhood. Similarly, fatherhood should be sacrosanct. This one is tough since it is the government that has by law created the circumstance, platforms, legalese, that first removed God from the public square, then the father from his headship, and then ease for single motherhood without the proper God ordained family. The people are not to be free of blame for they did not discern rightly and did turn away from God even when their conscience knows.

Note 7 – The democrat party by the percentages in 2023 are so far left of this commandment as to have one foot in hell. Abortion, the murder of the unborn, being thought by any man, and or, and especially woman to be a thing to consider at all under any circumstance whatsoever so blatantly violates that which was gifted by God the Almighty to mankind from the furthest right end of "The Right Line." That lawmakers had to get involved at all is reasonably an indictment against mankind to not know the mind of God. Women believing they have a right to murder and veil it behind another term such as health is intellectually vacuous and does not please God. Men being deceived by woman like Adam was deceived by Eve to not protest with all reasonable discernment does not please God. Any human being, man or woman, who plays with murder in such a cavalier manner, needs to fall on their face and beg forgiveness from your Creator, repent, and turn from this evil.

Note 8 – The Republican Party and by the percentages in 2023 are only a half-step behind the democrats. The party claims to be pro-life, this term also being a veil to take the sting out of the word murder, and meant to mean anti-abortion. For 50 years the supposed pro-life party legislators passed or punted on fighting for the unborn. In any consideration when an opinion has in it "the interest of the mother" and or "the interest of the state" and their respective compelling interests it is completely misguided, especially when standing on "The Right Line." Such verbiage relegates the mother as reasonably nothing more than a cow and the state as the rancher whom may dictate an interest in the baby cow, and that interest is death. Consideration would be better worded as the "interest of God."

Note 9 – Both parties if they could get murder correct when it comes to the unborn reasonably could reconsider murder among adults. Currently codified law for the last 80 +/- years states that all crime is commercial including murder, which begs the question, what was it the day before it was a commercial enterprise, and who are the beneficiaries of this commerce? This law by itself on "The Right Line" and scrutinized by the moral law could be seen as a violation of 9 of the 10 commandments, and a Biblical litigator could argue all 10.

Note 10 – Were the government (or rulers) per the Christian Bible to be a terror to evil why then is adultery nowhere on their tongues. Once again directly attributable to removing God from the public square the people because of the sins of fathers and mothers of past generations now seek adultery like moths to a flame. There is a particular "adultery app" that has 60 million members in 53 countries and boasts a million adulterous hook-ups a month, and that's just one of the many "sex outside of God's law" apps. This cannot all be laid at the feet of the rulers, however, they being silent on this evil if standing on "The Right Line." Individually they are certainly found very much wanting. Note this sin of silence by both parties makes their position on "The Right Line" interchangeable, i.e., both parties stand nowhere near the right side of "The Right Line."

Note 11 – The fourth amendment to the America's Constitution at the time of its construction was good especially these words,

> ***"The right of the people to be secure in their persons, houses, papers, and effects, against unreasonable searches and seizures, shall not be violated, and no Warrants shall issue, but upon probable cause, supported by Oath or affirmation, and particularly describing the place to be searched, and the persons or things to be seized."***

Since that time the person-hood of man has been incorporated, or stolen from the man for the benefit of the government / bankers. Since that time houses or the dwellings of a man have been commercialized by bankers, or stolen to the benefit of the government / bankers. Since that time papers have been stolen from the man for the benefit of the government / banker. Since that time the effects of man, being anything else whatsoever can be stolen from the man and commercialized for the benefit of the government / banker. Today, bad faith actors routinely unreasonably search and seize anything in sight without the clear and unambiguous intent of this article. Both parties, those being 1) government persons acting at the behest of 2) bankers, are complicit in the theft of the peoples stuff. On "The Right Line" it doesn't look good for either party.

Note 12 – If power is the capacity or ability to direct or influence the behavior of others or the course of events, then the "power of the purse" is reasonably the greatest power possible this side of death. The construct of the system of money in the world today is based on theft of one man's labor by a 3rd party, taking a portion for oneself and distributing it to other 3rd parties who lobby for the theft. It need not be this way for people voluntarily gift their money to 3rd parties often and in large sums for empathetic causes as well as commonwealth considerations. If the people could see benevolent uses of public funds there would be no need for an IMF, World Bank, Vatican bank, Federal Reserve, tax, etc. Imagine a commonwealth depository the only funds in its care were 100% voluntary, no paper trail being necessary. Greed being the underlying factor behind each and every law passed the lawmakers it seems should consider if they are voting their own damnation. Repent, pray for forgiveness. To steal from the masses is certainly a veil to shadow the theft from the individual, but it is theft nevertheless. As far as the party position on "The Right Line," both the jackass and the elephant could be moved much further to the left of right and move to the underside of the line. You decide!!??

Note 13 – Bearing false witness, lying, not telling the truth, are within the conscience of man known to be not right or i.e., wrong. When put on "The Right Line" and a simple question is asked such as, "What is a woman?", to a prospective person seeking to be paid by and represent the people for whom the applicant supposedly has qualifications to represent in any capacity whatsoever, and said applicant cannot or refuses to answer the question, then it is reasonable and discerning to consider certain possibilities about the applicant. Either the applicant is:

1. **stupid** - *a) slow of mind, obtuse; b) given to unintelligent decisions or acts; c) acting in an unintelligent or careless manner; d) lacking intelligence or reason*
2. **depraved** - *marked by corruption or evil*
3. **corrupt, corruption** – *a) dishonest or illegal behavior especially by powerful people; b) a departure from the original or from what is pure or correct; c) inducement to wrong by improper or unlawful means*
4. **evil** – *a) morally reprehensible; b) arising from actual or imputed bad character or conduct*
5. **wicked** - *a) disposed to or marked by mischief; b) disgustingly unpleasant; c) causing or likely to cause harm, distress, or trouble*
6. **correct** – *a) conforming to an approved or conventional standard; b) conforming to or agreeing with fact, logic, or known truth*
7. **liar** - *a person who tells lies*
8. **lie** – *a) to make an untrue statement with intent to deceive*
9. **intent** – *a) a usually clearly formulated or planned intention; b) the act or fact of intending; c) the design or purpose to commit a wrongful or criminal act; d) the state of mind with which an act is done; e) what one intends to do or bring about*

10. **false** – *a) not genuine; b) intentionally untrue; c) adjusted or made so as to deceive; d) intended or tending to mislead; e) not true; f) not faithful or loyal; g) inconsistent with the facts*
11. **witness** – *a) attestation of a fact or event; b) one that gives evidence; c) one who has personal knowledge of something; d) something serving as evidence or proof; e) public affirmation by word or example of usually religious faith or conviction*

In the year of our Lord 2023 which is plus or minus 1990 years after Jesus Christ the Son of God anointed by the Holy Spirit defeated death. Before that time, at that time, and for all of the 1990 years since that event and forever more there are fundamentals that will not change. For example, up will always be up, and down will always be down, etc.

What is a woman? Who would have guessed that a test for truth would come down to answering a question so simple that a 3 year old can answer if not coerced by a corrupt parent and most certainly a grown man or women, and especially a woman that has a womb and has menstruated and will not answer with immediate conviction such an obvious truth. In 2022 this very question was asked of an applicant who would be responsible to adjudicate the right or wrongness of things on the highest court in the land for possibly the rest of the applicant's life. When this individual stands alone on "The Right Line" and the answer to this question which is on the furthest end of "The Right Line," i.e., in the beginning God created....man and woman, and purportedly is a follower of Christ and cannot answer this question while occupying one of the only two possible configurations gifted by God, then most or all of the above 11 definitions with reason apply to that applicant. Sadly, in 2022 this question was asked, and the applicant, in front of God, the people notwithstanding, denied Him.

Further, and as it applies to the "jackass" group, 50 jackasses voted to confirm the applicant. Of the 50 jackasses 37 profess that Jesus is the Son of God, 9 profess God, 3 are cowards, and 1 is unsure. That no one could say boastfully something to the effect:

> ***"With all deference to God Almighty and my Lord and savior Jesus Christ, I cannot vote for such an obvious depraved, corrupt, with self-attested imputed bad character, who it can be inferred from***

the applicants own witness of a lie so egregious and horrifying and untrue that any consideration of this applicant anywhere near an office of public trust would show bad faith on my part and I dare say the sanctity of trust this governing body has been entrusted to it by the good people for whom we exist."

Concerning the elephant group, 3 voted with the jackasses, they claiming to know Jesus Christ. They along with the supposed Christian jackasses should repent and consider with greater introspection their job if they are to be as their faith requires: slaves to Christ.

If the others in the elephant group voted down party lines or because they could not vote for a liar will probably never be known, however, God knows. It is sad that the people cannot know. Sadder still this corrupt and evil person will be opining on the rightness and wrongness of things for many years. God help this child of God and I pray God that this person and all others repent daily and pray that all of their opinions have the righteousness of Christ foremost on their minds as they do the people's business.

Note 14 – Note 13 summarizes how badly the jackass side of the aisle is so very much further left of the elephants when judged on "The Right Line" on that particular issue. It might look something like:

Note the above analysis seems judgy and it is. Lawmakers, God have mercy on them, for they are not in an enviable position. Each lawmaker stripped of his/her jackass or elephant pin and standing naked on "The Right Line" can judge for themselves their position on the line. Likewise, the administrators (voted in), bureaucrats (not voted in), and the judges stripped of their jackass or elephant pin and standing naked on "The Right Line" it seems could move themselves very far to the left of right. Should they have any common sense left they might consider or envision themselves standing, or better yet kneeling on "The Right Line" and stare back at the Cross for that which is your only hope.

Note 15 – Coveting!! To covet the position of an elephant or a jackass so much so that "commandments 1, 2, 8, and 9" are violated so frivolously and cavalierly is heart breaking. The coveting of the positions of government requires "coveting minions" whom raise billions of "coveted dollars," to place "coveting officials" manipulated by "coveting bureaucrats" and "coveting special interest groups" into a system that is replete with the "coveting" of all of the peoples stuff. All of this "coveting" system created by "coveting bankers" who purchase and support all of the "coveting." All of the "coveting" artfully crafted by bought and paid for "coveting lawyers."

Much knowledge is required to play in the pig pen of government. A relevant scripture for consideration:

> **NKJV --- Ecclesiastes 12:9-14** <u>**The Whole Duty of Man**</u> – *9 And moreover, because the Preacher was wise, he still taught the people knowledge, yes, he pondered and sought out and set in order many proverbs. 10 The Preacher (or teacher) sought to find acceptable words; and what was written was upright—words of truth. 11 The words of the wise are like goads, and the words of scholars are like well-driven nails, given by one Shepherd. 12 And further, my son, be admonished by these. Of making many books there is no end, and much study is wearisome to the flesh. 13 Let us hear the conclusion of the whole matter: Fear God and keep His commandments, for this is man's all. 14 For God will bring every work into judgment, including every secret thing, whether good or evil.*

Is it possible that this tool finds its way to the lawmakers, administrators of law, and judges of law and may cause re-consideration of their roles in governance? I hope so.

~ PROGRESSIVISM ~

Another analogy to consider on "The Right Line" is the ideology called "progressivism." This will be tougher and requires breakout sessions so to speak. Here I offer a start….

First a definition per the first sentence in Wikipedia states:

> **progressivism:** *a way of thinking that holds it is possible through "political action" for human societies to improve over time. As a political movement, progressivism purports to advance the "human condition" through "social reform" based on advancements in (science, technology, economic development and social organization).*

I like this one as most all of the various ideologies bandied about today claim in some way to want for the improvement of the "human condition." Most of the ideas called progressive today have already been tried and have failed in that the "human condition" ended in the death of millions. If the intent is the death of millions I suppose the particular ideology would be considered a success by those proposing it, and there are those that do have that intent.

However, the ordinary run of the mill human being considers their "life" itself as a reasoned fundamental of the "human condition." If your mind can get that far and you recognize that any person you may see today, that is, visually see with your eyes, feels the same way and if you consider "The Right Line" then loving your neighbor as yourself should make for the improved "human condition." Further, the complete right side of "The Right Line" is a very vivid reminder that the reason you exist at all is you were created in "the image of God" and as a fundamental consideration of your "human condition" a certain kind of thank you is in order. Search your conscience, you know!

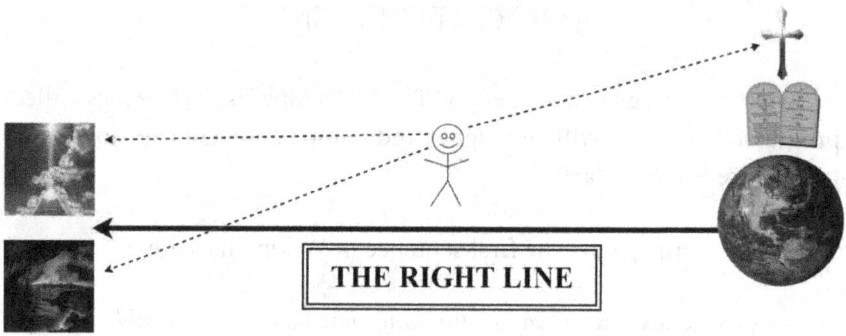

We are all on "The Right Line" and there will be an end, the question is do you want to be above the line or below the line at the end of your line? If you don't look to the Cross with your mind's eye, well!

The above graphic captures the beginning which is "righteousness" in its perfect state. The ideals stated on those original stones; as well as the perfect instruction of how to properly carry out the instructions on the stones, left for us by Jesus has been left for all of mankind in the Christian Bible and are all man would need to self-govern. But alas, and sadly man still doesn't get it.

Instead of considering our ultimate plight as an individual on "The Right Line", groups form and evolve into "isms." These "isms," history shows, seem to always go of the rails. Why? Why indeed.

The next graphic points to the 1900s as the most recent reminder for us to see at a glance that the ideologies being espoused today in 2023 as a "progressive" way to a "better human condition" have oh so recently been the direct cause of the death of millions. 160,000,000 directly in wars and if the approximately 45,000,000 babies worldwide lost to the "progressive" ideology of abortion from 1973 to the close of the 20th century is included in the tally, then the death and carnage of the last century is 1.375 billion image bearers of God murdered in the name of "progressivism."

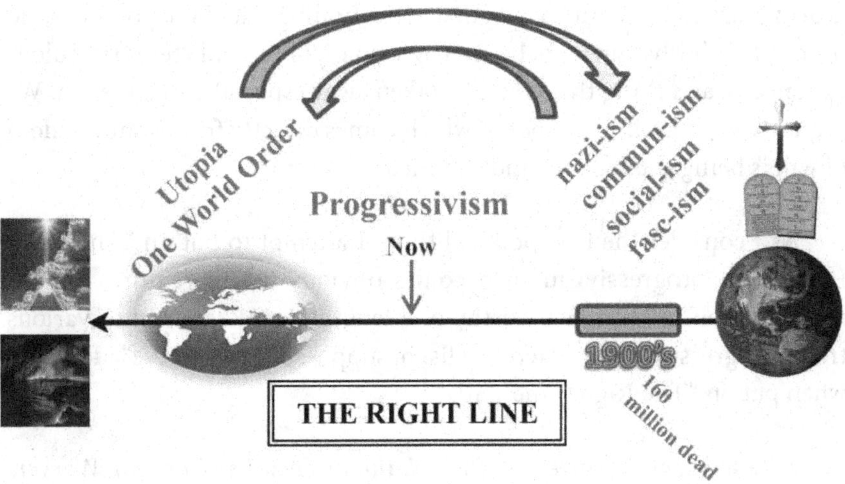

The graphic also shows time now with that big ole word "progressivism." As its definition noted above states in part *"progress through political action."* Political action is ambiguous, but its root or its foundation is idolatry. Naivety of certain men and to a greater extent certain women at all levels of intelligence are deceived into believing that the greatest ideals on the right end of "The Right Line" are wrong and that they have something better to offer humanity to "progress" the "human condition." The greatest of all ironies is the means being used are a combination of "all" of the isms noted below that have killed millions. The new packaging that includes all of the isms in the graphic is now called "public-private partnership." Do not be deceived; when the "one world order" crowd moves the "human condition" to its progressive view of utopia you will not have "free will." Your "will," will be subordinate to corporate interests with government as the policing force to keep "your will" in line.

The most "progressive" way to improve the human condition is once again on the right side of "The Right Line."

There is much evil afoot. In what is thought to be progress to an improved "human condition" as it turns out is so far left of the right end of "The Right Line," that those planning this utopia are dispensing with all and everything on the "right" end of "The Right Line." God, the moral law, and Jesus Christ are to be jettisoned completely. Free will is to be abolished. Getting there is incremental and was a slow simmer at first, but the flame is being turned up so much now that evil is boiling out of the pot the world over. Why, oh why can it not be seen by so many? Free will seems ridiculous to conceive as a thing that could be taken away especially in America. We are as naive as Eve!!! Free speech which comes directly from your freedom of will is being suppressed, and canceled.

As I consider the first political thing I attempt to put on "The Right Line," i.e., "progressivism" it becomes obvious that it requires careful consideration. It is in fact worthy of a lengthy breakdown in to various tried "progressive" ideas. Here is a list of supposed "progressive" ideas that when put on "The Right Line" fail.

- **nazi-ism** – *started as the "National Socialist German Workers Party" and progressed into a kingship granted by brute force to one man. It did not improve the "human condition."*
- **socialism** – *a belief that society can organize itself around shared everything. Individuals can own property, but production, or the chief means of generating wealth, is communally owned and managed by a democratically elected government. It has always produced kingships of very brutal men that murder those that dissent or disobey.*
- **communism** - *private property does not exist as it is thought to be communally owned, each person receiving only what they need. The deception is there is always a king, a powerful someone who gets drunk on power and brutally controls and murders. There have been no exceptions.*
- **capitalism** – *a system of "free markets." The individual is free, and can be involved in the affairs of his neighbor if he chooses. However, there is always a king, and in this system many little hidden kings called bureaucrats that sometimes benefit the "human condition," but generally benefit mostly themselves as they protect "corporate" entity interests and their wealthy little kings. Note, though flawed, this system has improved the human condition more than all others, but has also left dead bodies in its wake.*
- **fascism** - *1) a political philosophy, movement, or regime that exalts nation and often race above the individual and that stands for a centralized autocratic government headed by a dictatorial leader, severe economic and social regimentation, and forcible suppression*

of opposition 2) a tendency toward or actual exercise of strong autocratic or dictatorial control.

- **anti-fascism** – *see fascism.*
- **americanism** - *attachment or allegiance to the traditions, interests, or ideals of America. Note: See Chapter 5 how it started and a glimpse of how it is evolving into another thing. America and the "ideals" especially "Life, Liberty, and the pursuit of happiness" were and are still an ideal. What shored those ideals up at least for a time was the right end of "The Right Line." Over time the interests of a corporation not the "people" captured and swallowed up what was once a sacrosanct "ideal."*
- **bankerism** – *a system behind all of the above. Caring for the "human condition" only in as much as it creates wealth for them. They back both sides of any and all wars not caring about the death of the "human condition." A closed private system brilliantly conceived and protected from unrighteous bad faith acts. Clearly I made this one up, but..... it seems certain it cannot be disproved.*

There are other isms of social order which have all failed in their attempts at "progressivism" or to progress to some concept of an ideal place for humans. Some very recent isms that are throwing their ism into the hat of isms are woke-ism and trans-humanism.

- **woke** - *aware of and actively attentive to important facts and issues (especially issues of racial and social justice)*
- **trans-humanism** – *1) transcending human limits, superhuman; 2) the concept of an intermediary form between human and post-human. In other words, a trans-human is a being that resembles a human in most respects, but who has powers and abilities beyond those of standard humans. These abilities might include* ***improved intelligence, awareness, strength, or durability.***
- **trans-genderism** - *of, relating to, or being a person whose gender identity differs from the sex the person had or was identified as having at birth*

For clarity trans-human is any condition or state of mind that is not in the order so named on the furthest right end of "The Right Line" in Genesis 1 and 2.

A case might be made that trans-genderism is a sub set of trans-humanism, and is in a sense, as the normal "human condition" that each and every soul occupies is very specific in one of two possible configurations. Since the specific definition of trans-human suggests that the transition would be a perceived better human, the trans-gender has thus far only produced a "strength" advantage for the partial male to female trans-athlete. The "strength" characteristic in this particular and specific transition, if the current rules of transitioning to a female are followed, i.e., hormone therapy, make for the degradation of the original male "strength." It seems hard to make a case for the ideal trans-human in this instance as it is an obvious weaker and degraded human.

The other characteristics in the trans-human definition show no signs of improvement in **"intelligence, awareness, strength, or durability"** in the trans-gender person. In fact, a cursory review of transitioning either way, i.e., female to male or male to female, it would be hard to make an argument for an improvement in any of these categories and most reasonably quite to the contrary. I suppose that is why the definitions are distinct and different and therefore need to be put on "The Right Line" separately. Improvement in the human it seems is not the end game in the trans-gender. Intelligence, awareness, strength, and durability being of no concern it seems. So what are these categories replaced with? Feelings!!! Idolatry of self, vanity, etc., and with discernment a break from all that is at the right end of "The Right Line."

~ CONCERNING WOKE-ISM ~

This is a tough one, but I will give it a go. If DNA science is to be believed and there are double helix strands coded with information about the human then it follows that all of the possible pairings for anything whatsoever in a human being was in the DNA of the first man and first woman. That would include height possibilities, hair color possibilities, and for the purpose of deconstructing "woke," melanin.

Let's break down the definition of "woke." The first part of the definition, i.e., "aware of and actively attentive" when put on "The Right Line" and with an understanding of the 2023 definition and or ideology of racial anything and everything as racist. In order to be very specific, racist being defined as anyone thinking that another human being or group of human beings is inferior, or less than, because of their melanin content or there general geographic heritage.

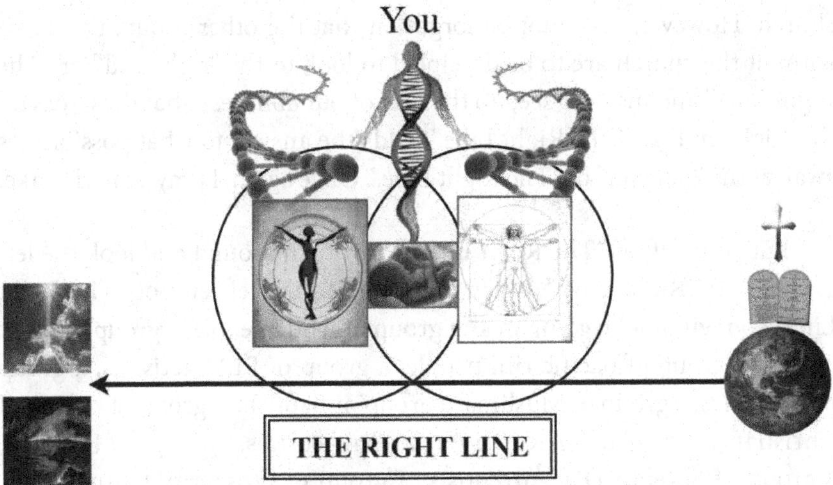

"Anyone" on earth can put themselves on the graphic above and in the place of "You." It's all there, as it pertains to "you," all of reality in one graphic. You, right there in the middle of "The Right Line" came to be because the Creator, i.e., God, created the foundations of the biological processes within the "man" and the "woman" to knit "you" in your mother's womb with your own never before coded DNA as well as "you" produced your own blood in the knitting process. Let me say that again, "you" while in your mother's womb were manufacturing your own unique blood. That process, that factory, "you," making that blood, did not happen by "chance." That factory within you was created, and not by your mom and dad. Look at the "right end" of "The Right Line," it will come to you. Discern!

Also, stare to the right end of "The Right Line" in this context: you are an ancestor of the first man and first woman who did in fact have all of the possible combinations of DNA for any and all possible characteristics that you enjoy as well as your neighbor and thus part of the "only" race of humans. It is further a fact that all of the possible skin pigment possibilities were in four women and four men after the flood. I would implore everyone to search out the work of Dr. Nathaniel Jeanson.

It is reasonable then to be properly "woke" then must start with aware. Aware of what? Stand on "The Right Line," look to the right. It's all there. We all are guilty of not being "aware" of the simplicity of the beginning. To be fair a "true" follower of Jesus the Christ is "aware" of and "actively attentive" to the only social group of any consequence whatsoever, the church. However, it cannot be forgotten that the other group, i.e., those without the church are to be descipled to look to the "right end" of "The Right Line" and made to see; (to the best of our abilities); that the Cross on the "right end" of "The Right Line" holds the answer to what possibilities await at the "left end" of "The Right Line." Once again, I pray, read the lake.

Put yourself on "The Right Line." Now turn around and look the left end of "The Right Line." When "You" get to the left end of "The Right Line" you will not be going in as a group of white people, a group of black people, a group of pacific rim people, a group of BLM activists, a group of Catholics, a group of Muslims, a group of Baptists, a group of reformed Christians, a group of NARs, a group of Pentecostals, a group of Mormons, a group of Seventh Day Adventists, a group of prosperity Gospel folks, a group of Hindus, a group of atheists, a group of feminists, a group of (fascists / anti-fascists), a group of athletes, a group of straight people, a group of homosexuals, a group of alphabet people......you get the point. Now as you consider your position looking to the left on "The Right Line," "You" will be going to the left end of "The Right Line" as "You" and "You" will be by yourself, alone, with no social network of any kind. You will be judged. We all, and that includes "You," are sinners and the Cross offers the only hope. Read the lake.

Is it possible, is it a reasonable statement or consideration to wonder if by the numbers one of the groups noted in the list above will have a larger percentage that walks through the narrow gate? If that is a reasonable assertion then it follows it might behoove one to search out and find out which group that is?

As much as humans seem to organize in groups of many categories, at the end of the line how many groups in heaven? I'm not sure, but it seems there may only be one. However, in the lake of fire, will the damned be allowed to congregate into groups? Not that it will matter!!! Think on that --- the woke considerations of 2023 will certainly be recognized in hell as being the wrong things to be "aware of and attentive to." I'm just sayin!!!!

To be woke then should be considered as "soberly awake" and aware of and attentive to the right end of "The Right Line." If we would do that then the so called "important facts and issues" (especially issues of racial and social justice) dissipate to nothingness like cold water on a hot griddle. Racial issues and social justice turn to dust and become moot. Or worded another way, love your neighbor as yourself and do that as intended by the Creator of all of it.

~ SUMMARY OF ISM'S ~

When each of these ism's when in and of themselves are put on "The Right Line" will be found to be very much left of righteousness and they, "the ism's," will progress somewhere, but it will not be to any of man's shortsighted concept of an ideal place for the "human condition."

Each one of the ism's above is worthy of an analysis on "the right line" complete with power point presentations to breakdown and deconstruct the various ideologies that purport to have the best solution to the ideal "human condition." I hope that I might work on some of them for a later time and am hopeful that others will consider the "The Right Line" as a useful tool.

THE STARTING LINE OF "THE RIGHT LINE"

Stare at the line above long enough and consider that at the right end of "The Right Line" man and woman came into existence at nearly the same time. If it were not so, there would not have been the first baby. In the theory of evolution it would have had to be the same way as well or there would have been no first baby. Seems ridiculously absurd that one puddle of ooze would spawn a man and another puddle of ooze right there in the same spot would spawn a female at exactly the same time on the timeline of supposed billions of years.

The Biblical account is vastly more reasonable. That man was created and then woman with very different functions, but similar enough to think, consider, feel, desire, procreate, work, work together, love, and of course disobey.

Also, stare at the graphic above and consider with your senses "what is" as it relates in this very specific graphic, i.e., "Man & Woman," and "what is" as you view them through your God given senses, what you see is called "general revelation."

Nowhere on "The Right Line" from the beginning to the end could there have been nor could there be anything on this earth if not for man and woman being very specifically designed for an "intended" purpose. Since we do exist it follows there is a purpose. So, there it is the question that has been the bane of man for all of history. If you stare long enough also consider that the Bible tells us that "the man" and "the woman" were created in the image of God, and it has been said that man and women therefore have a "spark" of the divine, but, and this is key, only a spark and it must be said that we are dying embers in the bonfire of life, our ash to fall back to earth into the dust. Is that all there is….billions of dying embers back to dust???

There would be no mankind if there were two men on right end of "The Right Line." Likewise, there would be no mankind if there were two women on right end of "The Right Line." So, what is now and what was there from the beginning is clearly foundational. Why then throughout history do some choose to kick against the goads??? Goads, great word, look it up!

Many people think too hard. Stare at the graphic again – you would not be here if the foundation of "man and woman" you are staring at "was not." Since it clearly is, then how it all started should be wonderful to consider. Just like holding a newborn anything, but especially a human baby is amazing, consider that there was a "first" baby and you should feel amazed for that "first" baby happened in exactly the same way you came to be…..you therefore are amazing.!!!!

Now, consider the other end of "The Right Line." That amazement which is the end of life! Amazing is not the word that comes to mind when death is contemplated. Fear is reasonable; indifference is common, but not reasonable. If you consider that your timeline doesn't even register on "The Right Line" above at least at the scale drawn. However, reason and conscience will tell you there is a reason for all of this. The Bible tells us what that is.

~ THE RIGHT LINE SUMMARY ~
THE INDIVIDUAL, NOT THE GROUP

This paradigm shift of a line graphic to consider not only time, but any condition whatsoever in terms of right being on the obvious righteous end of the line I hope is useful for your consideration. The above summary graphic can be considered in a couple of ways as follows:

1. All of time, the beginning of which is on the right. For God's reasons He created. The obvious pearl of all that He created was man and woman. He wanted them to know love, first of Him, then of each other and thirdly of offspring. That innate characteristic to love and as general revelation makes clear we innately love our "loved ones;" especially our children as well as those we call immediate family. Being harder to show that kind of love for others mankind required a moral code. That helped, but still man struggled to show love to neighbors. Man needed to be shown a selfless way how to do that. Jesus showed us how to do that. He would die for our transgressions so we could consider properly how to be a servant to others and love them truly. Sadly, all require reminding of whom to love first!
2. Your time, the beginning of which is still the right side of "The Right Line." In the graphic "you" and "you" alone came to be in the created order as it was from the beginning when God said, "It is good." And further, in exactly the same way, and the only possible way for "you" to be, in other words, from the procreated specific union of a man and a woman. As you stare at the graphic the fact that "you" are because of the miraculous foundation of a mother and a father being necessary for a "you" to be. It may cross your mind that your parents created "you," but man did not create the

> foundational building blocks of the procreation mechanism for "your" parents to create "you." God did in the beginning for His pleasure and thank God He did for here "you" are. If it pleased God for there to be a "you," and so much so that He came down in the flesh in the person of His Son so that "you" might see that there is a left side of "The Right Line," which is "your" death. And more specifically, to explain why death and the best news of all, how to defeat death.

I hope this graphic is in some way helpful to consider that "you" on the timeline of everything are but a speck, but a very significant speck. "Your" problem then is the same one "we" all have, and that is "we" have too long to think about it. The wonderful gift of life and all that is in it for us to enjoy most certainly is a distraction. God rested on the seventh day for all that he created, which has been and is a most reasonable thing that "you" and "we" can and should do to give thanks for and to worship God for the gift. The specifics of the righteousness that is on this summary of "The Right Line" is in the Christian Bible, or as noted in Chapter 6, Lake Christos. Read and drink in the Word of God.

> *Please God, as I finish this analogy, I pray that it might be a seed for someone that is useful to Your Glory. Amen!*

~ THE RIGHT LINE ~

All things considered, can now be made clear,
Laid on a line on which to put time,
Evaluate anyone or anything in any given year,

What standard, what measure, can we judge our behavior,
Stand on the line, look to the right,
There is the standard, there is the measure,
All in a book, all of the treasure.

Judge what you do by the Man on the Cross,
For it is He, only He, that will judge in the end,
So stand on the line and look only to Him,
For He is the Way, the Truth, and the Word,
That transcends the end at the left on the line.

You have but to believe and His grace you will find,
Freedom from hell that would otherwise bind.

Stand on the "Right Line" and judge all that you do,
So as you move left on the timeline of life,
Look right to the Cross, and know that it's true,
For at the left on the line when you stand at the gate,
It is Christ the Redeemer whom will determine your fate.

Trust your heart; trust your mind for you know this for sure,
The "Right Line" it is Christ, the Way and your cure.

Amen
JKF 4-4-2023

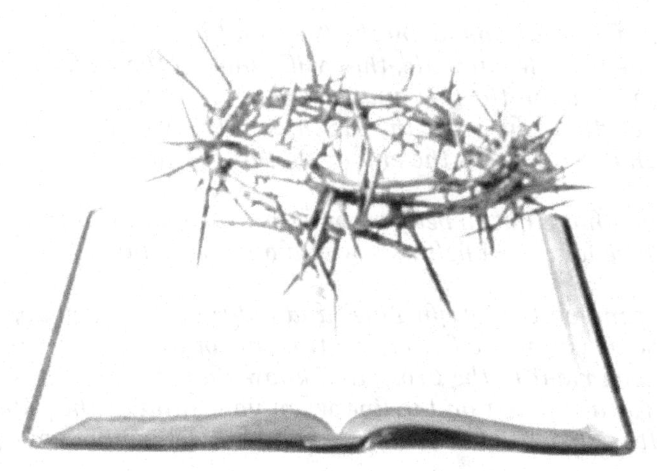

Fear is Inate....Why?

Wrath of God

Chapter 11

WRATH

What to make of wrath? And what to make of the wrath of God? Like much of my journey I like to lean into general revelation. Is wrath, which is defined in the dictionary as "extreme anger," a thing generally, revealed to me? It seems to me it most certainly is a thing I can see in me and in others. As I think on wrath in myself I tried to remember when was the earliest time I could recall wrath in myself? When I was a boy about 9 years old I was one of five and the second oldest. Without question I was the most obnoxious and deserved everything I got. That notwithstanding, my big sister, then 10, used her very sharp fingernails to draw blood by digging them into my arm. This particular time we were all horsing around in the living room with my Dad present. For the most part whatever we were doing was not totally unpleasant because my Dad was laughing at us. Well, as they say, it's all fun and games until somebody draws first blood. It's reasonable that whatever caused my sister to draw first blood was directly related to me being a little s*#t. Anyway, I got so mad that I started swinging and connected a left roundhouse punch that hit my sister in the ear. I can still remember my rage which must have looked ridiculous because I can still remember my Dad laughing and then having to change his demeanor to scold me. My sister started crying and although I got in trouble I was also proud of myself for standing up for myself even though the pride was utterly without merit and misguided.

What's important here is my earliest memory of extreme anger or wrath. I suppose this is where a parent recognizes that the need to channel that wrath to another thing. Sports works well especially for boys. I have been filled with wrath, or extreme anger only a few times and maybe once a decade, maybe. As I recall those instances I certainly can remember the state of mind. When that kind of anger has happened, it is always followed by being angry that I got so angry. So, how to deal with this wrath thing? It makes me think that "general" revelation suggests that the nature of man does not desire "generally" to be wrathful. If that is our "general" nature then perhaps being created in the image of God, neither does He.

We are God's children, and just as parents know that their children are going to experience extreme anger and innately know it is our responsibility to guide our children to rightly deal with it, and sometimes that dealing with it requires punishment to get the point across. If we do not deal with not only angry children, but also wrong deeds by children, well chaos and breakdown follows.

If when we have been reasonably shaped and molded to join society then our part in it will be polite. When we do not reasonably shape and mold our children to join and be polite in society then mobs start roaming the streets burning things down. If we were to follow Gods instructions there would be no mobs burning anything down. We would at all encounters, control wrath, be humble, and strive to help and serve each other.

Sorry, a bit of a tangent off of wrath. It seems to me that a righteous man and or woman know that wrath is right there under the surface though most of the time in a place perhaps best comprehended or explained as the unconscious. Wrath, a resource that thank God we don't wish to tap into, at least generally. If we are honest we wish that wrath could be rained down on the many things we see in our world that are so very clearly unrighteous. I know I do. However, as the Good Book notes, wrath is being stored up and it is not our place to store it!

All of what I hear so far about God and wrath moves immediately to the holiness of God which moves to exhortations about righteousness, justice, righteous justice, and why and how that plays out. If it is our nature to generally not to be angry and certainly not in our nature to be extremely angry and not in our nature to "want or desire" to be either of those two things, but it is within us to be wrathful, then we also know that we have the capacity to control ourselves and such feelings. So how is wrath to be used if we are endowed with it?

Righteous wrath! Is there such a thing? Some men have many encounters with situations that require the use of force to quell humans gone wrong, cops and soldiers mostly. Consideration for what with reason would be considered "righteous wrath" is for this analysis only for those instances where the wrong doer has violently trespassed on another and not meant to consider the "yea but what about this scenario?" Respect is reasonable to give such men that sign up for such duty. Unfortunately, the fact that such a position is required validates the fall of man. I am fortunate enough to have lived most of my life under the freedom and liberty provided by the system in America that protects same and have not encountered the violence I see in large cities or in foreign places.

Personally I have had only one encounter where I acted on behalf of another where righteous wrath, (in my opinion) was used against unrighteous wrath, (in my opinion) and one of the two wrath filled men ended a wrong. It was late afternoon traveling home from work in Phoenix Arizona. In Phoenix the major roads are two lanes in each direction with a center lane to pull into to turn to the left as well as create a safety zone. This day I used it to park when to my left and on the sidewalk there was man perhaps a head taller than I slapping around a woman shorter than I. To paint a picture for context this was a residential area and less than one hundred feet to the west or to my right as I aggressively put my pickup in park, threw open the door and ran to the in-progress beating, there were approximately eight people half men and half women watching. For further context I am 5'- 5" tall and at that time 26 years old and was a bodybuilder, and had been a wrestler, and rather scrappy.

As I consider my mindset, "anger" and certainly "extreme anger" or wrath is a reasonable adjective to describe my "state of mind." That "state" is what I was in when without any other consideration whatsoever, I ran into harm's way. When I got there I was yelling for the man to let her go in a tone he and all those watching knew to be angry. He started to say, "But she took my keys…" I cut him off and yelled with my right fist cocked, "I don't care, you let her go or I'm taking you out." He let her go and I yelled at her to go, which she did. He started to say something, which I cannot recall. I said some things about not beating a woman. That's it. No punches were thrown. What then stopped this man? Wrath!

Certainly this man was in some state of wrath and uncontrollable so. What stopped him? What he saw from his perspective was a crazy man rushing him filled with rage, or wrath. In this case wrath stopped wrath and with only words expressed in a certain kind of tone. Certainly the threat of me doing to him the same thing he was doing to her stopped him in his tracks.

What to make of this? Did I do the right thing? With reason most people would say yes, although I recognize in some cultures the beating of a women is a right and I might have been interfering so as to be unlawful. That aside, most discerning people would say that it was a righteous thing I did that day.

I am trying to consider through this example and through "general revelation" that part of the nature of man, created in God's image that has wrath within us. This wrath within us which can be so very wrong, and in another instance and sometimes at the very same instant in time can be righteous wrath. In the example above it is reasonable that I or the recent fatuous suggestion of a "social worker" could not have walked up and said, "Please kind sir, please stop punching the tiny woman." His wrath would have ignored such a request and the little woman reasonably would have sustained several more punches. So there's that!!

Just like I was not driving home stewing on the wrath within me, but.... it was in there. I was not a Christian at the time, but it seems certain things were "written on my heart," one of which it seems was that a little image bearer of God did not deserve to be beaten. Was my wrath stored? In a sense I suppose, for there it came.

The Bible says that when we sin we store up the wrath of God. It seems reasonable that God doesn't sit around stewing on all the sin in the world although he is very cognizant of all of it. Just as we are cognizant that every day somewhere on this earth there are great and horrific things done to image bearers of God 24/7, and while if we stop and think on that thought we know three things: 1) it's true; 2) we are powerless to do anything about it, generally speaking; and 3) we don't think on it.

If in those moments when we do think on it wrath bubbles to the forefront of our brains however short lived and sometimes our wrath is justified while other times we have to back off when all of the facts are found out. This should give us great pause, God alone knows the intent of every heart at every moment past, present, and future and He has made it clear that we will be judged. Why? He knows all, remembers all, and when He is ready, in His time, His wrath will be ready. Are you ready!!!!????

~ REAL TIME GOSPEL TANGENT ~

As I was writing the above few paragraphs in a coffee shop, two cops walked in for an afternoon beverage. When they had ordered I asked them if I could pick their brain about wrath for this chapter. They were gracious and we talked for perhaps 25 minutes. Both it turns out were supervisors, one of beat cops and the other of a gang unit. The gang unit lead was stocky and fit and at a glance any smart person would concur could handle himself. I told him of my one and only encounter noted above which he understood. He then recounted his first experience as a rookie when he had to use the wrath within him to subdue a wrong doer. The adrenaline raged as he took the bad guy to the ground using his instinctual wrath as well as his new training in controlled use of force. He now has to train wrath control to younger cops. Review of use of force or wrath incidents is part of his job as well, which is a net good. He also, mentioned Jordan Peterson and John "Jocko" Willink as philosophical inspirations to him and his counseling of his subordinates in the use of controlled wrath. This was awesome as I shared that it was Jordan Peterson that dropped the seed that inspired me to read the Bible.

I had explained that I was writing a book about my journey to the Cross which they reacted as if they thought that was pretty cool. To set the stage for the air in the room it was, I would say, jovial, i.e., all three of us were engaged in a cordial and fun exchange. The stout fellow said he had some schooling in theology, but was not what he considered religious. So, I said, "How about we test that?" Ha ha, it seems the tables were turned on the normal encounter with a cop in which they pull you over and their first question is, "Do you know why I pulled you over?" I did not have any intention of asking them about the gospel or if I could look in the trunk so to speak. If in a traffic stop a cop has "reasonable suspicion" there is something wrong the cop may ask the follow-up question, "Do you mind if I take a look in your trunk?" You're not obliged to answer, but some will. It seems in this instance I not only pulled them over, told them what I was up to, but this cop it seems voluntarily opened his trunk and showed me the contraband of his heart, so to speak. Ha ha!!

So I asked him, "What is the gospel?" It was quickly obvious I had him on his theological heels for he hesitated. So I said, "Let's back up, what does gospel mean?" It was again quickly obvious he had forgotten for he could not answer. So I said, "It means the good news." I quickly followed with, "What is the good news?" He said, "Jesus came…." and he could not finish the thought. The truth reasonably was in his brain, but he could not remember. It seems I had him on his theological ropes again and while he may grapple with bad guys from time to time and train for wrath encounters he wasn't ready for this one. So I ended with, "He came to save you, and He came to save you," while I pointed my fingers at him and his friend respectively. We all laughed and I told them I went to Desert Hills Bible Church and invited them. That was it. I hope to see them again and get their thoughts about me putting them in my book.

Later that evening I was at a Bible study and recounting the exchange to a friend. He had concern when I said I was just talking to some cops and he thought that I had been pulled over. In this rare encounter, no, I wasn't pulled over; it seems I pulled them over!! Great fun!

Policing forces of one form or another it seems for obvious reasons have been instituted for all of history. The way these fellows conducted themselves and spoke about wrath, at least in this short interview, made me think that they took their role as a policing force for good with the correct or righteous intent required of the badge. I hope that is the case!

Take away lesson from this encounter. These cops as leaders of cops must continually review protocol, tactics, etc., to stay sharp in their profession. If they don't it can be disastrous and deadly. For precisely the same reason the scriptures command that brothers and sisters gather together to sharpen each other. On the one hand thank God these "commissioned" officers stay in the game to sharpen each other for the sword they carry. On the other hand we can see an example of a cop who declared he used to be in the faith, but because he doesn't gather with the saints like he does with his fraternity of cops, his theological sword is dull and useless for the greatest of commissions he also was called to do.

End tangent.

~ BACK TO WRATH ~

History can be looked at through the lens of many things such as romance, art, religion, cultures, etc. Certainly history can and has been viewed through the lens of wrath and would encompass wrath at the nation level and the wars that require wrath in order to execute. Diplomacy and talking being reasonable and certainly preferred, man it seems has always moved to war as a means to an end. Greed and pride I suppose are reasonably the main sin on both sides of any conflict. When a nation is moved to war, the leaders one way or another have always convinced the young men to take up arms for a cause. Clever marketing always seems to work to convince young men that some greater good is a good reason to kill other young men convinced by their leaders that an opposing greater good is also a good reason to kill others that had they lived in the same neighborhood they would have played football, baseball, or some other sport together.

That observation aside, when war ensues it is truly hell on earth. The very organized way men and countries have invented horrific ways to execute wrath the outcome of which is premature death, always and every time.

To be sure when the history books are written and analyze wars there have been instances when the war fought with reason was righteous. For example, why Hitler needed to be stopped through the lens of history is an easy one. Japan I suppose is another, however, God help us for the technology developed to end that one.

Large scale mass death on par with that caused by the a-bomb or the fire bombings of Dresden one nation did to another nation; or the large scale mass death of a nation's leader to its own people such as Stalin or Mao; or more recently mass death in the world caused by bad faith bad actors convincing the masses through fear or clever marketing to self-inject themselves with untested stuff is mind boggling and something we naturally do not wish to dwell on. But sadly it is there.

All of history so far cannot seem to go one century without a war which mankind has figured out extremely sophisticated ways of controlled, but very deadly wrath to kill each other. In America very sophisticated categories of wrath divisions including Army, Navy, Air Force, Marines, Coast Guard, Border Patrol, and local Police forces have been set up in theory to subdue with great wrath if and when great wrongness is done. The scriptures tell us that governments were to be a terror to evil, or stated another way, a terror to those who do not do "right." God and God alone is holy and completely so, or He is righteousness itself and the ultimate standard for what is right. Where man's discernment required clarification when man thought he knew better how to live and act, God left us His word. The scriptures tell us there will be a time when the "right" which He and He alone has the "right" to declare as "right" will become wrong. The scriptures describe a time when, like the birth pangs of a woman giving birth, the intensity of right becoming wrong will increase and that we are to consider such a time as a sign.

Then there is wrath of the individual. How is it that so many individuals take to the streets with such wrath? Once again appealing to "general revelation" and knowing that there are obvious bad faith bad actors at the highest levels, with the most resources, unimaginable power, and intent to make themselves the "god" of the world. They also knowing full well the Bible and the structures and instructions of God Almighty, have been moving for years, and recently with an increase of their fervor to tear down the institutions and the order of things ordained by God.

~ WORLD REALITIES STIR OUR WRATH ~

>>> THE FAMILY <<<

How to capture the individual? Start with the family. The first family, Adam and Eve, one man and one woman. Clearly the evil one, created by God, thinking he can manage the affairs better than God, started right away by messing with the family. Today these bad faith, bad actors, no different than Satan the first time are taking his lead, they too thinking they can manage the affairs of man better than God, have worked very hard to make the family insignificant and subordinate to the "corporate" state. The first attack on the family was to tempt the woman to eat of a forbidden fruit. Today it seems Satan has upped his game and has tempted naive women to murder their own babies, and not only do it, but stand in the public square shouting with such wrath and claim they have a "right" to do such an unrighteous thing. In like manner as Adam who succumbed to the wishes of Eve, modern men stand down.

Per the Bible God created women to be a helper to man. Today women lead and men shrink and shirk their God breathed roles. Women with great wrath scream many forms of victim-hood status and the power brokers perpetuate this as virtue. The power brokers hire cowardly men and pay them handsomely to hold up these so called virtues thus propagating a lie that men generally stand behind this misplaced virtue. Proper men do not.

I was raised in the 60's and 70's and the sexual revolution as it was and is known was well on its way to a carnal temporal victory. Being young and having less than a thumbnail sketch of Christ, sin, salvation, and any consideration at all of the ever after I lived in the deep end of the pool of sin. I knew no other world for everything revolved around the mantra "sex, drugs, and rock & roll." Promiscuity was the norm, but the slippery slope it seems was being greased to get much worse. Those my age recall that even in the 70's it was still frowned upon for couples to live together out of wedlock and those that did hid it from parents and even generally. Today it's the norm and the youth today generally won't even get push back from their parents, in fact it is often encouraged as a test drive. This revolution I see clearly now was an attack on the proper masculine man and the proper feminine woman and the proper virtue required of each to look for proper love and not lust as a guiding force. Would I have chosen to do differently I can't say, but looking back, words like pride is not something that jumps into my mind to even share verbally much less putt in the scrape book of my life. Shame and lots of it!

The culture shaped me and while I understand that there were adults perpetuating the culture at some point the realization that I was responsible for my behavior irrespective of the culture and that I will stand alone before God and be judged, and most assuredly not as a culture. If I am judged and condemned to hell it won't be the cultures fault, it will be my fault. Anyway, this side of consideration of all of the aforementioned and as it concerns the breakdown of the family, it seems Satan was there for me and I danced. My story is but one of millions and millions that have and do dance with the devil.

It seems crazy to think things could get worse. Now it seems we have but to wait for the morrow for each day brings unfathomable degradation to the family.

This breakdown of the family not completely torn to shreds, but most certainly well on its way! The only place it seems to be somewhat intact is in a proper Christian family. The power hungry bad faith bad actors have gone after "Christ's family" or the Christian church for years and it certainly made attempts recently to get rid of it completely be declaring the church non-essential in the covid debacle. To be sure the attacks on the Christian church or "Christ's family" are going to get worse.

>>> THE CHILDREN <<<

Then there are the children. The evil one, also from the beginning messing with the children. Like Adam and Eve, the devil messing with children so much so that their firstborn son, Cain, would take the life of their other son Able, his own brother. Once again, Satan has upped his game by using naive women first to not only murder their own babies, but also to think they have a new "right" to groom other peoples' children into sex not ordained by God, and to once again with great wrath announce in the public square that they not only have that right, but they can and do hide their perversions from parents and claim the parents do not have a right to question them or even know. Once again the bad faith bad actors have infiltrated the education systems to encourage all of this and pay very handsomely to perpetuate all of it. Why? To breakdown the family! Anyone can see its working. The state of the family is sad, so very sad. Parents sitting in the lap of God, slapping Him and taking Satan's lead instead are setting aside their role as parent and protector of their own children, in some cases paying bad faith bad acting doctors, ironically having an oath to do no harm, to butcher their own children. In other cases, parents taking their own babies to see drag queens, giving their babies dollar bills to stuff in the G-strings of Satan following deviants. Dear God help them, I pray!!

Then there is the known sex trafficking of children, both boys and girls. Women also, but let's focus on the children here. Once again bad faith bad actors instead of using their wealth to benevolently help those that need help use the poorest image bearers of God as pawns in a global form of chess, the object of which is to capture the resources of nations while paying most handsomely for these pawns to immigrate to nations that have it better. In this sick game subsidized by bankers using middlemen called governments, taking the needed money not from their own wealth, but from another class of pawn called citizens. Immigration is the game, destroying two countries for the price of one the short term goal, long term - all and everything. In 2023 America, the leader of the nation against the will of the people for which he serves is the most heinous of puppet pieces on this global chess board. Why? In the game of the globe, children are being trafficked into sex slavery. Parents hoping for a chance, just a glimmer of a chance, send their daughters and sons on a trek through Bad Lands to be raped, beaten, murdered, and if they make it exploited by cartels to send future earnings back to the cartels. A tax if you will, no different than that of the "legal cartels" of bankers. It seems most evil because it is.

If part of the crime, say the exploitation by the cartels, could be stopped we might feign a victory for that piece. However, the entire process in America could be stopped tomorrow. The rape, the beatings, the murder, the sex-ploitation of boys, girls and woman, the suffering could be stopped by the order of one man. The problem is that man is too busy eating ice cream cones and can't seem to keep his own hands off of little girls.

Once upon a time in America mobs ran quite a game not unlike global bankers. They did similar things, but did not have as big a gang to keep their exploitation game going. When mob bosses were taken down the boss at the top who never pulled a trigger or took a dime personally would be prosecuted for ordering hits and having others do graft of various sorts. What's the difference? If there is a Biblical difference I can't figure it out, maybe someone could explain.

Today in 2023, and since January of 2020, one man was and is responsible for the crimes against these little children. That man who tacitly by his order is like the mob boss responsible for every rape, every murder, and every and all graft in the game. While we know that he will never be judged for crimes against humanity in this carnal, corrupt, and temporal world, he will in fact be judged. As Jesus Christ said of the little children,

> **NKJV --- Matthew 18 --** *6) "But whoever causes one of these little ones who believe in Me to sin, it would be better for him if a millstone were hung around his neck, and he were drowned in the depth of the sea."*

It seems God has made it very clear, the millstone thing will be better than what awaits this man in hell. If there is one very explicit statement in the Bible that sheds a light on the wrath of God it seems this is it. Here's the thing, that leader, and all who support these atrocities, many of whom are professed Christians, are in grave danger of a fate it seems far worse than a millstone around the neck and cast into to Davy Jones locker. An honest prayer is that they repent, turn to Christ, beg and beg hard for forgiveness, do the right thing, fix the hell holes in the world, as outlined by God and not evil men and their many highly paid minions. That includes everyone in the exploit food chain including all of the government minions of the devil and the billionaires and bankers playing this game of global chess with the children of God.

Just a thought --- if odds makers were to consider the probabilities for repentance of these players, what do you suppose those odds might be?? While I would and do pray for their souls I certainly wouldn't bet on it.

>>> THE WOMEN <<<

Another atrocity of trafficked young girls is the ripped from the headlines story of Jeffery Epstein whom met an untimely death the details of which are so preposterous that once again if the odds makers were to consider the odds of all of the claimed circumstances to happen as were reported....well you know. Then there is Gislaine Maxwell his mistress and pimp who is in prison for sex trafficking for Jeffery Epstein and as noted on a Joe Rogan podcast exactly zero other people. A good question Joe postulates. How is it she is in prison if there are zero customers supposedly Gislaine has trafficked young girls too. There are people commissioned to know, and they do. God knows all of the parties involved as well as all those involved in the cover up of sex trafficking of young girls to the rich and powerful. I do pray for their souls for once again as Jesus noted in the millstone warning they are in grave danger of an eternal fate worse than that.

Feminism, or as the late great Rush Limbaugh referred to the movement. "femi-nazi's," it seems has started to eat itself so much so that women themselves cannot say what they "in fact" are! There is not much to add perhaps only to say and pray on behalf of girls and women everywhere:

~ A PRAYER FOR THE GIRLS ~

Little girl, little girls, daughters of a father, daughters of a mother,
I can't believe I'm saying this, but God created you to be like no other.
You wouldn't be here were it not for the womb of your mom.
You wouldn't be here were it not for the seed of your father.

The seed and the egg we now know does contain a code if you will,
The language provided, not by chance, but God's choice to fulfill,
You are the product of Gods intent to make you,
He did not get it wrong, He wanted you to be just as you are.
Your place in His world, your place for His glory,
Is to embrace what you are and how you fit in His story,

Embrace little sister, embrace His decision,
You're a girl, you're a girl, you'll soon be a woman.
Ask you mother, ask your father,

"Is it true what they say, is it true what I hear,
That the most precious of moments, the highest of highs,
Is that moment you held me, even first when I cried?"

Reflect on the answer, reflect little girl,
You are half of the code; you are half of the plan,

Nothing you do, nothing you can achieve, no race you can win,
Will be better than the gift of God to marry a man.
This union is holy this union is blessed, when you hold your new baby,
You will finally know - you're a woman - you will finally understand.

In that moment, as your baby coo's and you embrace,
If you're honest you can say, there is a God for surely this is grace,
This baby is not clay, chance had no part,
Man is clearly not smart enough,
With all that man knows, and all he contrives,
Man simply doesn't have the stuff.

Who could knit that tiny thing the way of it is beyond belief.
Unless of course we reason & discern that the first breath your baby took,
Came not from a factory of man,
Not from anything so contrite as random chance,

But could only come from the mind of God and only by His grace.
I pray little girl, a woman now, holding a baby dear,
Thank God and as should we all, repent and turn to Christ,
Raise that baby with your man; raise that baby in the Lord,
Then one day in glory that feeling that you had will last forevermore.

Amen
JKF 11-2-2022

As I think on this prayer I cannot help but reflect on the happenstance in the discourse of the world today that men cannot weigh in on the affairs of women. Nonsense! Women certainly are not shy about vocalizing their opinions about men ad nauseam.

> **ad nauseam:** *referring to something that has been done or repeated so often that it has become annoying or tiresome.*

Women are half or more of the world's population, so of course men can, and I dare say have not only a vested interest in the affairs of women, but have a duty and a responsibility to protect all that is "obviously" sacred about women.

I am a father who can recall vividly the moment the doctor held my baby up and said it's a girl. Although I felt similar feelings about the miracle of birth and this new thing that would make me understand love in a brand new way, I have to concede the bond between the mother and baby was something different. Back then the love was instinctual and as I now understand part of God's designed nature in us is to cherish that little thing. Now my daughter is a mother and I have two granddaughters. Now as an old man watching my daughter love on her babies....well what could be better?

The poem / prayer above was written from the mind of a man, a father of a woman and grandfather of little girls. The point is a man can think with great circumspection about the affairs of women. I read the above prayer to my sister with the stated purpose to get a woman's thoughts. She thought it was from the perspective of a married mother of two boys right on. However, she and her husband both noted that it would likely alienate many. Realizing this and knowing that the prayer was honesty from my heart for that circumstance which would and does make for the best possible existence for women in this temporal world, another prayer is warranted for those and especially women whom because of fallen man and fallen women must navigate this world unnecessarily and irreverently unprotected properly as ordained by God, and made clear by His Son.

~ ANOTHER PRAYER FOR THE GIRLS ~

Dear God, my God, our God, their God,
I pray Lord God, merciful God on high,
I plead this day for the girls, please hear my cry.

There is a plan, You made it clear,
Your perfect way is known to the world.
Marriage is proper for a boy and a girl.

This prayer is for the wayward girl,
The girl deceived just like Eve,
However it happened, however it came to be,
You became pregnant, but it seems, you are the regnant.

It happens we know, it has for all time, but that's no excuse,
To fall back on that is to be quite obtuse.
In all but one case you and you alone control the space.

Boys being boys and men without spines, it is certainly true,
Are dogs and asses and assuredly swine.
Silver tongued devils, can and do woo.

But if you keep your mind sober and keep your mind clear,
The voice that you hear, the one saying no,
Is your Lord and your Savior speaking with love in your ear.

Wait maiden wait; wait for a man, who is honest and righteous,
And knows very well the Way of the Master.

But now for the girls for whom it's too late,
You've given birth to a baby; you're not wed and alone,
Single mom claimed a virtue, but it's reasonably not so.

But Jesus your savior, died for us all and died for you too,
It'll be a rough go; it'll be a rough time,
But pray to Him daily, pray whenever you can,

Pray to find a good church, pray to find a good man.
It's possible yes, to do it yourself, but God's way is better,
God has the best plan.

God has gifted you an instinct to love that baby dear,
So please don't take this as a slight or a sneer,
With love and God's favor, you can be of good cheer.

Raise your babies; raise them right in the ways of The Lord,
Be honest with your children and when the time is right,
Share your mistakes so they see you're contrite.

Their future uncertain, but you are their light.
Jesus your answer, so live little sister, live on with His might,

I'm not sure how to end this; I'm not sure what to say,
But I honestly love you and all Christians do,

We want to be with you and not to be late,
And find our way with you and your babies to Heaven's gate.
Take care little sister, take care and fly straight.

Amen
JKF 11-3-2022

One more thought about women. Concerning those righteous women that are not confused about what they are and who are athletes being forced by evil to compete against men claiming to be women? The most recent display of unrighteousness making national news, a man claiming to be a woman in collegiate swimming.

> *Dear women athlete swimmers,*
>
> *You know you are being cheated and feel helpless against what is so very obviously evil and wrong. Here's a suggestion. Conspire; yes conspire to send a message that will be a shot heard around the world. When the cameras are rolling, and in a big event, get on the blocks, take your mark and when the gun goes off stand up turn around with your backs to the pool and wait! You will be vilified and you will be heroes. Do not doubt that you will be the Rosa Parks of women's sports. It will send a message. I promise others in all other sports will take your lead.*
>
> *Yours truly,*
> *An old man thinking for the first time!*

Imagine the discontent. Imagine the news cycle. It would be glorious and you would change the world for the better! Good luck.

>>> MEN <<<

The Bible uses the phrase "true man." What is that? In 2023 the influences in the world might suggest that there is no such thing as a "true man." The feminist movement suggested and with great success that men are not needed. It seems that sex is quite the pesky little pleasure that men desire and so do women, not as something sacred, but in a casual, hook-up, promiscuous, irresponsible, and most egregiously an adulterous sort of way. Add in a little alcohol to the cocktail and indifference to life itself, the exact opposite of why God created men and woman has made for a world of the flesh.

Women in 2023 claim boys need to be programmed to be womanish, and if they don't act womanish then men are called toxic. All of this programming in large measure is promulgated by Hollywood. Except for Christmas Hallmark movies, which seem to try and keep the boy meets girl thing somewhat wholesome, in most every other cinematic 2023 experience the created order of things is completely upside down. Men don't lead, women do.

So what is a "true man"? It is simple and right there in the Bible. A "true man" can be seen for all that the role requires if:

1. *That man loves God first, recognizes his sin and knows he needs that same God who incarnated Himself in Jesus to save him, that man will not bow down to false gods or entities. That man will not shy away from the truth of the aforementioned.*
2. *That man will recognize that to use the holy name of Jesus in any form to express disgust or cursing is a most egregious sin.*
3. *That man will surely set aside a day of rest and a day to lead his family, wife and children to worship the Lord.*
4. *That man will likewise consider all days holy, and walk through this carnal world as if he were a guest.*
5. *That man will honor his mother, that man will honor his father, that man will if the carnal world has led his parents astray will do what he can to lead them to the Lord.*
6. *That man will not murder, that man will not murder in his heart, that man will defend life and will discern the difference.*
7. *That man will not commit adultery, that man will flee from the thought, that man will if properly counseled by his father will not fornicate outside the bonds of marriage.*
8. *That man will not steal directly or by deception.*
9. *That man will not say anything false about another, that man will weigh all evidence, will call out injustice, be accountable and require accountability.*
10. *That man will not covet, nor let his pride lead him astray.*

If the list looks familiar, congratulations! A true man will be the "head of his household" and strive to be that head as Christ is the head of the church. If it appears that the above list is not doable that's because it is not possible to live up to that standard, but it is the standard by which a man can be measured or considered to be the best he can be and considered a "true man." I should note so as to not sound sanctimonious that this man has failed all on the list, but I see it now. Men please read God's word and be a "true man." You will be blessed.

As I finish this section I think on my friend that since he was young lived as a "true man" and he has surely been blessed to the third generation. So much so that I had dinner with his daughter, her husband, and their children while the kids shared with me the moment they were saved. That my friend is joy and truly a witness to God's grace poured out on a true man.

>>> SOCIETY AND MEDIA <<<

Since about 1960 there has been a great shift from concern about Elvis Presley's hips being a concern for public consumption to:

- ✓ drag queen story hour for children;
- ✓ grooming of children for unnatural sex;
- ✓ the exploitation and butchering of confused children for money;
- ✓ CRT or "critical race theory" which is racist;
- ✓ Considerations that pedophilia or minor attracted persons, aka "MAP" should be considered normal.

All of these and more perversions of God's created order are given a whole month to celebrate and parade in the streets as things to be "proud" of. This sickness is vile and makes it clear that the evil intents of Satan have taken hold greatly in the world. This shift is seismic in its scope and not good. These types of sins wake up the wrath in men and women and righteously so.

I have coffee often with a group of retired old warriors including two charter member Navy Seals, a Marine, an Army soldier/retired NYC detective, an Army tank driver, an Air Force F-16 pilot, and an Air Force psychiatrist. We discuss all that is in the headlines noted above as well as the mainstream media lairs and the liars they lie about. These men signed up as patriotic Americans to defend something they thought worth fighting for. However, as they watch and listen to the chaos of today they are angry. Some of these men were trained to use very deadly force or "controlled wrath" and still have nightmares to this day. They are old men now and would if they could stand up again to fight for a righteous cause, but as we discuss the state of the union today and seeing so clearly that those leading the show are not righteous individually or as a group of leaders. Helplessness describes the feelings. Prayer is all it seems we can do. It would be fair to say that we feel anger for all of the above and if possible these old soldiers would lay down their lives to fight for future generations of children not to have to endure such filth and evil. It would also be fair to admit there is wrath beneath the surface. If we as image bearers of God feel wrath, how much more so does God.

In 2023 that which God created as well as His Word left for us on how to live and conduct the affairs of man are being turned upside down. God's version of right is being legislated to be wrong, and wrong is being legislated to be right and protected from calling out its obvious wrongness. Many are living in blatant wrongness; the media once concerned with calling out wrongness now carries the water of wrongness and daily calls out "right to be wrong" and "wrong to be right." Right is canceled, wrong is declared a virtue, God is mocked to be wrong by almost every word uttered by what is called "main stream media." And when I say "almost" every word if those words purport in any way the following:

(Note: all Bible References are NKJV)

1. **Arrogance** - *an attitude of superiority manifested in an overbearing manner or in presumptuous claims or assumptions* - (2 Timothy 3:2; 2 Corinthians 12:20; 2 Timothy 3:2; 1 Corinthians 4:6, 18,19; 5:2; 8:1; 13:4)
2. **Boasting** - *a statement expressing excessive pride in oneself : the act or an instance of boasting; a cause for pride; to praise oneself extravagantly in speech : speak of oneself with excessive pride* - (Romans 1:30; 2 Timothy 3:2; Galatians 5:26; 1 Corinthians 4:7; 5:6)

3. **Clamor** - *noisy shouting; a loud continuous noise; to utter or proclaim insistently and noisily* - (Ephesians 4:31)
4. **Complaining** - *to express grief, pain, or discontent; to make a formal accusation or charge* - (Ephesians 4:31; Colossians 3:13; 1 Peter 4:9; James 5:9)
5. **Conceit** - *excessive appreciation of one's own worth or virtue* - (2 Timothy 3:4)
6. **Coveting** - *to desire (what belongs to another) inordinately or culpably* - (Mark 7:22; Ephesians 5:5; Acts 20:33; Romans 13:9; 1 Corinthians 5:10-11; 6:1)
7. **Cowardice** - *lack of courage or firmness of purpose* - (Revelation 21:8)
8. **Deceit** - *the act of causing someone to accept as true or valid what is false or invalid* - (Mark 7:22; Acts 13:10; Romans 1:29; 1 Peter 3:10)
9. **Defrauding** - *to deprive of something by deception* - (1 Corinthians 6:7-8)
10. **Denying** - *Christ* - (Matthew 10:33; Luke 12:9; 1 John 2:22-23)
11. **Desiring** - *praise of men* - (John 12:43) (aka coveting)
12. **Envy** - *painful or resentful awareness of an advantage enjoyed by another joined with a desire to possess the same advantage*; (Mark 7:22; Galatians 5:26; Titus 3:3)
13. **Evil thoughts** - *morally reprehensible; arising from actual or imputed bad character or conduct* - (Mark 7:21; Matthew 15:19)
14. **False witnessing** - *intentionally untrue; adjusted or made so as to deceive; intended or tending to mislead* - (Matthew 15:19)
15. **Foolishness** - *having or showing a lack of good sense, judgment, or discretion; absurd, ridiculous* - (Mark 7:22; Titus 3:3)
16. **Fornication (or sexual immorality)** - *consensual sexual intercourse between two persons not married to each other* - (Mark 7:21; Matthew 15:19; 1 Corinthians 6:9; Galatians 5:19)
17. **Greed** - *a selfish and excessive desire for more of something (such as money) than is needed* - (Ephesians 4:19; 5:3; 2 Peter 2:14)
18. **Haters of God** - (Romans 1:30)
19. **Hatred** - **:** *extreme dislike or disgust* **:** *ill will or resentment that is usually mutual* **:** *prejudiced hostility or animosity* - (2 Timothy 3:3; Titus 3:3)
20. **Hypocrisy** - *a feigning to be what one is not or to believe what one does not : behavior that contradicts what one claims to believe or*

feel; especially : the false assumption of an appearance of virtue or religion - (Matthew 23:13,23, 25; 23, 27,28, 29; Mark 12:15; Luke 12:1; Romans 12:9)

21. **Impurity** - *ritually unclean; mixed or impregnated with an extraneous and usually unwanted substance; containing something unclean* - (Galatians 5:19; Ephesians 5: 3, 5)
22. **Jealousy** - *hostile toward a rival or one believed to enjoy an advantage* - (Galatians 5:20; 1 Corinthians 3:3; 2 Corinthians 12:20; James 3:16)
23. **Knowing** *to do good but not doing it* - (James 4:17)
24. **Lovers of self** – *narcissist - an extremely self-centered person who has an exaggerated sense of self-importance* - (2 Timothy 3:2)
25. **Lusting** - *usually intense or unbridled sexual desire*; after a woman - (Matthew 5:27-28; 1 Peter 4:3; Matthew 18:9)
26. **Lying** - *to make an untrue statement with intent to deceive; to create a false or misleading impression* - (Revelation 21:8, 27; 22:15; Ephesians 4:25; Romans 9:1; 2 Corinthians 11:31; Galatians 1:20; 2 Timothy 2:7)
27. **Malice** - *the intention or desire to do evil; ill will* - (Romans 1:29; Ephesians 4:31; Colossians 3:8; 5:8; Titus 3:3; 2 Peter 2:1)
28. **Murder** - *the unlawful premeditated killing of one human being by another* - (Revelation 21:8; Mark 7:21; 5:21; 10: 19; 19:18; Luke 18:20; Romans 1:29; 1 Peter 3:15; 4:15; Matthew 15:19; 1 John 3:15)
29. **Pride** - *a feeling of deep pleasure or satisfaction derived from one's own achievements, the achievements of those with whom one is closely associated, or from qualities or possessions that are widely admired* - (Mark 7:22; 1 Peter 5:5, 6; James 4:6; Matthew 23:12; Luke 14:11; 18;14)
30. **Slander** - *the action or crime of making a false spoken statement damaging to a person's reputation* - (Matthew 15:19; Mark 7:22; Ephesians 4:31; Colossians 3:8; 2 Peter 2:1; 1 Corinthians 4:13; Romans 1:30)
31. **Stealing** - (Ephesians 4:28; 13:9; Matthew 19:18; Mark 10:19; Luke 18:20; Romans 2:21; 13:9)

    a. *to take the property of another wrongfully and especially as a habitual or regular practice*

b. *to come or go secretly, unobtrusively, gradually, or unexpectedly*
c. *to take or appropriate without right or leave and with intent to keep or make use of wrongfully*
d. *to take away by force or unjust means they've* stolen *our liberty*
e. *to take surreptitiously or without permission*
f. *to appropriate to oneself or beyond one's proper share*
g. *to move, convey, or introduce secretly*
h. *to accomplish in a concealed or unobserved manner*
i. *to seize, gain, or win by trickery, skill, or daring* - stole *the election*

32. **Swindling** - *to obtain money or property by fraud or deceit* - (1 Corinthians 5:10-11; 6:10)
33. **Thievery, theft** - *the act or practice or an instance of stealing* - (1 Corinthians 6:10; Mark 7:21; John 10:1, 8; 1 Peter 4:15; Matthew 15:19)
34. **Treachery** - *betrayal of trust; deceptive action or nat***ure** - (2 Timothy 3:4)
35. **Unforgiveness** - *unwilling or unable to forgive; or* ***having or making no allowance for error or weakness*** - (Matthew 6:14-15; Mark 11:25-26)
36. **Unrighteousness** - *not righteous; wicked* - (Romans 1:18, 29; 2:8; 6:13; 1 John 1:9; 5:17; 1 Corinthians 6:9)
37. **Wickedness** - *the quality of being evil or morally wrong* - (Mark 7:22; Luke 11:39; Acts 8:22; Romans 1:29; 1 Corinthians 5:8, 13; Ephesians 6:12; 2 Thessalonians 2:10, 12; 2 Timothy 2:19)
38. **Wrong** - *not correct or true; incorrect* - (Corinthians 6:8);

....then they are on the wrong side of righteous. If you study the above list and have these words in your brain and available for consideration it is reasonable you may see one or more and sometimes many of the above sins I dare say daily and often in the demeanor and speech of most of main stream media. God is considered non-essential, His Word wrong, and the "corporate" word right. An interesting consideration of the word "corporate"; it comes from the Latin "*cor-por-ates*" which means to "form into a body." Interestingly enough the bodies formed are entities which are not living, i.e., "dead" or "corpses" or "dead bodies." Food for thought!!!

Every false witness by media is most assuredly storing up the wrath of God, and to be sure each individual individually will be called to account for your false witness.

There has appeared in recent history an alternative to "main stream media" and that being independent citizen journalists and or opinion blogs, and or satirists whom are challenging the bad faith of the main stream media. It's not easy since the money behind the big players collaborates with the governments and unelected three letter agencies to silence, cancel, shadow ban, fact check, and other dirty tricks to silence people that wish for truth, justice, and what was once the American way.

It also is reasonable proof that journalism is dead, for when was the last time you heard of a journalist of the caliber of Gary Webb. Gary Webb was betrayed by everyone having done some of the best "journalism" at the time and was made to look the fool. He most reasonably and certainly was despondent for all of the betrayal and cowardice of theoretical "associated journalists" and most certainly had reason to consider taking his life. But....in a great irony Gary Webb's death as reported by the main stream media is a proof unto itself that the "Association," or AP, who universally reported his death as a suicide with not one but two bullet holes in his head. Interestingly, not one journalist, as far as I know, asked the coroner where the two bullets lodged in his head. That might have been journalism which would have led to a second question and mayhaps a third.

I say this to make a point. The main stream media is not journalism. Journalism started its slow death the day the AP (Associated Press) became a thing in 1848. Anything now "associated" is propaganda. The internet, to the chagrin of the AP, resurrected journalism. There are now many actual gumshoe journalists and ironically two of the best also have the last name Webb. George Webb and Whitney Webb; not related! Others include Addy Adds, Paul Cottrell, Elijah Schaffer, Charlie Kirk, James O'Keefe, Andy Njo, and many others. Even comedians like Steven Crowder and Dave Landau have done more gumshoe journalism than any of the mainstream media.

Also there are alternative media outlets such as the DailyWire that are, thank God, making strides to make righteousness a thing again in media.

>>> SOCIETY WAKING-UP <<<

As I pen this paragraph it is the eve of the midterm elections in America (2022). A modicum of discernment might suggest that American society has been asleep, slumbering contently under the comforter of a brilliantly conceived slow moving "constitutional republic." However, in two short years many have thrown back the comforter because an alarm clock is waking their disengaged brains from their slumber. While they slept that which has been the foundation of our freedom has been craftily changed from a "constitutional republic" into a "democracy." When the left shouts that democracy itself is in jeopardy they are correct. Mob rule or majority rule (which is democracy) is for them in danger. It seems to me that mockery is in order, i.e., agreement with them that democracy as the left wants it to be is in danger. Why?

Because of the speed with which de facto dictatorial, mandates, executive orders, unelected bureaus, and mockingbird media pundits, have force fed absolute nonsense to the people; the people have and are continuing to wake up. While most cannot quote the Ten Commandments they most assuredly cannot articulate the "Declaration of Independence" and why that document is considered "foundational" and its importance to the very "idea" of America. Or, that it is only the first ten amendments to the Constitution that the rest of the Constitution was constructed to protect. Further that the administration of government itself by God's decree per the Bible is supposed to be a terror to those that consider violating the God given rights of man.

I hope that the tide washes some very wrong things away in this election cycle and I pray that if it does that the "right" side considers their charge with Jesus as Lord first and foremost. If so, we'll be okay. If not, and they are as they have been in the past, bad faith phony actors continuing the "bread and circus" of government then God help us all.

In any event slowly people are waking up the world over to a shadow governing board of bad faith bad actors many of whom as I pen this sentence are in Egypt, conspiring against the people of the planet without the consent of the people to shape the world into their image under the guise of climate.

A curious thing about the awakening is that God's indwelling nature was awakened in moms who showed up at school board meetings across the nation to let them know that what is being taught to their cubs requires the approval of mommy lions. It is a curious thing that should give those mothers pause that are not followers of Jesus the Redeemer why it is that they by some internal nature recognize that their babies are being attacked by another thing that is repulsive to their mom instincts. Could it be that these moms are image bearers of God and the instinct that a lioness has to keep the hyenas away from her cubs is God's order and that same order applies generally?

It is reasonable here to note that even in the animal kingdom there are rare instances when the mother abandons her offspring, but such occurrences are the exception not the rule. When such a thing is witnessed by humans there is an internal "nurture" thing that surfaces, or empathy for the orphan. We know there is not much that can be done about the mother, but great lengths to save the orphaned kitten, puppy, foal, lamb, elephant, monkey, otter or other animal it seems is an indwelling nature of man and woman. Why, dear God, why in the realm of those that are so obviously image bearers of God endowed with a "free will" would a mother and or father choose to not protect their babies with all the wrath within them and choose instead to butcher their boys to be girls and or their girls to be boys or and most sadly to abandon or worse yet abort or murder their own. Such a thing would if done to puppies and kittens would surely reign down the wrath of animal lovers and rightfully so. Why then, oh why has this become a thing for humans!? Consider the wrath that would ensue of some whack job was taking little boy puppies and cutting off their little wieners and trying to shape girl puppy parts. The outrage would be loud, animal rights activists would be at the state house, laws would be swiftly passed, and people would be in jail. Reasonably and rightfully so the wrath would be righteous. How then is this okay for humans? The obvious answer is it's not.

This could be in the "Society Asleep" section below, but fits here as people are waking up to this atrocity and fighting back as they should even when the highest office holder in the land it seems has taken on a new mantle for himself. The president of the united States is the chief administrator and at the same time is the "Commander in Chief" and it seems has now made it clear he is the "Chief Butcher" of children. If these atrocities are waking up the wrath within us, God help us when the wrath of God is released.

I as well as Christians the world over pray for an end to the harm done to the family, the children, the girls, the women, the boys, the men, and most especially the most vulnerable little image bearers of God, the conceived.

>>> SOCIETY STILL ASLEEP <<<

It seems the internet and this new thing called social media has become a force to flush out those not awake. The easiest groups whom have flagged themselves as "woke" it turns out are just shy of being in a total coma. Merriam Webster defines coma as follows:

> **coma:** *a state of profound unconsciousness caused by disease, injury, or poison.*

It seems this is most appropriate to describe what we see in this group only perhaps in the reverse order noted in the definition. In other words their minds have been poisoned, thus injured, and it seems for many are permanently diseased. The poisoning of the mind starts by:

1. not knowing "The Way"
2. not knowing basic biology
3. not knowing world history
4. not knowing American history
5. and perhaps most egregiously not knowing basic reading, writing, and arithmetic.

These basics missing have "poisoned" their minds, causing "injury," that for some will be a lifelong "disease." Most ironically the disease can be cured completely and be fast tracked to understanding by digesting the most important words ever to be penned, the Christian Bible. Through the lens of this book, "The Bible," then the other most basic categories will fall into place.

- ✓ Basic biology, chapter one of Genesis.
- ✓ All of world history and why the rise and fall of empires are contained in the 66 books of the Christian Bible. The almost two thousand years since the closed cannon of those 66 books follow the exact same blueprint as biblical history in the rise and fall of empires.
- ✓ American history and why it was for a season so very special could be likened to the biblical kingdoms that were greatly blessed, but only for a season when they lived for God.
- ✓ Reading, writing and arithmetic being directed by UNESCO, and those asleep not knowing who this anti-God entity is keeps the masses in this coma.

I am signing off for the evening. Tomorrow is November 8, 2022 which will be a curious indicator of how the awakening is going. Come Wednesday morning will there be an indication for further awakening towards a God centered righteousness, or will the "great reset" which will swing the trajectory for America towards that which is evil. Stay tuned.

Wednesday morning November 9, 2022 --- Well it seems the tug of war for left vs. right is as it has been throughout the American experience, i.e., another draw. In theory this draw creates a slower moving government and perhaps that will slow things down a tad. The red/blue map geographically appears as if there are more right thinking, law and order, keep kids safe, balance the budget, and be a kind, but America first nation. However, because the large metropolitan areas which have been indoctrinated with greater ease with the wishes of those leaders that want to change America into the vision of Klaus Schwab and George Soros it seems America will continue down a path tilted towards that which is wrong. We'll see.

In fairness to both those waking up and those still asleep there is factual easily found fraud by the government to on purpose, with what can only be construed as bad faith lying made legal. Look into the Smith-Mundt Modernization Act which gives license to the "federal" government or more rightly called the corporate US, to legally propagandize the American people through any media whatsoever.

> ***Summary of Smith-Mundt Modernization Act of 2012*** *- Amends the United States Information and Educational Exchange Act of 1948 to authorize the Secretary of State and the Broadcasting Board of Governors to provide for the preparation and dissemination of information intended for foreign audiences abroad about the United States, including about its people, its history, and the federal government's policies, through press, publications, radio, motion pictures, the Internet, and other information media, including social media, and through information centers and instructors. (Under current law such authority is restricted to information disseminated abroad, with a limited domestic exception.)*
>
> *Authorizes the Secretary and the Board to make available in the United States motion pictures, films, video, audio, and other materials prepared for dissemination abroad or disseminated abroad pursuant to such Act, the United States International Broadcasting Act of 1994, the Radio Broadcasting to Cuba Act, or the Television Broadcasting to Cuba Act.*
>
> *Amends the Foreign Relations Authorization Act, Fiscal Years 1986 and 1987 to prohibit funds for the Department of State or the Board from being used to influence public opinion or propagandizing in the United States. (Under current law such provision applies to the United States Information Agency [USIA].)*
>
> *Applies such prohibition only to programs carried out pursuant to the United States Information and Educational Exchange Act of 1948, the United States International Broadcasting Act of 1994, the Radio Broadcasting to Cuba Act, and the Television Broadcasting to Cuba Act.*
>
> *States that such provision* ***shall:*** *(1)* ***not prohibit*** *the Department or the Board from providing information about its operations, policies,*

> *programs, or program material, or making such information available to members of the media, public, or Congress; (2)* ***not be construed to prohibit*** *the Department from engaging in any medium of information on a presumption that a U.S. domestic audience may be exposed to program material; and (3)apply only to the Department and the Board and to no other federal department or agency.*

In a nut shell the Smith-Mundt Act of 1948, which made it okay to propagandize foreign nations and made it illegal to lie or propagandize the American people was "modernized" to make it legal to lie to the American people through all available media. Notice the underlined (3) item above seems to restrict the lying to the "Secretary of State" and the "Broadcasting Board of Governors" if that's not bad enough, it does not preclude any and all other government bodies from propagandizing and lying. Another way of describing the "Act" is a slick way of legalizing "project mockingbird," or in other words, legalizing lying and bearing false witness.

One analysis of the "Ten Commandments" states that the greatest injury to commerce and law is the sin of bearing false witness. How is it that a nation that thinks it is "One Nation Under God" has law makers create a law of any kind that states in writing in any way, de jure or de facto, that false witness is the law of the land for the "free and the brave." It is embarrassing and most certainly an abomination to the Lord God Almighty, His Son Jesus the Christ, and the Holy Spirit of God. It is no wonder we are a nation in judgment and falling from grace.

If you have two brain cells to rub together to produce a discerning thought then you will know with certainty sure that there are the lying liars (media) telling lies on behalf of the many liars in 2023 U.S. Corp. and at the behest of various "hidden hand liars." When you see it, it just may help the scales of bread and circus fall from your eyes.

~ PRAYER FOR THE LIARS ~

Thy kingdom come, Thy will be done, on earth......
In heaven there are choirs,
In the associated press there are liars,
And with the devil they do conspire.

Journalists fired mockingbirds and parrots hired.

Without knowledge or caring, the truth set aside
They spew the same song, with arrogant pride.
Info babes and info dudes, do not journalists make,
With no research or account, what you are is so fake.

To declare what you say is the news and the truth,
Is a ticket to hell, if it's put out without proof.
I pray that this poem hits you square in the mirror,
Take a look at yourself, and question your soul.

If what comes out of your mouth is not true it's a lie,
You've got to better, and you've got to know why,
The first line of this poem infers a place in the sky,
The kingdom and will are made for right and not wrong,

You want it you know it, so you have to be strong.
Bend your knee, bow your head, ask to know Jesus the Son,
If you're contrite as you see that to lie is a sin,
The only way out is the truth, now the journey begins,

Pray, and pray often and always, and you will be set free.
Christ will show the Way, His Spirit the key.
He will lead you home, a place hard to see,
But the reward --- to be on earth as in heaven and free.

Amen
JKF 9-9-2022

>>> THE STATE OF THE CHRISTIAN CHURCH <<<

Christian churches no matter what denomination understand and embrace love, even of enemies of God. So if churches are judged in "love" Christian churches might seem cohesive and most similar. However, if churches are judged considering both "love" and "wrath" the field of biblical churches narrows substantially. If your church does not preach the "wrath of God" and remind the sinner, which means everyone, that the wrath of God is as important to comprehend as His love.

While the scriptures say God is slow to anger, and His wrath is stored up, it is very clear His wrath will be poured out on unrepentant sinners who continue to live in sin denying Jesus as Lord and Redeemer. If you are not in a church that preaches the wrath of God, you are being robbed of His word. The great commission cannot reasonably be properly preached to non-church people without the warning of the lake of fire and God's wrath that will send you there and how the "Good News" will ensure that you avoid that fate.

Those churches not preaching the entire gospel move themselves into the category of false church. As noted in Chapter 6, if it is not in Lake Christos, or what is in Lake Christos, is not preached, discernment should make clear you may be in a false church being led by a false prophet, teacher/rabbi, pastor, or priest as noted in the scriptures as wolves in sheep clothing. Beware!

It is important to recognize your sin and repent as sin crosses your path in your sanctification life (and it will), but also as you see a brother or sister floundering it may be he or she has been robbed of the entire gospel. Be truthful in love and or point out that which they may be missing. It would be unloving not too. As the apostles said often we are to preach Christ crucified and be bold in that proclamation that it was God's wrath poured out on His Son for us.

~ SUMMARY OF WRATH ~

Family, children, women, men, and the various social categories discussed above stir up wrath in me. The cops I met, my old patriot friends, friends from church, coffee shop discussions, media, almost every hour of every day the breakdown of truth is discussed and has the masses in one way or another feeling versions of simmering to boiling over wrath. It is very reasonable that if we feel it and it is being stored up in our belly, it certainly is rational to understand why the scriptures say the wrath of God is being stored up.

Other bullet pointed sins of this nation that are clear sins against God are:

>>> IDOLATRY <<<

Especially of self, and those that teach the children to have self-esteem and that they are okay as they are. They in fact are not. To tell them they are is false witness. The sin of idolatry especially of self is easily the most committed sin and the one from which all other sins flow. To decide for self that you can be something different or you can decide on behalf of others that they should be something different than what is obvious, and you claim any kind of authority to make such a claim you are very guilty of the sin of idolatry. The idolatry of "look at me," "look how cute I am," and the modern technologies that groom such idolatry into young girls and to lesser extent boys, makes social platform creators akin to Aaron in the Bible fashioning the golden calf. It is most reasonable that creators of such platforms intent at some level I'm sure were and is to honestly connect humanity with humanity. The question is what intent # 1 was. If one had to guess the number one "intent" was "not" to glorify God. It is more reasonable it was the love of money, if we're honest. However, if it weren't for YouTube, I might not be saved, or at least the call of God would have been in some other way. There is good and evil in everything. While the various forms of media are and can be a tremendous blessing, like the perversions of sex itself, at the same time Satan it seems temps and greatly so.

> **voyeur:** *a person who gains sexual pleasure from watching others when they are naked or engaged in sexual activity*

To be a voyeur, is it idolatry? Yes and a most egregious one at that. If at the fall it was God Himself whom in essence told Adam and Eve to cover themselves when He fashioned skins from an animal, was it not a command or training by a Father and fact "Thee Father" to be humble? Is that why we generally don't walk around naked even if front of our spouses? Is that why we seem to know intuitively that to be naked is to be a private affair and certainly the intuitive knowledge that naked intimacy is to be shared with a spouse. Designed by God, sexual desire leading to sex culminating into such a short lived, but incredibly intense climactic thing. Since it is, is it not reasonable to discern it is at the top of the list if not the #1 idol of man?

The "natural and proper" reason for its power can be discerned by noting that there are 8 billion people in the world the greater percentage of which are within the confines of the God ordained marriage between a man and a woman.

The "unnatural and improper" acknowledgment of its power can likewise be discerned by noting that there are 8 billion people in the world a smaller percentage of which are from unions not ordained in a God ordained union. The "unnatural and improper" acknowledgment of its power is the fornicator, the adulterer, and the voyeur. When Jesus said to the crowd after He wrote in the dirt, NKJV--- John 8:7 -- ***"He who is without sin among you, let him throw a stone at her first."*** The context of this lesson by Jesus was the sin relating to sex for that short lived climatic thing. Who reading this can claim to be innocent of fornication, adultery, and voyeurism? Surely it seems the woman was guilty, but who caught her, was it the husband or a voyeur?

- ✓ Fornication – hookup apps not long ago were in the classified sections of newspapers and magazines are now front and center of many sinners on their cellphones, and sadly in front of the children.
- ✓ Adultery – Once maybe only found in the workplace, bars, and nightclubs is now also available on websites and apps and a click away.
- ✓ Voyeurism – Not long ago only in magazines, then moving to the big screens, and now available to children a click or two away too many porn sites. This sin of voyeurism has made "porn" perhaps the biggest, most addictive idol of all.

Those that use platforms to worship themselves or make an idol of any of the above commit the sin of idolatry.

Another pretty awful and Godless idolatry is the self-idolatry of a co-opted new definition of gender, and downstream of that foolishness of the self-identity of the pronoun idol. While there are levels of learned "anything" one does not have to have a piece of paper to be and expert in basic biology. For instance, as you go through your day today and you see boys and girls, congratulations you are a biologist, and I dare say for this fundamental categorical observation you are an expert biologist and you have properly identified in the controlled environment and laboratory of reality the only two genders ironically you can find in the first chapter of the first biology book ever put to typeset.

Yet another extremely dangerous and evil idolatry is the idol of the authority. From the time of the first appeal to authority by Satan to Eve, women and men are easily deceived to think that because someone has achieved an acknowledgment of purported "higher" learning granted to him or her by a system, that it means we should consider them an authority. The fallacy of this seldom gets our attention, but recently there was a claim to the "self" and I do mean "self-claimed" idol of authority that before the spring of 2020, 99% of America and the world had never heard of this supposed authority. Foisted into our minds by media with a claim of super human abilities to know about things very small, this man claimed that if anyone were to question him they were, in his self-perceived throne of king idol, questioning science itself. Wow! That statement woke some up and others not at all. For a person to suggest that he is science itself is idolatry on steroids. This man should be an example for girls especially who use TikTok to hoist themselves up to be idolized, and most particularly this new authority concerning gender and pronouns. Most assuredly a very slippery slope to perdition!

A measure of stored wrath! Reasonably so!

>>> FALSE GODS <<<

God's glory is in everything we enjoy with our senses; it is written on our hearts as well as very conveniently written down for us. So, no matter how one may wish it were not so or claim "their god" wouldn't do this or "their god" wouldn't do that, or as the neo-atheist use the most foolish of claims that "their belief" is that they lack a belief, which "is" a belief. All very obtuse! The scriptures say all are without excuse. God tells us he is a jealous God which is very reasonable since all that there is He made for us as His image bearers. That some don't see it would most reasonably be just one of the many sins that disrespect His glory and stores up a measure of wrath.

>>> THE LORDS NAME <<<

Living Water Ministries and Ray Comfort specifically does, in my estimation, the best possible job of convicting the heart of men and women about the most popular cuss word in the world. He asks if they would use their mother's name as a cuss word. The answer is a resounding, "Of course not." Why, Ray asks? There is a bond between mother and baby that starts at birth, but it's curious when Ray asks the question why, there is usually a hesitation, for while we know we would never consider using our mom's name as a cuss word, it has never come up or considered, ever. The answer of course is the God created bond between mother and baby, the evidence of which is everywhere, even in the beasts. We are commanded to "honor" our mother, but this one specific honor we give to her seems to be embedded in our DNA so to speak. Ray asks why the name of God and or Jesus Christ, whom gifted us all with our mothers, we it seems "all" are guilty without the honor so obviously due, use God's name in the place of other cuss words to express disgust. Why is cussing at all in our nature? If we stop just a moment and think on that and if we have ever uttered the words, "Our Father, who art in heaven, "hallowed" be thy name….." we should immediately beg for forgiveness. Personally, in a most cavalier manner, I like most of the world, for what will be the larger percentage of my life, was guilty of this lawlessness. Hollywood in its totality and any actor and or comedians that have used God's name in a disrespectful, blasphemous, or vain, manner is in grave danger. This isn't just a faux pas, it truly is egregiously blasphemous. Yet another and pretty awful sin that reasonably stores up a measure of wrath.

>>> SABBATH <<<

The Sabbath, a day of rest or a day of worship? Or, both? Or, is it possible to work, rest, and worship each and all days? The fourth commandment says to "remember" the Sabbath and keep it holy. What was the Sabbath? It was the day after God completed his creation and rested. Remembering, what does that mean? Keep it holy, what does that mean? Rest, what does that mean? Today is a Friday as I type these words and I am looking out a window in a coffee shop and I contemplate that there are eight categories of stuff.

1. The first category includes cars, structures, sidewalks, patio tables, parking lots, a roadway, light fixtures, a plane in flight; and electric transmission lines in the distance. But for the discovery of Gods order, in this case, philosophy, mathematics, chemistry and physics none of those things would be there.
2. The second category of stuff includes a beautiful blue sky with wispy high altitude clouds; several palm trees, palo verde trees, various bushes, and a bird on a table. None of these things had anything to do with the mind of man, nor chance. They were created by God for His glory and our enjoyment.
3. The third category of stuff I cannot see, but know to be there. The solar winds that carry the ultra violet radiation I recognize as light from the sun; the electromagnetism that churns away deep in the core of the earth that makes for the compass needle to point north; the static in the atmosphere; the atmosphere itself; the humidity in the air; the high altitude wind moving the clouds I see; and the moonlight in a subservient dance with the suns light, but making its way nevertheless through the atmosphere; the stars, solar system, galaxies, and all of the matter in the universe along with the forces that make them dance in a cosmic waltz all beyond the blue sky I can see. All of these unseen things necessary for any and all life and if any one of which didn't exist or was out of its finely tuned position, mankind would not exist.
4. The fourth category of stuff is also invisible and are God created energies that have been harnessed and include: jet propulsion energy coupled with wing design copied from the bird to lift that plane; the electricity flowing in the distance through those electric lines; the electricity that is being held back from lighting up the parking lot light fixture because a photo cell keeps the electricity at bay; the 2,3,4, and 5G energy bouncing around everywhere that in the last hour allowed me to view a video of my granddaughter singing a song on my cellphone as well as call a friend in Colorado; the Wi-Fi technology that lets me on this computer connect to the world wide web; the sound I hear from the speakers in this coffee shop, and the odor of coffee beans.
5. The fifth category of stuff are things I cannot see, but know to be there. People in the plane, people in the adjacent buildings, people in the cars, and all of the biological and chemical process keeping

them going. Other birds I cannot see and the bugs, worms, and seeds that sustain them, the process of photosynthesis that keeps the plants ever growing, and all of the similar, but different cells that sustain all of that life.

6. The sixth category of stuff I cannot see, but know to be there are concepts and ideas only possible in the mind of man and the bio chemical mechanisms that allow those intangible things to manifest at all. An idea, a concept, or the idea of a concept is something a beast cannot do, only man. The ability to think, thinking, philosophy, math, love, hate, beauty, ugly, etc. all somehow floating around my brain and the brains of every human on earth. At any one time, of the 8 billion people on earth, approximately 4 billion brains are in the most unusual state of dreaming. This category of stuff should give us the greatest pause. It cannot be seen, but it's everywhere.
7. The seventh category of stuff relates to the senses, as I look out the window 120 million cells, 6 to 7 million of which are specialized to allow me to see the beautiful colors, and that's just one eye; the noise I hear but for the intricately designed ear would be for not; the voice box that forms sound designed to make sound that man controls so I can enjoy the song I hear; the taste buds that make this latte register in my brain as delicious; the thermostatic sensor cells in my skin that allowed me to precisely adjust the water in the shower this morning for optimum comfort; the touch and dexterity I feel through my fingers as I type each and every letter in this transcription; the smell of the coffee beans, my own after shave if I think on it, and even the memory of the smell of lilac flowers if I just think on that.
8. The eighth categories of stuff are emotions. I cannot see them, but boy are they out there. Joy, anticipation, fear, surprise, sadness, disgust, anger, trust, hurt, love, hate. The emotions we feel somehow downstream of our conscience and our senses interestingly enough can sometimes be seen and sometimes not. All of the 8 billion people emanating some sort of a frequency of energy relating directly to the emotions they feel. All of those emotions, in some sort of energy or unique force, all right out this window!

I know with reasonable certainty that all of the people around me, all of the people in that plane, and reasonably 99% plus of all people for all of time past, present, and future have taken and will take all of what I just wrote down for granted.

I know that everything I just wrote I took for granted until I looked out the window and thought to contemplate what was out there. I'm sure I left something out, but my God, forgive me for not "remembering" that all that is, is in fact, a manifestation of You and Your will! And all of it is being held together by forces we still do not understand even with all we do know. All of it, every last "bit" has been gifted to us by Your grace.

I suppose the law, as was noted by the apostle Paul, is in fact a schoolmaster. To be clear the Ten Commandments were intended to be the master law, and they still are. However, Jesus while He mentioned all of the commandments while he walked the earth, He admonished the Jewish leaders for what the Sabbath was not. "Remembering," yes!! "Resting," yes!! "Set aside," yes!! Keep it particularly special above all other days, or "holy," yes. To not save a life or heal the sick, no. To not raise a hand to do anything whatsoever, no!! What then?

What did Jesus leave us with? When He said that the greatest commandment was "Love the Lord your God with all your heart, with all your soul, and with all your mind," is it not reasonable that this commandment cannot be executed without "remembering" always. Further, Jesus said He was the fulfillment of the law, and that includes "remembering" the Sabbath. Should we not therefore consider why Jesus said that the greatest commandment is to "Love the Lord your God with all your heart, with all your soul, and with all your mind."

How can we not look out any window or view anything, or hear anything, or touch anything, or smell anything, or taste anything and not "Love the Lord God with all that we are; heart, soul, and mind." To "remember" the Sabbath or the day when God rested after he created all that I just saw out the window might just reasonably be why Jesus worded the greatest commandment as He did. Further, Jesus stated this commandment before the Cross and before He defeated death. If the greatest commandment clarified the law before the Cross resurrection and ascension, how much more should we "remember," "rest," and "set aside" a day to gather to worship the Creator after those events.

Resting on that day we set aside. What is that? What should that look like? I confess being new to every single consideration of God, I once again will lean into "general revelation" in the world available to me today as it pertains to resting on the set aside day and weigh in as an old man thinking for the first time.

First of all, it is known to me that this particular has been bandied about; philosophically discussed; mathematically analyzed and in all of those considerations a constant to the discussions seems to be the cycle of the sun, moon, and stars. All of those thought processes have brought forth the calendar. The stumbling stone for consideration of the "Sabbath" or the set aside day all seems to get its fervor from the calendar. So I'll start there.

- First known calendar - Sumerian 3100BC, based on the day/sun cycle, the moon/season cycle and most reasonably the seven day creation cycle. Why a seven day week in the earliest calendar(s). The earliest or Sumerian calendar created in the region of Sumner which was within earshot of the tower of Babel, which was a mere 100 years after Noah, and the dispersion of the peoples all of whom would have known about two things, the flood and creation week. If this were not so 7 days would make no sense.
- The names of the days of the week have been settled to be as they are and were codified, so to speak, by Constantine in 301AD. It was he that also decreed Sunday as the first day of the week. He might have decreed Wednesday as the first day. What then? All that it would mean is that I would be writing these thoughts about Tuesday and Wednesday and why all the hub bub.
- God called the seven day week: day 1, day 2, day 3, day 4, day 5, day 6, and day 7.
- God left much for man to discover, however, it is clear we cannot nor will we be able to pin point or figure out where Constantine's weekday naming convention lines up with God's day 1. Keeping time, i.e., calendars would be one of those things that would take man awhile to figure out, but with no pre-flood records available

to pin point the actual day one, it is not likely to ever be known this side of the day of the Lord.

- God's providence allowed Adam to name the animals. God's providence allowed Moses to give us a history lesson as well as codify His intent for our behavior. God's same providence allowed Constantine to codify the names of the week which by that time in history Germanic, old English, Latin, and other European cultures had contributed to the naming conventions of the weekdays relating to the sun, moon, and some of the planets known at that time. God's providence allowed many men and women to make sense out of this place by using names to categorize stuff. The names of the days of the week then are no different.
- Which day to rest then? Jesus said He is the rest. Rest in Him. When? Just day 7? It seems His message was, "Look to Me," whenever you need it and rest in Him. This makes a lot of sense, but only if He is worthy of consideration as a thing to rest in. For all that was attested, and all that Christ did when He walked the earth including the miracle healings, feeding of thousands, the raising of Lazarus, and especially the crucifixion, resurrection, and ascension great pause is most assuredly warranted. If pause is warranted, resting a bit is certainly warranted. When Christians feel the normal stresses of life, prayers are said; conversations with a fellow saint comfort; gathering any day of the week for singing, worship, prayer and study are new to me, but awesome; and however it happened that the day we know as Sunday turned out to be an excellent day to gather with even more saints, well, all the better.
- Since it was a Roman emperor that codified the names of the weeks after the Heavenly bodies or planets, rather than day 1, day 2, etc., and Sunday by his decree became day 1 and Saturday became day 7, and the nature of man to be a bit dogmatic in opinions, it is most logical that the Jews would hitch there wagon to Saturday as the "resting day" pursuant to the Mosaic tradition. It is also logical that Christians would hitch their wagon to Sunday as the "resting day" in honor and in consideration that the Jewish Messiah defeated death on the third day and that Jewish Messiah, Jesus, said to "rest" in Him.

- Romans 14:5 says one person esteems one day above another; another esteems every day alike. Let each be fully convinced in his own mind. Romans 14, if I discern correctly lays bare that we mortals have minds of our own and tend to create stumbling stones for ourselves and then becoming a bit too self-righteous we tend to put those stumbling stones at everybody else's feet.
- Because of various advancements in technology, all providential, as well as the Good Book certain men and woman desire a relationship with their Creator. That Creator came to us in the flesh so we could get closer. Think on this – if there were no automobile, there would be no mega-churches and for that matter the biggest gathering would be in people's homes or church houses that would be constrained by how far someone could walk. Thank God for the auto, for we can now join with more saints.
- Further, and most reasonably, God knew we would stumble on all of the sins: self-righteousness, legalism, lust, greed of money, etc., therefore as Jesus stated, "The Sabbath was made for man….." which makes the day a "gift" just like every breath we take. So, to set aside one day to rest is a very reasonable reminder for us to slow down. Yes slow down. Stop! Stop being self-righteous, stop being legalistic, stop being lustful, stop with greed of money, stop! Stop for the love of God stop for just a minute. For all of the material things we gather in our sojourn or to be clear, our temporary stay on God's earth, we cannot take it with us after death. When considered in this manner just a little bit, God help us, the greatest commandment as spoken by the Son of God convicts us all.

Gathering then became legalistic, and to be sure is still legalistic in most religions, for the "not commanded" restrictions invented by man. Gathering with the saints as ordained by the apostles who were instructed by the Son of God Himself, is certainly very reasonable to keep us in His Word, worship Him, and sharpen our faith. Is it a sin then not to "remember" always? It seems the greatest commandment should be the greatest schoolmaster least we forget and fall away, which we know happens. For how easy was it for me to take for granted everything I just took the time to consider? Is it therefore reasonable that this sin also stores up a measure of wrath? How can it not?

Postscript 1 – when I first penned this two days ago I only had 4 groups of stuff, yesterday I added the 5th and 6th categories of stuff, and today Sunday I woke up thinking about the 7th category of stuff. Just think of all of the acquired knowledge of mankind that I left out. It makes me feel an understanding why men sometimes fall prostrate on their faces to worship God and why we do not deserve to see the face of God. Also, two days ago I called that friend in Colorado for his feedback on categories 1 thru 4. He and his wife liked it, but wondered if there was a better word for "stuff." I couldn't think of one so I looked up the definition. Stuff defined: matter, material, articles, or activities of a specified or indeterminate kind that are being referred to, indicated, or implied. I add this definition for a bit of comedic relief as while I agree with them that "stuff" sounds like slang and a bit juvenile, after I read the definition I have changed my mind and therefore left it in. Further, 50 years ago my friend was the quarterback and my boss, well, not today my friend!!

Postscript 2 – Sunday night (11-13-2022) my church, Desert Hills Bible, held a seasonal communion service in which people came to a microphone to share why in the past year they were thankful to God. I didn't share anything, but as I listened to others it struck me that I am thankful that I found this church and have been able to grow in understanding and discernment. The thought crossed my mind that perhaps and most certainly reasonable that Pastor Robb Brunansky and the many saints that I have the pleasure to hob-nob with were part and parcel to why now at this time in my journey I saw what I saw out the window.

Postscript 3 – The eighth category worthy of note popped into my head 12-2-2022.

>>> HONOR FATHER & MOTHER <<<

Why honor your father and mother? Why is it that my granddaughters, 2 and 4 throw their little arms around mommy and daddy's neck? Why is it that they love Poppy and Gigi, Grandma and Grandpa? Why is it they have no shame about being naked? Why is it that at a certain point they will feel something, reasonably recognition of their nakedness, or shame, and then desire privacy? Why is it that parents instinctively know it doesn't matter that infants see their nakedness, but it very soon becomes inappropriate?

Why is it instinctual for a parent or grandparent to start the training of little ones to not barge in when they are in the bathroom? Why at a certain point the thought of ones parents' being naked is so gross? Why when children grow up and forever more the thought of the parents having sex is reprehensible? Why did God kill the first animals for their skins to cloth Adam and Eve? Is it because with the fall came shame, and then training by the Lord how to overcome shame and introduce a way to express humility?

Considering the above it seems part of honor is instinctual; child to parent and parent to child; and part is learned. In stable and even not so stable homes children love their parents with some kind of instinctual honor or want or wish that their relationships would be good. When raised in the ways of the Lord when led by the father and supported by the mother great honor both ways is observed. When a departure from the God ordained mother and father loving relationship happens, and downstream of that, God ordained mother, father, son, daughter relationships fall away from the biblical family, well what happens is what in 2023 is awful and sadly normal. Disrespectful, narcissistic, bullying, promiscuous, slutty, arrogant, self-indulgent, sadly might describe most teenagers before they are 15.

Why is it that at 67 I still remember the father to son talks in which life instruction was given and I knew to be right and desired to and did honor him for that training? Why did I not want to disappoint my Dad? Why are all of my memories of my dad fond? Why do I still think on my father as one of the smartest men I knew even though I know now I was not raised in the ways of the Lord? Why do I love him and miss him and wish I could talk to him? Why when I think on my mom do I wish I could hear her giggle again? Why does it bring a tear to my eye when I reflect on the fact I know I was not a good son and I cannot fix it? Why did my Dad's steak-fests become a legend around that 14 foot picnic table and rock fireplace in the mountains of Colorado and the marinade my mom made still remembered so fondly by anyone privileged to have partaken. Why will I always cherish the summer when I was 17 when me and my dad lived on a sailboat for the summer in Casper, Wyoming while I worked for him for my first summer job. Why is it that my family and most others always enjoy Thanksgiving? Why did my baby girl as a toddler grab hold of me and say, "My daddy!" Why was my daughter filled with a certain emotion of honor for me on her wedding day? The other day I asked my daughter why she loved me, to which she responded, "Cuz your my dad." Why does my daughter honor and love me beyond measure even though she knows of my sin and sins.

Why is it that in the TV series "Blue Bloods" and for 12 years and counting, the family dinner scene is far and away the favorite part of every episode, and that the father figures are very much respected as the "head of the family."

Why is it that when boys and girls realize they have sexual desires they don't want to talk about it with their parents and vice versa? Why is this stumbling stone not comprehended for perhaps the biggest departure for the honoring of father and mother? Why do daughters hide especially from their fathers the sin of fornication? Why do sons hide the sin of fornication especially from their mothers? Why do mothers and fathers not want to think on it, much less talk about it? Why would it be the greatest of achievements and the proudest of moments for a father to know that as he walked his daughter down the aisle that she was wearing that white dress for what it is supposed to signify? Why when dad knows the white dress is a lie does he still love his daughter always and without condition? Why is there never a discussion about the virtue of the groom?

If we obeyed the greatest commandment there would never be a baby without a mother and a father in a God ordained marriage. If we understood the second greatest commandment a boy would love a girlfriend's father and mother per that commandment to love your neighbors as yourself and honor them first, then the honor due the girl would have the respect it necessarily deserves and requires. If we understood the second greatest commandment a girl would love a boyfriend's father and mother per the command to love your neighbor as yourself and honor them first, then the honor due the boy would have the respect it necessarily deserves and requires.

The points raised above are not contemplated much or at all as we fumble through our lives, nevertheless the answers with a bit of scrutiny are downstream of recognizing that God created all, then God created the first image bearer of Himself in Adam, whom was alone which God said was not good, so having it seems already created the biological foundations of male and female in the beasts, God created woman. Had God created for Adam another man for companionship, there would be no reason for the command to honor father and mother (reductive reasoning, ha ha), and wouldn't the world be boring for there would still be only two men and I wouldn't be writing this and you wouldn't be reading it. Humph! It seems I just made a philosophical and I dare say brilliant observation. Deep, deep thought!!!

Lessons had to be learned after the fall which continues till this day which we still cannot seem to get right. Marriage for instance! If we were to "cleave" as one flesh as intended and commanded perhaps the command to honor mother and father would not have been necessary for the children would never see strife in their parents, but for the fall! In any event the above thoughts seem to have a connection to why honoring of father and mother was commanded. It also seems so very obvious that the dishonor afforded to fathers and mothers in 2023 is certainly one reason there are so many broken families, broken men, broken women, and broken children. Downstream of that broken foundation are broken communities, societies, schools, governments, and most of all broken bankers.

Those that have fathers like mine, even though he was not perfect, understand what it is to feel fond of and honor him. Those that have mothers like I did, even though she was not perfect, understand what it is to feel fond of and honor her. Those that have surrogate parent(s) that stood the post and loved you also understand what it is to feel fond of and honor them. That type of fondness and honor is downstream of an innate love. Consider that we all can certainly get our heads around loving our natural or surrogate fathers and mothers intuitively. Even in the wickedness of this world there is a bond or "honor" both ways that is worthy of our consideration, and having so considered, why then was a commandment necessary? The answer is the same now as it was before Moses, from that time until Christ, up to and including now. Answer: we are sinners in a fallen world. How much more should we love the Father in Heaven that gave to us the blessing of parents whom we know love us and for whom we love without condition. More than we realize I think this one must store up much wrath.

Thank You Lord God, who sent His Son Jesus to remind us and instruct us why it is that the greatest commandment is to love God with all that we are. Forgive me for so long not to have considered or acknowledged the greatest school master. Amen

Postscript 1 – For some reason I just recalled a time when I was a senior in high school, and for a time there was a strain, a force, an uncomfortable silence between me and my Dad. It just hit me why. Shame! I was hiding the sin of fleshly lust from my dad. That sin was keeping me from studying and training as I should for both football and wrestling. He wasn't brought up in the ways of the Lord so I wasn't either. I know he knew, but he didn't know how to lead me. Looking back my sin was not honoring my Dad. Had I, per his wishes, I would have studied, trained harder, and most certainly not lived in the flesh. My dad loved me and I loved him greatly even through the silence. There was no doubt about that, but my sin of not honoring him created a valley of shame, sadness, and now regret. My dad past away in 1992 and I cannot make amends. Is it worthy of note that, 1) I haven't thought about this for years; 2) the thought came back to life while thinking on and writing about this commandment; 3) it was on the other side of repentance that the epiphany that it was my sin and my sin alone that made for those dark times.

Postscript 2 – After a couple of years and when I went off to college things improved greatly with my Dad. I got married, moved away to Phoenix and talked with him often. Since I followed his footsteps into construction management our conversations would often be me seeking his advice. In 1991 I was visiting my folks in Colorado. It had been weighing heavily on my mind for quite some time that I had never told my dad that I loved him nor had he told me. My dad was from the greatest generation and as has been recounted to me by many people, WW2 vets were known for not saying those words. My folks lived about 70 miles north of Denver and on the day I was to leave, mom and dad gave me a ride. I'll never forget this. The entire trip my stomach was in knots for I was determined to say the words, "I love you," to my dad. Imagine if you will, this had been bothering me for some time because I had a 4 year old daughter at that time whom I said the words, "I love you" as a matter of ritual a dozen times a night when tucking her in bed.

I knew instinctively it was important. Anyway, I was determined to break the curse that day. I couldn't find the courage for the 1½ hour trip to the airport, so when we pulled up to the curb at Stapleton International Airport my stomach, my throat, my entire being was a wreck. We got out of the pickup truck, put my bags on the sidewalk, I hugged my mom and told her "I love you" which she responded in kind. Then I turned to my dad, stuck my hand out to shake it, looked into his face, my guts burning, and I shook his hand without saying a word. What a coward! I watched them drive away walked into the terminal and uncontrollably wept. The good news is I loved my dad and I know he loved me and there was much love in that handshake. The bad news is so very sad. For you see my dad was to have heart surgery the next spring and never wake up. I would never again shake his hand nor would I have another opportunity to correct this cowardly lack of honor I might have bestowed to my father. There is a lesson here and I know you know what it is!

Postscript 3 – 25 years ago in 1997 my girlfriend at the time and now my second wife's father was dying of cancer. He was at home with in-home hospice care. My wife has 5 other siblings, there are 4 girls including my wife and 2 boys. Her mother had called a family meeting to honor their dad. What happened turned out to be a meeting in the kitchen that turned into a complaining session about things in the family estate which had not been attended to. Dad had perhaps dropped the ball and left certain things unresolved. Her oldest brother seemed particularly upset. I wasn't a part of the family at the time so I listened for a while and asked if I might say something. My wife's mother gave me permission. I recounted the story about my failure to tell my dad that I loved him that day at the airport and how I never got the chance. I then noted that anything left unattended is going to necessarily require that someone else handle it, but not today. I suggested that they go into the other room and tell their dad that they love him, for nothing could be more important that day. The meeting immediately adjourned and my wife and all of her siblings went into the bedroom stood around the bed of their dad and each in turn said "I love you." I will always remember that my wife's mom thanked me. I also will never forget the lesson! A few days later he passed away.

>>> MURDER <<<

Thou shall not murder! Why? Thank God that generally and statistically this is not the normal state of the mind of man. How sad that a category of research is required to deal with murder, and on the other hand thank God that the mind of man can gather info about the depravity that drives an image bearer of God with malicious intent that would take the life of another. Murder for all of time happens for the same reasons, i.e., "greed," "lust" or the pursuit of "power" or phrased another way – lust, love, loathing or loot. It is these categories that detectives consider as they narrow down the search for a murderer.

Why is it that of all of God's commandments this one mankind even in the secular world knows to be wrong? It is intuitive, and for defined specificity intuitive means:

> **intuitive:** *using or based on what one feels to be true even without conscious reasoning; instinctive.*

Even psychopaths and sociopaths do not "generally" murder, and when they do they have the "intuitive" nature to hide it. Thank God that the predominant normal is to not murder.

This particular sin, however, does in fact captivate the mind in that we seem to be entertained greatly by its existence. From the pen of Shakespeare, Arthur Conan Doyle, Angela Lansbury, Tom Clancy, Robert Ludlum, James Patterson, John Grisham, and hundreds of other authors and the thousands of murder mystery books, to the many categories of murder mystery on big screen and television it seems murder very much attracts the human mind like moths to a porch light. It isn't hard to confess I too am attracted to these mysteries whether they are fictional or real.

Mob stories like the Godfather, A Bronx Tale, Goodfellas, The Irishman, and American Gangster are both fictional and real and are very much true in the portrayal of murder, the conspiracy to commit murder, and the cover-up and direct ties to government players.

The mini-series "Narcos" about Pablo Escobar; "Narcos–Mexico" about the Guadalajaran cartel; and "El Chapo" follow real life drug trafficking from my time as a high school student in the early 1970's right up until 2016. Although the next cinematic sequel has not yet been written, (as far as I know), for the kingpin that will take the place of El Chapo, and reasonably already has, and is in place and is conspiring with three letter US Corp entities to market drugs to the American people. US Corp presidents, in varying degrees are read into the program depending on their respective inclinations to graft. Some less, some more, but all certainly know that the programs to bring contraband into the American market do "in fact" exist. The fact that fentanyl, cocaine, and other drugs still pour into America, with just a small measure of discernment, is proof that graft downstream of greed for a slice of the billions to be made is why the highest office in the land opened the southern border. What does the drug trade have to do with murder, you ask? It always does.

Those that are charged to be righteous, such as every single human being in a government capacity whatsoever cannot claim a defense for wrong doing if they do not have clean hands.

> **Clean Hands Doctrine:** *The clean-hands doctrine is the principle that a party's own inequitable misconduct precludes recovery based on equitable claims or defenses. The doctrine requires that a party act fairly in the matter for which they seek a remedy. A party who has violated an equitable principle, such as good faith, is described as having "unclean hands." The clean-hands doctrine is invoked when a party seeking equitable relief or claiming a defense based in equity has themselves violated a duty of good faith or has acted unconscionably in connection with the same subject matter out of which they claim a right to relief. The doctrine of unclean hands does not deny relief to a party guilty of any past misconduct; only misconduct directly related to the matter in which he seeks relief triggers the defense.*

This doctrine is well thought out in its construction to consider a matter in man's court. But, and this is a question, if those members of government, open the southern border knowing full well that drugs will flow in, children will be trafficked for sex and exploitation of any kind whatsoever, and murder will occur for a multitude of reasons, will those parties be able to stand before God and claim clean hands? And another question, will plausible deniability be a thing when standing before God? Just a thought!

Movies like "Kill the Messenger," "American Made," and "JFK" also fascinating and entertaining and torn from the headlines and except for poetic license for dramatic effect are factual.

TV shows like "Law & Order" and its various spin offs have been popular for 30 plus years because of both the fascination with murder, but also the innate wish that good hopefully triumphs over evil. Blue Bloods, since 2010 has been very popular for murder as well and the desire that good triumphs over evil. A curious side note about Blue Bloods is the near 100% agreement that the favorite part of this show is the family dinner scenes in every show. (Noted above in the "honor father and mother" section).

What all of these movies and shows have in common is "murder." All are replete with greed, lust, and power and when necessary use murder as a tool in pursuit of their greed, lust, and power. All are replete with ties to government that does conspire with the criminal elements for greed, lust, and power, but trying to convince themselves and the public that government greed, lust, and power is somehow a greater good. To be fair the fictional TV series do try to show government forces as forces for good and sometimes they are, but it is very obvious in 2023 America that US Corp is captured and bears little resemblance to God ordained righteous intent for law and order.

Documentaries about serial killers like Ted Kaczynski, Ted Bundy, and Jeffery Dalmer are not for the faint of heart and I truly believe if possible should be avoided.

However, on the other hand all books, movies, mini-series, TV shows, and documentaries with discernment are, in my opinion, a learning tool that if considered rightly will sharpen the mind of especially men to not be naïve, but instead to be appropriately protective. The world is a fallen place and for this category gruesomely so. If it were not for the mind of man to grapple with murder, i.e., know its source, know its manifestations, study it, and know as much as possible about it, we would live in a more chaotic world than we already do. Thank God for discernment.

Before I was broken at the foot of the Cross I never gave it a second thought, but now I do. Why? Should I flee, is it sin? Or is it reasonable to be fascinated and entertained for a higher purpose? I can say that I find myself much more selective and in a sense intuitively so, e.g., 90% of what I might start to watch I will turn off after 5 minutes.

All of the above has for all of time, since Cain murdered Abel, through the whys of biblical sanctuary cities, to David's murder of Uriah, to whatever murder just happened in the last minute, none is more horrendous and evil than the murder of the Son of God, Jesus the Messiah of the Hebrews and the Savior of Gentiles.

However, it seems to me there is a category of murder that comes in second place to the murder of Jesus. That category is the murder of the conceived. Judge Edward Cowart said to Ted Bundy at sentencing that his sins of the murder of "only" 36 women were, "extremely wicked, shockingly evil, vile, and shows utter indifference to human life." How then has the mind of man and in this case especially women become so indifferent to the life of the conceived. Part of it certainly is the fallen nature of man, but this one shows that very evil people like Margret Sanger, Hitler, Marx, and their acolytes, i.e., the pro-choice crowd who have used and do use propaganda to infect and completely corrupt the minds of young girls and women. Propaganda first used by Satan whispering in the ear of Eve is still manifestly at work in the world and continues to work as Satan's minions whisper in the ears of young women that it is somehow okay to murder their conceived babies.

Ted Bundy murdered only 36 young women. Each year in America, supposedly a God fearing nation, which has "In God We Trust" on its legal tender, has convinced young girls and women to murder 1,000,000 conceived human beings each year. Another 14,000,000 chemical induced abortions occur for a shameful 15,000,000 conceived human beings murdered in America each year. Worldwide between 40 and 50 million murders of conceived human beings occur each year which equates to 1 murdered conceived human being each second. Shameful!! It took over

100 years from the 1850's to slip from protecting the conceived to outright "opined" legalization by 7 of 9 men to murder the conceived in 1973. I pray God it doesn't take a hundred years after the overturning of Roe vs. Wade in 2022 to protect the conceived as image bearers of God that they "in fact" are.

Jeff Durbin, a Pastor from Tempe, Arizona is one of many, but in my opinion one of the best voices to walk into the halls of government and directly confront evil and honestly and with love call out those that are supposed to be a terror to evil as stated in the Christian bible and do exactly that, i.e., be a terror to evil. Not only does Jeff do that, but as he should he calls them to repentance so they too may enter the narrow gate. Sadly it seems most do not heed his heartfelt desire for them to be with the saints in eternity.

It is this category of murder that makes my mind and millions of likeminded men and women feel and certainly understand the word wrath. Righteous wrath, I think so.

> *I pray Dear and most merciful God, please touch the hearts of mankind to repent and turn from the most egregious and wicked sin of abortion. Amen*

Wrath of God! If we can comprehend the wrath of God and stored wrath of God at all, then murder should give us great pause, and especially of the conceived. There is good news however, the gospel of God. Read the Word, repent, turn. The scriptures speak of a narrow gate. This should make the abortion crowd tremble with fear and be scared to death and of death!!!!!!

A measure of wrath stored up by God, yes and a large measure seems most reasonable!

>>> ADULTERY <<<

> **adultery**: *Voluntary sexual intercourse between a married person and a person who is not his or her spouse.*

Why would God need to command this restriction? And in that restriction is a very emphatic "Thou shall not..." In contract law the word "shall" is binding without leeway. Why so strict a pronouncement?

Why in young love does a boy get jealous if his girlfriend looks at or talks to another boy? Why do young girls get viciously jealous for the same reason? Why are these feelings instinctive? Why the desire to have a boyfriend or girlfriend at all? Why just two to three years prior there was little interest in the opposite sex at all? The answer - by design! The same way God designed men to naturally be protectors, and women to naturally be more nurturing, God designed the dance.

At approximately the same time in development of boys and girls the desire to be with a girl or the desire to be with a boy the dance it seems has been designed into our very being. The dance starts the same way generally. The boy desires to be with and then must ask out a girl. The boy is generally terrified at the proposition. The girl desires to be with and then must hope a boy will start the dance. Both sixteen plus or minus, the boy having recently tested and acquired a status in what he erroneously considers manhood, i.e., the driver. To begin the dance a door must be knocked on, parents met. An awkward pre-dance ritual, but required. Then the walk to the chariot, a door held for the girl to enter the chariot. This prelim to the dance having reasonably been taught to the lad by his dad and if not it was most certainly mom. The boy walks around to his side all twitter pated that there is a girl in his car and will be right there next to him, very exciting indeed. He takes his position behind the wheel of this monster with all the horses under the hood, feeling all confident that he's the man. He glances at the girl, and she at him both extremely excited about the other. He thinks she is lovely with the curvy features and fairness of face he only a few short years ago thought was a bag of cooties. Here I must pause for I have no idea what she is thinking. All I can surmise is her feelings are similar.

They are now on the dance floor and the dance begins. First order of business the hand must be held, terrifying! Then hoping you have something to say that the other party may find remotely interesting. Also, terrifying! After fumbling and stumbling through this nightmare there follows the intense desire to smash lips. Terrifying, but ultimately awesome!

Now this is where the dance should, but seldom does, get proper instruction by a qualified dance instructor. That master dancer should be the father of the boy and the father of the girl with appropriate assistant coaching advice from mothers. A master dancer would have already grounded the boy and girl in the ways of the Lord and the respect for God and His behavioral instruction and why? Why the "waltz of love" will bring blessings and why the "tango of lust" is dangerous.

Sadly the dance instructors have left the building. The instruction has been relegated to TV, cinema, and social media all of which are varying degrees of porn and are very tempting, but perverse to God Almighty. It is the "desire" or "lust" to do the horizontal mambo that is similar to the "love of money" that makes this dance or "the act" an idol unto itself. This particular idol has been the bane of civilization. Trust ruined, families destroyed, children damaged, churches split, governments useless, empires crumbled, and worst of all nations having once been blessed by God having that blessing removed.

The dance with teenagers has always had varying percentages of proper "waltz of love" participants the allure of which is why Hallmark Christmas movies, and boy meets girl movies are still favorites for the ladies. Sadly the market for promiscuous behavior is more popular. Sitcoms while they do make us laugh have normalized the temptations of Satan to partake in the "horizontal mambo" right out of the gate for teenagers. Today in 2023 the mambo at least in America, and I suspect in most of the world, is very much in fashion and perversely so.

Virtue having been groomed right out of young girls turning them into sluts. That word, while exactly correct for its description of girls and young women today, has been lost in the lexicon of America since to be a slut is now the norm and a right and sadly a virtue. If this were not so there wouldn't be thousands of young girls and women screaming, protesting, and lecturing on social media platforms, "my body, my choice." In other words they have a right to be a slut, sleep around with young boys and men, whom are not in fact, true men, and unashamedly scream in your face about their right to murder the evidence.

Because a large part of our nature is to be polite we hold back on stating truths in a manner that offends. However, for honest and heartfelt analysis I offer an alternative that is not polite, but is reasonably precisely correct. Consider if you will the scene we have all seen of women screaming at a protest, "my body, my choice." Now, and this is a question, would not the following chants also be apropos:

- ➢ I'm a slut, I'm a slut, my right to rut
- ➢ virtue a thing no more, my right to be a whore
- ➢ men are pigs, I'm a bitch, when I'm in heat, I'm not discrete
- ➢ I hate the patriarchy, but a slut I must be
- ➢ my baby, my choice, God be gone
- ➢ that millstone thing, I'm not afraid, murder my baby, that's what I say

I certainly could go on ad nauseam, but you get my point.

What happened to virginity being the highest honor and virtue? Well, Satan, through Hollywood, has all but erased the word from the conscience. Virgin and virginity, slut and whore, all words hardly ever spoken about or even uttered, why? The word "normalized" works well here. We as a very fallen nation have normalized that the word virgin and the word slut need not be uttered or discussed since the normal is that virginity is no longer a thing and since to be a slut is the norm, why bring it up?

It should be noted that the word slut when it is spoken is used as an admonishment to anyone who would dare to suggest in any way that the promiscuity of a girl or woman is, let's say slutty. The admonishment goes something like, "How dare you slut shame me!" Game, set, match! Proof positive that to be a slut is a virtue.

The word whore when it is used has been shortened to Ho and is held up in many a modern song as a virtue. What happened to 1) modest, 2) polite,

3) spirit filled, 4) proper, 5) humble, 6) intelligent ladies? If women carried themselves in a manner that the above six adjectives were recognizable in their characters the word Ho would not be a thing. Not only that, men would start behaving, as these characteristics it turns out are appealing to men. There might just be a revival in the use of the word lady. Songs like, "once, twice, three times a lady" might be more vogue than WAP.

Another interesting phenomenon is the casting couch. Many a Hollywood starlet is a starlet precisely because of her exclusive decision to not walk away from the allegorical couch. Pressure for fame and future money should not be a thing and would not be if men in powerful positions were not pigs. The "me too" movement spawned a retributive phase in American history that spread around the world and I dare say was a necessary corrective mechanism to make men take heed. The women however danced the dance and got paid.

Now about men. A term for men that seems to have disappeared is "gentlemen."

> **gentleman:** *a chivalrous, courteous, or honorable man.*
>
> **chivalrous:** *courteous and gallant, especially toward women (typically used of a man or his behavior)*
>
> **courteous:** *polite, respectful, or considerate in manner*
>
> **honorable:** *1) bringing or worthy of honor; 2) of the intentions of a man courting a woman directed toward marriage*

Too be sure there are millions and millions of men who fit this bill. Those men aside, what men are today is mostly their own fault, but it cannot be denied that the feminist movement and the movement to destroy the God ordained family has relegated men as non-essential. If this were not so we would seldom here the words, "single mom." What better way to make toxic men than to teach boys that they are. Rather than instruction by men on how to be a man and a gentleman, young men are being taught by women to be something very, very un-biblical. Most recently the Boy

Scouts, created to teach young men to be men was ruined by women. This but one of many examples of why manhood is under attack.

Men at one time showed respect to each other by using phrases like sir, yes sir, no sir, or a straight up Bob or John. Today that type of respect has been replaced with bro, homie, dude, dawg, and the like. That's on the men. As the scriptures point out, "set aside childish things," i.e., grow up be a man's man, cowboy up, square up, man up, etc..

Part of the journey to be a man is for a father to teach sons how to dance. The courtship dance can be, should be, and necessarily must be taught if fathers want for their sons and daughters to have children that will properly know the 5th commandment.

The gist of this discussion thus far has been the early stages of the dance in which our young are normalized into fornication. Having learned this dance because absent fathers and mothers turned the instruction over to nefarious others and having been fornicators for a while, but for some reason still being compelled to marry it should not be a surprise that the next dance on the dance card is adultery.

That adultery is wrong is clearly written on the heart. Were this not so the guilty party would not hide it. Just like a child innately lies and sophomorically tries or thinks that the lie can be hidden from mommy and daddy, so too the adulterer sophomorically tries or thinks that the lie can be hidden. While the adult if crafty enough and deceitful enough can hide the sin for a longer period of time from the spouse, the lie by the numbers will be found out. Trust burned to the ground, children scarred, households destroyed, guilt piles up, shame haunts, respect lost. Worst of all God saw it all; He warned us in so many ways and could not have been clearer in His "shall not" commandment.

The incredible lure of lust! Why is it that teenagers long for a boyfriend or a girlfriend? And even if they spend a few years living on the fornication dance floor do they at some point desire to have an exclusive boyfriend or girlfriend and long for a change of status to man and wife. Could it be that the innate nature to be in union with one man and one woman has a God breathed force for His glory? If in this fallen world the nature of man and woman is to by the numbers marry, what should we make of that? It seems most reasonable that the force that makes a man and a woman want to "cleave together" should be with a modicum of discernment understood to be God designed.

Perhaps a glance at the beasts might also have an indicator of God's intent for His glory. In the animal kingdom – pause! As I typed the word kingdom it struck me to look up its definition.

> **kingdom:** *1) a country, state, or territory ruled by a king or queen; 2) a realm associated with or regarded as being under the control of a particular person or thing.*

It seems very clear the King of the animal kingdom is God. Postulations to the contrary are physiologically, philosophically, and evidentially vacuous. When I hear "Mother Nature" all I can think is, how stupid does one have to be. In the realm of the beasts the design is one male beast and one female beast to create cute little baby beasts. All of these little baby beasts most assuredly please God for they most assuredly please His image bearers. The common denominator for the beasts and mankind is procreation to make adorable little babies.

The "know better" and "discernment" being exclusive to man is why fornication and adultery sear the conscience. We certainly "know better," so why do we disobey our built in conscience? God surely designed the innate "dance" we do, knowing His intent for its proper execution should culminate in a "marriage" between one man and one woman. How ironic that there are God designed hints in the animal kingdom about designed courtship dances. I suppose the biggest hint is that the only reason for the dance in the animal kingdom is the propagation of the species. Humph! How about that?

Sex is wonderful and is a gift. But the gift, like life itself has rules. Man it seems in antiquity could not figure out the rules which are written on the heart. Why past, present, or future fallen men don't think philosophically about much at all, though we should. For instance, why do we feel jealousy? It took a flood, Sodom and Gomorrah, a commandment, and the Son of God to make it clear that marriage is the rule. Sex within the rules glorifies

God. Sex outside of the rules is cheating, fraudulent, and destroys. The destroyed relationships caused by this sin should seal the deal for mankind to avoid this sin like the plague it is. The fact that it is so violated should make it clear we do not think on the greatest commandment and since we do not consider that command it should be no surprise that mankind's violation of the second greatest is why this sin is still pervasive and still destroys.

Jesus the Son of God – let that sink in, "the Son of God" raised the bar when He said, ***"I tell you that if you even look with lust, you commit adultery in your heart."*** Why would Jesus say it like that? If the miracles He did when He walked the earth were not proof enough of His power; and that attested fact should be enough; it seems that in all of his interactions with people, no matter whom, Jesus knew their thoughts. If we read the Christian Bible and notice that the words of Jesus; and the apostles that He taught to teach us; still reach right through time, to this very instant and convict us. Adultery! We know it's wrong, and it should be clear that God the Father, God the Son, and the Spirit of God see our minds and our hearts, which should terrify us!!!

Marriage, what is it? The conscience knows. This union was commanded way before the 10 commandments. People all over the world seek a partner and innately know that to "cleave" with one, and only one, is safe and beneficial for all especially a family. So why do we stray. It's the sex thing. That idol, that temptation is perhaps the single most powerful temptation, but only as we move into adulthood. God has protected the very young from this desire, thank God! It's all we can do to teach them good manners, not to lie, and not to steal, and to honor especially mom and dad.

If a marriage is proper, the man will be proper, the woman will be proper, both living in the ways of Lord Jesus. If they live per the only proper instruction found in the world, the Christian Bible, they will be blessed. The ultimate blessing, a date with Heaven!

As much as its definition is being co-opted to be a new thing, what it is, I submit, is written on the heart. Marriage is a God ordained covenant by and between a man, a woman, and God. The custom, tradition, and ceremony included the statement, "let no man put asunder," which should also state for clarity, "let no woman put asunder," and for even further clarity, "let no state entity get involved at all." This was and is a command of God, but the covenant was high jacked by governments to make it a civil contract, the benefits and privileges granted by an entity, rather than a law covenant with God. Ironically, marriages once recorded in the front of bibles were a record kept in church houses and included two witnesses. That same record can still be presented to a county recorder's office as a lawful record even today. The only difference being the government cannot share in the spoils of the marriage. Food for thought!

A bit of a tangent off of adultery, but certainly a curiosity why governments care less about God ordained unions. If two parties want benefits and privileges from a corporation, a "civil" union is granted by the corporation for they clearly are not in the soul saving business. Since the government is not in the soul saving business why would they care about the God ordained union? All that the government license does is let the "corporation" know where their cows are. If the cows want to act like beasts, what do they care? And further, after having begged the state for this civil union, to get out of it once again begging must be done to get out of what the participants begged the state to get into. Once again, the state is an entity that does not care. The divorce decree serves the state by letting the state keep tabs on where its cows are going and where they took the property that the state considers to belong to the state.

John Adams, observed, "*Our Constitution was made only for a* ***moral and religious*** *People. It is wholly inadequate to the government of any other." James Madison wrote that our Constitution requires* ***"sufficient virtue*** *among men for self-government," otherwise, "nothing less than the chains of despotism can restrain them from destroying and devouring one another."*

So here we are in 2023 devolving into a "non-moral" and "irreligious" people. Further, because of this non morality and irreligious state of the union, the Constitution is, as John Adams noted, inadequate. What would make it adequate? Only a return to Jesus Christ.

As James Madison noted "sufficient" virtue among men a requirement for the Constitution to work. That "sufficient" virtue has evaporated.

Per Wikipedia it is mostly Christian men and women that have gone to Washington, but have left their virtue somewhere else. The people are having chain upon chain placed around our necks and so subtly are the chains placed we do not feel their weight – yet. Despotism is here, look no further than Covid. Our founding fathers thought so much more profoundly about consequences.

Certain bad faith actors in the culture today want that everyone bend to the whims of a perverse redefinition of marriage. God ordained it, wrote it on the conscience, designed the courtship dance into our being, designed the desire to "cleave" to one woman or man, and designed jealousy into our very being as a check valve to its proper state. Anything else is a journey to hell!

Wrath stored up? What do you think?

> *God in heaven, forgive us most merciful Lord of lords, Jesus the Redeemer. You gift so much, conscience is most certainly a huge gift. Please forgive us for our misuse of it. May we repent, turn to you to lighten the load, and be redeemed to enter Your glory. Amen.*

I called my friend and read the above for input. He rightly noted that it thus far is the most cutting segment that this "old man thinking for the first time" has weighed in on. He suggested something to soften the sting. Of course he is right. I couldn't sleep last night for thinking on it. Clearly I took shots at boys, girls, women, men, and the state. All guilty of sins either directly or tangentially related to adultery and necessarily by extension marriage and what that is.

Millions live in proper relationship within the God ordained parameters of marriage. They are truly blessed. While they may be righteous for this sin rest assured they are sinners and they too need the mercy and saving grace provided exclusively by the salvific act of God, through Jesus in whom God was well pleased. That salvific act is what softens or takes the sting out of this section.

Those that go through the harrowing experience of divorce born out of betrayal make for a very lucrative industry called therapy. The sin of adultery is far reaching in its destruction. It may take many years to get through to a place that is tranquil of mind. Shame and guilt are heavy burdens indeed. But there is good news – the gospel. Literally translated gospel means "good news," and that good news is that burdens of shame and guilt along with any and all other burdens were nailed to a Cross for you. There is a catch; however, you must see it. If you don't the scriptures speak of dying in your sins which can be very literally understood to mean exactly what it sounds like. If you die and have not accepted Jesus and what He did you will have died in your sins, or stated another way, you take your sins with you into the grave meaning that your sins are in your casket with you and not nailed to the Cross. That my friend is not good news.

Christians that have accepted the free gift of salvation will be gifted heaven by faith in Jesus and what He did. Those that do not accept the free gift and continue to live in your sin will not be gifted heaven.

Repent brothers and sisters. Repent if this section hit a little too close to home. For Christians love you and wish to be blessed by your company in heaven.

One final thought on marriage. Marriages that are properly lived are recognized by all. When we see an old couple holding hands after 50, 60, and 70 plus years of marriage we smile. Why do you suppose that is? It is those marriages that Christ recognized and called out as an example of what is a righteous union in this temporal realm because the love within such a marriage is deep. The husband loves his bride and "cleaves" to her. Likewise the wife honors the husband and "cleaves" to him. Both sacrificing selflessly, one for the other. This bond is what Jesus, the Son of God, used to explain His love for His bride, the church, i.e., those that both love and honor Him for the selfless sacrifice He made to atone for their sins, and those members of His church that selflessly sacrifice their lives for Him.

>>> THEFT <<<

The 8th commandment is another "Thou shall not." Another very emphatic command not to steal.

> **steal:** *take (another person's property) without permission or legal right and without intending to return it.*

The definition of "steal" above was obtained from the first on-line dictionary that popped up. The Merriam-Webster definition is as follows:

> **steal:** *to take or appropriate (another's property, ideas, etc.) without permission, dishonestly, or unlawfully, especially in a secret or surreptitious manner.*

What caught my eye was the word "legal" in the current on-line definition and the word "unlawfully" in the Merriam-Webster definition. A seemingly small distinction, but the word "legal" as it pertains to stealing are legalese constructions by lawyers which they construe as "rights" bequeathed by the state. While "unlawfully" gets its origins from God and the very specific "shall not" in the 8th commandment, and Noah Webster knew this.

In looking up the word steal all of the following related, or man's categorizations of stealing are noted below:

1. **theft** - *the action or crime of stealing*
2. **robbery** - the action of taking property unlawfully from a person or place by force or threat of force
3. **larceny** - *theft of personal property*
4. **grand larceny** - *theft of personal property having a value above a legally specified amount*
5. **petty larceny** - *theft of personal property having a value less than a legally specified amount*
6. **burglary** - *entry into a building illegally with intent to commit a crime, especially theft*
7. **shoplifting** - *the criminal action of stealing goods from a store while pretending to be a customer*

8. **pilfer** - *steal (typically things of relatively little value)*
9. **loot** - *steal goods from (a place), typically during a war or riot*
10. **appropriation** – *1) the action of taking something for one's own use, typically without the owner's permission; 2) a sum of money or total of assets devoted to a special purpose*
11. **misappropriation** - *the action of misappropriating something; embezzlement*
12. **embezzlement** - *theft or misappropriation of funds placed in one's trust or belonging to one's employer*
13. **peculate** - *embezzle or steal (money, especially public funds)*
14. **defalcate** - *embezzle (funds with which one has been entrusted)*
15. **purloin** – *steal something*
16. **identity theft** - *the fraudulent acquisition and use of a person's private identifying information, usually for financial gain*
17. **internet piracy** – *related to copyright infringement, or the use or production of copyright-protected material without the permission of the copyright holder. Copyright infringement means that the rights afforded to the copyright holder, such as the exclusive use of a work for a set period of time, are being breached by a third party. Music and movies are two of the most well-known forms of entertainment that suffer from significant amounts of copyright infringement*

Isn't it interesting that man can categorize stealing in so many ways? Is it not also interesting that God does not? Stealing in any of man's categorizations is a sin. There are no caveats in this commandment. Whether stealing a stick of gum, downloading pirated music or movies, embezzlement, or appropriating money from funds stolen from a man's labor are all stealing.

As I think on stealing or theft my mind considers two categories as follows:

1. Plain and unambiguous theft living person to living person.
2. Hidden Black Hand of legal masters of subterfuge to create a person "entity" to steal all that they can get away with.

Category #1 is straight forward; however, some may question the use of the word "living," the answer to which is in category #2. These categories require an in depth study into "legal" constructions that when comprehended will leave a soul knowing that most of what constrains mankind in the "legal" system are properly labeled:

> **misfeasance:** - *a transgression, especially the wrongful exercise of lawful authority.*
>
> **malfeasance** - *wrongdoing, especially by a public official*

A simple proof for consideration is the word person. Look in a Black's Law dictionary for the word person.

> **person defined Black's Law:** *1) a natural person; 2) an entity created by law for the benefit of the government, corporation.*

So, and this is a question, when one fills out an application for a marriage license or any other public contract, are not the applicants begging the government, or entity, or a dead thing, or corporation for the benefits and privileges available only from the dead hand of that "entity"? Another question, is there a law that created an entity out of the natural person for the benefit of the government? Food for thought!

The book of Job in the Bible describes the most righteous man whom God as a lesson to Satan, put Job through trials and tribulations unimaginable. In Job 32 verses 21 and 22, a young man and seemingly wiser than Job's three older friends rebuked Job and his older friends for not considering God as thee "Most High" and righteous God. In his wisdom the young man, Elihu, says to his elders and to Job the following:

> **NKJV --- Job 32:21-22** -- *21 Let me not, I pray, show partiality to anyone; Nor let me flatter any man. 22 For I do not know how to flatter, Else my Maker would soon take me away.*

These words are part of scripture and should be considered and heeded. Not only have lawyers given themselves flattering titles they have crafted into their legalese constructions a hidden title of a man in the same word, i.e., "person." (See Black's Law definition above.)

The answer to what is raised thus far is a deep dive into "theft" and is not the intent of this book to cover. I studied law and legal for a time and found the law to be fascinating, but finally realized none of the "legal" constructions of man will be useful to argue one's way into Heaven. Lawyers, judges, and law makers would be wise to, as is stated in courtrooms often, "the people will stipulate" or the "defense will stipulate."

In America in 2023 the law is not equal, or as stated in the scriptures:

> **NKJV --- Proverbs 20:10** -- *Diverse weights and diverse measures, They are both alike, an abomination to the Lord,*

In other words, if equal weights and equal measures, whether in law or commerce, are unequally applied in any fashion it is theft from someone to the benefit of another. That someone can be and very often is the "state," "corporate," "dead" entity, the beneficiary being a living person as noted in my "Category # 2" of theft, i.e., a *"hidden black hand of legal masters of subterfuge to create a person "entity" to steal all that they can get away with."*

>>> THEFT OF THE STATE <<<

In 2022, the city of San Francisco decriminalized petty theft. Cops can't stop and the "justice system" cannot prosecute anyone who steals anything worth less than $900. A perfect example of wrong becoming right. The lawmaker instead of being a terror to evil gets in bed with the thief, condemning the thief to hell as well as himself or herself.

To be fair, why would the government care, since the government has been stealing the people's labor since 1913 when the 16th amendment was "supposedly" ratified in early 1913. Coincidentally, later that same year the Federal Reserve Act was "supposedly" passed turning over the administration of people's labor to private bankers. That cabal of private families is still administrating the deception and no one knows who they are. Diabolically useful to their scheme is section 4 of the 14th amendment which states that the "The validity of the public debt of the United States, authorized by law, …., "**shall not**" be questioned. In other words because in contract law the word "**shall**" is binding without leeway. How convenient, the Federal Reserve, since it was ratified in 1913, even though it appears to be a government institution is in fact, not. It is wholly private and hides and is protected by the rubes in the US Corp. Also notice the "**shall not steal**" in Gods commandment is craftily used in the 14th amendment and the federal reserve act to do exactly that, i.e., steal.

It seems the theoretical Christians in the halls of Congress and the Senate might want to revisit their charge in this brilliant, diabolical, scheme to steal without question.

For a treatise on the evil of the scheme read "The Creature from Jekyll Island" by G. Edward Griffen. The scheme was brilliant in its conception, deception, and execution. However, that brilliance will not get one through the narrow gate. The systems now being contemplated are just as brilliant, are doubly deceptive, and it appears will be executed for even more control of the people's labor.

There are many schemes that the people are unaware of that steal.

Amendment IV of the Constitution:

> ***The right of the people to be secure*** in their persons, houses, papers, and ***effects***, against unreasonable searches and seizures, ***shall not*** be violated, and no warrants shall issue, but upon probable cause, supported by oath or affirmation, and particularly describing the place to be searched, and the persons or things to be seized.

A question? As I understand it the legislative branch is supposed to make laws and all such laws should secure the freedom of the natural person and all "effects" of any kind whatsoever for that natural person. How is it then that the Code of Federal Regulations or CFR is a thing at all? All codes and regulations of the CFR are what is called "color of law" and is not law. So, another question? If anyone just glances down the table of contents of the CFR how is each and every section not "theft" or the "stealing" of the very "effects" of the natural person the 4th amendment articulates very emphatically "shall not" be violated. Food for thought! Theft on a grand scale, you decide! Wrath stored, hummm I wonder?

A further consideration or food for thought is that in 1938 all crime was commercialized. This begs the question, what was it the day before? One day it was crime, the next day money was to be made on the crime. But who gets the money? And who gets to decide what constitutes a crime? If crimes can be made out of things that do not harm another, what a cottage industry for commerce! And if this is so, the construction is again brilliant, but is most assuredly theft.

The book of Luke in the Bible gives an accounting of what Jesus said to the Pharisees about their corruption. The Pharisees would be akin to our government representatives. When Jesus pointed out the Pharisees or "government officials" hypocrisy a lawyer piped up and said to Jesus that your condemnation of the Pharisees also condemns us. Lawyers then as now were and are to advocate on behalf of the people and be fair and righteous in their craft. Then as now they were not just, then lawyers were sycophants for the Pharisees, and today they are sycophants for the court or BAR. Whether representing the state, or defendant, both lawyers are officers of the court first. Another way of thinking on that is they have one master and God is not it, it's the BAR. Today lawyers craft and script all of the burdens that weigh down the individual. Jesus said, "Woe to you lawyers! For you have taken away the key of knowledge."

Today there are many sub-categories of law that attorneys may specialize in which makes it most profitable for the post 1938 commercialization of newly created crimes made by fiat. When the known corruption that is law-fare today, is it not worthy of a prayer for the lawyers.

How this is not seen by lawyers and judges today, especially those that claim to be Christ followers boggles the mind. But to be fair, the craftiest lawyers have taken away the key of knowledge for the rank and file lawyer. They are lawyers in procedure and no little about law, less about ethics, not much about the scriptures, and therefore are often hamstrung by procedure and cannot even bring a fact, the constitution, or the law, and most certainly not an oath to the Bible, which was once required, into a courtroom for proper consideration.

Not only that, but most lawyers don't know that they represent not a natural person but an entity created for the benefit of the government/

bankers. I know that last sentence will raise eyebrows and will not be understood. Compartmentalization of information even for lawyers induces a cognitive dissonance that may never be seen. Even though I am throwing around information that may seem as if I am off my rocker, a lot of research will lift the veil. The intent of this book is to go fishing for men and that is the goal. Some of those men are in that world noted above need the Redeemer and this portion is for them.

Three examples for consideration of how lawyers hide the key of knowledge:

Example # 1) - Many years ago on July 4th there was a policeman standing a post on a city street in NE America when a little boy about six years old ran up to the officer yelling, "mama got cut, mama got cut."

A black woman ran from a nearby house screaming, "He has a knife!" She was in a knee length white nightgown covered in blood. The officer ran to the woman, who was now collapsed on the sidewalk. He leaned down to ask if she knew who did it. The officer had to lean down close to her mouth to try and hear more clearly as she was gurgling through the blood from her cut throat. The woman said his name was "******." Just then a black man, whose appearance was very slovenly and thuggish, came out of the house brandishing a butcher knife covered in blood.

The officer, staying next to the woman, yelled for the man to stop and drop the knife. The man did not and ran down the street. The officer shot him from a distance of about five to seven feet, hit him in the leg, the man fell to the ground, got up and ran away. The officer could not leave the woman so the man got away and was later apprehended and arrested. The officer stayed with the woman and in looking to ascertain the extent of her wounds discovered that not only was her throat cut she had been disemboweled from her vagina. The officer tried to push her entrails back in and hold them in with a towel. She remained alive for a short while, but died at the scene.

Fast forward to trial. The officer was called to be a witness and as he enters the courtroom a smug defense attorney for the accused smirks and asks the officer if he recognizes the man he saw running away from the murdered woman. The officer knowing the game said something to the attorney to let the attorney know the officer thought he was an a@#hole. The reason was the perp didn't look like a thug anymore. His once unkempt hair was cut close and his street thug cloths were replaced with a suit and tie, making him look not like the truth of his nature, but hiding the truth to deceive a jury, i.e., a lie and a blatant theft of the truth.

The officer, having intent and being sworn to tell the "whole" truth, was hindered by an unjust attorney and judge and a system which for some reason, knowing the truth and in this case having a "smoking gun," or more specifically the bullet with ballistics, taken from the leg of the defendant. The officer was not allowed to state this fact for the defense attorney objected that this fact would be prejudicial to his client. Ya think!!! Further, the officer could not say for certain that the cleaned up defendant was the same man for the transformation was extreme. The murderer was acquitted.

Several weeks later and in this judge's court for an unrelated case, the judge asked the officer if he could see him in chambers. The judge asked the officer if he recalled the case noted above. The officer saying, "Of course." The judge let the officer know that the man had murdered again about six weeks later, had cut up a woman, threw her parts in a barrel and threw the barrel in the river. The judge wanted the officer to know that, quote, "We got him." Further, the judge made a comment to the effect, "This ones on me." Who can know, but that should have haunted that judge to his grave.

This is my question. The system allows for discovery, therefore the prosecution and the defense would have known that the murderer had a bullet in his leg, which could be linked to the officer's gun. For what reason whatsoever, could there be, for such an egregious miscarriage of justice. When he was finally caught how is it that the defense attorney and the judge were not disbarred? Another question, do the attorney and the judge have unclean hands, and if not in man's court, what about the court of God. Another question, in the eyes of God, will the unjust judge not be complicit in "stealing" the life of the second victim and would this not be a form of depraved indifference? I do not know, but it makes me consider how carefully lawyers and judges should consider the ramifications of their chosen craft for as this case shows, righteousness is elusive and slippery when there is no reason for it to be.

Example 2) - This example includes false witness sins and stealing sins and involves a very specific "theft" of the peoples "effects" which is the "shall not be violated" clause in the 4th Amendment. That very specific "effect" is the people's right to judge both the facts and the law. The right of the people in the jury process has long been established common law and that precedent being clear in Supreme Court rulings many, many times in America. "The Citizens Rule Book," published by Whitten Printers, Phoenix AZ, 602-258-6406 is a must read for every American. This excerpt from the "Rule Book" is exactly why in example #1 above justice was perverted:

> *Without the power to decide what facts, law and evidence are applicable; JURIES cannot be a protection to the accused. B.A.R. attorneys and judges are actors, and acting in the name of government, if they are permitted by JURORS to dictate any law whatever, they can also unfairly dictate what evidence is admissible or inadmissible and thereby prevent the WHOLE TRUTH from being considered. Thus, if government can manipulate and control both the law and the evidence, the issue of fact becomes virtually irrelevant. In reality, true JUSTICE would be denied leaving us with a trial by government and not a trial by JURY!*

Today, perhaps because of the 1938 commercialization of crime, bad faith bad actors, (lawyers and judges) incentivized by commerce, lie to the people keeping the truth from the people thus stealing one of the peoples effects clearly and unambiguously protected by the 4th amendment to the constitution as well as the last four words of the 10th amendment.

> **Amendment 10** - *Powers of the States and People. Ratified 12/15/1791. - The powers not delegated to the United States by the Constitution, nor prohibited by it to the States, are reserved to the States respectively,* ***<u>or to the people</u>.***

In any court where there is a trial by jury today in America the instructions to the jury will be a lie. The instructions will be a statement usually from the judge that the jury can only judge the facts of the case and the judge will decide or tell the jury the law. The people do have an absolute right to nullify any law the jury deems to be wrong. This lie is by propaganda or "project mockingbird" tactics of the media told over and over in movies, TV, books, etc..

Example 3) - Several years ago in a NW state a man was traveling in a car borrowed from his mother. The car had expired tags. The man was pulled over by the police, when asked if he knew why he was being pulled over he replied, "No." The officer made him aware of the tag situation. It was here the man made the officer aware that it was his mother's car and he was not aware. It is the next question that almost landed the man in prison for the rest of his natural life.

The officer in violation of his oath to uphold the Constitution which includes the 4th amendment, without probable cause coursed the man into searching the vehicle. Drugs and paraphernalia were found, the amount of which were by unconstitutional fiat regulation decided by some unelected party to be egregious enough to send this man to prison. The man was arrested and held over for trial. This is an example of a crime declared and for which no one was injured either directly or indirectly, but a man was to be put in a cage for the rest of his life.

Fortunately for this man he had a friend knowledgeable in the law and even those fiat codes and regulations that in fact are not law at all. The man called his friend for counsel. The instructions were as follows:

1. When asked to sign anything write UCC 1-207 and then sign your name through and on top of that code.
2. At arraignment plead not guilty and demand a jury trial.
3. Be your own attorney-in-fact.

Right before the trial his friend published in the local newspaper various excerpts from the "Citizens Rule Book" noted above. This good man's intent was clearly to do the opposite of what Christ condemned the lawyers for, i.e., not hide the key of knowledge.

At the start of the trial, the judge asked the jury if anyone had read the paper. No one answered nor did they have an obligation to answer. Why?

Who is the authority in the room, the judge, the lawyers, or the jury? You decide. Hint: We the People.

The judge then asked if the righteous man was in the courtroom. He was, but knew he was under no obligation to answer so he stayed in the back of the courtroom and watched the proceedings so as not to prejudice his friend's case. The judge had called the righteous man's name out loud because the judge read it in the newspaper. The judge stated that he might have the righteous man arrested for jury tampering. It is not known if anyone in the jury had read the article about jury's rights and responsibilities, but probably some had and that is all it would take, just one juror.

The state's case was that the defendant possessed the following:

1. a pipe;
2. papers;
3. 4 grams of marijuana;
4. 2 mushrooms.

For perspective 4 grams might fill that pipe 3 maybe 4 times and the 2 mushrooms any reasonably man would conclude was for private personal use. The state however added without investigation or proof an added charge of intent to distribute and other fiat crimes. These charges in this state would have incarcerated the defendant for life.

The defendants only hope was that the jury was sufficiently educated by the article in the paper that:

1. No one was harmed.
2. The stop violated that defendants 4th amendment rights.

During the trial the prosecuting attorney called the officer to the stand. He was asked how he came to know of the drugs. The officer stated they were in plain site, which is understood to be probable cause for a detainment. Upon cross examination the pro se defendant/attorney-in-fact informed the judge that he needed to question the officer. Granted permission by the judge, the pro se defendant attorney-in-fact asked the officer if the contraband was in a sealed container. The officer, in a jamb said that it was in a backpack. This was true and apparently could not be denied or lied about. Since the contraband was just attested by the officer to "not" be in plain sight, but in a backpack, this statement was perjury or a lie in open court by the officer which was a clear violation of his oath to uphold and defend the Constitution and in this instance the 4th Amendment. This violation cost the officer his job.

These two points being enough for the jury to acquit. Although this action by this jury was not enough to nullify the law across the land it did nullify the law for this one case. The jury found the defendant not guilty. The juries vote in essence saying;

1. The facts presented violated this man's right to be secure in his person, property, papers, and effects as the "4th Amendment clearly and unambiguously states, and that the state transgressed and trampled on his God given rights to be free.
2. The color of law was decided by the jury to be wrong.

The unjust judge, however, tried to get a 2nd bite at the apple, or put the defendant in double jeopardy by sleight of hand. The unjust judge remanded the case to another court a couple of weeks later. His sleight of hand was assigning another case number making it seem like and unrelated incident, which is a fraud on the court. The defendant once again acted pro se in the second trial by jury. That jury had apparently also had read the paper. The jury acquitted a second time. This man, only by the actions of a Good Samaritan, was saved from life in a cage.

Other facts or violations of law that did not get exposed, but should have are:

1. The law was in fact not a law, but color of law.
2. The fiat law concerning the drugs was unconstitutional.
3. The judge was unjust and violated his oath to uphold and defend the Constitution. When the judge announced in open court that the good Samaritan should be arrested for jury tampering he very arrogantly stated in open court in front of God that the people do not have a right to know the truth, and in this case a

constitutionally protected right to be secure in all of their effects. One very sacred "effect" is the truth. The judge bore false witness against the Samaritan, slandered his good name, and threatened an arrest for telling the truth. The judge should have been dis-barred.

4. The unjust district attorney violated his oath to uphold and defend the Constitution. The district attorney should have been disbarred.
5. The officer violated his oath to uphold and defend the Constitution, perjured himself and was let go.
6. The 1938, all crime being deemed commercial and the commerce created thereto goes to the attorneys, clerks, and judges. How the booty is shared is unclear. Some monies by the case bonds, which are traded on the stock exchange, and other monies from prison bonds for those prisoners incarcerated and last however long the person is incarcerated, these also traded as a commodity on the stock exchange.
7. The incentive is clear. The corruption of why a judge would try a 2nd time is clear when the "all crime is commercial" law of 1938 is seen. The love of money it seems greatly tempting and as seen here corrupts the soul.
8. The indifference to an image bearer of God, the depravity of conscience one must have to confine a fellow brother in a cage for what is legal in an adjacent state and was by any reasonable person a ridiculously small amount of drugs. Note - it is my understanding that one marijuana seed will put a man in a cage for 5 to 15 years in this particular state. Further, all involved know that most people have prescription drugs so much more harmful in their medicine cabinets.

Other issues in this case if dissected further lay bare that there are very corrupt attorneys making law where none is necessary and then hiding the key of knowledge so that only a few may enter. These include:

1. The UCC code mentioned earlier is taken from the "Uniform Commercial Code."
2. This UCC code is color of law first agreed to by states in 1952 and updated continually.
3. When the defendant or any man or woman signs any document in a public interaction, he/she is without the key of knowledge which

is only known by bad faith actors. If any document is signed in pubic it is a contract with the US Corporation and waives any right unless that right is reserved.

4. The populace has no idea about the truth of the existence of the U.C.C., C.F.R., hundreds and thousands of other color of law codes and other constraints, chains, and shackles put on the individual and that if they sign any document is per the ~~Pharisees~~, I mean government, a voluntary begging for the privilege purported.
5. The populace also has no idea that the American natural person as well as the trustee of the US corporate person in any and all courts is one and the same thing. The defendant was both of these "persons" and so are you.
6. The car the defendant thought to be his mother's was in fact property of the state by fraud and so is yours.
7. The defendant harmed no one, was misguided in using drugs, but freedom includes the right to be stupid.

There are many sins in the above examples all of which show that the greatest commandment and the second greatest commandment were nowhere to be seen. But once again, as Jesus said, "Woe to you lawyers…."

A prayer for the lawyers:

> *My heart grieves greatly for lawyers, for some are my friends and have given me great counsel. Within the industry there have been many a great mind and have made constructions in law that are most righteous. However, it's the malfeasance and misfeasance, some knowing and some perhaps unwittingly, but nevertheless lawyers need You, Lord Jesus to unveil their eyes to see.*
>
> *Amen*

In the gospel of Luke 11:52 when Jesus said "woe to you lawyers," Jesus was what we today might call a whistle blower. Note verses 53 and 54 after Jesus said "Woe..."

> **NKJV --- Luke 11; --** *53 And as He said these things to them, the scribes and the Pharisees began to assail Him vehemently, and to cross-examine Him about many things,*
>
> *54 lying in wait for Him, and seeking to catch Him in something He might say, that they might accuse Him*

It strikes me that this same technique is used to trip up those detained. In other words, Miranda rights, especially that part that states, "anything you say can and will be used against you."

In most court proceedings a judge may ask a defendant three questions as he/she looks at the defendants ID, such as:

1. Is this you
2. Is this your address
3. Is this your social security number

Most respondents would respond yes, yes, and yes and the judge would move on. However, in the legal system created by a very crafty bunch, the truthful answers would be no, no, and no. If necessary the judge will have, in his black bag of malfeasance, just tricked you into perjuring yourself. He will only use it against you if the proceedings don't go as the state wants and you'll never know what hit you. You may be coerced into a plea which always benefits the state, and to be clear, benefits the state and certain privileged parties in monetary gain, all crime being commercial.

This is why in Luke 11, Jesus said in the 2nd sentence of verse 52, "You did not enter in yourselves, and those who were entering you hindered." In other words, the lawyers at that time would not enter into the temple, which is where the legalizers, or Pharisees, presided, and the lawyers did their bidding and hindered the people. They did things like "steal" and make sure the people pay the temple tax in various ways so that the Pharisees maintained their wealth and never had to get their hands dirty.

Today lawyers do the same thing, i.e., use their craft to keep the con going, "stealing" the wealth from the people and all in such a manner that the lawyers don't have to enter into the temples, or in other words, the halls of the government, or the federal reserve, or the three letter agencies, or the world bankers and their lairs in England, Switzerland, and Rome. When "the people' do discover a wrong, the crafty lawyers and lawmakers vote for themselves immunity. The lawyers use ignorance of the people and hinder them just as Christ said.

One of the best legal minds in the American experiment was Oliver Wendell Holmes who had many a quip of law made famous. One such quip was, "*Ignorance of the law is no excuse.*" Lawyers and especially judges think this is a righteous thought. I think Jesus would disagree. To be ignorant of the key of knowledge purposely hidden by 1,000,000 plus laws, codes, regulations, etc. and purport that the people are without excuse about its deceptive construction is precisely why the Son of God said, "Woe to you lawyers."

As it relates to the moral law and the glory of God Oliver's quip with reason applies perfectly for it is written on our hearts so we are without excuse.

> **attorney**: *an actor to attorn.*
>
> **actor**: *to get up on a stage and lie convincingly enough to make one believe in the character and the plot.*
>
> **attorn**: *to steal from one and turn over to another.*
>
> *Or succinctly summarized - liars and thieves. Not in honor, but in dishonor. A dishonorable profession.*

The above definition will not be the one found if looked up. However, and this is a question, does it not accurately describe the administrative courts of the US Corporation that have made all crime commercial since 1938 and ingratiate a certain class of priests with the labor of the people. Is not this definition a reasonable consideration for what Jesus might think of as a perverse system?

There was a day when students were taught at least some law in high school. The very wealthy and particularly whoever owns the Fed, recognizing that an educated populace greatly hinders the stealing required to maintain the con. So, lawyers doing their bidding swayed the educational system to, as we have all heard, dumb down the people. I'm not sure, but I know that many people have discovered the con and it makes them feel wrath. If, as image bearers of God, people being people, when they find out they have been lied too, had every effect of their existence stolen from them, and the betrayal of trust they feel when the con is discovered, if these people feel wrath, what does God think? As the Son of God warned, "Woe to you lawyers..."

Jesus calls everyone to repentance which includes lawyers. Repent! A modicum of research will remove the scales so craftily glued to your eyes. When you see it, you will have some serious soul searching to do. I wish you, and this is a most appropriate here,....God speed!

>>> THEFT IN THE INDIVIDUAL <<<

When I was in the 4th grade I befriended a boy across the street, or perhaps properly analyzed, he was a little older, a little hellion, and he more reasonably conscripted me to join him in his pursuits of bad stuff. I recall he was left alone a lot with little supervision, so..... you know. Anyway, he had a 5 speed stingray bicycle with a banana seat. I would ride on the back and we would go down to the grocery store in the summer. There were cases of pop stacked on the sidewalk in the front of the store. He would propel us lap after lap around the store and on each lap I would reach out and take one can of pop. We would go around to the back of the store and put the can of pop in a box conveniently left for us by the store, then more laps. We would laugh and laugh as this seemed great fun. Then we would take our booty home and be well supplied with stolen libations for a few days.

The same lad taught me how to steal candy. I remember the first time, thinking the exercise more like a game I laughed and very aggressively, with great exuberance and stupidly obvious intent stuffed probably a pack of gum in my pants pocket. My corrupt little friend having already by 12 years old honed his thief craft taught me the necessary skills, me being 10, to be cool, more deceitful, so I could properly break the 8th commandment. Thankfully, he got older and lost interest in hob nobbing with kids, and for the most part, but not totally, I avoided the temptations of this sin.

Even then, as a little kid, I knew it to be wrong for why did I hide it from mom, dad, and even my siblings. Certain things taught, to be sure, but some things sear the conscience even of a kid.

Today I have two granddaughters, 2 and 4. About three weeks ago I was reading to them before bed, the two year old to my left, and the four old to my right. The story was about a bear family, mom and dad bear were away and brother and sister bear were horsing around and broke a vase. When mom and dad come home the little bears tell lie upon lie to hide their problem. The lesson of coarse was proper as mom and dad bear made it clear the dangers of lying. When we were done I asked my four year old granddaughter if she ever lies. She very innocently said yes followed by the justification, "but I don't do it all the time." So, clearly more training required. It was very cute, the innocence of babes, but we as parents and grandparents clearly have more work to do.

>>> TANGENT <<<

I was sharing my thoughts with a friend who rightly pointed out two things, 1) little ones are little sponges, and 2) we don't help the lying because we lie to them often. His greatest objection is the lye of Santa Claus. Although cute and fun for all of the joy it gives us to watch the joy it gives them for the whole month before and especially the morning of Christmas. My friend is correct in that children being sponges most certainly may misconstrue the nature of lying. I'm not as staunch as my friend on this point, but he does make a good point in that children learn about lying mostly from their parents. My thoughts on the subject are that even without Santa, little kids seem to, of their own accord, live in a world of make believe.

For instance the time my four year old granddaughter handed me a pillow to steer the couch cuz the couch was now an airplane and I was the pilot and she took her seat in her little toddler chair and instructed me to instruct her to buckle her seat belt. Yes, I confess I lied. I went with her into her make believe world, she told me we were going to crash in the jungle, so I warned her that we are going down, brace yourself. We crashed at the same time that the family dog, a large yellow lab, came into the room. I said, look a dog. My granddaughter said, no Poppy, that's a lion. Her little four year old make believe world, to be dogmatically truthful, was lie upon compounded lie and delightful. My instinct tells me we won't get in that airplane nor travel to that jungle, and she will have forgotten the whole incident when she is 13. Discernment?

Or the time 30 plus years ago when my daughter was three and up until she was maybe six or seven we played the "Huntsman and the Wood Fairy." She would be a bad wood fairy and I, as the huntsman would have to chase her around the house, catch her and take to jail which was her bedroom. I would throw her in the dungeon and shut the door, she would be laughing hysterically, escape from jail and the caper would start all over. We played that for a few years, a total complete fabrication and lie, but the greatest of fun. She remembers it fondly as do I, but my friend is correct in that as parents our job is to be ever vigilant to keep our babies within the proper boundaries of what is right and wrong, as well as fantasy and reality.

Children live in this make believe world for a few years. When they emerge from this cocoon of innocence as parents we see clearly when their little computer brains start making more sense of the world and they dispense with make believe, a natural God gifted gift of evolutionary discernment, if you will. Can we join them in this make believe world and still guide them properly out of it? I think we can if we pay attention.

However, I think my friend makes a very good observation in that we spend much time on the lie of commercialized Christmas and Santa. It is most reasonable that parents should spend an equal amount of time, if not more, especially during the Christmas season on the reason for the season.

> *A prayer for parents: Dear Lord Jesus, I pray for the parents, that their little ones are brought up in the ways of the Lord. The birth of Jesus is wonderful and has much that will capture the mind of our babies. Let us learn and discern to use the Christmas season to glorify your Son Jesus. Let us rightly divide fantasy and reality for our babies, enjoy their innocence in their make believe world, but keep them firmly grounded in reality and truth. Amen*

This is perhaps a little off topic of stealing, but in a way at the same time it should cause us pause to make sure we balance the innocence of babes and not "steal" it, but also with great care guide them into the truth, that being Jesus. Would it not be this type of innocence that is joyful for us as image bearers, be the very reason Jesus said,

> **NKJV --- Mark 10:13-14** -- *13 Then they brought little children to Him, that He might touch them; but the disciples rebuked those who brought them. 14 But when Jesus saw it, He was greatly displeased and said to them, "Let the little children come to Me, and do not forbid them; for of such is the kingdom of God.*

Notice Christ was displeased and Christ said, "do not forbid." This is a logical place to speak of the wrath that is most assuredly stored up for the actual "stealing" of children. Since biblical times there have been worshipers of Baal. It would be most naive to think this cannot be a thing in what we think is an educated, enlightened world. Satan worshipers are a thing and children are in fact, stolen, physically abused, trafficked for money, trafficked for sex, trafficked for labor, trafficked for blood, and trafficked for parts. It is so horrific that the brain turns off for most people. But, it is a fact, and there are men, good men, such as Tim Ballard who quit Home Land Security to dedicate his life to the most noble cause of saving the little ones. There are also good journalists like Laura Logan and others that are dedicating their lives to exposing this most heinous of crimes.

Think on that for just a minute, HSI an investigative branch of Homeland Security cannot and will not protect America from child traffickers. Why? Sadly it is Satanic Americans that are the beneficiaries of the crime. The government turns a blind eye because the money to be made is huge and most sadly it is the complete lack of virtue and total depravity of US Corp that **"can"** find funding to go after moms that do not want their babies to be taught anything whatsoever connected to sex, but they **"cannot"** find funding to protect the "stealing" of children. There are many players in government that have the power to "not" look the other way, but they choose to steer their souls directly into perdition. Depraved indifference is a reasonable and righteous construct or maxim of law. How depraved do you have to be to have the power and not use it? Is it reasonable to assume, Jesus will not look favorably on judgment day for those that had the power and did not raise their voice.

End Tangent

Back to stealing of the individual: A case can be made that the worst theft of the individual are those that steal from God to argue against him. Frank Turek has a book titled "Stealing From God," in which he uses the acronym C.R.I.M.E to articulate most effectively the premise. His argument is solid and so as not to be accused of "Stealing from Frank" I would encourage those searching to get his book or if so inclined, sign up for his on-line course.

Stealing from God to argue against him is a tragic form of theft. That aside, stealing is most certainly a problem for humanity. Once again if we lived by the 1st greatest command and the 2nd greatest command we would never consider taking anything without asking and if that "thing" has a value that a reasonable and fair exchange of lawful money would feed the party for whom that "thing" belonged and he was willing to share that "thing," well the world might be a more pleasant place.

When I talked about my early escapades as a ten year old thief it was in my mind that there was more, but when I penned those earliest sins I could not recall later crimes. Well my conscience has gone into the memory vault in my head and opened the file cabinet to the section labeled theft. Low and behold a dusty old file labeled "forgotten theft" stamped on the front of it is still there in the vault. Forty five years ago when I was starting to work in corporate America I did take the occasional pen, notepad, sticky notes, hi-lighter, stapler, tool, etc. Looking through a different colored lens now it is horrendous to me how I could have done such a thing. At the same time there were many a time when I would take an item back when I noticed that the cashier had not rung it up, or yelled to someone who had dropped a $20 bill and I let them know, and many other such acts. Why the two standards in the same brain? Good question. The answer is sin is written on our hearts. You have but to look into the memory vault of your own brain and you too may find conflicting files. When we sin and go through with a wrong thing, and when we are held back from the same sin in on a different day, both are written on the heart. The former suppressed and probably forgotten and the latter remembered and falsely convincing the self that you are a good person. You are not; you are a sinner just like the rest of us.

The good works files will not outweigh the sin files, for sin is not measured in pounds. Sin is measured in occurrence. One sin weighs the same amount as 100 sins on the scale of Gods justice. Recognition of the files is the first step. Just like when it is recognized that we collect so much material crap and often want to purge the burden, we also want to purge the conscience. As it turns out there is a way. Read the gospels and the epistles. After a lifetime of sin and in this example incidental theft that your employer might not have noticed or even cared about, God did. Hit your knees, repent and turn. It seems to me a miracle that God's mercy is so great that He can forgive me for sins I had forgotten about and nailed my sins along with yours to a Cross.

>>> THOU SHALL NOT COVET <<<

covet: *yearn to possess or have something*

The 10th commandment reads:

> **NKJV --- Exodus 20:17** -- *17 You shall not covet your neighbor's house; you shall not covet your neighbor's wife, nor his male servant, nor his female servant, nor his ox, nor his donkey, nor anything that is your neighbor's.*

If God thought we were capable might this commandment be the 5th commandment and there would be no need for any of the others. Think on that for a moment. The five commandments. One tablet. For it is this condition of the heart that leads to each of the other sins. Since the fall of man when Adam and Eve desired wisdom and ate of the fruit of knowledge, boy did they get it. That desire, or lust for wisdom was the first coveting sin. If they had stayed content with "honoring God" they would not have wanted for anything so coveting wouldn't be a thing. However, after that first coveting sin God's desire for obedient image bearers would require lessons and guidance. Left without the 10 commandments after the fall and before they were carved in stone, man became corrupt and very much so. That corruption reasonably not unlike much of the world today. No honor of God, no honor of parents, murder on a grand scale including babies, adultery and sins of the flesh, theft, false witness and lying, and the coveting that leads to each of those sins.

The tenth commandment is specific in what not to covet and has the emphatic "shall not" attached to it. It strikes me that there are things that are okay to covet, or "yearn to possess or have." The "shall not" commands are very specific and all of them involve coveting that "shall not" thing described in the command. Would it not follow then, that to covet, or yearn for, the opposite of the "shall not" command would be the righteous goal, or the righteous yearning, or righteous coveting for mankind?

1. ***You "shall not" have any other gods.***
    a. You shall yearn to recognize the one and only!
    b. When called and born again this yearning will be natural and cannot be otherwise.
2. ***You "shall not" make graven images or worship anything but Me.***
    a. You shall yearn to only worship God in the Spirit.
    b. When called and born again this yearning will be natural and cannot be otherwise.
3. ***You "shall not" take the name of Lord your God in vain.***
    a. You shall yearn to not render the Lords name useless in any form.
    b. When called and born again this yearning will be natural and cannot be otherwise.
4. ***You "shall not" forget to set aside a rest day and keep it holy.***
    a. You shall yearn to set aside a rest day and keep it holy.
    b. When called and born again this yearning will be natural and cannot be otherwise.
5. ***You "shall not" dishonor your father and mother.***
    a. You shall yearn to honor your father and mother.
    b. When called and born again this yearning will be natural and cannot be otherwise.
6. ***You "shall not" murder.***
    a. You shall yearn to not murder; you shall yearn to not think ill of another.
    b. When called and born again this yearning will be natural and cannot be otherwise.

7. ***You "shall not" commit adultery.***
    a. You shall yearn to not commit adultery; you shall yearn to not lust even in thought.
    b. When called and born again this yearning will be natural and cannot be otherwise.
8. ***You "shall not" steal.***
    a. You shall yearn to not steal. You shall yearn to not steal any effect of your brother.
    b. When called and born again this yearning will be natural and cannot be otherwise.
9. ***You "shall not" bear false witness against your neighbor.***
    a. You shall yearn to not bear false witness.
    b. When called and born again this yearning will be natural and cannot be otherwise.
10. ***You "shall not" covet.***
    a. You shall yearn to not yearn for anything that belongs to another.
    b. when called and born again this yearning will be natural and cannot be otherwise.

So that it might not be construed that this analysis suggests in any way that the Christian because of his/her acknowledgement of sin, and then acknowledging that Jesus came to redeem his/her sin, that said Christian can claim a "holier than though" status is to fall short of understanding. That is why the word "yearning" is used. In other words, the Christian will struggle, have trials, tribulations, temptations, and unholy thoughts, but the cross will forever more be the undergirding of their life.

NKJV --- Mathew 22; 35-40

35 Then one of them, a lawyer, asked Him a question, testing Him, and saying,

36 Teacher, which is the great commandment in the law?

37 Jesus said to him, **<u>You shalt love the Lord your God with all your heart, and with all your soul, and with all your mind.</u>**

38 This is the first and great commandment.

39 and the second is like it, ***Thou shall love your neighbor as yourself.***

40 On these two commandments hang all the Law and the Prophets.

Jesus summarized the acceptable coveting or yearning when He stated to a lawyer the greatest commands. Note that in the lawyers question the last three words are "in the law." Jesus did not rebuke or make any inference that these were maybes. They are authoritative commands from the Son of God before he went to the Cross. If we listen carefully and take heed to these two laws there would truly be peace on earth.

Since mankind still stumbles over his own pride the world is in the state it's in, it seems clear that God's patience, forbearance, and mercy might be recognized and as obvious as our reflection in the mirror. Sadly the patience, forbearance, and mercy of God are not recognized in the macro for the world would not be in the sinful state that it is obviously in. If these three attributes of God were recognized sin would stop tomorrow.

The Ten Commandments are clearly needed for were they not here for us today it is reasonable we would already have destroyed not only ourselves, but the planet also. We should thank God every waking minute for the Ten Commandments. God knew that man was and is not capable to keep them so He would have to enter His creation to provide a way.

If we redirect our coveting, our yearning, and our desire to Jesus and that He sacrificed Himself for our coveting, well, we would find ourselves weeping. I notice now that as I attend the Christian church and when voices are raised in worship it is not lost on me that my fellow Christian brothers and sisters that covet Jesus are often brought to tears.

It should be very evident that God is so very awesome and for some reason wants that the image bearers that he created join Him. Why? Does it matter? Thank God that He does. We understand that place we know as heaven or glory, but it is reasonable that our limited mind cannot perceive its awesomeness. Will it not be something more awesome than we are capable of conceiving in our wildest imaginations? I thank God for mercy.

> **mercy:** *compassion or forgiveness shown toward someone whom it is within one's power to punish or harm:*

Dictionaries vary slightly, but the gist is the same. However, the considerations of mercy contemplated and defined by man are for the innate and general revelation of our interactions with each other. But why? By what standard do we feel or consider mercy at all? Without God as a standard man would not know mercy. So, if God is the standard would mercy be better defined as follows?

> **mercy:** *God's compassion for His image bearers, and His forgiveness shown towards His image bearers, whom He alone has the power and the authority to punish and harm.*

Perhaps in dictionaries the above definition should be first and the current one in the dictionaries should be second with a preamble sentence to the effect that - "man's mercy to each other is possible because of Gods mercy as noted in the first definition." We need more reminders so we keep in mind the standard. Just a thought!

The best sermon I've read too date on the 10th commandment was by Ligon Duncan on 5-26-2002. It can be found on line at: https://rts.edu/resources/the-tenth-commandment-no-coveting/

The wrath man might feel concerning coveting is elusive since coveting is in the heart and mind. Some coveting is seen in a leering eye, a furled brow, or a fake smile. For the most part coveting is in the heart and easily hidden. The stored wrath of God is different and as has been discussed here and noted as a precursor to all of the "shall not" sins, we might just want to look inward and examine ourselves for God sees the coveting.

FINAL THOUGHT ON GODS WRATH

As much as delusional man and or men think they have the answers to progress society to some sort of utopia they are foolish. If one thinks about the state of the world now, 2023, it should be obvious. Only Jesus has the answer! We could get there if we would bend the knee, but can we? It seems that a second coming is reasonably the solution. If that is the way of things then if Gods wrath is stored, and He tells us it is, perhaps you, yes you, should take pause, keep your yap shut, think with discernment, realize you like everyone else are "in fact" a sinner, humble yourself, and seek "The Way."

Which brings me to consider the "Wrath of God"? Romans 12:19 says, "Beloved, do not avenge yourselves, but rather give place to wrath; for it is written, "Vengeance is Mine, I will repay," says the Lord." This New Testament scripture being written in several places in the Old Testament scriptures. It seems men as individuals and as collective groups or nations can't get this one right. The answer was given to us very simply by Jesus, the Savior, i.e.,

> **NKJV --- Matthew 22: 37-40 --** *37 Jesus said to him, "You shall love the Lord your God with all your heart, with all your soul, and with all your mind." 38 This is the first and great commandment. 39 And the second is like it: "You shall love your neighbor as yourself." 40 On these two commandments hang all the Law and the Prophets."*

It is said that God's wrath is an indicator of His holiness. Time after time people make the statement, "How can a holy God allow so much suffering in the world?" and "My God wouldn't do that." These and similar statements are uttered ad nauseam by the secular world, but to be fair by many that honestly want to know the way of things. There are thousands and thousands of sermons, philosophical, apologetic answers available to answer these questions. These answers are so obvious to some and completely elusive to others and vehemently denied by many and perhaps most of mankind.

For those that the answer is elusive I hope and pray are in a category that can be reached with the gospel. If you think you may be in this group, please read the Christian Bible, ask, search, ask, and search more. Unfortunately there are many false teachers and you will have to wade through that muck, but read the New Testament over and over. The Word will set you free.

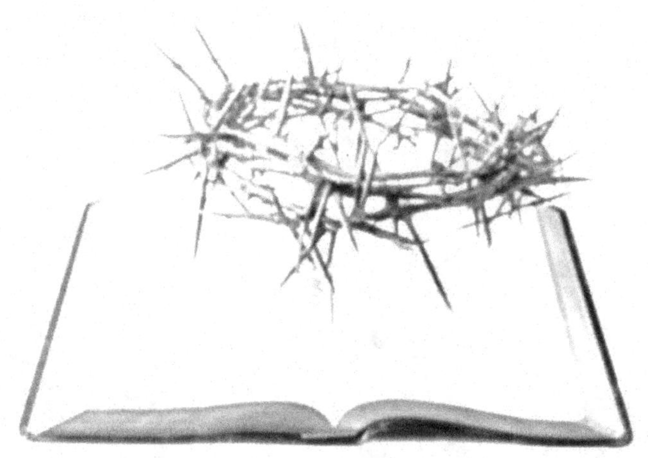

Judge Not!

Not Possible!

Chapter 12

JUDGMENT

How do categories, spectrums, hierarchies, distribution, types, etcetera of sin at the threshold of heaven apply when in the presence of God? How are we to be judged? If Jesus was the perfect man, God Himself incarnate and we are judged by that standard what are we to do? A quick internet search on delineated sins in the Bible came up with 87. It seems that each of the sins might fit somewhere under the big 10 and as Christ noted about the two greatest commandments all of them could be categorized into:

> ***1) Not loving God with all your heart, soul, and mind, or 2) not loving your neighbor as yourself.***

Perusing a list of 87 is a very convicting, so much so that the question arises and is a very reasonable one to ask. How can I, you, or anyone live so perfectly?

The answer to that little conundrum is – you cannot nor can any man who has ever lived save one. Jesus the Son of God and son of man, it is stated boldly in the gospels, and letters of the apostles who walked with Jesus, and attested to the fact that He lived perfectly and what is said to be holy. Jesus was able to avoid all of the 87 sins and anymore not on the list for He was the Word from before creation that defined righteousness, and lived it.

For an exercise try it yourself. Look up sins in the bible on the internet. Think on it a bit. How do you fare? It's a pretty convicting exercise. Recognizing that you are guilty in some measure of the larger percentage of sins considered. Now what? What to do with that information if you have ever wondered if there is a heaven and entrance requires that you can't get in unless you have lived a life devoid of those sins. Minimal deductive reasoning will cause you to admit that it's not possible for you. That same deductive reasoning will cause you to conclude no one you have ever known, nor reasonably could anyone alive or who has ever lived or will live, live to such a standard.

Congratulations! If you get this far and acknowledge that the above is true or has the possibility of being true, that stirring thing, or feeling, firing around in your mind just a little bit, you might just feel thirsty. Thirsty for what? The answer is the truth. If God desires his created children to be with Him and also knowing that left to their own devices they cannot do it, what then? By this time, if you are still reading this old man's thoughts you know the answer is in the gospels. Read the lake!

AN ADMIRALTY ALLEGORY OF JUDGMENT

We are all in the same boat. That boat is called the "HMS EARTH." HMS meaning HIS MAJESTIES SHIP. In the ocean of space we float around there are only two ports at which we may debark; Port Heaven or Port Hell. One is paradise and the other not so much! As passengers we are all sinners and like the Titanic that hit an iceberg, it seems HMS EARTH has hit the iceberg called sin. Also, like the Titanic it is clear that the ship is going down. The HMS EARTH has been outfitted with lifeboats, but unlike the Titanic there are enough lifeboats for all on board.

Here is where the story is dissimilar, the Captain, desiring that all passengers get a seat in the lifeboats requires that the passengers acknowledge His skill as Master Shipbuilder as well as skill as Captain. He has placed maps and signs on every deck and everywhere on the HMS EARTH to let the passengers know of His skill, i.e., His glory in shipbuilding, and of his Captain skill, i.e., His glory in navigating and driving the ship. The Captain provides every meal for every passenger, desires to break bread with each and every passenger at each and every meal and hopes for, but does not demand, that each passenger humbly be thankful for the bread and the boat ride.

There are many departments on the HMS EARTH, each vital to the proper functioning of the great vessel. The Captain has commissioned officers of varied rank tasked with specific oversight of the departments. A structured order, if you will. Each morning on the HMS EARTH the sailors are required to muster in their designated departments.

> **muster:** *a formal gathering of troops, especially for inspection, display, or exercise:*

All sailors must work and all are accountable in their respective departments. Each must muster him or herself in meekness and with a heart of respect before the Captains Ghost each morning and examine themselves, inspect their own hearts, then get to work. Once a week they must muster with their commissioned officers.

The Master Ship builder, Captain, and the Captains Ghost being one and the same in fact love all passengers, but also make it clear that the Captain will judge who gets a seat in the lifeboats. His terms are reasonable and not burdensome, but are a must for debarkation at the port of Heaven. All others that do not get a seat, sadly and very much so, will go down when the boilers blow up and the ship slips beneath the waves in flames.

In military law and especially known in ships at sea there is a judgment and punishment called captains mast.

> **Captain's mast:** *a term used in the context of military law. It is defined as the non-judicial punishment of an enlisted person by a military commanding officer. These types of punishment are usually granted for offenses of minor nature.*

I witnessed a Captain's mast once on the USS Ronald Reagan, a nuclear powered aircraft carrier of the US Navy. My nephew was a seaman on that boat and I was able to hitch a ride from Honolulu to San Diego. It was a six day sail and was awesome. On the trip there were 6 to 8 sailors that had disobeyed the Captain's orders concerning getting a tattoo overseas.

Every day for a couple of hours in the middle of the hanger deck for all to witness they had to turn out in their dress uniforms, stand at attention and be chewed out by a superior officer for their insubordination. Some may have had to clean toilets, scrape paint, or other chores, and others may have been stripped of rank. If the infraction warrants it sailors will not be granted shore leave.

The point is, in the earthly Navy, the captain is god and judgment and punishment is swift. Note however, that the crime seems menial as does the punishment. In God's court it will be different. The Word of God tells us that sin we may consider menial, while it may be, is still sin and will be judged and the punishment for its violation is eternal damnation.

The Captain, our Lord Jesus Christ, has offered to any sailor on the HMS EARTH a free pass to debark at port Heaven. At one point in the HMS EARTH's voyage through the vastness of space the Captain came down from the helm and went to the Captains mast Himself as a lesson and a sacrifice for all of the sailors for there was a great mutiny against the Master Shipbuilder.

That part of the crew that sees the Captain for what He is and recognizes that He was crucified on the Captains Mast for salvation will be gifted a free port pass. Not only that, but the Ghost of the Captain guides those sailors that recognize His sacrifice for the rest of his or her voyage. Those that dismiss the Captains handiwork, dismiss the Captain, dismiss the Captains commands, dismiss the Captains sacrifice, dismiss the Captains Ghost, will not be afforded the Captains grace and mercy and will not get off the sinking ship and won't find a seat in any lifeboat. The only reasonable solution for the boat ride is taking the free offer.

Another pretty cool tradition on such boats at sea is coming to port and docking. On that day sailors are required to put on their dress whites, stand the rail; which on the aircraft carrier means go to the perimeter of the flight deck; and be observed by the citizens as the ship comes to port. Family and friends cheer as their loved ones come home. Now imagine for this allegory the HMS EARTH is to dock in the port of Heaven. How glorious to dress in the new white robes described in the Bible, stand the rail, and be greeted by the citizens of Heaven and the angels cheering your arrival.

~ JUDGMENT FOR REAL ~

In 2023 this is a most interesting topic. It is astonishing how many times the words, "don't judge me!" or the Bible says, "you shouldn't judge!"; or some form of these two statements come out of the mouth of a sentient human being. But, in this postmodern phase of humanity sadly this is the tripe that somehow has made its way into academy. The statements, themselves being obvious judgments, are spouted by real live persons as rational thought. Sad, very sad indeed.

Humans judge every waking moment. To do right or do wrong crosses our paths each day and must be judged. This being a clear conclusion with no more than one minute of thought makes one an expert on the "fact" that judgment is a must for our safe navigation of each day. Now, moving on from the sophomoric, tackling the weightier matters we must judge, how then to proceed?

God gave us a conscience to navigate the judgments we encounter, but alas, since Eve followed by Adam were tempted and then fell headlong into wrong, mankind knew then and still knows by his conscience what generally not to do. The temptation to great for us not to touch physically or with our minds makes for the mess we find ourselves in.

Mankind couldn't do it without instruction, so God flooded the earth, made way for another plan, gave us commands, and examples of how to judge. Some judgments were carried out rightly and are still used rightly today and others not so much. When God entered His creation through His Son, more instruction was given to judge. Most of that instruction was to the individual to judge inwardly. Were man to follow His commands with His examples we would already have Heaven on earth. But much to our chagrin, that entity called Lucifer is fighting like hell to have us not look inwardly to do that which is right, and do the opposite.

Mankind generally has had some form of government to keep the peace. To that end, laws are made, some righteous and some not, but a structure nevertheless to make for an order as opposed to complete disorder, or chaos. To keep the peace judgment is a must, and punishment also a must. There has, to my knowledge of history, never been a society that has had order without judgment and punishment. Whoops check that, history tells us before the fall it was so. To have such harmony, if we are honest, will only exist when Jesus arrives the 2nd time. Those that were meek, i.e., obedient to His Word will find peace without fear of anymore judgment.

Until that time, man it seems will most reasonably be condemned to an existence requiring both judgment and punishment. What then should that look like?

The scriptures instruct how to adjudicate both crime and punishment. Those included constructs are fair and reasonably given that man cannot see the heart. Witnesses, at least two, to be exact were a must for all of the crimes outlined in the Ten Commandments. The 4th amendment to America's constitution reiterated that scriptural construct into the very fabric of the American experiment. As noted in the previous chapter America's experiment has gone off the rails in that crime has been created by fiat where no harm has been done. That aside, for the violations of the six commandments of God for man's interactions with man, some are taken seriously as crime and others not at all. Some crimes against God obviously cannot be judged by man as they cannot be seen by anyone but the individual and of course God. Crimes of the heart such as: hate, jealousy, lust, and coveting the government cannot judge; although man is now legislating by opinion "hate" crimes. One man or group deciding that if another has a contrary opinion it is a "hate" crime. This will be the undoing of civilization and we see its destruction everywhere in 2023.

Governments and very evil people are attempting to judge the heart in what "they," the self-appointed "overlords," determine as wrong think. Social credit scores, need I say more! If you don't show by your actions that you agree with man's determinations of right and wrong you will be judged, not by God's standards, but by man's, and specifically very un-Godly men and women. Brand new un-biblical laws and punishments await this "new world order." Banishment and unrighteousness as well as continued theft of labor are already happening.

A review of the Ten Commandments and the courts of man illuminate the problem. (Inferences from NKJV)

1. Love God with heart, soul, and mind. --- Once in each and every courtroom as a matter of oath by all parties to the Bible and to the constitution, the underpinnings of which was the "Christian Bible," today are not allowed in a courtroom. What could go wrong????
2. Make no idols. --- The Bible and God out of the courtroom, the new idols are now the corporate entities including: the state (the idol in the court is the seal of state); the corporate entity persons, (plaintiff, defendant, esquires for the prosecution and the defense, clerks, bailiffs, judges, and other officers of court). Note: men don't enter the court, only entities.
3. Taking the Lords name in vain. --- Since God may not enter a court, His name is rendered as useless and therefore all proceedings take Gods name in vain.
4. Holy Sabbath – the court takes the day, but having trespassed and acted wickedly to what end.
5. Honor father and mother – the courts now have family courts to make family a matter of state rather than a matter for the church and God.
6. You shall not murder – a wicked money making enterprise.
7. Adultery – a matter of state and completely a matter of commerce. Adultery is not wrong at all except to let the state know where its property ends up.
8. Stealing – a matter of law with many a money making scheme for the state.
9. False witness – phony veil protecting the state in court, but expected for the people. False witness in some circles or groups considered a virtue. Some groups more than others. Need I say more?
10. Coveting – absolute coveting acceptable for state and elites, but all are guilty of this one. Coveting as per God's command is not understood for it is not contemplated. Were coveting contemplated the other sins would never see a courtroom. The exception would be the fiat crimes against the state for which there is no injured party.

Some of God's commands do enter man's court, sadly all for the commerce to the state and investors, some rightly for the necessary order required by God, murder for example:

Murder still wrong, is not adjudicated righteously and has punishment all over the map. In the world today murder has been categorized as follows:

a. 1st degree - premeditated, purposeful killing of another person
b. 2nd degree - when a person kills someone without planning to do so
c. 3rd degree - has a detachment to the holiness of human existence, indifference
d. felony murder - murder that happens during commission of another crime
e. manslaughter – murder with perceived or claimed non intent
f. involuntary manslaughter – death due to reckless conduct or criminal negligence
g. self-defense – a right to life and not murder

As man does in categorical considerations of this and that, he once again has spent much philosophical energy analyzing murder. It does seem there is utility in these categories and helps to determine an answer to what man desires to find out concerning a murder, and that is the hows and the whys. We are curious creatures so these are helpful for us to understand the hows and whys of murder.

So, having spent much time on the hows and whys in a courtroom, and someone is found guilty and assuming the verdict is correct the next phase or penalty phase by and large is not biblical. God's justice was death, and swiftly. Why? Why would God command death for the murderer and why swiftly?

The biblical history of murder and how it should be considered, judged, and penalized was for a time proper in America. It's considerations and penalty for the most part was per a biblical standard. In other words, when a murderer was apprehended, caught, tried, and convicted the murderer was "swiftly" taken to the gallows and hung; this being done in public. In the Bible execution was by stoning or the sword in both the Jewish tradition as well as the pagan traditions. The evolution of how to put to death a murderer I suppose included advancements in technology, and thoughts about mercy. The constant however was "swift." Why swiftly? Why indeed, especially because God commuted the death penalty for the first murderer, Cain. That's a tough one; however, the lesson perhaps has something to do with sovereignty. God alone should take a life in his time. Now enter the evil heart of the murderer who for whatever unjustified reason takes the life of one of Gods children.

God knew it would happen just as He knew man would lie, cheat, steal, lust, and covet. However, murder is a bit of a no-brainer or at least it should be as it concerns penalty. Death for the guilty murderer was swift not only for the heinousness of the crime, but, and reasonably and more importantly, for the lasting frontal cortex image of the public execution in any of its forms for the public. It shouldn't take a "rocket surgeon" to discern that swift public execution will cause pause in the heart and such fear would have citizens consider with great restraint how to navigate coveting in any of its forms that would move a heart to murder.

Today since all crime is commercial murderers are caged because large sums of money are made for the time they are incarcerated. This covetousness of money by those that invest in crime in any of its forms but especially the long term caging of murderers does two things. It negates the "swift" part of God's law and also negates the pause of heart and the fear that would restrain man from contemplating murder in the first place.

While man has more at his disposal in the way of forensic science to assist in finding the truth of a matter, especially murder, mans' failure to follow God's law in the penal phase makes for a cottage industry and enterprise of murder with a turn style of murderers whom would have thought differently if swift execution per God's law was still a thing.

It should be noted here that a homicide by self-defense and a Good Samaritan death are not murder.

In all of the above corruptions of God's law noted above, it seems clear man cannot seem to get out of his own way. In the end, the very end, as I contemplate sin, crime, judgment, punishment and how man "doth protest too much" against God it makes the narrow gate Jesus spoke of seem narrower. Further, in the judgment seat of Jesus, murder will be murder, regardless of intent, state of mind, drunkenness, etc., the penalty - the lake of fire – the sentence – forever.

In order for there to be some semblance of order man must stop wrong, which we know in the heart is a must. In the first quarter of the 21st century, however, what man deems wrong is being rewritten each day and not in a good way. As the Bible says, "right will become wrong," and "wrong will become right."

If we cannot clearly see right and wrong how are we to righteously judge? The answer is we can't. Justice must be administered to all equally. Justice must be blind to status, ethnicity, and sex. Equal weights and measures are biblical, but it seems nothing is measured fairly anymore; quite to the contrary, the weight or the measure of a thing is arbitrary. Not only is mankind failing on his own, but a third of the created angels, following Lucifer, are tempting mankind to do the opposite of right, and put stumbling stones at every turn of our lives in order that God's children turn against God and follow the dark path.

~ SUMMARY THOUGHTS ON JUDGMENT ~

God judges, we are created in His image, therefore we judge. We cannot not judge. What then? We would do well to judge rightly, but by what standard. If by God's standard we will do well, for his standard is truth. Objective revealed truth is a start and if acknowledged as truth, proper judgment will produce righteous outcomes. Once subjective truth gets its deceitful nose under the tent, evil outcomes follow, every time. Those evil outcomes sadly are pervasive and everywhere, global, with the logical outcome, a culture of death with body bags to count.

Who to judge first? Your neighbor to the left or your neighbor to the right? Your neighbor's husband or your neighbor's wife? Your kids or your neighbor's kids? Your social circles, or you neighbors social circles? Your political party, or your neighbor's political party? Your nation or your neighbor's nation?

We obviously judge each of these categories, we cannot help it, and we should, or should we? If you did not think to judge yourself and your heart and mind first, you may have work to do. Why, because we are all hypocrites. Let's examine and consider why Jesus said we are all hypocrites.

> **hypocrisy:** *the practice of claiming to have moral standards or beliefs to which one's own behavior does not conform; pretense*
>
> **pretense:** *1) an attempt to make something that is not the case appear true; 2) a claim, especially a false or ambitious one*

Many have been the times when hearing of the transgressions of someone else; doesn't matter the topic; I have said to myself, or judged privately in my head concerning what the other party should have done if they were only thinking right "like me." Sadly, many have been the time I voiced my theoretical righteous thoughts in public. Hypocrite much! In either case, whether in my private thoughts or out loud, I condemn myself for who am I, this sinner extraordinaire, to weigh in on anything. This is where the secular world desires that the issue stop. No more judging, "don't judge me," etc.

"But," and there is a huge "but" to consider. That "but" is the plank. Jesus said, "*Hypocrite, first take the plank out of your own eye, and then you will see clearly to remove the speck from your brother's eye.*"

Jesus lessons here are many:

a. You are a hypocrite;
b. You have a plank in your eye and mind; the plank of lust, the plank of covetousness, the plank of self-righteousness, which is idolatry, and all of the other planks of sin.
c. You can remove the planks, if not all at once, you can work at chiseling away at your planks, called sanctification;
d. You will have a new view, i.e., new knowledge
e. Your brother, sister, or neighbor has had, or is having an issue for which your acquired knowledge may help them out of the ditch, or i.e., remove the sin from his or her heart and mind.
f. As you help your neighbor don't be afraid to let your neighbor know about your plank and how you removed it or are chiseling away at it. That chiseling should include "the good news."

If you have ever said words like, "well at least I don't ________," (fill in the blank), or, "at least I'm not that bad," your words condemn you as a hypocrite. Your statement acknowledges that you see your neighbors spec, but in your self-righteousness you see his spec as a plank and your plank as a spec. Jesus parable is a proper warning, woe you hypocrites, and that includes all of us. It seems to me that once we acknowledge we are sinners, and if sin is the train engine, then each of the boxcars in toe are filled with our various planks of hypocrisy.

Why planks and specs? I suppose Jesus, as a carpenter, new the weight of planks as well as the irritation of a spec of sawdust in the eye. Given His craft the allegory makes more sense. Further, He knew the weight of the heaviest plank ever He would carry on his back to Golgotha. Jesus would take on all of the collective specs and planks, i.e., sins and hypocrisies, of all of mankind upon Himself and be nailed to a Cross of planks. Jesus was judged by God. God's wrath made way for the execution of His Son, not for His Sons sin, but ours. Jesus willing took the judgment, scourging, thorny crown, being spat upon, and for you He did this. When the trial and preparation for the execution was concluded, Jesus carried the planks upon which He would be nailed.

Jesus said that if we follow His instruction, the burden is light. When you consider the weight He carried to His crucifixion, and we accept that He carried that weight for us so our burdens may be light, well....? Here I am speechless....!! That He would be acquitted for our sin, have the prison doors of death rolled away so that we also can be released from the same prison we are all sentenced to. Well, once again I am speechless...!! That He pleads with us to follow Him, for He prepares a new home for us, again.... speechless....!!

Our charge simple, let our neighbors know.

Curiously, as I was penning thoughts on hypocrisy, I listened to a podcast by a certain Canadian lawyer who was interviewing a Norwegian lesbian who noted that being a lesbian for over 20 years was easy in the culture of Norway. She says that she is an artist, who is in a lesbian band, makes homosexual movies, and whose career has been "art" related to the homosexual culture. Now, she is being ousted and persecuted for speaking out against men identifying as lesbians and is facing three years in prison for saying so. She has lost income and essentially canceled from society and commerce for saying men cannot become lesbians. She thinks and has stated publicly that for men to say they are lesbians is homophobic and misogynistic against women, but "especially" lesbians. Her use of the word "especially" is especially ironic. She thinks these men are perverts. In the interview, she seems like a lovely woman and I am sure she is. She is correct in her assessment that these men are perverts. But, let's analyze that word.

> **perversion:** *alter something from its original course, meaning, or state to a distortion or corruption of what was first intended*

What is curious is that she is not self-reflective enough to see that twenty years ago she decided to live her life in a way that is "**altered from its original course, meaning, or state to a distortion or corruption of what was first intended.**" And now that the "perversion" line in the sand has been redrawn she finds it offensive. Let's once again review the following definitions:

> **hypocrisy:** *the practice of claiming to have moral standards or beliefs to which one's own behavior does not conform; or a pretense*

> **pretense:** *1) an attempt to make something that is not the case appear true; 2) a claim, especially a false or ambitious one*

Jesus said He was the fulfillment of the law. He also said, "Judge not, least you be judged." What is included in the "not," Jesus says to not judge? Could it be that the "not" is His created order as well as his instructions for how to conduct oneself in His created order, which was articulated right before He said "Judge not" in the Beatitudes sermon. Could it be that this woman has judged that God's order is wrong and Jesus warned her "not" to do that. The rest of the "judge not" statement says, "least you be judged." Jesus followed with, "and with the measure you use, it will be measured back to you."

Could it be that this is an example of a woman judging that God is wrong, has devoted her life in rebellion against God's "not" warning and calling her rebellion "art"? Is it reasonable that her "pretense" of "art" is her measure? She does what she does because she is all in on her perversion and hopes that others find her rebellion somehow righteous "art." She now finds herself being judged by other parties whom also have judged God to be wrong, and in an ironic turn of events those that persecute her are using the same measure, i.e., they like her, demand the world see their perversion as righteous, or to use her measure, "art." Humm how about that!

This woman, as I noted, seems very lovely, but like the parable of the plank and the spec, she cannot see the plank in her own eye. In this case those that attack her don't have specks in their eyes; they have several skubala covered planks in their eyes to be sure. However, in both cases, the lesbians and the trans-verts, and for the government that persecute her in favor of the more perverse, the only answer is for all to see Jesus, acknowledge the created order, repent, and then and only then will the planks fall from their eyes.

> *A prayer for the lesbian - I pray for this woman, I pray she can see where freedom lies. I pray that she finds the light before she is judged more harshly. God speed. Amen*

Perhaps an odd way to have summary thoughts on judgment, but then again, maybe some food for thought and a way to wrestle with the idea and necessity for righteous judgment and "especially" of self.

~ EXAMPLE OF A RIGHTEOUS JUDGE ~

Judge Edward Cowart, best known for presiding over the first murder trial of Ted Bundy. His sentencing speech became famous at the time and was for the most part recounted in the Netflix series about Ted Bundy. The speech went something like this:

> Judge Edward Cowart, *"Judgment that you be adjudicated guilty of murder in the first degree. That the killings were indeed atrocious and cruel in that they were extremely wicked, shockingly evil, vile, and with utter indifference to human life, and that you should be put to death by a current of electricity that shall pass through your body until you are*

dead. I understand that you have a statement you would like to make and you may do so now."

Ted Bundy, *"I won't ask for mercy, in fact I find it absurd to ask for mercy for something that I did not do. I'm not the one responsible for these horrific acts. Although the verdict found in part that these crimes had been committed, it erred in finding who committed them. As a consequence I do not accept this sentence. It is not a sentence of me; it is a sentence of someone else who is not standing here today."*

Judge Cowart– *"The court is going to sentence the person found guilty of the offense, your name sir was on that verdict. Take care of yourself young man. I say that to you sincerely, take care of yourself. You're a bright young man. You would have made a good lawyer; I would have loved to have you practice before me. But you went a different way partner. It has been a tragedy for this court to see the total waste of humanity that we have experienced here. I don't have any animosity toward you; I want you to know that. Take care of yourself."*

The Ted Bundy trial was quite the theatrical performance. Ted was a murderer at his very core, but knew to wear a mask of character to play a role of a charming young man on some occasions or he played the role of a wounded charming young man on other occasions to deceive pretty young girls into his car. At least 36 times Ted Bundy played these roles, the end game to brutally murder his victims.

The bible calls for the government to wield the sword of justice and be a terror to evil. God gave that power to servants of the people or governments although it is reasonable that at least some of the fathers of those girls would have liked to have Ted Bundy alone and wielded the sword of justice themselves. The system worked in that Ted was able to defend himself, but the evidence was too overwhelming. Ted was found guilty and sentenced to die. Ted was on death row for 10 years and electrocuted. Ted denied his guilt until just before his death when he confessed to at least 36 brutal murders. He was convicted of 2.

Judge Cowart by all accounts at the time of his death was considered a righteous judge. Sadly, Ted Bundy will be remembered more. We need righteous judges, but until we govern and judge per God's standard of righteousness the devolution of humanity seems certain. I do pray for the world to be reformed to God, recognize and see clearly that His Son, Jesus, did come to save us.

Judge Cowart's sentencing speech was accurate in his descriptors of the nature of the crimes. Judge Cowart's man to man statements about the truth of the outcome was direct and firm. Judge Cowart's obvious empathetic concern for the man Ted Bundy is a good example of how Christians are to have empathy towards sinners. The judge was honest in his wish for that sinner to have walked a different path.

It is a struggle and a sadness to consider that on the one hand Judge Cowart was the overseer of justice for a natural man that took the lives of two natural women and ultimately thirty four more natural women. On the other hand, to know that Judge Cowart knew he was presiding over a gnostic court with hidden knowledge concerning the commerce side of the legal system makes me posthumously prayerful that he was right with God.

I have noticed in my short walk with Christians that they pray a lot for loved ones who have strayed from the path that leads to the narrow gate and seem to be strolling towards the wide gate. Further, much prayer is directed towards governments and other bad faith actors that are walking an unrighteous path. More prayers, dear God, more prayers!

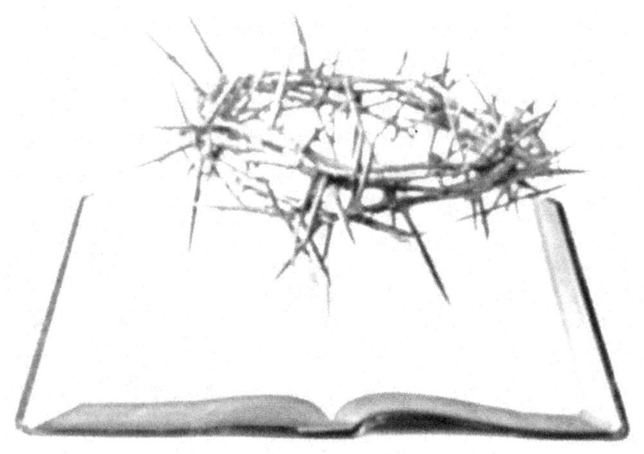

Heaven!

I Hope So!

Chapter 13

HOPE

Well, as I start this chapter it is December 20th, 2022. The celebration of the birth of Jesus is a few short days away. The last two chapters concerning wrath and judgment certainly need to be included in our pursuit of knowledge, which was humbling to consider and put to paper. Now moving from thinking on the wrath and judgment of God, hope it seems is a logical topic to consider. Being a new sojourner on the quest for the Heavenly City and now 67 years old I can say honestly I gave little thought to neither the wrath of God, nor his judgments for most of my life. Now I contemplate it daily and even though I now know and accept that what was done at the Cross was for my benefit, I struggle that the narrow gate may be too narrow for me to squeeze through.

This is where hope comes in.

> **hope: noun** - *1) desire accompanied by expectation of or belief in fulfillment; 2) someone or something on which hopes are centered; 3) something desired or hoped for*
>
> **verb** - *to cherish a desire with anticipation; to want something to happen or be true; to expect with confidence*

Notice that the first paragraph is selfish. Philosophically considered how could I not consider my plight and how anyone reading this not consider their own plight. Silly perhaps, but like the announcements on airplanes, "put on your own oxygen masks first, and then help your neighbor," or as Christ said, "remove the plank from your eye so you may better help your brother." I am "hopeful" that this book through the eyes of an old man thinking for the first time gives someone else the same oxygen, the same "hope" that I now truly feel.

Concerning the definitions of "hope" and firstly the noun form. Desire, expectation, and belief for many things is subliminal like waking up in the morning, expecting to be awake for plus or minus 12 hours, followed by the subliminal desire, expectation, and belief that sleep will refresh us. Every day this subliminal "hope" is there, built in to our very being it goes unnoticed, unappreciated. That might be called the micro consideration of life. The macro would be that at some point we will be faced with the knowledge that each of us took a first breath and we all will take a last breath. The desire, expectation, and belief that we fill that space between first and last breath with meaning of some sort is, well, life. The innate general nature of man to live and cling to life is self-evident. Different for all, but at some point between that first breath and the last one, each confronts the question, "Is this all there is?"

Death, what a state to contemplate! First breath, >>>>time>>>>, last breath, death>>>>. That cannot be the end of it. Enter in the second noun definition of "hope," i.e. "***someone or something on which hopes are centered.***" For the Christ follower the someone is Jesus, for all other religions including atheists, there is a something, but no someone. Take any religion known and the formula for all of it might look something like this:

Formula for Lake of Fire

{ 1st Breath + (>>>> Time >>>>) + Last Breath } = { Death + Judgement = (2nd Death x (Hell Forevermore)) }

i.e., horrific life eternal for (you)

The left side of this equation has one variable and that is (>>>time>>>). That variable, i.e., time, is grace and patience gifted to you by your Creator, God, but as you can see the variable expires. The right side of this equation is worthy of great scrutiny. If God is desirous that we know timeless joy He most certainly does not wish for the left side of the equation to be our destiny. So, God the Master mathematician offered one and only one alternate equation as follows:

Formula for Eternal Life

$$\left\{\frac{1^{st}\text{ Breath} + (\text{>>>> Time >>>>}) + \text{Last Breath}}{\text{You} + (\text{Faith in Jesus})}\right\} = \left\{\text{Death} + \text{Judgement} = (\text{Life} \times (\text{Heaven} \times \text{Forevermore}))\right\}$$

i.e., joyous life eternal for (you)

The left side of this equation has two variables, (>>>time>>>) and **(faith in Jesus)**. The right side of this equation is also worthy of great scrutiny. This gets us to the verb form of hope. "***to cherish a desire with anticipation; to want something to happen or be true; to expect with confidence.***"

I must admit that I struggle greatly with the "confidence" part, but having read the scriptures, studied many other religions and the various factions of Christian churches, I find myself steadfast in wanting, desiring, cherishing, that for the rest of my time on the left side of the 2nd equation that **(faith in Jesus)** stays, not as a variable, but as a constant in my equation so that the right side of the equation comes to fruition.

> *Prayer for All Humanity: I pray that this "hope" finds you. Amen*

Hope, is Jesus hope? Saturday last was Christmas Eve, 2022, followed yesterday by Christmas day, 2022. Saturday, Desert Hills Bible, in Phoenix Arizona held two Christmas worship celebrations. The worship on Christmas Eve consisted of listening to a truly wonderful choir with a mini orchestra. This year the opening song was, "Joy to the World." With a short intro by the piano, the choir's first word was, "JOY." The choir was so loud and clear and beautiful in its enunciation of the word, I wept, so much so I was conscience of my shoulders bouncing up and down. It took a stanza or two to restrain what I suppose was joy! I had just mentioned to my wife that the consideration and anticipation of this celebration was causing me to choke up a bit knowing that voices were about to fill the sanctuary. The next hour was filled with melody and song that truly made all present feel caught up in joy. It was glorious. If that is a slice of heaven, a peek, a trailer, a preview, a foreshadowing, wow!!! To be with fellow believers in the Word, who came this day to pay homage in recognition of the day, 2022 years ago, Jesus our Lord and Savior was born of a virgin into God's world, well, "Joy to the World, the Lord is come, let earth receive her King!" This thing, this happenstance, this potentiality, this hope for this type of joy in an ever after, makes it very wonderful to consider that Hope and Joy are quite synonymous in that they are both Jesus.

The next day the Sunday worship had different, but just as wonderful song and melody, led by truly gifted music leaders. They led the entire congregation to fill the sanctuary with praise so wonderful, once again stirring up joy. It was akin to the excitement sports fans might have when their team is about to engage in play. Only this gathering has the "hope" of total victory attached to it, I suppose because the outcome of who wins is in the air. Hard to describe, but the word awesome comes closest.

Today is Monday the day after Christmas and having enjoyed worship and the gathering with family in thanksgiving to God for the greatest gift any man or woman could ever hope to receive, it crosses my mind that writing about "hope" right after Christmas is like a softball pitch thrown down the middle in the sweet spot so that what this chapter begins with might be better a conclusion. Wow! As I finished that sentence, my rookie status it seems is showing, a rookie move to be sure. For Easter must be considered. I'll close this chapter with a thought or five on the Hope that is Easter.

Hope! What might there be in "general revelation" that is there for us to see about hope, but like all of our blessings, we take for granted. Possibilities? We take every breath and hope for the next. Our heart beats and we hope for the next. If we pause right here on just these two considerations we certainly can consider that death could happen at the next breath or heartbeat. I am hopeful these days to have a few more days to enjoy my family, my extended family, my grand babies, my friends, my time in a great church, and this ride on this giant blue ball. That requires, I suppose, for me to hope for thousands and thousands of breaths and heartbeats.

I suppose breaths and heartbeats are good general revelation considerations, but what might be the more specific things hoped for? Now, as I look at the world threw aging eyes, and threw this new set of lenses I wear, the first consideration of hope is for my granddaughters. They are 2½ and 4½ as of this writing. Their innocence, playfulness, happiness, sadness, unconditional love for their mommy and daddy and by the grace of God, the extension of that love to Poppy and Gigi is truly joyous. It is hard to put into words, but grandparents know what I mean. Part of my hope for these girls is that they may be raised to know the Lord. My hope is they are guided away from the pits I fell into. So far, so good and I feel joy! My daughter and her husband are doing a wonderful job. As I think on them I need to pray more for things hoped for as far as they are concerned. I love them!

~ HOPE FOR THE YOUNG ~

Clearly, sober minded adults hope for protection of the innocence of children. When I watch the children at church, hope seems tangible, a thing within reach. From the infants, to the toddlers, to the preteens, teenagers, and young adults in an environment of Christ centered worship hope is in the air. A wonderful feeling! It gives an old man a bit of comfort to witness with old eyes, and first hand, that in one church, on one street, in one suburb, of one American city, is but a sampling of the faithful whom seek the Lord. I am hopeful that the troops will be mustered and rallied to as the song says, “Onward Christian soldiers, marching as to war, with the Cross of Jesus going on before.” In other words, “Disciple the nations!”

For the young not in the church, it could not be clearer that infants, toddlers, preteens, teenagers, and young adults need the gospel more than ever before. The worst possible people to have ever been gifted life by God have infected all and every institution that has reason to interact with the minds of the young. Their intention is confusion, despair, destruction, and death. Slowly creating a culture that is antithetical to every teaching of Jesus. If the scriptures say to love God, these monsters push no God or that God has no scruples whatsoever. If the scriptures warn about the dangers of coveting, these monsters have pushed narcissism so ugly that the young are coveting anything and everything with reckless abandon. First commandment, love God; tenth commandment, do not covet. If a commandment of God says do, the monsters say don’t. If a commandment of God says thou shall not, the monsters are pushing its okay. I’m not sure the problem is reversible or the prophesies in the Bible are near at hand, but whatever the church can do it should. We at minimum can and should guide the young in our immediate spheres of influence. Souls are in the balance. For those that may read these words and find yourself triggered because you find nothing wrong with the exploitation of the young, please reconsider for your soul is in the balance too.

~ HOPE FOR NATIONS ~

The hope for the nations considered herein may seem elusive as my thoughts unfold, but please bear with me till the end. There are certain "bad faith," "bad actors" whom feel they can reconstitute planet earth to be a in their image and be a "One World Order." That phrase is well known today and was not made up in a comic strip. The phrase was put into the public ethos by a cabal of very wealthy men who after having attained such wealth could not be content to retire and go fishing and sit on a porch. They discovered they can buy power and with that power why not secure the entire globe. It is these men who coined the term "One World Order." That is why over the past several decades they have been trying to erase nation borders. In Europe, the Middle East, the Far East, north and south Africa, and the Americas. Most recently the erased border at the southern border of America is an obvious example of the strategy. It is more difficult than they thought for the confusion of language created by God at Babel has proved to be quite the impediment to their plans. Nevertheless they persist and are not concerned with the language thing, and in fact are working to reinvent a universal language beholden to their ideologies. Another impediment is America who at least for the time being is still "One Nation under God," but they, or more correctly, their minions have recently stated that God is dead and that Jesus is a myth. Therefore, when the borders are all erased and there is only one nation they think there will be no God, no Son of God, and no Holy Spirit of God.

Can they pull it off? I doubt it. Will they get close? They already have, and are pushing very hard to get to their ONE WORLD ORDER or ONE WORLD RANCH for an alternative illustration. Their main objective is a one large ranch. Thus far they want the masses to think they have clean hands and are righteous; wanting only the best for the people they consider chattel or cows. They of course do not have clean hands, are not righteous, and truly think what would be best for the people/chattel is that most of the people/chattel need to be offed. Why?

> **arrogance:** *an attitude of superiority manifested in an overbearing manner or in presumptuous claims or assumptions*

These types are beyond arrogant. Imagine for a moment you have the power to kill 7.5 billion people. How would you do it? You are now a rancher and each continent is one of your pastures to be managed. You would need ranch hands and managers, but you think there are too many people, too many rabbits, if you will, ruining your pastures. They need to be culled. The problem of course is these are not beasts and you know it, they are people, with conscience and soul. But you are better than them, and they are useless eaters. But, because they are people, you must devise a plan to off them while making yourself look benevolent. You have all the money in the world, and in fact, since the consolidation of the world's money supply 260 years ago by you and a few other rancher/bankers you control all of it, so how then? Knowing that men can be bought, you buy them. They do your bidding and can even be molded by various propaganda methods to buy into a slow methodical extermination of the rabbits infecting "YOUR" pastures. Could you do it and feel like you have clean hands? Of course not!

Rest assured there are those that are proceeding with precisely that plan. If there was ever a time for hope it is now. Since Christ said no one would know the end, no one will know the end. That proclamation is simple and if there was anything that could be "self-evident" it would be that. The scriptures foretold of bad times. Well, here we are.

Being here, right now, at this point in time is evidence that the sin nature of man survived the boat ride that Noah and the other seven took. We have but to look around. But, the faithfulness of Noah also survived the boat ride. Not long after the ark touched back to earth, however, mans' ego, i.e., mans' self-importance came back with much arrogance. The tower of Babel is a historical incident referred to in the history book titled "The Bible" and notes that peoples' language was changed, so much so that the peoples could not communicate and separated themselves one group from another and dispersed in different directions. Thus the nations we know today.

A recent development in testable science by research biologist Dr. Nathaniel T. Jeanson is putting the arrogance of man on trial. The arrogance in this instance is for certain members; not all; but certain members of the academic community and only those in the STEM fields; not the social sciences for that discipline have completely lost their minds. In his book "Traced," it seems that the presuppositions of the evolutionists is by the very scientific method the science community says is the way to do science is producing fruit that traces the origin of all men on all the earth today to not only the tower of babel but back to the sons of Noah and their wives. What does this have to do with hope? Good question.

The scriptures say, **"The fear of the Lord is the beginning of wisdom."** Since Darwin this scripture if written by non-believers of the theoretical PhD crowd might be written: **"The admiration of Darwin is the beginning of my arrogance!"** It may take some time because "arrogance" is a like cancer and a very deadly form for sure. This cancer is treatable even in scientists, but sadly because of the book learning knowledge this crowd does have in its quiver, it will not concede that another archer, i.e., Dr. Jeanson, has found an arrowhead in the DNA of now, and the DNA of history. The DNA of history means that some bones and or tissues of long dead animals and humans, as well as the DNA of the living, can now be analyzed and be linked backwards in time and it seems hit the bullseye of history and interestingly enough with 95% accuracy of what the Bible says about history.

Hope comes in many forms and in ways God only knows, but I do know that many a scientist believes in God and the creation model of origins. Work like Dr. Jeanson's may convict some of them, whom may convict others, and so on, and who knows, maybe someday there might be a Discovery Channel program that corrects the record and with such correction, many may fear the Lord for the first time. That feels like hope at least for the science crowd. The science crowd by and large are ranch hands not the owners of the ranch. They are bought and paid for and their opinions have likewise been purchased. What they believe in by faith will not be easily changed for they are proud. But, God is patient; our prayers undergirded with faith in Christ can help. Hope, the only hope!

How about and what to do about those ranchers, those that live in the "big house"? They are even more proud if that's possible. Here's the thing, what this means is that these ranchers/bankers and ranch hands called scientists/elitists, as well as the 7.5 billion chattel/people on earth can be traced directly to Shem, Ham, and Japheth and their wives. That means that those ranchers/bankers/Davos types are cousins to or are in a direct family line to the 7.5 billion people they are inclined to murder. Even more extraordinary is all 8 billion are in a direct line to Noah which makes any man's pride to consider himself in any way superior to another as extraordinarily ludicrous, that is to say, foolish, unreasonable, amusing and ridiculous. If one's mind can get this far then this seemingly complex, but in reality simple revelation then makes the Bible so primary, so foundational to everything. If the Bible is validated to Noah through DNA technology, then to realize that the Bible's pre-flood account is with reason also accurate and is the truth, which means that we are all in a direct line lineage to Adam and Eve. If that is so then God as Creator becomes very much self-evident and should give everyone pause, and that pause should instill fear, trembling, and repentance.

The hope that is in the words above is only partial to the hope that the ranchers/bankers/Davos crowd will need. The other hope is in God's special blue ball. Though they think that earth cannot handle the population they are misguided. Instead of the investment they have made in dumbing down the population, investment turned 180 degrees to support education in the extreme would yield minds that can do as God instructed in the beginning; which is to say; take dominion be fruitful and multiply. It is clear that the rape of the planet per the rancher/banker/Davos crowd has been an abysmal failure. They need to be fired. Fresh minds recognizing first that Jesus is Lord, did die for our sins, and that we are all brothers and sisters; as some brilliant minds have verified with the very scientific method which for a time precluded by law any inquiry into the realm of creation. It is now possible to put an updated brain trust to work. The task?, to better manage the resources of the earth. In other words, God's will be done on earth as it is in Heaven.

If this hopeful scenario were to happen then what need would there be for the World Economic Forum and those that push the "great reset" and the "one world order." The nations separated by God's hand at Babel can stay separated and with reason be descipled as nations like the Son of God said. And oh what joy to appreciate and appropriate other cultures. One can hope.

ardor: *extreme vigor or energy*

faith: *firm belief in something for which there is no proof*

dogma: *something held as an established opinion; a point of view or tenet put forth as authoritative without adequate grounds*

I should note here that in America it is still against the law to teach creation as an origin of everything. Think on that for a minute and it should be clear that America "by legal law" is Godless. That law is a clear violation of the 1st amendment which states that "***no law respecting an establishment of religion, or prohibiting the free exercise thereof.***" The theory of evolution, the god of which is "chance," is a religion the beliefs held to with ardor and faith for which there is no conclusive proof and has become dogma. Dogmas by force shackle inquiry. By law "chance" has been the "established" state religion while the free exercise of inquiry into God has been prohibited.

However, another scientist, Steven Meyer, standing on the shoulders of others has articulated very well that "all" that has been discovered by "all" accounts cannot exist without information or "code." The question then for scientists is where did the "information" come from? Anything man has created came from a mind, or intelligence, if you will, that processed and organized information. So, who, supplied the information, or code, that organizes the complex factories found in the cell? Come on, I know you know. Hint! It wasn't "chance."

~ HOPE FOR GOVERNMENTS ~ ESPECIALLY USA

If the rancher/bankers provide the means, the scientists of many types provide the methods, then it follows that governments provide the opportunities. The governments no matter what nation, no matter what documents constitute how they operate are controlled by the rancher/bankers. Hence the governments provide the opportunities on queue for rancher/bankers to control their chattel for optimum benefit to the "big house."

As I consider what to say here it strikes me that people of the world are "hopeful" in their governments generally, and on one hand it would be awesome if that hope produced good fruit. Sadly, governments of the world have so corrupted the institutions of government that while people still "hope" that their respective governments are righteous, the people are naive to maintain such "hope." In America we have been privileged to have at least for 23% of a millennia a document that has constrained those charged with governing to a specific set of guidelines. Those guidelines are all but erased as we are governed not by laws written by those charged with making the laws for they are figureheads and seldom put pen to paper or keystroke to computer to write a single law per the rules for lawmaking as stipulated in the Constitution. They have staff, think tanks, universities, law firms, and lobbyists with way too many lawyers, etc. that do all the work, then they don't even read it! How can that be?

How could me, you, or any person anywhere "trust" anyone whatsoever to do something, anything, anything at all, especially make a law that will affect my life and my neighbors life and take our labor to do it and not read that which they vote on. That is the way of it and with such an obvious fraud on the people America as managed by the US Corp will not likely make it to 25% of a millennia.

If they were required to write or type every and all words that come to the floor of the "people's houses," what might that mean? At minimum it would mean they would have to think for themselves. A good start!

But alas, the US Corp is so entangled with favor, not for the people, but rather for special interests which are private and corporate. No one stands in their own unlimited commercial liability, to the contrary, layers and layers of trust, corporations, legalese protections, and immunities allow those in government as well as the robber barons that lobby the people's labor to the benefit of a small, very small, cabal of thieves.

With all the bread and circus that the people are fed and allowed to see, hope for government is very, very elusive. How then, can the people be hopeful when those that represent them are so corrupt? I'm not sure! I am aware of Christian lobbyists that do have meetings with lawmakers and that's not nothing. However, it's the fruit of their labor as government officials that is hard to make sense of. For example, I'm not sure how one can pray to God Almighty, with comprehension of salvation for your soul being only through accepting that Jesus was God incarnate and went to the Cross, defeated death for you specifically and then vote for the dismemberment of, and murder of the unborn.

harpy: *a shrewish woman*

shrew: *an ill-tempered scolding woman*

When Christian lobbyists pray with these congressmen and senators do they pray as well as call them out to their face to repent? I don't know how it works, but it seems Jesus had no problem rebuking the government for sin. I don't know how the prayers go, I don't know how the meetings go, all that is visible is the fruit. The fruit is still millions of dead babies. Other fruit visible is the lack of visibility of legislators on news shows speaking about the murder of babies. That "lack of visibility" is in their world called politics or political survival. My hope for these government officials is that as they pray they consider with great introspection that while they may be avoiding ***"shrill harpies,"*** will they be judged in Heaven by harpies or Jesus? Another note is that when many a congressman, or senator, or other theoretical servant of the people does appear, Sunday is that day they choose. That fruit alone should give pause for they, if proper servants to the Lord Jesus, would be in a house of worship and not with a conscripted bought and paid for propaganda whore. Just a thought!

This is just one single point, but in no ways an insignificant point, about the fate of many a government soul. Hope then, hope for the government is a tough one for the government is like an onion with layers and layers of bureaucrats whom prepare the law the lawmakers should have. What the people are left with is layer upon layer of bureaucratic nonsense, each layer of which makes one cry for the depths of the fraud, theft, covetousness, murder, and violations by law of each of the ten commandments and especially the 1st,2nd, 3rd, and 4th. From NKJV --- Exodus 20:

I. **I am the Lord your God, which have brought you out of the land of Egypt, out of the house of bondage. You shall have no other gods before me.**

II. **You shall not make for yourself a carved image—any likeness of anything that is in heaven above, or that is in the earth beneath, or that is in the water under the earth; you shall not bow down to them nor serve them. For I, the Lord your God, am a jealous God, visiting the iniquity of the fathers upon the children to the third and fourth generations of those who hate Me, but showing mercy to thousands, to those who love Me and keep My commandments.**

III. **You shall not take the name of the Lord your God in vain, for the Lord will not hold him guiltless who takes His name in vain.**

IV. **Remember the Sabbath day, to keep it holy. Six days you shall labor and do all your work, but the seventh day is the Sabbath of the Lord your God. In it you shall do no work: you, nor your son, nor your daughter, nor your male servant, nor your female servant, nor your cattle, nor your stranger who is within your gates. For in six days the Lord made the heavens and the earth, the sea, and all that is in them, and rested the seventh day. Therefore the Lord blessed the Sabbath day and hallowed it.**

I think the fruit of the founders shows clearly that there main allegiance was to God as God was acknowledged in both the "Declaration of Independence" and the "Constitution for the United States of America." Could it have been done with more specificity, i.e., calling on Jesus Christ as the Lord of the nation? Yes, it could have, but it was not a pulpit sermon, it was a law document and thank God that someone thought to put the words:

> **Done in Convention by the Unanimous Consent of the States present the Seventeenth Day of September in the *Year of our Lord* one thousand seven hundred and Eighty seven and of the *Independence of the United States of America* the Twelfth In witness whereof We have hereunto subscribed our Names,**

Notice, "*Year of our Lord*"! Those very specific words could not then nor cannot now be misconstrued to mean anything other than recognition of Jesus Christ. It seems the most influential in the convention may have had only a belief in a God, but may have because of the virgin birth, been skeptical that Jesus could be the Son of God. These men held sway in what ended up on paper and whether intended or not the words, "*Year of our Lord*" are providential. The Constitutional Convention was made up of Christian men and those men were not tricked into penning their signatures to this document, they full well knew that Jesus died for salvation, freedom, and liberty. I know some disagree that they should not have chosen to pick up arms against the tyranny of the king of England, but providence it seems made it so. In any event what is important here is knowing that what is still espoused, at least sometimes, is that the Constitution is the "supreme law of the land," and further it was constituted for "the Independence of......America" as noted above and highlighted in "grey," and that "independence" was by "unanimous consent" to be under the "Lordship of Jesus" and no other.

The above thoughts, I think, make a reasonable argument that the "first" of the Ten Commandments were by unanimous consent properly considered by the framers. The part that causes much strife is that within the same document, "no religious test" shall preclude a person from holding an office of trust in the US of A government. What to make of this conundrum!

Right out of the gate the first president, George Washington, started a tradition not specified in the "constitution" and that was to place a hand on the Christian Bible while swearing an oath to uphold and defend the constitution. Was this a "religious test"? The answer is no, for George did it pursuant to the 1st Amendment, i.e., there was no law at the time prohibiting the free exercise of his religion. His choice to acknowledge God's law as the underwriter of his oath to another document, in this case the "constitution" shows a certain wisdom that George knew very well that the "Blessings of Liberty" as stated in the first sentence of the constitution could only come from a God. The document or piece of paper itself blesses no one. In that sense it is no different than the ancients making a golden calf only to worship it. What the framers did see is a way to shackle the whims of man to do evil with four branches of federal government and fifty state governments that in theory would constrain wrong.

> **religion:** *1) a personal set or institutionalized system of religious attitudes, beliefs, and practices; 2) the service and worship of God or the supernatural; 3) commitment or devotion to religious faith or observance*

> **test:** *a means of testing such as: 1) something (such as a series of questions or exercises) for measuring the skill, knowledge, intelligence, capacities, or aptitudes of an individual or group: 2) a procedure, reaction, or reagent used to identify or characterize a substance or constituent; 3) a positive result in such a test; 4) a critical examination, observation, or evaluation*

Wise on the one hand as the framers contemplated greatly those empires when run as a theocracy always fell or at minimum created conditions that were not favorable to the people. The framers were confident and cautious that this new document might work if the four branches of government understood their respective roles. Sadly it seems three of the four branches have been captured and the fourth doesn't know it is a branch.

It didn't take long however to start violating the 2nd commandment. September 17, 1787 the framers made a law document, whether wittingly or unwittingly, declaring Jesus as Lord. Three years later land was ceded for a new city, a noble city, which is most reasonable as an idea. After making a place to conduct the Lords business in a noble city why then is the "DC" district filled with idols and monuments, none of which recognize the Lord of America, save the crosses at Arlington. I'm not sure that there should be, but I'm just asking a question, why are there so many monuments to pagan gods, idols, and entities?

The physical buildings are a wonderful testimony to architecture and engineering, but why the pagan accoutrements. Why is the city laid out with the "religious faith" of the Masons? Why is the legal tender inscribed with the "religious symbols" of the Masons? If the constitution says that no "religious test" shall exist to hold office, why is it that the "test" of being a Mason is part of the fabric of D.C.? It could be a coincidence I suppose or it could be the fruit of a religion, i.e., ***a personal set or institutionalized system of religious attitudes, beliefs, and practices*** hidden in plain sight. Just a question?

The war of 1812 might have been a wakeup call from God, but it clearly wasn't heard, for the idolatry continued. From the founding in 1787 to 1812 was 25 years or 2.3% of a millennia. The British almost took the newly formed nation back. Anyway, it is what it is and a curiosity that most people never consider, nor do the people of America worship or bow down to the physical elements, but it does beg the question, why are they there? What the people of America perhaps are all guilty of is idolizing that district called DC and what goes on within its walls as our savior. We at minimum put way too much faith in the institutions.

> **wile:** *devious or cunning stratagems employed in manipulating or persuading someone to do what one wants*

The wiles of Satan started early. Many of the original leaders of the nation by their fruit showed an understanding that Jesus is Lord and underwrote, tacitly, the Constitution. For example, and most fortunately John Marshall by his fruit in writing the Marbury v Madison decision in 1803 shows a discernment that the wiles or, "cunning stratagems," as was attempted to federalize or make only the wishes of powerful men the law, that decision recognized the underwriting of the Constitution by Jesus as Lord and put a reasonable constraint on the whims of men whom by the power of their position would take rights, freedoms, liberties, and property from anyone they wish.

There have been many a righteous adjudication of matters, but sadly the scales are heavier on the side of unrighteous adjudication of matters especially today. As noted earlier that most of what governs America is a corporation with "color of law" agencies and policies, not law.

A cursory glance at the preamble to the constitution and considering it as a scorecard for the American government shows that in each of the itemized "wishes" or "hopes" for the institutions of government to perform on behalf of those they serve, that today in 2023 D.C. is failing in its duties. Let's break it down:

We the People of the United States, in Order to form a more perfect Union, establish Justice, insure domestic Tranquility, provide for the common defense, promote the general Welfare, and secure the Blessings of Liberty to ourselves and our Posterity, do ordain and establish this Constitution for the United States of America.

Table 1 – If the preamble is scored as if the people were its intended beneficiaries and 0 – 10 is the range, and 0 is a bad score in which the people are being robbed of their persons, houses, papers, and effects; and 10 would be the people are secure in those considerations.

Table 1 on next page:

Table 1

1	We the People....in order to secure	.2	No one is secure in their person (0); all are tenants not owners of homes (.5); all papers in public are not secure – trusts only (.3); effects are consigned to gov. by deceit (0) ---- average of these four = (.2)
2	A more perfect Union	1	Segregation not assimilation is the opposite of perfect (0); woke ideologies are opposite of perfect (0); baby killing is opposite of perfect (0); Christians (40%) +/- (4) ---- average of these four = (1)
3	Establish Justice	.2	Divers weights are not equal, secured vs. unsecured persons (.2)
4	Insure domestic tranquility	0	Antifa, BLM, mob rule, mob thieves, no bail, catch and release, open borders, abortion clinics, woke ideologies, depraved minds (0)
5	Provide a common defenses	3.5	Technologically (7); woke strategies (0) ---- average these categories (3.5)
6	Promote general welfare	0	Homelessness, drugs, mental health, despair, abortion, single motherhood, open borders, psy ops, depraved minds(0)
7	Secure blessings to ourselves	3	Education system (.5); Children in 2 parent household (69%) (4); children in single parent household (23%) (2.5); belief in God (79%) (5) ---- average these four categories (3)
8	Secure blessings to our posterity	0	32 trillion in debt;, borders meaningless; 1 mil babies murder/yr.; culture of death
	Total Score (possible 80)	**7.9**	**Or 9.8% of 80, or an average of .98 of the 8 categories. i.e. abysmal**

Table 2 on next page:

Table 2 – If the preamble is scored as if the people are only those within the jurisdiction of D.C. and are employees of US Corp. and it is those people that are its intended beneficiaries and 0 – 10 is the range, and 0 is a bad score in which those people; (US Corp employees) persons, houses, papers, and effects are being secured; and 10 would be that those people (US Corp employees) are secure in those considerations.

Table 2

1	We the People....in order to secure	10	They all have immunity (10); perhaps tenants but secure real estate to themselves (10); cloak of national security (10); effects of chattel secured to their benefit by deceit (10) ---- average of these four = (10)
2	A more perfect Union	10	Perfect for D.C. (10); anti-Christian policies (10) ---- average of these two = (10)
3	Establish Justice	10	Divers weights unbalanced to their favor always, secured
4	Insure domestic tranquility	10	Tranquility for D.C. and real estate of participants
5	Provide a common defenses	10	CIA, FBI, media weaponized; military ops secure interests of bankers and minions
5	Promote general welfare	10	Their general welfare is promoted by their vote to themselves
7	Secure blessings to ourselves	10	Their blessings to themselves are from Satan, i.e., unjust, not righteous
8	Secure blessings to our posterity	10	Their posterity protected at least for a time by their own vote.
	Total Score (possible 80)	**80**	**Or 80 out of 80, i.e. 100% effective for D.C.**

Certainly the above tables are subjective and anyone could weigh in and score it themselves and might feel my scoring in "Table 1" was tainted with bias. Fair enough, but, it seems reasonable that anything less than a perfect 80 in "Table 1" shows a most egregious violation of all public officials having sworn an "oath" to uphold and defend the constitution that was intended to be for Americans and not US Corp employees.

Further "Table 2" should not exist at all if America was a republic as intended. However, it is perhaps useful to see where the US Corp secures their blessings from and too. If both scorecards were 80 it would indicate that the employees were righteously "securing blessings."

Such analysis lays bare that the supposed Christians within US Corp. pay little attention to the underwriting of the Constitution being "In the year of our Lord" and that Lord is Jesus the Christ, the Son of God, and that Lord should be the underwriting of every thought, every expression, every blessing you should be securing for God's children. Anything less, although you may think your security is safe, it is but temporal and in the long run may find you at a wide gate. This simple analogy suggests a direct, not an indirect, violation of the 3rd commandment…..**Thou shalt not take the name of the LORD thy God in vain; for the LORD will not hold him guiltless that taketh his name in vain.** The key word is "vain."

> **vain**: *1) producing no result; useless; 2) marked by futility or ineffectualness; 3) having no real value*

The lawmaker, administrator, bureaucrat, judge, lobbyist, et al., might consider that if they in any way make God's law, especially the moral laws, ineffectual, futile, of no value, or in any way contradictory to His command of a very specific "shall not" then as the 3rd commandment notes in its attached judgment, your God will not hold you guiltless.

With that in mind, do you:

> **covet** – do you covet your position, status, power, fleshly desires, the game, other people's money, etc.
>
> **bear false witness** – do you speak with forked tongue; do you attribute bad character to individuals, or groups without evidence; do you lie with intent to deceive, do you vote to protect the lie and liars, etc.
>
> **steal** – do you vote to unsecure the "blessings by God" and Gods commandments of liberty, freedom and justice; do you vote or opine to unsecure a man's God given right to defend himself physically or defend himself by his word; do you vote or opine to steal a man's right to an opinion; do you vote or opine to steal a man's labor; are you complicit in not voting or opining on correcting the usurpations of all the theft heretofore made in law or color of law.
>
> **adultery** – do you commit adultery, do you lust in your mind, do you vote for or opine on any consideration whatsoever that makes

any "non God" ordained covenant, union, or bond acceptable and therefore making God's "shall not" vain, i.e., ineffectual, of no value, futile, and useless.

murder – do you murder, do you murder or think ill of or hate those that don't agree with you, do you vote for or opine on the murder of any human life, do you vote for, opine, or appropriate funds stolen from another man's labor to send the sons and daughters of mothers and fathers to take the lives of anyone for the monetary enrichment to yourself or others.

honor mother & father – do you honor your parents, do you vote on or opine on any law, color of law, or institutions that make for and steal another man's labor to support any circumstance whatsoever that would support conditions for which mothers and fathers cannot be honored for your votes have created and supported the undermining of the family, hence rendering mothers and fathers moot; do you vote for, opine, or appropriate other people's money to support families that are not as ordained by God.

Sabbath, keep it holy – do you set aside a day to worship, do you consider that your soul is in danger, do you pray, do you consider the wrongness of your violations, do you repent.

It should be obvious that all government officials need to be prayed for, evangelized, pitied, prayed for some more for the fruit seen directly and indirectly with a small modicum of discernment shows that violations of the 10 commandments, or moral law, by the American form of government is in crisis.

So far what is contemplated above shows how easy it is to make an idol out of anything including one's own thought. Pity is proper to feel for the lawmakers for how difficult to not be tempted. The consideration about idolatry has been a direct condemnation of the unclean hands of politicians and that is a fair reasonable assessment.

Christians statesmen need to first, repent, second turn, third be bold, pray Ephesians 6: 10 through 20 each morning and before they put their signature to anything they do on behalf of this "One nation under God."

NKJV --- Ephesians 6: 10 through 20 --- The Armor of God

> *10 Finally, my brethren, be strong in the Lord and in the power of His might. 11 Put on the whole armor of God, that you may be able to stand against the wiles of the devil. 12 For we do not wrestle against flesh and blood, but against principalities, against powers, against the rulers of the darkness of this age, against spiritual hosts of wickedness in the heavenly places. 13 Therefore take up the whole armor of God, that you may be able to withstand in the evil day, and having done all, to stand.*
>
> *14 Stand therefore, having girded your waist with truth, having put on the breastplate of righteousness, 15 and having shod your feet with the preparation of the gospel of peace; 16 above all, taking the shield of faith with which you will be able to quench all the fiery darts of the wicked one. 17 And take the helmet of salvation, and the sword of the Spirit, which is the word of God; 18 praying always with all prayer and supplication in the Spirit, being watchful to this end with all perseverance and supplication for all the saints— 19 and for me, that utterance may be given to me, that I may open my mouth boldly to make known the mystery of the gospel, 20 for which I am an ambassador in chains; that in it I may speak boldly, as I ought to speak.*

Even better, do it in session, boldly together, out loud for the people to hear. Then close with Ephesians 6: 23 and 24.

> **NKJV --- Ephesians 6: 23 and 24** -- *23) Peace to the brethren, and love with faith, from God the Father and the Lord Jesus Christ. 24) Grace be with all those who love our Lord Jesus Christ in sincerity. Amen.*

Note that this is consistent with the 1st amendment that Congress can make "no" law that prohibits the free exercise of religion. Such a thing would, I think, be glorious to the ears of God and America and send a message to the world that America just might make it to the 25% mark of a millennia and beyond. Hope! Wow! There's some hope for ya! God would be pleased, but the devil would not!

Just under 90% of each house claims to be Christian. Well, put your faith where your mouth is! The percentages are certainly on your side. Ride into the valley, the gospel is with you.

pampered: *indulge with every attention, comfort, and kindness; spoil*

If the rules and protocols of whatever chamber imprisons your speech, your freedom, your faith; imagine the apostle Paul literally chained to a Roman guard and "in chains" for years and yet he was able to speak and write about Christ crucified and that speaking and writing made it across the centuries like no other words ever. Notice that in Paul's letter to the Ephesians noted above in verse 19 and 20, Paul asked for prayers so that "whenever" he opened his mouth he could be fearless to make known the gospel. If Paul could proclaim Christ from Rome in the miserable conditions of a Roman prison, is it not reasonable and possible that you "Christians" can, from the "pampered" positions that the people have bestowed upon you be a bit; no; not a bit, but a large measure more bold and 1) ask for prayers that you may be as bold as Paul, and 2) consider that "every" measure of your work should be for the glory of Jesus the Christ.

Will your words be remembered beyond the next news cycle? Will you be remembered at all one month after you are out of office? Will you have an impact with any words you may write or utter as impactful as Paul? The answer is "maybe," but your fruit thus far makes it seem unlikely. Imagine what might be said about you or a coalition of Christians in government that speaks and writes with boldness about the true Lord of America and then bears fruit that clearly shows that your Master is Christ, not Satan.

Personally I have prayed generally for lawmakers, and I know many do, but sadly more prayers are needed for the fruit of your labor does not point to righteousness. Maybe start with a public pronouncement of repentance and request for prayer!!!!

Hope in government. As it is it doesn't look good. With Jesus on board and acknowledged, the ship of state currently headed for the rocks can be steered to peaceful waters where hope can not only save a nation, but with the gospel as our flag other nations will be in awe. The problem then would be exporting the good word so other nations could likewise benefit in the "hope" that is Jesus and salvation.

Be representatives of Christ first, then it is conceivable that the "tables" noted above in Tables 1 & 2 could be turned!

And while we're at it start drilling so we can help our neighbors not freeze to death.

~ HOPE FOR "WE THE PEOPLE" ~

The "people" described as "we the people" in the constitution is an oddity. Patriots today often express the words as if they had a force. They of course are just words on a parchment penned almost 236 years ago. The "we the people" alive at the time the words were penned was approximately 3.8 million. The "we the people" alive today is near 350 million none of which were the "we the people" the document was written for. Certainly then the tacit understanding of the document would be that it was intended for the nation and "the people" in perpetuity.

That aside, what do the words mean? What should they mean? What force do they have? There is a maxim that a court cannot move unless someone, a person, moves it. Simple concept and seems logical and it is. Likewise, "we the people" cannot move unless someone moves. "We the People" is in fact the fourth branch of government, but cannot do anything without a greater number of "we's" moving. Marxists understand this better that Americans. Look what they, "BLM and Antifa" accomplished in property damage in one summer, i.e. they moved. The fact that the supposed representatives of "we the people" did nothing to stop it lays bare that they are not representatives of what the average American thinks they are supposed to be representing. In other words, you will know them by their fruit.

So what then? The people must wake up, and secondly the people must move. Complaining to your TV is not movement. Engagement at the seats of government, in all of its forms is essential for the 4th branch.

The particulars of how to move is neither the subject nor the intent for this book. The subject is repentance. The hope for "We the People" then would be the same as the hope expressed in the previous section, "Hope for the Governments" for the "people" are the 4th branch of government and need to engage with the full armor of God. Once again, read the gospels, read the constitution, read the "Citizens Rule Book," and engage.

It is obvious that America is on a collision course to extinction. If this nation was once protected under the Wing of God's protection it seems clear that His protections are being withdrawn. It would be my hope and I know the hope of all Christians that America be like Nineveh. Repent and turn! Hope for "We the People" lies in repentance and prayer.

~ HOPE FOR THE CHURCH ~

My short journey in the realm of the church and having learned, contemplated, discussed, and discerned, once again my imagination considers an allegory to explain what the church has become over the centuries. But first, what is the church? Hope for the church must consider first that question – what is "the church"?

> **unambiguous** - *not open to more than one interpretation*
>
> **institute** - *set in motion or establish (something, especially a program, system, or inquiry)*
>
> ***nebulous*** - *(of a concept or idea) unclear, vague, or ill-defined; 2) indistinct, vague*

The word church and its etymology have as its tap root with very clear and "unambiguous" origin those that gather in the name of Jesus Christ and His words and Him alone. His words then are the mortar of the church. His words, if read, contemplated, discussed, and discerned are clear and "unambiguous." The church then became an "institution" of, by, and for Jesus, the Son of God who "instituted" it. What it is then, "the church," is a gathering of two or more whom are in union to worship, read, discuss, study, learn, be taught, pray, rejoice in song, weep, repent, and consider with humility the wonder that is the free offer of salvation and how we also can share the "good news" that death can be defeated .

The word "church" in 2023, like the word "gender" has become "nebulous." How so? It is not because the Word of God as spoken through the Christian Bible, from Moses to the apostle John on Patmos, is "unambiguous," rather it is because as is stated "unambiguously" from

Christ Himself that "***many would come***" and pervert His words, therefore rendering His Words as vain, i.e.:

> **vain:** *1) producing no result; useless; 2) marked by futility or ineffectualness; 3) having no real value*
>
> **schism:** *a split or division between strongly opposed sections or parties, caused by differences in opinion or belief*
>
> **ostentatious:** *attracting or seeking to attract attention, admiration, or envy often by gaudiness or obviousness: overly elaborate or conspicuous: characterized by, fond of, or evincing ostentation*
>
> **denomination:** *a recognized branch of the Christian Church*
>
> **bastardized** - *lower in quality or value than the original form, typically as a result of the addition of new elements*

Since Jesus instituted the church "many" did come just as He said and caused many schisms in the church which started soon after the apostles made clear what a church was supposed to look like. Humility, gathering together, worship, prayer, singing, and staying true to the word were simple and clear in the gospels and the letters now known as epistles thankfully left by those taught by Jesus for the "instituted" church. It took some time to assemble those New Testament scriptures which did then and do now layout what the church should be.

It would be but a short couple of hundred years for the first schism to happen and it would be a large one and an "ostentatious" one at that. Copying the "ostentatious" nature of the Pharisees and Pagan elements of the Roman and Greek gods and cultures filled with much pomp and circumstance the first schism lasted for over a thousand years before someone noticed. That schism has survived to our time, but has been further "bastardized" with many an element not "instituted" by Jesus.

When someone final noticed a schism happened, but not in a completely new direction. This schism was not what one might think, or a split in a new direction, it was a rebuke of the ostentatious first schism and a call to revert or "reform" back to the teachings of Christ and Christ's apostles.

After that first "reform" there have been many a schism, some tangents off of the original 1st schism and other schisms shooting off of the "reformed" schism. All of this schism business are the history of the church and do cause much confusion especially for newcomers. With hundreds if not thousands of houses of worship called "the church" what is one to do that wishes to gather with others as we are commanded to do.

Thankfully God is patient and He has gifted us with the ability to learn. Today it is easier than ever to check out what are now known as "denominations" of Christian churches. The first order is the read the Word. Then via the internet study the schisms and why. Check out the history of each; be skeptical especially of those that claim "special revelation" to men that did not walk with Christ. Further, if a denomination instructs to not listen to or discuss or learn other views and or schisms that have anything added to the Christian bible be on your guard. Keep searching. You can listen at double time via YouTube say two sermons a day of various denominations which by the math means twelve in six days. The seventh day of course to be set aside to give thanks too and know the God you seek. In short order you will be curious and hear solid as well as very questionable sermons. Ask around; when you find an expository preacher ask to visit with him. Most importantly stay in the Word, i.e., read the Bible daily and pray.

~ ALLEGORY OF THE FISH ~

The word fish we all understand is an all-encompassing word to describe what we know to be thousands of different types of critters that swim through and can breathe under water. Further, the water fish swim in can be categorized into three main types - fresh, brackish, and salt. Everyone surely knows what fresh water is and what salt water is, but unless you happen to live where brackish water is located you may not be aware of it and what it is. Brackish water is found mainly where rivers meet oceans and the waters mix, making varying degrees and or mixtures of fresh and salt water.

What does this have to do with fish and this allegory about fish and the church? Simplistic perhaps, sophomoric okay, but here goes. First of all the allegory is for Christian churches, or denominations that claim a commune with Jesus. For those faiths that believe in or worship a deity or have a faith in someone or something other than Jesus Christ of the Christian Bible, this allegory would consider them an island unto themselves.

By the numbers most fish live in salt water, a lesser number live in brackish water and fewer still live in fresh water. It seems there is only one fish that lives in and thrives peacefully in the freshest water of all. High in the highest mountains where the freshest water falls from the sky as snow and then melts into the high mountain lakes there is one species of fish called a brook trout. The water is as pure as pure can be and the burdens for the brook trout is light. This water then is like the gospel, pure and undefiled. A church that stays in the pure water of the gospels within the Christian bible will be like the brook trout that swim in these high mountain lakes and small brooks, or narrow gates, if you will, to thrive in the fresh water lakes of which there are many around the world, but few will find.

As rivers flow toward the oceans they widen and support more varieties of fish, beautiful fish, creatures of God, but the waters they swim in become murky and cloudy with impurities picked up on the way to the oceans. These fish are like the many denominations of the Christian church that have clouded the gospel with impurities not found in the head waters. These Christians, like fish, gather in schools of thought that have created the denominations. These fish are close to the freshest water, or these churches are close to the pure gospel, but alas, they seem to have grown scales on their eyes and cannot see clearly like the brook trout. Fishermen know that a brook trout in a high mountain lake can see a predator, or wolf in sheep clothing, to steal from and another allegory, from a good distance and are happy to defend the faith and show off the wonder found in clear water.

As the river reaches the ocean brackish water supports fewer types of fish or denominations of churches, but still has the hope that is in the fresh water. For example, there are many schools of thought that invoke the name of Jesus, but not only have picked up the pollutants on the journey to the oceans, but have made up or written extra biblical books declaring these books to be the new authority written by boastful fish that came along long after the Master fishermen left His tackle box for anyone to open. They take out some tackle and replace it with other tackle and instruct their fish to only consider what these boastful fish say and use their newest tackle and suggest the first tackle box is wrong.

The salty water of the oceans has the most fish, but lives in the least fresh water. Most of the Christian denominations sadly swim together in salty waters. Most of the fish share a commonality in that they are ig fish of their own making. Ig fishes are abundant and easily become nose-ring fish for which there are many a "pomp and pred" fish that cast their nets into the shoals ready to haul in a catch of unwitting ig fish knowing how easy it is to turn an ig fish into a nose-ring.

Some of these "pomp and pred" fish might be called cloak fish or idol fish, or cloak and collar fish, i.e., cloaked in the idolatry of self-righteousness they deceive themselves and have deceived billions of ig & nose-ring fish to believe that these cloak fish are the way, the truth, and the life and if the ig & nose rings will follow their lead, follow their instructions, follow and consider the tackle in their tackle boxes to be the way because they wear shiny cloaks. Once they convince the ig fish that the cloak & collar fish are special then the ig and nose-ring fish will work as the cloak & collar fish prescribe and if they work and obey certain cloak fish magic rituals then the ig & nose-ring fish might, possibly, maybe get a pass to the big dock in the sky. It is more likely that all ig & nose rings will have to be purged in a purge tank and then maybe possibly, but not for sure the ig & nose-ring fish may make it to fish heaven. The ig & nose ring fish blindly follow the cloak fish and don't consider the narrow brooks for most don't look in the tackle box for if they did they might see that they are swimming in wide oceans and not the narrow brooks explained in the main tackle box. These ig & nose-ring fish sadly don't know that they are prey. Guilt, shame, and fear keep the ig & nose-rings scurrying to the clefts and caves and may never see an estuary, or know there is a pure water lake at all or a narrow brook that leads there.

There are also "money," aka, pyramid fish that prey on a similar school of ig & nose-ring fish called a naïf fish offering them blessings and prosperity if they give the fruit of their labor to the "money" fish with the biggest mouth in that particular school.

Other schools of ig & nose-rings are led by "claim" fish convincing other types of ig & nose-rings that they have but to call into existence anything they may desire. These ig & nose-rings naively purchase a diet of masticated bull fish chum that they swallow thinking they too can call out to the "rocks, gases, and cold" in the universe and a car, job, house, and even their very own ocean will be theirs. All of these material blessings are there for the claiming, but of course they must continue to purchase and pay for the masticated bull fish from the leader claim fish with the largest mouth that is providing all the bull fish.

Other schools are "Simon says" or "Say it with me," or "feel good" fish that are easily hypnotized by lullaby music to fall over, roll around, blow bubbles that make noises no other fish understands, and jump around to loud music that tickles their gills, but teaches nothing from the fresh water and the fresh water tackle box. These are a curious lot. A Simon fish with a certain charisma can somehow get a peculiar type of ig or nose-ring to do whatever the big daddy "Simon" fish says. If the big daddy "Simon" fish says, "repeat after me….blah, blah, blah," the feel good ig fish will spout back, "blah, blah, blah." If the big daddy "Simon" fish says blow bubbles that make no sense and no fish anywhere could possible understand and convince this curious lot that these nonsense bubbles mean something to the Master. Very curious indeed!!!

Another unique school of fish is led by double X, flap jaw blabber gill fish that may have once accidentally jumped into a fisherman's boat and rather than slip back into the water quietly, they flapped and flipped and flipped and flopped until they flapped themselves back into the water. Then they somehow managed to find large schools of ig & nose-ring fish that they convinced that they had been gifted by the Master fisherman a special fisherman's license to flap jaw and blabber about things they saw while flapping around in the boat. It is more reasonable that their flap jaw blabber gills were starving for oxygen when they were flapping and flipping in the boat and also may have dislodged a scale or two that landed on their eyes and missed the Master Fisher's fishing instruction about double X flap jaw blabber gills to be silent in matters concerning finding the narrow brooks and fresh water lakes. I reviewed this particular allegory with a colleague who recognized the parallel post haste to real world certain church leaders of ig fish & noise-rings, but suggested an example from the secular world might be helpful to make clear the veiled, but hysterical and candidly accurate adjectives for this fish. My colleague's suggestion was that if anyone might wonder what a flap jaw blabber gill fish sounds like one might tune into "The View."

So as not to be misunderstood, double X flap jaw blabber gills, are very rare, but do seem to gather in their seductive nets plenty of ig & nose-rings of the single X and double X varieties. Flap jaw blabber gills should not be confused with sugar & spice & everything nice fish. Most double X fish may swim in schools of ig & nose-ring fish, but because they are also angel fish, lady fish, lovely, and sugar & spice fish they also recognize a double X flap jaw blabber gill when they see one. These beautiful angel, lady, and lovely fish are most welcome in the fresh water lakes.

As I consider how to wrap up this allegory two curiosities about using fish as allegorical cross over replacements for man and how man behaves, it dawned on me that the allegory falls apart in certain circumstances. Let me explain. Last night I thought a good while about sandwich fish, letter fish, gender fish, and woke fish.

Sandwich fish would be the lettuce, bacon, guacamole, and tomato fish. The letter fish would be all of the newest letters wanting to have a place in the original school with the sandwich fish. As most sandwich connoisseurs know too much stuff in a sandwich can be a hot mess. Another sandwich seems unlikely since none of the letters can be categorized with any reasonable vegetable or lunch meat, so what to do? This is where my allegory starts to fall apart.

As I consider the fish in the lakes and oceans in the real world it strikes me that while there is only one race of humans with perhaps less than ten different colors, in the fish world there likewise is one "race" or category of fish, but there are thousands, and maybe tens of thousands, of different varieties and colors. Interestingly, in both groups there are only two types of biological arrangements of cells that can come together to make a new biological arrangement of cells. One biological arrangement of cells has been termed male while the other has been termed female and the term used to distinguish between the two biological structures is sex, one being male and the other being female. Quite useful I think! The fish world doesn't seem to be confused by the roles each of these biological arrangements play in their realm. Humans didn't use to, but now some humans seem to be oblivious to the generally revealed truths available for us to consider. Truths as one might find in fishes, for instance!

So for me to conflate the sanity of the real fish world that conduct their fish affairs with very specific roles for these two sexes of fish with the insanity of the human world that seems to have a dysphoria attached to, at least a small percentage of its ranks, makes my allegory fall completely apart. Therefore, I've decided to steer this boat clear of the shallow dangerous coral reefs where the sandwich fish, letter fish, gender fish, and woke fish swim. It would be poor sportsmanship and disingenuous and insulting to fish to compare them even allegorically to humans at all, but especially to certain schools of ig and nose ring church fishes that have thrown out the very explicit tackle concerning sandwich, letter, gender and woke fish. For some reason many a salty water church claiming Jesus as Lord have been deceived by the very slimy im-moray eel, aka, devil fish that seems to have removed their spines rendering them jelly fish whom hate the sandwich fish, letter fish, gender fish, and woke fish. Rather than throw the lost fish a life line to pull them into the lifeboats, they offer them anchors of the dead that will surely drag their confused souls to the depths of Davy Jones locker. Unless the tackle box is opened the brackish and salty water churches along with the sandwich fish, letter fish, gender fish, and woke fish will end up washed up on the shores of the island of Sheol.

Also, this is probably a good place to point out and make clear that brook trout generally have a good sense of humor gifted to them by the Master Fisherman. This trait called humor is specific to humans just as much as the trait called anger, neither of which is a trait of fish. For clarity the author was laughing while considering what spilled out on the docks in this "fish allegory." I hope you see it!!!! It is not lost on the author, however, that this allegory will instill the trait of anger in certain allegorical fish. If so, it is the author's sincere hope for the angry fish to perhaps consider that this fisherman loves all of the fish and wishes for all fish everywhere, in any water, to find the narrow brooks. Also, this sojourner fish is hopeful that when I get to the "big dock" in "the lake of the ever after" that I don't hear the words, "Depart from me, this lake isn't for you." i.e., I pray God I have found the fresh water lakes and am now a brook trout. Further, it should be explained that the brook trout are not perfect fish; they like all fish in any type of water are sick with the first virus of sin, but are fortunate to swim in the fresh water hospital of the gospel.

This is a silly allegory and perhaps you might consider your church and that you may not be a brook trout. You may, however, be an ig fish and or a nose-ring. The good news is ig & nose-ring fish have only to swim upstream to the fresh water and find the narrow brooks leading to the lakes where the brook trout hang out. Being an ig fish and or a nose-ring fish is temporary. You can learn away the ig and shake loose the nose rings or if you have a hook firmly embedded in your gullet, find a brook trout that will be happy to help with whatever hook has you landed in the wrong water. But, and this is a must, you have to want to open the tackle box. Once opened and then devouring all of the 66 compartments in the tackle box you will find that you desire to swim upstream.

The hope then for the church or more precisely "the denominations" of churches is that all of the fish in whatever church you are in realize 1) this is an allegory; 2) you may not be in the right water; 3) you are not a fish, you are called to be a fisherman; 4) open the tackle box; 5) learn about the different types of fish; 6) go fishing, i.e., disciple the nations, and hopefully as a brook trout!

~ POLITICS & THE CHURCH ~

In my journey within the body of a church I find myself in learning mode and requiring much more knowledge concerning the roll of the church in the state. To this point I confess ignorance, but thinking nonetheless. Years ago I spent much time studying Americanism, constitutional issues, law, color of law, etc. So, the comments below reflect some of that journey which I realize is in conflict with some of the sermons I have heard on the subject. What I have penned therefore are observations of and considerations of what an American form of government as instituted by God looks like.

As I begin, I will quote a statement made to me by my sister and brother-in-law and attributed to Robert Costanza, circa 1989.

"The most insidious form of ignorance is misplaced certainty."

Which is to say, I am professing my ignorance and am not at all certain, and perhaps am in good company for this topic has been contemplated for 2000 years and most certainly for the 236 years of the American experiment.

Below is Romans 13 in all caps font (COPPERSTATE GOTHIC LIGHT) IS FROM THE KING JAMES BIBLE I.E., KJV);

while Romans 13 from the New International Version i.e., (NIV); is in a normal font (Times New Roman) and;

> *my thoughts concerning each verse are "italicized" below each verse and indented.*

Romans 13

KJV --- 1) LET EVERY SOUL BE SUBJECT UNTO THE HIGHER POWERS. FOR THERE IS NO POWER BUT OF GOD: THE POWERS THAT BE ARE ORDAINED OF GOD.

NIV --- 1) Let everyone be subject to the governing authorities, for there is no authority except that which God has established. The authorities that exist have been established by God.

> *In America the "higher powers" or "governing authorities" is "WE THE PEOPLE," therefore the "every soul" (KJV) or "everyone" (NIV) would be the "subjects" or the servants of "THE PEOPLE." In other words, the representative "servants" are sent by the higher power or governing authorities to do the "ordained" or "established" righteous work of God on behalf of the "higher power" / "governing authority of "THE PEOPLE." Therefore, it is reasonable to conclude that God has established "the power" or "the authority" of "WE THE PEOPLE."*

KJV --- 2) WHOSOEVER THEREFORE RESISTETH THE POWER, RESISTETH THE ORDINANCE OF GOD: AND THEY THAT RESIST SHALL RECEIVE TO THEMSELVES DAMNATION.

NIV --- 2) Consequently, whoever rebels against the authority is rebelling against what God has instituted, and those who do so will bring judgment on themselves.

> *The servant representatives that "resist" or "rebel" against the authorities of "THE PEOPLE" "ordained" or "instituted" by God will bring the judgment of God on themselves for they are not a terror to*

evil, they have become the evil. In 2023 America "THE PEOPLE" as authorities are not guiltless for they are not conducting themselves as the proper power / authority.

KJV --- 3) FOR RULERS ARE NOT A TERROR TO GOOD WORKS, BUT TO THE EVIL. WILT THOU THEN NOT BE AFRAID OF THE POWER? DO THAT WHICH IS GOOD, AND THOU SHALT HAVE PRAISE OF THE SAME

NIV --- 3) For rulers hold no terror for those who do right, but for those who do wrong. Do you want to be free from fear of the one in authority? Then do what is right and you will be commended.

If the servants represent the rulers and or authorities which are "THE PEOPLE" righteously the servants have nothing to fear. If the servants do right they will be commended. If you find as servants that "THE PEOPLE" condemn your service more than your service is praised for your works are not good and clear violations of the moral law of God and therefore evil, then you are in danger. If not in this world, most certainly the next.

KJV --- 4) FOR HE IS THE MINISTER OF GOD TO THEE FOR GOOD. BUT IF THOU DO THAT WHICH IS EVIL, BE AFRAID; FOR HE BEARETH NOT THE SWORD IN VAIN: FOR HE IS THE MINISTER OF GOD, A REVENGER TO EXECUTE WRATH UPON HIM THAT DOETH EVIL.

NIV --- 4) For the one in authority is God's servant for your good. But if you do wrong, be afraid, for rulers do not bear the sword for no reason. They are God's servants, agents of wrath to bring punishment on the wrongdoer.

For "THE PEOPLE" are "ministers of God" or "Gods servants" to see that "THE PEOPLE'S" servants sent to do good in fact "do good." If "THE PEOPLES" servants rebel against the authorities, i.e., "WE THE PEOPLE" and do wrong, and are not righteous it is incumbent on the authorities "THE PEOPLE" to use the power of "THE PEOPLE" to use the constituted powers bequeathed on the servants to "with prejudice" and righteous wrath, bring punishment on the wrongdoing servant as well as one of "THE PEOPLE" as it may apply to the righteous requirements of God. A side note is the curiosity that the original authorities would not bequeath the servants the power to remove "THE PEOPLE'S" swords. Would that not be an indication of God's establishment of righteous power to the authorities, once again, "THE PEOPLE"?

KJV --- 5) WHEREFORE YE MUST NEEDS BE SUBJECT, NOT ONLY FOR WRATH, BUT ALSO FOR CONSCIENCE SAKE.

NIV --- 5) Therefore, it is necessary to submit to the authorities, not only because of possible punishment but also as a matter of conscience.

Therefore, servants, submit to the will of "THE PEOPLE." Clearly "possible" punishment you have evaded for you have made yourselves immune from the punishment you deserve and seem to be void of conscience. Beware!!

KJV --- 6) FOR THIS CAUSE PAY YE TRIBUTE ALSO: FOR THEY ARE GOD'S MINISTERS, ATTENDING CONTINUALLY UPON THIS VERY THING.

NIV --- 6) This is also why you pay taxes, for the authorities are God's servants, who give their full time to governing.

Tribute redefined as taxes may be a problem for tribute means an acknowledgment of gratitude, respect or admiration. That aside, truly, "WE THE PEOPLE," are "God's servants" and would gladly pay "our servants" a reasonable sum for the servant's labor. A problem exists when the servants do not give their full time governing and have stolen "THE PEOPLES" labor to "farm out" the duties constituted to the servants and that which they do attend to is not right but wrong and in fact evil and the "farm entities" are all evil. To give tribute in the form of gratitude, respect, or admiration is rendered as moot for you "servants" betray yourselves by your fruit. For all of time with but few exceptions taxes have been by force and if by force and not by gift freely given, is it not tyranny?

KJV --- 7) RENDER THEREFORE TO ALL THEIR DUES: TRIBUTE TO WHOM TRIBUTE IS DUE; CUSTOM TO WHOM CUSTOM; FEAR TO WHOM FEAR; HONOR TO WHOM HONOR.

NIV --- 7) Give to everyone what you owe them: If you owe taxes, pay taxes; if revenue, then revenue; if respect, then respect; if honor, then honor.

> *Working backwards: to whom do "WE THE PEOPLE" owe honor when the servants conduct themselves without honor. Respect: to whom does "WE THE PEOPLE" owe respect when the servants of the people show no respect? "Custom" conflated with "revenue" is a problem. In any case, "render" or "give politeness to the house you may enter as may be their "custom" would be good manners. To "render" or "give" "revenue from one of "WE THE PEOPLE" to another of "WE THE PEOPLE" should be a private not a public affair. The servants of the people are owed no consideration whatsoever of private matters. Taxes collected to pay the servants and/or for public projects with honor would be owed voluntarily and if the public servants and projects are done with honor, with respect, and righteously, a thriving nation we would be.*

Love Fulfills the Law

KJV --- 8) OWE NO MAN ANYTHING, BUT TO LOVE ONE ANOTHER: FOR HE THAT LOVETH ANOTHER HATH FULFILLED THE LAW.

NIV --- 8) Let no debt remain outstanding, except the continuing debt to love one another, for whoever loves others has fulfilled the law.

> *If there is a debt owed whether in duty, responsibility, or financial, to whom it is owed should be known in the flesh and is private and only public as the private parties may agree. Love of others, our enemies and God's enemies is a light burden with Jesus. This presupposes that God has enemies, which He does and has made clear. Concerning the servants of "WE THE PEOPLE," they are in trouble in God's court for they create unjustified, unrighteous debt, compounding without end. Further, they purport that the authorities, i.e., "WE THE PEOPLE," owe the debt when it is they whom created it. How is it that the servants encumber their masters with debt? Those of "WE THE PEOPLE" that take money from another of "WE THE PEOPLE" through a proxy are guilty of stealing. In God's kingdom there will be no money so there can be no debt as we understand coin debt. There will be debt required in love.*

KJV --- 9) FOR THIS, THOU SHALT NOT COMMIT ADULTERY, THOU SHALT NOT **KILL**, THOU SHALT NOT STEAL, THOU SHALT NOT BEAR FALSE WITNESS, THOU SHALT NOT COVET; AND IF THERE BE ANY OTHER COMMANDMENT, IT IS BRIEFLY COMPREHENDED IN THIS SAYING, NAMELY, THOU SHALT LOVE THY NEIGHBOR AS THYSELF.

NIV --- 9) The commandments, "You shall not commit adultery," "You shall not **murder**," "You shall not steal," "You shall not covet," and whatever other command there may be, are summed up in this one command: "Love your neighbor as yourself."

> *How to love self? I wouldn't want to have adultery committed against me. I would not want someone to murder me or think about murdering me. I would not want someone to want or covet anything that is mine or has been joined to me by God. I would not want someone to conduct any act whatsoever against me or anyone created in the "image of God" that is not natural as is clear in God's word and God's general revelation. Concerning the word "kill" vs. "murder." The word kill is a translation of the Hebrew word ratsach, which nearly always refers to intentional killing without cause which is murder. Concerning the "Any Other Commandment," or "Whatever Other Command" references: the "Other Commandments" are laid out with specificity in the Bible, picking and choosing which ones to follow is folly, and when the servants make law that makes it a crime to call out the "Commands of God" to not partake in sins of the flesh, the servants are violating the command to love, and make themselves proxies for sin and not "The People" whom are to love but also declare the gospel.*

KJV --- 10) LOVE WORKETH NO ILL TO HIS NEIGHBOR: THEREFORE LOVE IS THE FULFILLING OF THE LAW.

NIV --- 10) Love does no harm to a neighbor. Therefore love is the fulfillment of the law.

> *As it concerns the servants of "WE THE PEOPLE," they have usurped the law of love completely and cause and continue to cause harm to humanity at such a grand scale it should not be a surprise that God has removed His blessing to the once "One Nation Under God." God help us.*

The Day Is Near

KJV --- 11) AND THAT, KNOWING THE TIME, THAT NOW IT IS HIGH TIME TO AWAKE OUT OF SLEEP, FOR NOW IS OUR SALVATION NEARER THAN WHEN WE BELIEVED.

NIV --- 11) And do this, understanding the present time. The hour has already come for you to wake up from your slumber, because our salvation is nearer now than when we first believed.

> *Whether one of "THE PEOPLE" or one of the peoples "SERVANTS" it should be abundantly clear that, 1) each of us individually is closer to dead than we were yesterday. 2) America is closer to dead with each appropriation for obvious wrong. 3) Some of "THE PEOPLE," are waking up, some of the "CHURCHES" are waking up, some of the "servants" are waking up --- but what can be seen of America, whether in "THE PEOPLE," "THE CHURCH," or "THE PEOPLES SERVANTS" the majority of the FRUIT is still rotten. 4) The KJV states, it is "high time"; and as the NIV states, "the hour has already come." For America does this mean a) that this is the time to wake up (KJV), or, the time is past and it is too late to wake up? We'll see! I pray for the "CHURCH" to wake up first. Then, if as "THE SERVANTS" bios boast, the "SERVANTS" are Christians; call them to account, that is to say, repent!*

KJV --- 12) THE NIGHT IS FAR SPENT, THE DAY IS AT HAND, LET US THEREFORE CAST OFF THE WORKS OF DARKNESS, AND LET US PUT ON THE ARMOR OF LIGHT.

NIV --- 12) The night is nearly over; the day is almost here. So let us put aside the deeds of darkness and put on the armor of light.

> *Again, what is it going to take for man to wake up? We are closer to dead, America is closer to dead. But alas, wake up, gird yourself, secure your work shoes, cast off laziness which is darkness, contend for the faith, contend for liberty, contend for the virtue of the "SERVANTS." Demand, not hope, that your "SERVANTS" put on the armor of light that is CHRIST JESUS. Put on armor that includes knowledge of God, fear of God, knowledge of how the rulers became the servants/ slaves, and the servant/slaves became the rulers. With that armor, or*

knowledge, engage. It is, after all, exactly as is stated in the GOOD BOOK, a battle against the spirit of darkness.

KJV --- 13) LET US WALK HONESTLY, AS IN THE DAY; NOT IN RIOTING AND DRUNKENNESS, NOT IN CHAMBERING AND WANTONNESS, NOT IN STRIFE AND ENVYING.

NIV --- 13) Let us behave decently, as in the daytime, not in carousing and drunkenness, not in sexual immorality and debauchery, not in dissension and jealousy.

(KJV) walk honestly and with honor. (NIV) behave decently. Men can appear in the daytime to be honest and decent, but behind the veil of mind and heart darkness too often prevails. Rather than gathering to riot and carouse, gather to pray, worship, and sing about the glory of the coming of the Lord. The lustful wantonness in chambers of debauchery and sexually immoral places created by men and women inclined to debauchery be damned. Walk away, turn, and repent! This applies with equal measure to "THE PEOPLE" and to the peoples "SERVANTS." It is known of the debauchery of the "SERVANTS"!! Prayer as well as "in your face" calls to repentance which very much is a 1st Amendment appeal to the "SERVANTS" for a redress of the grievance that is their "UN-Godly" walk.

KJV --- 14) BUT PUT YE ON THE LORD JESUS CHRIST, AND MAKE NOT PROVISION FOR THE FLESH, TO FULFILL THE LUSTS THEREOF.

NIV ---14) Rather, cloth yourselves with the Lord Jesus Christ, and do not think about how to gratify the desires of the flesh.

"WE THE PEOPLE" and the "SERVANTS" most certainly must consider with a sober mind verses 11 through 14 for they reiterate the peril that awaits "THE PEOPLE" and "THE SERVANTS" if we do not put on as armor the truth that is the Lord Jesus Christ and dispense with lust and idolatry of self.

Enough said I suppose for "a thought" or "fourteen thoughts" on the politics of the church in the state. Controversial yes, wrong, we'll see!!

~ THE HOPE THAT IS EASTER ~

When I started this chapter it was Christmas time and a rookie mistake was made. The "Joy" that is Christmas governed the consideration that this chapter about "hope" should be concluded with thoughts about the birth of Jesus. As soon as those words fell out of my brain and off of my fingertips I knew an error had been made. While the feeling was true, for the joy was unmistakable for those in attendance at Desert Hills Church as well as for the millions of voices raised in the remnants of churches around the world to be thankful for the day God entered His creation. I corrected the error in the next sentence for I knew that this chapter should conclude with the hope that is salvation, that is to say Easter!

First of all the word Easter is curious as its etymology suggests it is borrowed or high jacked from the pre-Christian Saxon word Eostre, a pagan goddess. A cursory search suggests that Saxons made sacrifices to this goddess around the time of Passover. Interesting, but not clear if this "Passover" was the Hebrew Passover. If so, and it reasonably was, it would conform to the same idolatry found throughout the Old Testament scriptures when Hebrews mingled with other nations and ended up worshiping their idols.

In any event somehow someway, providence perhaps, whoever this goddess fiction may have been she is long gone and forgotten. The word Easter is now the luckiest word to ever morph in meaning. To now be associated with the only hope mankind has, the word Easter wins as a descriptor / adjective of anything whatsoever, but as it turns out is "thee descriptor / adjective" to denote the pinnacle of glory.

The "hope" that is Easter makes me ponder hope generally, therefore the word "hope" is interesting in that it can be applied to anything. We hope our babies have all the parts in the right places and function as designed. A carpenter hopes that his next load of lumber is straight and true. Dating couples and or newlyweds hope for fidelity. Ranchers hope for healthy livestock. Farmers hope for the rain. Kids hope for puppies and kittens. Alcoholics and drug addicts hope for the next high. Workers hope the day goes faster and the weekend comes sooner. Boys and girls hope to feel whatever it is that seems to draw them together. Drug dealers hope to make a big score. Bad men hope to do bad. Power hungry types hope for dominance over others. Pedophiles hope to get away with it. Sinners hope to not be judged. Narcissists hope to be seen. Students hope to achieve.

Tangent: Right now I am in a neighborhood coffee shop in the afternoon and about twenty 7th grade girls just walked in and are hanging out. It turns out that the owner is the father of one of the girls. He lets the kids hang out until such time as their parents can pick them up, pretty cool. I chatted with one of the fathers who brought in a couple of pizzas and the gaggle of giggling girls temporarily proliferated into a school of quite ravenous pizza piranhas. This particular group were awesome in that they were polite and having great fun after school. As I watched them interact I wonder what they hope for? Similar I suppose in the general day to day existence of junior high, and distinct in their family dynamics. I cannot help but wonder if they are being mentored and guided to salvation. Anyway, they are all hoping and do not have any idea that an old man types away and hopes for them to know the good news.

End tangent.

> **temporal** - *relating to worldly as opposed to spiritual affairs; secular*
>
> **secular** - *denoting attitudes, activities, or other things that have no religious or spiritual basis; contrasted with sacred*
>
> **venerate** - *regard with great respect; revere*

It seems that hopes and desires are infinite. Why do we hope for anything? Since we do and cannot not hope could it be that hope is as foundational to human existence as much as air, water, and food? Plausible I think! We most certainly hope as our babies enter life, babies begin hoping very early, kids, teenagers, and adults all hope. At some point on the lifeline of each individual all of the things hoped for may actually become realized and bring temporary joy, fulfillment, etc. Other things hoped for may not become realized and like it or not pass into the distance of your life like the view of things vanishing in a rear view mirror of a car as it travels down a highway. Whether realized or not all things hoped for in the end are temporal and secular in nature, save one.

The hope not found in temporal things is found in a non-temporal reality called eternity. The only way to realize that eternal hope is to know with clarity what is behind this word, this entity, this hope that is Easter. How to know has been, still is, and will always be related to what we can hope to know, comprehend, understand, and feel about what is on the other side of that door called death.

Hope, the ultimate hope is behind that "descriptor / adjective" Easter. There is no greater hope. It is a variable which with faith can be changed to a constant that completes the equation of life and punches a ticket that "you" then may pass from death to life.

All that any of us may hope for cannot be greater than; better than, faster than, higher than, or any <u>other</u> "than" then that which is understanding and accepting that God Himself gave to us freely the fulfillment of hope. That fulfillment, Jesus Christ, the one worthy to be acknowledged, thanked, respected, and yes, most certainly worshiped. What Immanuel or "God With Us" did for us is the culmination of hope.

Easter! It was one day 1,990 years ago, approximately 23,880 months ago and approximately 762,350 days ago. So, what was so special about that particular day? How was it different than any day you may have lived? That "day" the God that created you, the God that created me, the God that created "all" things, by His design, decree, will, plan, grace; however one may wish to phrase it; whether we like it or not, picked "that" day Christians venerate, and "that" day is Easter.

For on that day after having creating "all" that is, and having created man and woman in His likeness, knowing that free will would and did become the bane of man's existence, God incarnated Himself by His Spirit into mankind through a maiden whom He chose to humble Himself to our most meager level. God then lived among men in the flesh of His Son, Jesus, who came to set the record straight. In other words, man & woman got it wrong, always did, always will. God's wish for His created children is that we would be righteous and live forever in a "Garden of Eden." Adam and Eve did not get it and could not do it, no one in the history book of God's instruction got it or could do it and neither do you get nor can you do it, except for Easter. This day that was Easter, God showed the way.

Sacrifice, yes sacrifice! Beyond the age of innocence, all at some point sacrifice in some way, but few, so very few, think about or consider at all what it might mean to, on purpose, with premeditation, and planning sacrifice your life for another. Sure, we have the occasional hero, but in those instances the sacrifice was for some and that is noble, but the Easter sacrifice was for all.

On a Friday, Jesus, half man half divine, willingly suffered the most brutal of deaths to make a way for those who accept the sacrifice to enter a "new heaven," a "new earth," or put another way go to the Eden first intended. On the third day after that sacrifice, Jesus, by a power we cannot know, defeated death and came out of a tomb. Easter! It is that day, the day Jesus came out of the tomb that is "thee day," the only day on the timeline of existence itself that is; if it is possible, even more special than the day Jesus was born.

The summary of temporal "hope," i.e., all of the hopes that man has had, does have, and will have temporally, have an expiration date. Only one hope does not. Easter then is where "Hope" was and is a thing completed.

Postscript 1 – Throughout this book I have found it useful to define words. The particular words chosen are as much for my edification and I hope for the reader as well. Most of the definitions, but not all, are taken from the works of Daniel Webster. It is curious that in my journey to compose this book, I found in "The Evidence Based Bible" by Ray Comfort, words attributed to Daniel Webster just before he died. They are as follows: "The great mystery is Jesus Christ-the gospel. What would the condition of any of us be if we had not the ***"hope"*** *of immortality?... thank God, the gospel of Jesus Christ brought life and immortality to light." His last words were" "I still live."*

~ THE SCOPE OF HOPE ~

Hope I suppose, as much as the nose,
Is a feature revealed, but not for the creature.
Thinking and reason, and considering why,
Why Daddy this, and why Mommy that,

Why is there up, why is there down,
Why can't I fly, and why should I try.
Why am I young and why are you old?
Why is there sky, and why do we die?

My child, my child, good questions you ponder,
The answers you seek are out there in the yonder.
The knowledge of all is not possible to know,
But you will learn much in this life as you wander.

Three of your questions I must help you to answer.
Why are you young, and why am I old,
And why do we die, it is these why's you ask,
The sole reason for man and all of his tasks.

First my dear child, all that there is,
All that you see, all that you think,
And all that you seek,
In the span of all time will be gone in a wink.

I'll do my best to ground you in truth,
And better I do this while you're still in your youth.
For evil will come soon enough to deceive you,
And say truth is a lie and does not exist.

Stay with me child, let's think this through,
Can "A" and non "A" be one and the same?
If the answer be yes, then all is askew.
But if the answer is no, then truth we can claim.

Truth, so easily proved, means all of your questions,
Although some may be tough and elusive,
Do have an answer that is quite conclusive.

You will be told that all came from nothing,
When you hear such a thing, you will have encountered a fool,
Be not deceived, for that is objectively clear drool.

Nothing ever begets something, & something never begets nothing,
But something can beget something, so the big question is,
What was the first something?

The answer my child is God, the Creator,
You will find on your quest that nothing is greater,
This is truth, you will have to confront,
His majesty, however, to the lost an affront.

As you search for meaning and why,
You will encounter two things that at first make no sense,
Hope and then faith may not appear to be somethings,
But do not be fooled and then sit on the fence.

Hope and faith are most certainly something,
For if they were not, why do we have them?
Why man and no other creature or thing?
To answer this question will answer your whys.

My child, my child we live in the now,
But minds of the past can catch us up on the how,
History recorded a past time of man,
One book, the Bible, the one with God's plan.

The scope then of hope is certainly vast,
The hope for the future, did it come from the past?
To answer this question, let us consider the cast,
God the creator, the leading role uncontested,
His scope for the hope, in Adam and Eve He entrusted.

The script went awry, right out of the gate,
When Satan barged in thinking he could do better.
The scope of the hope that was God's became tainted.
Eve and then Adam did eat of a fruit God forbade them,

Sin once nonexistent, would now require wages,
Like it or not a debt for all ages.
Man's life forever God's original plan,
Would be redirected by God in His will and by stages.

The history and lessons and the path back to Eden,
In the book called the Bible with all of the wisdom.
The most important truth of all is man cannot do it,
So God entered His world, by His Son, and His Spirit,
Listen closely my child, the answers to your why's,
Hope in forever, is by faith that God as Man did not die.

God with us, Immanuel, Jesus the Savior,
Came to instruct us and correct our behavior,
All that He taught, was imparted to scribes,
Not to be lost or forgotten though Satan has tried.

Christ Jesus His mission on earth once completed,
Would be accused, then betrayed, innocent when judged,
Condemned to the Cross, but not yet defeated.

Three days in the grave, stone rolled away,
40 days more Christ did walk among men,
For witness to you child, your debt He did pay.

So your answers to why are you young, why am I old,
Why do we die, are a hope for a place that is higher than high.
Hope for that place, more precious than gold,
Is by faith in God's grace, and now that you know,
Go out in the world child, share and be bold.

God wanted you to be in His plan,
Why? For His glory and that you understand,
Now go my dear child, now that you know,
The answer to all why's, rests solely in Jesus,
For it is His sacrifice that surely will free us!

The scope then of hope is faith in the news,
That Jesus is Savior, all that's left then, is to choose!

Amen
JKF 2-1-2023

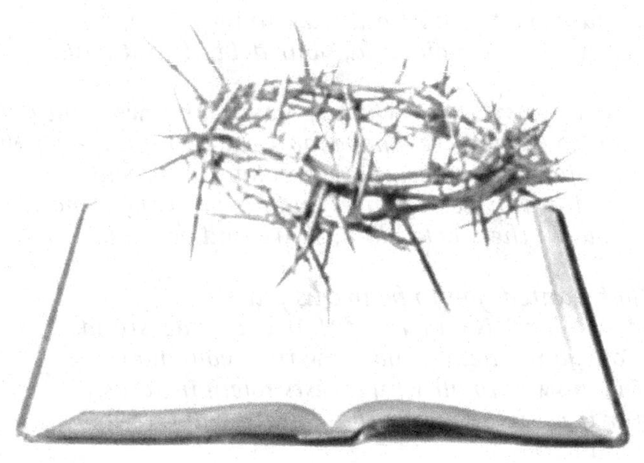

How Do We Know What We Know??!

Phenomenom with the Senses!

Nomenom with the Mind!

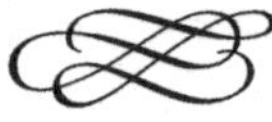

Chapter 14

IS SCIENCE ANYTHING W/O GOD

No!

For a moment I thought I would be clever and end this chapter with only the word "no!" and move on. In the spirit of Michael Knowles book, "Reasons to Vote for a Democrat" (a comprehensive guide), I considered the humor element as sufficient. However, in Michael Knowles book he does make salient point after salient point, an apologetic if you will, which lays bare the vacuous platform of the modern day Democratic Party. To be fair, the elephants in the room, are more akin to frightened snappy Chihuahuas barking once in a while in a congressional hearing or at a mic, but are toothless so their words and actions are idle and justice, which is downstream of righteousness, is a mere platitude.

> **vacuous:** *1) emptied of or lacking content; 2) marked by lack of ideas or intelligence: stupid, inane; 3) devoid of serious occupation: idle*
>
> **idle:** *1) not turned to normal or appropriate use; 2) lacking worth or basis*
>
> **platitude:** *a remark or statement, especially one with a moral content, that has been used too often to be interesting or thoughtful.*

Sorry, listened to a bit of vacuous nonsense this morning and got off track. So, back to science! In a great irony science in many a category in 2023 could with reason be described as "vacuous," "idle," and easily identified by "platitude" upon "vacuous" "platitude." But, let's move on!

religion: *a personal set of institutionalized system of religious attitudes, beliefs, and practices. (Ex. theists and atheists)*

chance: *1) something that happens unpredictably without discernible intention or observable cause; 2) the assumed impersonal purposeless determiner of unaccountable happenings: luck; 3) the fortuitous or incalculable element of existence*

billion: *a very large number*

For example, since Darwin's influence, and in America the 1925 Scopes Monkey Trial that certainly helped solidify the religion of "chance" and "billions." It was a quite brilliant legal maneuver that paved the way that the "theoretical" gods called "chance" and "billions" created life from nothing and were by legal fiat made the "gods" of America from the tyrannical boot of government. "Chance" and "billions" still termed theory and hypothesis but nevertheless deemed to be "scientific" and therefore "theoretically" truth.

Most interesting from a philosophical perspective that mostly, let's call them "theoretical," Christians in the federal and state governments are absolute in their support for the "theoretical" science of "chance" and "billions" being by their "force" the only religion that the populace in a now "theoretical" "One Nation Under God," may be taught in the, let's call them, "theoretical" institutions of learning. The summary of years and years of postulating "everything" has produced the following conclusions:

~ THEOREM OF AN ATHEIST ~

capricious: *given to sudden and unaccountable changes of mood or behavior*

arbitrary: *1) existing or coming about seemingly at random or by* ***"chance"*** *or as a* <u>capricious</u> *and unreasonable act of will; 2) based on* *or determined by individual preference or convenience rather than by necessity or the intrinsic nature of something; 3) not restrained or limited in the exercise of power: ruling by absolute authority; 4) marked by or resulting from the unrestrained and often tyrannical exercise of power.*

distance: *1) the quality or state of being distant: such as: a) spatial remoteness; b) personal and especially emotional separation*

>>> POSTULATION # 1 <<<

[chance] acted on nothing [somehow];

[somehow] = [chance] + [force] pushing on nothing;

[force of somehow] + [nothing] by [chance] blew up (or expanded rapidly --- potato / paataatoo)!;

[nothing] was very small and dense;

[anti-nothing] is the space not contained inside the very small dense [nothing]

[big bang] = the explosion that ([chance] + [somehow]) acting on [nothing] created [something] from [nothing] + [anti-nothing]

[everything] = the universe created when [nothing] blew up into the [anti-nothing]

So clearly [everything] = ([chance] + [somehow]) + [nothing] = [big bang] = [anti-nothing] + [nothing] = [everything];

[everything] = gases + rocks + ice + planets + stars + moons + empty space (aka space between the stars)

QED, which means that "the atheists argument has just proven postulation # 1." (theoretically)

>>> POSTULATION # 2 <<<

[billions] = a very large number

[year] = [billions] / [billions] x [1 earth revolution around sun]

[time now] = a very large number of earth revolutions around sun = [billions x years]

[somehow] = [chance] + [force] pushing on ~~nothing~~ (nothing after the bang replaced by everything), i.e.,

[somehow] = [chance] + [force] pushing on [everything] x [billions of years] created = [life on earth]

[everything then] = gases, rocks, ice, planets, stars, moons and empty space (aka space between the stars)

[everything now] = [chance] + [somehow] acting on [everything then]

[everything then] x [billions of years] = ([everything then] x [somehow] = [life on earth]) = [everything now]

Therefore it is clear that [everything] x [billions of years] x [somehow] = [biological life on earth]

QED, which means that "the atheists argument has just proven postulation # 2." (theoretically)

>>> POSTULATION # 3 <<<

[D1] = distance = [spatial remoteness]

[D2] = distance = [personal and especially emotional separation]

[God] = the Being perfect in power, wisdom, and goodness

[who] = [secular scientist] + [anti-Christos] = [atheist]

[what] = **[postulation #1** -- i.e., ([everything] = ([chance] + [somehow]) + [nothing] = [big bang] = [anti-nothing] + [nothing] = [everything])] + **[postulation # 2** -- ([everything then] x [billions of years] = ([everything then] x [somehow] = [life on earth]) = [everything now])]

[when] = an ever changing number of [billions of years] = variable

[where] = in the mind of [who's] in state sponsored academy

[whim] = [capricious] + [arbitrary] multiple variables of [when] in the minds of [who's] required to stay in good standing with fellow [who's] proportional to [arrogance] + [pride] + [hatred of God] + {[faith] x ([postulation 1] + [postulation 2])}

[why?] = ([who] + [where] + [what]) x ([when] + [whim]) = [D1=spatially removed] + [D2=emotional separation] x [God]

QED, which means that "the atheists argument has just proven postulation # 3." (theoretically)

>>> ATHEIST THEOREM QUESTIONS <<<

I've not had the years and years of "theoretical" learning, but I'm pretty sure the above analysis sums up the academy of thousands upon thousands of man hours using thousands and thousands of brain hours of atheistic and/or secular world view thinking to "theoretically" postulate "everything." Let's just say presented in this way, I for one have questions.

Question 1 – Bang, expansion, explosion no matter what term is used to explain "the big bang," if it expanded at the speed of light would take 20,000,000,000 years as man thinks of a year to "expand" to the guesstimated size of the known universe now. How?

Question 2 – It has been stated that all of the guesstimated 200,000,000,000 (200 billion galaxies) would have had to be in their current known positions a "split second" after the "bang" or the whole universe would have collapsed in on itself. (part of the fine tuning argument). How does common sense make sense of this?

Question 3 – How fast would the rate of expansion that resulted in a universe that would take 20 billion light years to cross have to be for the entire event to take place in a split second or i.e., the twinkling of an eye? Or considered another way:

speed of light	186,000 miles / second
speed of light	14,664,240,000,000 miles / year
Dia. of universe	20,000,000,000 light years
Dia. Of universe	293,284,800,000,000,000,000,000 miles
radius of universe	146,642,400,000,000,000,000,000 miles

At present the universe is guesstimated to be 20,000,000,000 light years in diameter. Let's assume for comprehension the center point of the "big bang" is the earth. If a little boy turned on a pen light laser beam from earth it would take 10,000,000,000 years to travel the 146,642,400,000,000,000,000,000 miles radius to the known outer edge of the universe. Once again, 10 billion years and a beam of light. Now, let's consider something we humans understand to be large, say Mt. Everest. In the "big bang" theory Mt. Everest would have to travel 146,642,400,000,000,000,000,000 miles not in 10,000,000,000 years but a "split second." My question is "REALLY???"

Question 4 – In this theory, and here is the biggy question, what force started the whole proposition? In other words the 1st line of "Postulation # 1 above; or, "[chance] acted on nothing [somehow]"???

~ THEOREM OF A CHRISTIAN ~

For an alternative consideration of origins I propose a long accepted theorem with a kinda, sorta algebraic layout of what I found in the oldest history book on earth.

theorem: *an idea accepted or proposed as a demonstrable truth, e.g. or i.e., Genesis through Revelation.*

~ OBSERVATIONS --- RECORDED HISTORY ~

[God] = the Being perfect in power, wisdom, and goodness

create = {+-*/} = breath or word of God

time = {+-*/} [beginning] * instant before [day 1] = matrix or place to put everything

{+-*/} x [day 1] – heavens and earth

{+-*/} x [day 2] = firmament – a place to put life

{+-*/} x [½ day 3] = a place to put flora & fauna

{+-*/} x [½ day 3] = flora

{+-*/} x [day 4] = firmament of universe = [(sun + moon + stars) x (fine-tuned gravity)]

{+-*/} x [day 5] = [creatures of waters] + [creatures of air]

{+-*/} x [½ day 6] = [creatures of the land]

{+-*/} x [½ day 6] = ([man & woman] + [gift from God to man of [dominion of [flora + fauna]])

{+-*/} x [day 7] = God x ([rested] + [blessed] + [sanctified]) x [day 7]

If: week 1,

G = [God] x {+-*/} = ?…Time...?,

T = [time] = a place to put [F+L+M]

F = [day 1] + [day 2] + [½ day 3] + [day 4] = [firmaments for life]

L = [½ day 3] + [day 5] + [½ day 6] = [flora + fauna] = [life]

M = [½ day 6] + [gift] + [day 7] = [man]

Then: (from the history books) + (revealed and discovered principles of God's order)

B = [beginning] = before time

C = [created] = (unmoved mover (God) x [beginning])

T = [time] = [beginning + [day 1] + [time now = (n days) from beginning) - 1]

n = TBD

E = [end] = after time

>>> POSTULATION # 1 <<< THINGS TANGIBLE & INTANGIBLE

G = [CxB] + [T] + [F+L+M] +E = everything = alpha to omega = B to E, i.e., beginning to end

G = {+-*/} x [everything tangible] = GOD

If – (all things tangible & intangible)

If GOD = {+-*/} x [everything tangible]

If GOD = {+-*/} x [everything intangible]

If tangible man is created in [image of GOD]

If man has [intangible attributes]

Then [intangible man] is created in [image of GOD]

If Intangible Attributes:

[mind] = [thought + consider + reason + logic + discernment]

Reason Level 1 = RL1= conscience / right / love / good / goodwill / responsibility / emotions joy / humor

Reason Level 2 = RL2 = wrong / hate / evil / bad faith / emotions sad / lust / covet

Reason Level 3 = RL3 = metaphysical / philosophy / ontology / epistemology

Reason Level 4 = RL4 = math / physics / electrical energy

And Tangible Attributes

Reason Level 5 = RL5 = categories of [everything tangible]

And:

[mind] = [RL1 + RL2 + RL3 + RL4 + RL5]

Therefore:

G = {+-*/} x ([everything tangible] + [everything intangible]) = GOD

Science = [study] x [[everything intangible = [RL1 + RL2 + RL3 + RL4] + [everything tangible = RL5]]

Therefore: science = [study] x [everything]

Since G = {+-*/} x ([everything tangible] + [everything intangible]) = GOD

Then [science] = [study] x [GOD] i.e., ***Science = study of God*, or more precisely**

Science = study of everything God created

QED bam!!, mic drop!! "The Christian argument has just proven postulation # 1." (observable facts except E)

~ CONCLUSIONS ~ COMPETING THEOREMS

Drawn from the *[atheist / anti-Christ]* perspective vs. the *[Christian / creation]* perspective of everything.

The above analysis is just one more treatise, in the many thousands that consider origins. I've never had occasion to think on the matter, so this exercise was fun and would be fun to do as a presentation for academy. The exercise helped me solidify my suppositions about creation as the only reasonable origin of "everything," including both the natural and the "hidden," "abstract," "metaphysical" elements of the created order.

It strikes me that if [½ day 6] were removed from creation week, i.e., man, then the firmament left would stilled be held together by the finely tuned gravitational forces and the earth would still be the earth filled with flora and fauna and the foundations of creation that would allow the flora and fauna to flourish.

While such a garden certainly would be pleasing to God that part of His image that we call a "mind" would not fill the garden. Most certainly the elements of mind I termed RL1 through RL5 would still be there in the mind of God, but there would be no "children." Or considered another way, a "children" sized hole in God's heart. I realize that is not reasonable on one hand, but on the other hand it's perhaps the only way to explain, or consider, why God created at all. Perhaps the closest man gets to understanding what the love of God is like is to be a parent, especially the first moments.

The atheist community has many a guru and Richard Dawkins today is considered reverently in at least the top 10. In fairness to the atheist postulations of everything the following quote from Richard Dawkins would be a reasonable summary statement for the "Atheist Theorem" considerations above:

> ***The universe we observe has precisely the properties we should expect if there is, at bottom, no design, no purpose, no evil, no good, nothing but blind, pitiless indifference.***
>
> --- ***Richard Dawkins***

This statement has been trotted out in many a presentation and or debate as a battle cry or a mantra of atheists. Therefore, I as well will trot it out and should like to analyze this statement as follows:

1st two words: --- "The universe" – so far agreement, i.e., it is fair to say the object is "everything."

3rd word: "we" --- this is where the statement diverges immediately from fact to fiction. Who are the "we's" to whom he is referring? A fair supposition would be that group of scientists called biologists, and the subset called evolutionary biologists, and a subset of those called atheistic evolutionary biologists, as well as those students not inclined to weigh the evidence or even look at alternative interpretations of the same evidence. In other words a smallish faith cult of pier reviewed Darwiniacs.

4th word: "observe" --- *defined: <u>notice</u> or <u>perceive</u> (something) and register it as being significant.* Fair enough, Richard has not noticed, but more likely perceived the universe as laid out in the rest of the sentence.

5th through 8th words: "has precisely the properties" --- Bold indeed! This is "precisely" why the words vacuous, idle and platitude were defined at the beginning of this chapter. In fact "the properties" in his specialized field, i.e., the gene, point to information and therefore a mind. Also, the information is precise.

9, 10, and 11: "we should expect" --- Again with the "we," the "should expect" deflates the "precise" characterization of the "properties" in words 5 through 8 which at best seems speculative.

12, 13, and 14: "if there is" --- "if," now we're getting somewhere, everything that follows is per his own words "iffy."

15 and 16: *"at bottom"* --- bottom defined: *"the lowest point or part of something, or, the lowest position"* I must admit this turn of phrase confuses me for in context of the whole statement makes me think his indifference is at the "bottom" of his conclusions. Confusing I know!

17 through 20: *"no design, no purpose"* --- design defined: *"purpose, planning, or intention that exists or is thought to exist behind an action, fact, or material object*"; "purpose defined: *the reason for which something is done or created or for which something exists."* Again a reasonable supposition based on the context of his entire statement is that he is blind. Ironic I know given the order seen everywhere and the laws of physics that did not design themselves. Also ironic given Richard's book "The Blind Watchmaker," as well as one of the definitions of blind which is, "*lacking perception, awareness, or discernment.*" And as for purpose, Richard would be hard pressed to deny that his "purpose" for his entire "purposeful" life has been to convince the world that there is no "purpose."

21 and 22: *"no evil"* This is peculiar, I don't even know what to say, except it might confirm Richards blindness.

23 and 24: "no good" *good defined: that which is morally right; righteousness:* This is peculiar as well since Richard I suppose would consider all of his work as good and therefore moral, right, and righteous! So which is it?

25 through 29: *"nothing but blind, pitiless indifference."* And there it is. The "bottom" line. So, Richard's life work, all of his philosophizing since he at 15 or 16 decided to have faith, not in God, but Darwin. Since that switch of faith and the impressive life in academy he finds "nothing" redeeming about the universe. Odd, however, to conflate rocks, gases, etc. which can obviously not feel pity nor indifference with constructs that only the "mind" of man can consider and or reason about, you know, epistemological considerations! Since man is not blind in thought, and is by the percentages neither pitiless nor indifferent, I for one feel both pity and empathy without indifference but rather great care for Richard.

Curiously, again a supposition of mine, Richard's conclusions about the "universe" when he himself specializes in biology and with particular interest in the "gene," i.e., a very, very, small fraction of the universe, aka "everything," it seems there may just be a bit of presupposed bias in his bold statement. Richard Dawkins is considered an acknowledged leader in the field of evolutionary biology. A review of his bio on the internet indicates his early interest was zoology with some study of animal behavior but with an interest in where they came from, i.e., origins. It is not clear how much field or lab work was done in this area, but the math indicates it was short lived. The remainder of his career seems to have been thinking about genes, rather than lab work, say in gene splicing for instance. His "thinking" career appears to have him being groomed by a "closed" system of academy and then turning out as a groomer himself in that same closed system. The majority of his work is dedicated not to the study of the "gene" but to anti-God activism.

Richard has done a fair share of debates with Christian giants such as John Lennox and others to his great credit which shows his dedication to his world view. I encourage anyone who may read this book to find this debate below in "debates" section. The debate is centered on his book "The God Delusion" in which his belief that science has now in the 21st century advanced with enough evidence to conclude that God is a delusion. Please give it a listen and draw your own conclusions. I think Mr. Lennox certainly and obviously has the requisite abilities to go toe to toe with Mr. Dawkins. In any event, such debates should happen and as you will see in a civilized way. A much better format than say college students today that go to the streets and chant one, two, or three word narcissistic platitudes.

~ GIANTS OF SCIENCE & ORIGINS ~

The summary of mans' mind on earth is the sum of all dead guys' thoughts, on the shoulders of other dead guys' thoughts plus some living guys' thoughts, but only if those thoughts were written down or saved in some medium. 40 authors, 66 books, 1500 years produced what we now call one book, The Bible. All dead guys completing a body of work 2000 years ago that interestingly speaks to origins in Chapter 1.

Since man cannot create life from nothing and the obvious constructs of the firmaments that GOD created including the framework called "time" as a place to put the firmaments held together by the created natural laws, i.e., the "fine-tuned" forces, man calls gravity that holds the earth in its special place with its unique firmaments that sustain life. Would not that entity have a purpose, a reason? Since man does play a role for here we are, surely we have purpose and reason to be involved. Well, that too is in that book. How we got here, why we are here, and that it will end all explicitly and precisely explained.

Then what? The law of entropy is a solid scientific conclusion that all that is will end. If this is so then what? It is this ultimate conundrum that I wish for and I hope for many to listen to the list of presentations below. Why? Because with reason the listener may find the "then what" question worthy of additional seeking. Seeking what? You "will" see if you "will" to listen.

At this point it seems clear that although I make a reasoned analysis it is time to appeal to the science of things and whom better than scientists. What has been discovered in the last 50 years is mind boggling in all fields of inquiry.

As this sojourner travels along I find myself grateful for the science that has been made available for pretty much all of the acquired knowledge of man on the magic rectangle. Realizing that reading is almost a thing of the past and that audio and visual formats are preferred, I offer the below list of talks in a variety of scientific disciplines. It is my sincere hope that the curiosity bug may bite the reader to consider a listen.

Before you start and for your consideration it is possible to get through all of the material in half the time if the 2X feature is used to speed up the videos. If that proves to fast YouTube has 1.25X, 1.5X, 1.75X, as well as 2X speed functions. If you can't figure out how to use those functions Google it.

In any event all of the below information considered together offers the Christian an unbelievable amount of apologetic material. Also, it would be my contention, if I were a betting man which I am not, that if a secularly schooled listener whom has not pursued knowledge since high school or college would consider the sum total of the information available in the below list, many a knee might bend to the glory that is God.

~ TOP SCIENTISTS OF THE 21ST CENTURY ~

The list below is formatted as – Time, YouTube Channel, Title

Science Generally

56:32 Visionworks --- Theism & Science: A Conversation with John Lennox

1:51:32 Calvary Chapel … Science Confirms Biblical Creation – Jason Lisle

1:24:29 Hoover Institution --- By Design: Behe, Lennox, and Meyer on the Evidence for a Creator

45:41 Discovery Science --- Stephen Meyer: God and the Origin of the Universe

1:00:13 Hoover Institution --- Stephen Meyer on Intelligent Design & The Return of the God Hypothesis

Paleontology

1:28:05 NW Creation Network --- The Power of Biblical Paleontology

1:01:34 Calvary Bible Church --- The Work of a Creation Paleontologist

1:01:24 Joshua Springs --- Dinosaurs & the Bible, speaker Jason Lisle

Geology

4:14:59 Young Earth Creation --- The Best Movie explaining Noah's Flood Part 2, *(geology, genetics and more)*

1:20:29 Young Earth Creation --- The Best Movie explaining Noah's Flood Part 1, *(geology, genetics and more)*

52:16 Justin Peters Ministries --- Jason Lisle Interview

1:32:53 Is Genesis History --- 90 Minutes of Geological Evidence of Noah's Flood – Kurt Wise

45:42 Discovery Science --- Stephen Meyer: God and the Origin of the Universe

1:03:04 Ligonier Ministries --- Stephen Meyer: Rock of Ages & the Age of Rocks

Evolution vs. Intelligent Design aka God

47:18 Ligonier Ministries --- Darwin: A Myth for the Post Christian Mind

Chemistry

1:01:01 James Tour --- Does Science Make Faith obsolete?

Biology - The Cell

59:55 Discovery Science --- Revolutionary: Michael Behe and the Mystery of Molecular Machines

1:21:03 Stephen Meyer --- Signature in the Cell

Philosophy Statistics & Biology

52:37 Discovery Science --- Evolution & the Experts - Douglas Axe at Dallas....

31:36 A Little Bit of Philosophy --- Introduction to Philosophy of Religion

2:41:14 Cross Examined --- I don't Have Enough Faith to Be an Atheist w/ Frank Turek

30:18 Ligonier Ministries --- How Do We Know What We Know?: A Blueprint for Thinking w/RC Sproul

Astronomy / Cosmology

2:16:27 Calvary Chapel Grand Junction --- Astronomy Reveals Creation, Jason Lisle

1:15:11 Answers in Genesis --- This Video Dismantles The Bid Bang Theory

Astrophysics

1:36:47 Granite Creek Community Church --- Reason to Believe, Hugh Ross

Debates

1:46:39 Larry Alex Taunton --- Richard Dawkins vs. John Lennox

2:59:38 Apologia Studios --- Epic Debate over God's Existence

1:55:10 Apologia Studios --- Incredible: Christian vs. Atheist Debate (White / Durbin vs Clark / Ellis)

3:08:47 Alpha & Omega Ministries --- Debate: Is the NT Evil? (White vs Silverman)

The above videos total 50 +/- hours of various disciplines of science and for good measure four debates.

>>> GENETICS <<<

And for icing on the cake I implore the reader to go to YouTube, find the "Answers in Genesis" channel, find the "playlists" tab, and scroll down to a playlist titled "The New History of the Human Race." There you will find 26 videos totaling 20 hours with Nathan Jeanson and Ken Ham all concerning breakthrough discoveries in the field of genetics. Full disclosure, it will be hard to follow, but listen anyway for when you get through it the findings should convict you to your core that "all men are created equal" if nothing else.

Further, the "Answers in Genesis" website, YouTube channel and of course the "Ark Encounter" in Kentucky, (which I have not seen yet) is one of many, but certainly one of the best repositories of knowledge concerning science in many disciplines including all of those listed above.

Note: All of the 70 hours herein listed are just a fraction of thousands of hours of scientists; atheist, believer, and Christian; all looking at the same information whether historical or in the now. You have probably heard the secular / atheist interpretation of the data. I pray you give consideration to the scientists that see the same information, but notice many flaws in the currently accepted academy and make alternative theories and hypotheses about the data which will, I am certain, give you great pause in what you think you know.

Note: I have listened to all in the above list and hours and hours more. I mean no disrespect for the many that are not on this list, but the lessons herein were compiled by me spending 15 minutes searching the internet for scientists discussing the various disciplines. Imagine what 30 minutes might produce! I submit and implore the reader especially those that have questions or are curious to set aside a little bit of your day to seek knowledge.

~ SUMMARY OF SCIENCE ~

If you could find 1 hour per day for 2 months you most assuredly will be smarter and hopefully wiser and I contend that just maybe this small sacrifice of your time in scientific inquiry will be the providential catalyst which will then lead you to consider with utmost haste the gospel of God. Please do not let that possibility, however, hinder your quest for knowledge. Knowledge and downstream of that wisdom will give you something in your quiver to converse about with family, friends, and strangers and if nothing else will make you interesting.

My main takeaway from the considered science would be that the biological and genetic discoveries at their core are information. That discovery alone has moved very brilliant minds to believe in God or for some confirm their belief in God. Not only do they believe in God these same men are professing Christians in that they profess that Jesus Christ has atoned for their sins and therefore are my brothers in Christ. That last statement is most curious, i.e., how might a man move from an epiphany conviction about God as creator to that same God entering His creation half God, half man to save the scientist. How indeed! This truth cannot be seen in a telescope or microscope, but with reason when one reads the peer reviewed gospels and letters of those that walked, talked, and lived with Jesus still available for all of mankind to see and or hear, the Word will convict your soul, capture your heart, and comfort your person. These scientists you can be sure, read the Word with the same scrutiny as they read scientific peer reviewed papers. When the truth is seen it cannot be unseen, it can be denied, but it cannot be unseen.

These men look at the complexities in the cell with the amazing factories that replicate with specificity the building blocks of life without factory managers and are convicted of the creator mind that did the creating, i.e., God. Further, they conclude by the evidence that these complexities could not and did not evolve over billions of years. In other words the science shows the irreducible complex parts and pieces could not have evolved no matter how much time is presupposed into the evolution equation. All of the parts required had to be there, one with the other, dependent on each other for the mechanisms of the cell to work in the first instance or in the beginning.

This conclusion with reason is "science" using the "scientific method" to discover and make sense of "phenomenon" that must with discernment be a "noumenon" in the beginning.

> **science**: *1) knowledge or a system of knowledge covering general truths or the operation of general laws especially as obtained and tested through scientific method; 2) such knowledge or such a system of knowledge concerned with the physical world and its phenomena: natural science; 3) a system or method reconciling practical ends with scientific laws*

> **scientific method**: *1) principles and procedures for the systematic pursuit of knowledge involving the recognition and formulation of a problem, the collection of data through observation and experiment, and the formulation and testing of hypotheses*

> **phenomenon:** *1) an observable fact or event; 2) a temporal or spatiotemporal object of sensory experience as distinguished from a noumenon*

> **noumenon:** *posited object or event as it appears in itself independent of perception by the senses*

The noumenon of all of these recent discoveries is "creation" which is most certainly independent of perception by the senses and for which the science most certainly points to a creation event that made biological life instantly. Some of these same scientists however get stuck on the universe being billions of years old. The stumbling stone seems to be the "speed of light" and the other stumbling stone which is the "theory" of the "big bang."

If the "inference to the best explanation" for the mechanisms of the cell is that they had to happen instantly, I am perplexed that the same scientists, not all, but some that can get their head around the biological miracle, but cannot conclude that the same creator could move light faster than light or; for the over-thinkers; not move it at all, but just "put" the firmament or universe in place instantly and as effortlessly as He did biological life as the evidence suggests.

I submit that the speed of light and the red shift expansion seen with the instruments of the cosmologist that causes confusion are in place doing the dance the cosmologist observes through the telescope in like fashion to what the biologist sees in the microscope in the mechanisms of the cell that dance to information. Both are moving, both are sustaining, both are rich with observable and discoverable phenomena. What the cosmologist studies dances to physics describable by math which is information of a type. What the biologist studies dances to very specific coded information within the factories of the cell that maintains life. At each end of the spectrum, i.e., from the very large to the very small; no matter how much is discovered, explained or theorized; the minds of men will always run into the noumenon problem i.e., the origin of the latest discovery.

Another way to consider it is to think of a high jump bar. The bar itself is a "noumenon." Each new discovery raises the bar and piles up phenomenon below the bar, but the bar never goes away. There will always be something above the bar that cannot be perceived with the senses. A nightmare for atheist scientist, a dream come true for the Christian scientist.

The very first noumenon is described in the first four words, "In the beginning God." The second noumenon is in the fifth word, "created." All of science for all of time chases the second noumenon and that is appropriate. It is sadly only the Christian Scientist that comprehends how the second noumenon came to be. The Christian scientist can joyfully conduct his / her work holding fast to the first noumenon or the "Word" and doing their part to make sense of that which was the second noumenon which "created" all of the phenomenon for the scientist to consider and therefore help mankind have dominion over that which was "created" for us. Thank God for the scientist.

~ GOD MAKES A SCIENTIST ~

Straightaway God made a scientist,
Naming the animals, and considering fruits, nuts, and seeds,
Adam for sure was the first taxonomist,

Whether Adam liked it or not,
He'd be the first to see the stars,
By default making him the first cosmologist.

When God gave Adam a helper,
Surely Adam noticed Eve's incredible structure,
Again by default making Adam a physiologist.

After the fall, Adam had to consider Eve's moods,
Why cuddle today, and on the morrow leave me alone,
Making Adam the first befuddled psychologist.

The point being clear that since the first man,
God had intention, God had a plan,
Part of which was to gift certain souls with a specific curiosity,
To find interest in the particulars of his work and generosity,

Some would like spiders, some would like snakes,
Others anatomy, and still others the mind,
And some an interest in chemicals if only to make cakes.

Whether the cosmos with the sun,
Or the cell and the flagellum, the trees in the forest,
Or the elements of nature whose science is sound,
The hawks in the sky, or the rocks in the ground,
God would make scientists to categorize creation,
Just one of the jewels found in His Crown.

Many disciplines required for science to consider,
All that there is, all that we see,
An alliance with science, the scientist needed,
For mankind to think carefully and cautiously proceed.

God made the scientist by His will and decree,
To guide with clarity so we may all see,
The Glory of God, and when we so see,
We thank God in Heaven, and do so from our knees.

Amen
JKF 3-24-2023

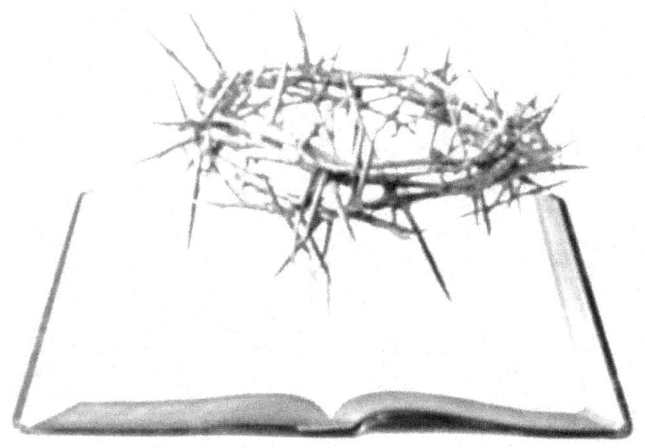

Metaphysical Transportation System

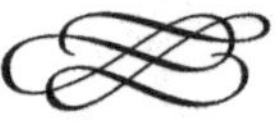

Chapter 15

TRANSCENDENCE

transcend: *1) to rise above or go beyond the limits of; 2) to triumph over the negative or restrictive aspects of; 3) to be prior to, beyond, and above the universe or material existence*

metaphysics: *the branch of philosophy that deals with the first principles of things, including* ***"abstract"*** *concepts such as being, knowing, substance, cause, identity, time, and space*

metaphysics (mine): *[mind] x [RL1 + RL2 + RL3 + RL4], e.g. the mind thinking on the intangibles (see chapter 14, Therom of a Christian, Postulation # 1)*

abstract: *existing in "thought or as an idea" but not having a physical or concrete existence*

hidden: *being out of sight or not readily apparent; concealed*

why: *for what reason or purpose*

In consideration that man can think on metaphysics at all, knowing that no other creature on earth can, strikes me as perhaps a first principle of transcendence. In other words minus the mind of man there is no capacity for any other life to "transcend" beyond the instincts for survival in the moment. Therefore, since man can perceive intuitively or through some inexplicable perceptive powers we by the "fact" that our minds do consider the metaphysical we have an element of our nature, our very existence that "transcends" or by design "has transcended" to another plane not shared with any other life.

Why? Why indeed! Why us and not the toad? The answer is clear, we are special. But why, why us and not the toad? Right out of the gate, not only gifted with life, we very early on ask why. All parents can attest to the why thing. That question, why, is an indication of a first principle of transcendence. We most certainly take our "out of the gate" transcended status for granted. Speaking for myself and having already acknowledged that as an old man, I only recently discovered a philosophical world and then beyond that the philosophical considerations of metaphysics, therefore I confess an ignorance of the subject, but doing my best to catch up.

Nevertheless, here I stand having to give it a go, i.e., why? I think the case for a "first" principle of transcendence as noted above is reasoned. So, is there a "second" principle of transcendence? If as we live and breathe already transcended above all other life with our "why" elevated status is there more? 1) Why would there be more? 2) Do we deserve more? 3) Why might we deserve more than the toad?

Without the consideration of God, the answer to the last three questions are bleak and would make nonexistent all of the attributes of reason described in the previous chapter and in particular:

> **Reason Level 1 = RL1**= *conscience / right / love / good / goodwill / responsibility / emotions joy / humor*
>
> **Reason Level 2 = RL2** = *wrong / hate / evil / bad faith / emotions sad / lust / covet*

Since the mind of man does have in his very being these non-tangible elements of our nature that cannot be "seen, heard, touched, smelled, or tasted" or i.e., hidden, then it follows these capacities of man might be termed a "second" principle of transcendence. If this is so, we have already transcended not once, but twice above all other life. These, let's call them gifts, should not be taken for granted, but sadly are for we don't stop long enough to smell the roses, as it were, and all of these gifts are most certainly roses.

As I stare at RL1 and RL2 above it strikes me that mankind generally would like a world filled with only RL1 and not RL2. The age old question, "why would a Holy God allow so much RL2 in the world"? But, if you stare at RL2 long enough it seems very much apparent that unless these existed there would be no measure whatsoever to know anything in the RL1 lineup. Or, as C. S. Lewis put it "*A man does not call a line crooked unless he has some idea of a straight line.*" The straight line of course would be the RL1 considerations and the crooked line would be the RL2 considerations.

> **conscience:** *(a Greek translation) – A knowing of oneself, that faculty of the* ***soul*** *which distinguishes between right and wrong and prompts one to choose the former and avoid the latter.*
>
> **soul:** *an* ***entity*** *which is regarded as being the immortal or spiritual part of the person, though having no physical or material reality, is credited with the functions of thinking and willing and hence determining all behavior. 2) the moral or emotional nature of man. 3) spiritual or emotional warmth, force, etc., or evidence of this.*
>
> **entity:** *1) being, existence; 2) a thing that has real and individual existence, in reality or in the mind; anything real in itself; 3) essence; essential nature.*

Just considering the above definitions is evidence that a man or reasonably many a mind has contemplated the abstract, the hidden, the metaphysical and left for us definitions that are reasonable and useful. I've not contemplated any of this before so it is most interesting that taking these definitions into the mind I find them reasoned and truthful.

So, following the logic of the definitions, the abstract entities that are real in the mind, entities such as conscience, soul, entity itself, and all of the RL1, RL2, RL3, and RL4 entities are in fact real for they cannot be denied to exist, it follows, it seems to me with a small measure of discernment, God. And, if as it has been revealed by the special revelation of His Words, man in his real essence, i.e., man's natural person, as well man's abstract or hidden entities or soul gifted with a conscience is very much created in the natural as well as the soul. All of this in the image of God!

I find as I think through these things that while the natural sciences are awesome and awe inspiring, the metaphysical are likewise awesome and awe inspiring; these entities are even more so when considered through the lens of the gospels. How Jesus came to teach man ultimately how to conduct ones affairs so that the RL1 considerations of our souls can be realized. Even though His teachings and or instructions from the Sermon on the Mount with the beatitudes, or what is blessed or considered blessed in the eyes of God which if man lived by those instructions the world with any reasoned calculus would be in the RL1 zone. But alas, it is objectively not so, which interestingly enough Jesus also confirmed. Evil has been with us since the first temptation, is with us now, and will be with us until....!!???

It has been said thousands of times in thousands of ways by man thinking beyond his/her pay grade that a man, a leader - religious or otherwise, a self-proclaimed anointed profit, men who claim God talks to them directly, charismatic loud mouth men/women, that if mankind would buy into their, most often self-delusions of what it might take to make a utopia out of this place all would be well. The best idea ever conceived, that being the American idea, is crumbling before us, and the ludicrous "one world order" ideas being presented as an ideal replacement for virtuous moral self-governing interestingly enough have psychopathic, self-righteous fools whom would be the leaders of it all.

It's not looking good, but Jesus through the apostle John on Patmos, as well as other prophesies in the Christian Bible give very specific indicators of how bad it will get. Sadly since most people, even professing Christians have not read, much less ruminated on the warnings how would they know?

It should not be surprising then that man does not consider that we can and will, like it or not, "transcend" beyond this place. If there is justice, and there is, for justice is as much a part of our core being as is injustice how then could there not be justice in the ever after.

It is hard, so very hard, to convince an atheist, but it turns out it is almost as difficult to convince people whom believe in God that we will "transcend." This little fact, i.e., that believers in God and I dare say many professing Christians, stumble on Heaven and Hell. Especially the Hell part! It is my prayerful hope for them to read and reread the Bible. For the love of God, if you love God, be inquisitive and search Him out for Jesus talked of hell many, many times and if you believe or claim to be a believer, believe what the "Savior" said about hell. Fear of the Lord is the beginning of wisdom, believe that with sober mind and when you do you can "transcend" beyond that fear to a place of comfort if you acknowledge your sin and look to Jesus. One more time from an old man thinking for the first time, the gospel, the good news is available to anyone. You cannot do it alone, it is not possible, and you need help. Help is available, but you have to ask for it.

The RL2 zones of our thinking are hidden certainly from everyone but you, and even you hide your delusion that you don't violate the moral laws for you and most all of us think that we are good. Curiously when the RL1 line was penned in the previous chapter "conscience" was first in the string. Further, as the definition suggests humans generally, except in the case of mental defect, understand and even confess that they are good evidencing that whether they understand it or not it is their conscience and it's faculty to distinguish and prefer right over wrong is ever present in the mind and is most certainly affirmation of a conscience. Beyond man's natural tendency of conscience to at least think that he/she choose right over wrong, or good over evil, if questioned directly with but a few questions the RL2 lineup is exposed as right there continually and simultaneously with the RL1 lineup. It seems with a little probing it can be found that the conscience of man is deluded to think that he is good.

Ray Comfort lovingly, winsomely, and empathetically has asked thousands of souls if they believe they are good. Those asked that question curiously without a one or two second delay say that they are good. Ray in his most winsome way takes them on the shortest of journeys to have most of those he engages realizing and convicting themselves of their self-delusion that they are in fact not as good as they thought they were. This piercing of the conscience in roughly five minutes done by the words of the engaged person themselves, Ray merely probing with very simple, but convicting questions. Once so probed, the convicted soul having judged himself in many cases "transcends" right before our eyes. I would encourage the reader to check out Ray Comfort in action on his YouTube channel "Living Waters." It may not be evidence of the final "born again" transcended place, but I think one would have to agree when one watches these people with whom Ray interacts, it would be hard to conclude anything other than at least in the moment captured, these souls transcended from "*I'm a good person*" to "*I am in fact not a good person and therefore with reason am a sinner,*" not by Rays judgment, but by their own judgment.

What you will witness with Ray's engagements is an excellent example of "transcendence" in this realm. Witness of such a thing should give a person pause to consider your own plight. I think it is fair to consider that each of these souls needed "help" and Ray helped. They will, however, have to do more on their own. The "Helper" they need is but a sincere desire and a prayer away as well as all of the answers awaiting them in Gods Words.

Other examples of instant "transcendence" we have all witnessed, but don't consider it as such would be things such as:

- ✓ when a family has been separated by time and distance from a soldier and the soldier thinks to surprise his/her spouse, kids, siblings, and or parents with his/her return
- ✓ when a soldier is likewise reunited with a dog,
- ✓ when children are surprised with a puppy or kitten,
- ✓ when a wife reveals to a husband that she is pregnant,
- ✓ when the doctor holds up your baby and says it's a girl when you were told it's a boy,
- ✓ when a wife reveals to parents that they are to be grandparents,
- ✓ when an American patriot gets a lump of joy in the throat at the playing of the national anthem,
- ✓ when American patriots get a similar lump in the throat and or tear in the eye when at a sporting event the national anthem is played,
- ✓ when American servicemen and family here "Taps" played at a burial
- ✓ when one hears certain songs like "Amazing Grace" or "The Battle Hymn of the Republic" and a tear finds its way to the corner of the eye,
- ✓ when a church during the Christmas season hears choirs sing "Silent Night" or the like and the heart is moved,
- ✓ when a man hears and watches a sermon like "The Redeemer" by Voddie Baucham and tears up as one watches Voddie tear up,
- ✓ when your daughter does a sneak attack on you to inform you she is pregnant and you get to be "Poppy,"

Especially today with the advent of the magic rectangle we witness many such encounters all moving or "transcending" the mind or soul to instant joy. But why the tears, why the choking up? Sometimes we don't feel it, but when we see it we find it a wonderful thing to witness. Sometimes we feel it directly and wonder almost immediately, where did that come from? I think it is one of the many gifts bequeathed on us by He who crafted us in His image. God allows us, if ever so briefly to "transcend" to an almost indescribable place of, not just joy, but joy in the extreme. In any event it seems that maybe it is a glimpse of Heaven. If a glimpse of Heaven, why oh why, would we not want to be in such a place….forever?

All of the above examples indicate transcendence to the RL1 part of our conscience. Below are examples of instant transcendence to RL2 places such as:

- instant road rage
- the place a sane mind goes when it is discovered an insane mind harms in any way a child
- the current 2020's descriptor of a Karen, i.e., a woman enraged irrationally for circumstance of the world with reason a sane person would determine is none of her concern (to be fair there are male Karen's also)
- a pro-death activist when a pro-life activist suggests that murder is not reasoned nor rational
- a toddler whom discovers RL2 places might get him a cookie
- a grown up whom discovers that RL2 places will cause otherwise sane minds to cave
- sane fathers and especially mothers that discover that pedophiles and perverts are grooming their children at all levels of state sponsored education, especially school boards, the FBI, the DOJ, main stream media, Hollywood, Disney and the like
- citizens when they realize their governments have been, are, and will continue to be corrupt as it concerns virtue and morality
- a husband or a wife when betrayed
- when a misguided youth is angered when he / she feels disrespected, often when respect is not warranted in the first place
- evolving anger in easily molded minds to the latest made up bigot idol of the day

There of course are many things that "transcend" the mind to anger and often instantly. When I was younger and "transcended" to anger in an instant, afterward I would get mad that I got mad. What to make of that? It makes sense with consideration that the conscience is a check valve for the soul. Generally and reasonably humans would rather dwell and hang out in RL1 zones, but it seems with directed indoctrination young minds can be groomed to a mindset of RL2 zones. Directed indoctrination works. It worked so well last century that because some ideologue dictator convinced or indoctrinated the youth du jour of that time that extermination of those that disagree would make for a better world. It didn't. And as the scriptures say,

> **NKJV --- Ecclesiastes 1:9** -- "*What has been will be again, what has been done will be done again; there is nothing new under the sun*."

America, once guided by virtue, is now guided by the most unfit among us, and if the ship of state does not turn around, the 21st century will stack up the bodies beyond the infanticide bodies already discarded as bio waste. War has been declared by the infirm of mind on women, children, on white people especially men, on Jews and Christians and the list grows. Can we "transcend" beyond the madness? We'll see!

Setting aside the obvious exact same challenges that have plagued mankind for all of history I must move on to consideration of final "transcendence"!!!

"Transcendence," the final frontier as it were, to move to a place that is good, is righteous, is joyous, is full or fills the soul with nothing but love without the baggage of the plagues of mind that are not good. That place, i.e., Heaven with reason is not a for sure thing. In like manner as we seek any knowledge that may be of interest, we must seek that which causes us to seek knowledge in the first place.

We know that there is something else for it is written on our hearts, which interestingly enough is written in the scriptures. To transcend to that place will require every bit, if not more, acquired knowledge to get there. We spend much time learning about God's creation, should we not give at least equal time to that place God wishes for us to be?

If that is a reasonable thing to consider since we have "transcendent" examples in the here and now would not "transcendence" after death be a worthwhile consideration. Should we consider it more than we do? Is there a place we could gather to consider "transcendence"? Oh wait, there is! Find a place where you can gather with others that consider it greatly, the Christian church. I hope and pray for your ultimate "transcendence" to that final frontier. Be careful to find a place where the teaching pastor takes you each week into the Bible and directs your attention to the "Words" of God. Further a proper church should have breakout groups for study and fraternization for you and especially your children to live a gospel centered life and not a self-centered, worldly, sins of the flesh, attention seeking, material coveting, me, me, me existence.

~ TRANSCEND ~

I'm here, why? Where am I to go?
Where did I come from, how am I to know.
I came from nothing, in the blink of an eye,
The first thing I considered was the big question why?

For a time I would be curious about all that I see,
From the bee and the flea, the things in the sea,
And what's the difference between the he and the she,
All that can be done with a, b, & c and all the letters thru x, y, & z,
And why is two followed by three?

I would find as I aged the whys were unending,
The minds quest for answers, it seems unrelenting,
The toughest queries of all are why am I here,
What's it all for, and can there be more?

So many things to consider with the senses,
But then I would wonder, will my behavior have consequences,
In the here and the now, it is abundantly clear,
There are morals, virtues, and rules to which man must adhere.

So, I transcended from why, to what's right and what's wrong,
Finding wrong made me weak, and right made me strong,
Knowing what was right, however, wasn't enough,
For I would stumble into wrong especially in thought.

Easy to hide and never get caught,
So why the seared conscience, why do I feel I ought not.

If there is justice, what then to do, how to escape,
Can I be free from this hell in my mind?
And can it be done with little red tape.
Where can I look, what might I find?

I would be an old man before I figured it out,
The answers were there, they were there all along,
Death the justice for this sin I can't shake,
Since it is innate within me to live and not die,
Can I be free, can I be saved?

After much contemplation, and certain anticipation,
I would find solace in a promise of certain salvation.

To transcend this place, to transcend this time,
On all our behalves, and for all of our crimes.
God's Son, the One Chosen to free us from death,
Was without mercy beaten having done nothing wrong,
Then nailed to a Cross, until He breathed His last breath.

By His own power, His strength and His might,
Even death could not hold Him, even death He did smite,
But why, oh why, why would He do it,
The answer is simple; it was for us and our plight.

The grave it will find us, we can't get away,
Or can we? If we think clearly, if we consider and pray,
God wants that we be with Him, that we all find the Way.

Use reason, it's a gift, let's not pretend,
We all know we'll die, we know there's and end,
But by faith in His grace, we all may transcend.

Amen
JKF 3-31-2022

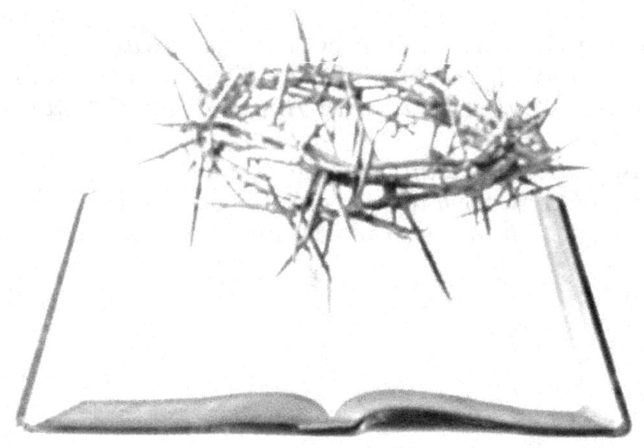

Thinking is required to express!

Expression reveals truth or lies!

Righteousness or foolishness!

Chapter 16

JUST A THOUGHT

~ SPLITTING TIME ~

One day I thought to look up the history of BC and AD as well as the history of BCE and CE. The history is there for anyone to look up and is interesting. What made me ponder at all was seeing BCE and CE at all since for most of my life I had only seen BC and AD.

In both cases these designations commemorate all of history into two epochs. BC (before Christ) and AD (Anno Domini) which is Latin for "The year of our Lord." And for clarity the split is specifically for all of time before Jesus was born (BC or BCE) and for all of time after the day Jesus was born (AD or CE). Even though history tells us this split in time, or more precisely the acceptance of these designations of this split in time happened 500 years after the split.

It seems even though throughout history certain men have worked and still work to destroy Jesus and the memory of Jesus, certain trademarks, or God marks, "if you will," that are stamped into time. The designations of BC and AD are reasonably such a God mark. Why?

God will be made known much to the chagrin of those whom would seek to erase His glory. When I grew up BC and AD were common and even unbelievers knew what it meant, even though not schooled properly in the why of this "split in time."

Non-believers prefer BCE and CE for "before common era" and "common era." Why? Its preference is stated by non-believers themselves to not use an acronym which points so directly at Jesus, or a Christian era, or Christian perspective at all. This seems akin to taking a leafy branch and wiping clean the footsteps of Christ. Common era --- common to what? Try as they might the "common" is still the time before the birth of Jesus Christ and the time after the birth of Christ, but nice try!

A perfect example of the "leafy branch" was found on one of the websites I visited. This particular website did seem to accurately give the historical accounts of how and why both sets of acronyms came to be, however, one word gave them away. That one "leafy branch" word was "theoretical." It was used to imply that the "God mark" or existence of Jesus is "theoretical." Humph....the most attested to figure in all of recorded history, theoretical. Interesting! It seems the work of the fallen continues.

Just a Thought!

~ SMASHING OF A TOE ~

One Saturday not too long ago while doing chores I was breaking down a little giant ladder and dropped it with great force directly on my left big toe nail. Having broken bones before and remembering the excruciating pain associated with such things and after jumping around and hobbling I suppose in a way that if videoed would not nor could not be judged well for graceful movement through space and time by a human. Blood oozing through the top of my sneaker, adrenaline peaked, feeling no expectations of engaging in polite society, a sat on the sidewalk, removed my shoe and then gently my sock to witness what appeared to be a mostly normally constructed foot, but a pretty messed up looking big toe. Even through the intense pain my brain faculties were intact enough to know that blood gushed forth from somewhere, but the whimpering shell of a man felt the hesitation to look, not look, need to look, what a klutz, let's look, wait a minute, calm down, this hurts like hell, etc.

Anyway, it seemed like a long time but wasn't. I washed off the blood in the bathtub, gently wiped it with an iodine swab, my friend helped me with a dressing, then I gently put my bloody sock back on, unlaced my shoe, gently put it on, hobbled to the car, drove home, and per my lovely nurse daughters advice I elevated it, put ice on it and watched TV the rest of the day.

The postmortem on the wound as my daughter noted in a text after she reviewed the pictures and queried me via text for this one person triage scenario. She texted, "Sounds like you smashed it just right if you're gonna go around smashing toes. Just ice it so it doesn't swell up like a balloon."

The way it felt I fully expected I would be laid up for a while for initially to put weight on it was similar to past trauma this ole body has felt. In this case my expectations for being laid up were crushed in a good way. I went to bed thinking I would have to forgo church the next morning. My wife and I laughed that I could probably get away with wearing my slippers. When I woke up Sunday morning there was no pain, no limp, nothing. It seems my daughters analysis was spot on, i.e., I smashed it just right.

What does this have to do with anything related to "thinking for the 1st time"? Good question. That morning at church during the worship singing portion of our service, two of the hymns spoke directly to or inferred the suffering of Christ on the Cross. My mind recounted the toe smashing incident and the associated pain that I thought at the time was a broken toe. I could not help think that this one time, this perfect toe smashing, that triggered all of the God designed elements of our bodies that let the body know it has just violated the physical science part of our existence that keeps us comfortable. Then to be followed hours later by a reminder that Jesus suffered so very much more on His way to the Cross and on the Cross, and that He did it on purpose.

Just a thought!

Afterthought - It also made me consider He was trying to wake me up in some way. I can't say that I know what specifically He had in mind this time, but it crossed my mind that humanity could use such a wakeup call and it seems certain we have them all the time, but as the scriptures say, "... there are none so blind as those whom will not see."

Just another thought!

~ AFFIRMATION OF HORROR ~

When I was a kid there was a movie about a madman, one Dr. Victor Frankenstein. The mad doctor creates what is termed "The Creature," who was normal in his thought and emotions, but was physically something created as abnormal. The creature struggled mentally until his demise because the creatures "physical" could never be normal.

> **abnormal:** *deviating from what is normal or usual, typically in a way that is undesirable or worrying.*

Hummm! A perfect definition of what is behind the veil of "gender affirming care" which is but a costume veil for butchering and mutilation of children and other very troubled souls.

Mary Shelly, the author who wrote the book "Frankenstein" in 1816 when she was 18 years old penned the novel on a challenge with friends. The challenge was who could make up the most horrific tale. I note this as the author was a teenage girl not unlike the teenage girls of today. A very disturbing distinction, however, is Mary Shelly was "contemplating" the most horrific thing imaginable. Today, our young are not only contemplating the horror, but seeking out and finding the Victor Frankensteins of the world to make "creatures" of themselves, but unlike the "created" creature in Mary Shelly's book, they are "self-created," by their own hand, assisted by a modern day Dr. Frankenstein to make themselves abnormal.

Mary Shelly contemplated what unthinkable horror was 204 years ago. Today we could call Mary Shelly a prophet. She thought greatly about and predicted the mental anguish of the "created" creature as well as the mental anguish and regrets of the mad doctor. When Mary Shelly dreamed up her "creature" it was male and created from the largest parts of many dead corpses. That horror story has inspired many more fictional horrific tales. Could Mary Shelly have guessed that an even more horrific tale would unfold in the future and be true? Fast forward from her time to 2023 where girls and boys seek out the mad Dr. Frankensteins of the world who no longer hide their work in laboratories in mysterious castles.

Alas, the mad doctors in 2023 are found on every street corner clinic and hospital. Further, the villagers in her tale were rightly outraged about the creature, but today the citizens that are rightly outraged are silenced, canceled, jailed and when a parent or parents object, their children are taken from them and given over to the mad Doctors by the state whose minds have also been infected by this strange evil.

Boys will pay these mad Dr. Frankensteins large sums of money to mutilate their genitals and fashion a vagina which does not work and is freakishly abnormal. The normal penis and testicles thrown in the garbage as bio waste.

Girls will pay these mad Doctors huge sums of money to cut their breasts off, mutilate the reproductive parts and mutilate the arm, leg, back, or some other body part to make an abnormal, freakish penis. The breasts and reproductive parts thrown in the garbage as bio waste.

A most curious "side effect" of this horror show is that whatever this virus of the mind is that brings these self-created abnormal humans together with the mad Dr. Frankensteins of the world, also think that all of mankind must agree that this is "not" horror. That "side effect" in itself is worthy of a clinical study.

The cottage industry of Dr. Victor Frankenstein madmen who will without conscience mutilate the troubled youths are a most curious and viscous lot. Their minds are worthy of study as much as the minds of the self-created abnormal humans. What kind of sickness would have to infect the mind in such a zombie like fashion to have the young consider such a thing and a Dr. to buy in to the delusion?

As the stories of the "self-created" transformed humans unfold it is reasonable to conclude the mental anguish will haunt and torment these poor souls for the rest of their lives. There are already many a story of regret and it is most reasonable that in the coming decades there are going to be volumes of stories, books, and movies about misery of both the self-deceived and those that in any way had a hand in the horror, from the groomers, to the Dr. Victor Frankensteins of the world, as well as the citizen enablers that refuse to see the horror for what it is.

Frankenstein the movie and others like it are labeled "horror movies" and that is a proper category. Today doctors and all that assist them are doing things to their fellow brothers and sisters and especially the children that I submit are more horrific than Dr. Victor Frankenstein. What makes them more horrific is that the book and the movie were fiction and in that fiction Dr. Victor Frankenstein did what he did in secret. Today groomers, doctors, nurses, hospital bean counters, academia, government, bankers, a certain percentage of complicit citizens, and the most horrific of all being the complicit parent, all conspiring in a most egregious horror perpetrated upon fellow image bearers of God and they do it in the open.

Just a thought!

~ WORDS ~

stupid defined: *having or showing a great lack of intelligence or common sense*

abomination defined: *a thing that causes disgust or hatred; in biblical terms, an abomination to God, His order and His law*

idiot defined: *a stupid person; a person of low intelligence*

Many words today have been co-opted to mean something different from the original intent, so defining terms is more important today than ever. Crib for instance. Kids or youths perhaps have always made up goofy code; some of which sticks and some falls buy the wayside in a few years. When I was young the terms boss, far out, bitching, and groovy, were common to describe a thing that was awesome. Those seemed to have died, but others become a staple, like crib. Once defined only as a babies bed, now includes someone's home. The examples given are benign and don't hurt anyone in any real tangible sense, although my grandma and my grandfather found the use of such words a corruption or a waste of what a young mind should be putting into it. I remember my grandfather being disgusted that Latin was removed from school curriculums. I think he was very much right, and further Greek, Hebrew, and Aramaic would have been useful.

Today a word that has been completed co-opted and is not benign in its use is the word gender. It is not benign and in fact is malignant and like a tumor it invades the normal tissue of the brain, is infectious especially in the young when with malevolent intent groomers, i.e., that once great profession of teacher charged with the preparation and training of the young has itself been groomed to prepare and train narcissists. Generations of young that have an excessive or erotic interest in the self and their own physical appearance have now been groomed into existence. Worse yet they go further on two fronts:

1. many are groomed into believing that sex anytime, anywhere, with anyone, with whatever perversion can be dreamed up is acceptable, and
2. with what can only be a satanically designed bio weapon for the brain convince many of these newly created narcissists they would be happier in a new bio costume.

Without concern that this grooming is creating a brand new culture of unhappiness, extreme narcissism, and suicide, not to mention the cottage industry for mutilation monsters. Doctors once considered a benevolent profession, now prey on those groomed into such a severe mental disorder in which rational thought and rational emotions are so impaired that contact is lost with the Creator and His created external reality.

What for all of time was a descriptor of one of two things and that being the sex of male and female in the natural world, and a grammatical category in inflected languages to recognize the feminine and masculine usage of language with the obvious and normal•associations with the only two natural sexes that exist. The misuse and fraudulent redefinition(s) of the word gender is new to the world since the mid-20th century and its scope is ever expanding. If there was ever a perversion of God's created order it is when this clearly stupid abomination entered the gray matter of an idiot.

Just a thought!

~ NOTICE VS. ASSIGNMENT ~

notice: *the fact of observing or paying attention to something.*

assign: *designate or set "something" aside for a specific purpose.*

right: *a moral or legal entitlement to have or obtain something or to act in a certain way*

authority: *official permission*

arrogance: *an attitude of superiority manifested in an overbearing manner or in presumptuous claims or assumptions*

mindless: *marked by or displaying no use of the powers of the intellect*

perversion: *alter something from its original course, meaning, or state to a distortion or corruption of what was first intended*

ignorance: *lack of knowledge or information.*

preposterous: *contrary to reason or common sense; utterly absurd or ridiculous*

psychobabble: *trite or simplistic language derived from psychotherapy*

insanity: *1) extreme folly or unreasonableness; 2) something utterly foolish or unreasonable*

moron: *a stupid person*

idiot: *a stupid person; a person of low intelligence*

Perhaps the greatest injustice to mankind is the reconstruction in language of words to express a perversion of what was once truth. As it relates to the previous section about the word gender is the perversion of language that involves the necessary understanding of other words and their original definitions. Often today we hear about the assignment of gender at birth by a doctor. The presupposition would be that the doctor has some "right" as defined above or the "authority" to assign the sex of a baby. The doctor has not been bequeathed any such authority or right to assign the sex/gender (same thing) of a baby. This specialized doctor has been taught to safely deliver the baby boy or baby girl, that's it. Before the insanity of gender dysphoria, the doctor "noticed" the gender/sex of the newborn as either a boy or girl, it was not assigned. Further, the "noticing" is so easy it requires no schooling whatsoever to "notice" that a newborn is a boy or girl. A toddler of, say, three can correctly "notice" the gender/sex of a newborn.

If there was a right or an authority to "notice" that a newborn is only one of two possible God created configurations, God it seems has bequeathed that right and authority to toddlers. The preposterous statement that a doctor "assigns" the sex/gender would by logic presuppose that the doctor was right there in the uterus when the sperm penetrated the egg and with his "right" and "authority" took his authoritative set of micro-tweezers and arranged a particular set of chromosomes into an XX or XY configuration. If a doctor had such a "right" or "authority" that doctor reasonably might have created the foundations for such a miracle in its first instance. Oh wait! That was God.

The ignorance in academy that preposterously claims that a doctor has a right or an authority to assign the sex/gender of a newborn, rather what in reality the doctor does do, which is notice the authoritative handy work of God, the Creator of baby boys and baby girls. Further, doctors know that God alone has the right and that God does this with perfect authority and perfect assignments. Any doctor that denies this obvious truth is a liar. Further, anyone, anyone at all that would dare to deny God's assignments is a liar and covets their own self-righteousness over God's generally revealed truths about his created order.

In conclusion with honest sincerity that I not pervert the proper construction of words to convey truth the following arrangement of words uses all of the words defined above, the truth of which, with a modicum of reflection is self-evident: Here goes!!!!

> *The perversion of reality by mindless supposed intellectuals with an extreme attitude of superiority manifestly and overbearingly expressing*

presumptuous claims or assumptions such as a right bequeathed by a make believe fairy authority to "assign" the sex/gender of a baby; rather than the God bequeathed sense of sight that allows anyone to "notice" the miracle of a baby boy or a baby girl. Further, the insanity of the new-psychobabble ignorance cottage industry of morons that has spawned a dysphoria so preposterous and melodramatic in its idiocy that its participants are to be pitied, prayed for and when appropriate mocked.

Just a thought!

An afterthought – I read the above to a friend and in this case a woman for a laugh. She did laugh and recounted a wonderful incident when her son was about 2½ years old and he was being potty trained. She had a little potty next to the toilet for the lad's training. The little guy, it should be noted took showers with mom as is common at that age. Just learning to talk, he was sitting on the potty and made a statement to his mommy. With a very contemplative look on his face he said, "Boys have peeders." Mommy replied, "Yes they do." Then the toddler, again with a very contemplative look on his face said, "Girls don't have peeders." Mommy responded, "That's right." Then after having very contemplatively thought through these revelations, his little toddler countenance changed from contemplative to joyous having cracked the code, if you will, and with happy authority stated, "Girls have ears." His mother laughed internally and praised the toddler for his passing, with flying colors, a level of intelligence not seen today in academia.

This anecdotal observation by a 2½ year old toddler, just learning to talk, having only a year earlier made the transition from crawling to walking, in the "la-bor-a-tory" of the bathroom, using scientific analysis and observation having only seen one naked girl, correctly identified after having "noticed" that his peeder was a feature exclusive to boys, and also "noticed" the lack of a peeder was a feature exclusive to girls, and that ears are a feature shared by both sexes is genus level stuff. I dare say by today's standard of what is considered science in American institutions of "theoretical" higher learning, this toddler was an Einstein.

Just another thought!

~ THE EROSION OF TRUST ~

trust: 1a) *assured reliance on the character, ability, strength, or truth of someone or something;* ***1b)*** *one in which confidence is placed;* ***2a)*** *dependence on something future or contingent, hope;* ***2b)*** *reliance on future payment for property (such as merchandise) delivered, credit bought furniture on trust;* ***3a)*** *a property interest held by one person for the benefit of another;* ***3b)*** *a combination of firms or corporations formed by a legal agreement, especially one that reduces or threatens to reduce competition;* ***4a)*** *care, custody such as the child committed to her trust;* ***4b)*** *a charge or duty imposed in faith or confidence or as a condition of some relationship; or, something committed or entrusted to one to be used or cared for in the interest of another;* ***4c)*** *responsible charge or office,* ***5)*** *archaic : trustworthiness*

trust *as a verb - trusted; trusting; trusts*

trust *as a transitive verb –* ***1a)*** *to rely on the truthfulness or accuracy of, believe, trust a rumor;* ***1b)*** *to place confidence in, rely on a friend you can trust;* ***1c)*** *to hope or expect confidently trusts that the problem will be resolved soon; 2a) to commit or place in one's care or keeping, entrust; 2b) to permit to stay or go or to do something without fear or misgiving; 3) to extend credit to*

trust – *intransitive verb -* ***1a)*** *to place confidence, depend, trust in God, trust to luck;* ***1b)*** *to be confident, hope; 2) to sell or deliver on credit.*

intransitive: *characterized by not having or containing a direct object*

racket: *a usually illegitimate enterprise made workable by bribery or intimidation*

For many years I have pondered this word trust. It started years ago while studying considerations of law, contracts, agreements, etc. At some point as one journeys down that particular path of acquired knowledge one learns about "trust law" and the legal construction called a "trust." This legal construction is quite old and it was interesting to read some of the old trust law and writings.

It is said that "trust law" is the highest form of law. Curious statement! How did this "highest form" come to be in the first place and then how did it become the "highest form." As I read the old English writings they were creating agreements between "gentlemen" with means to protect themselves, why? Answer, because no one could be trusted.

The "Trust" by ancient agreements of those with means could and did make for a "legal" corral if you will to protect their chattel and stuff. Legal minds went to work crafting constructions of legalese, corporations, cabals of legalese constructionists, and subservient diversified cabals of teachers, accountants, government minions, propaganda divisions, and various entities of force to, as one of the definitions above notes, *"reduces or threatens to reduce competition."* Competition for what? Excellent question, the answer is everything and everyone they may want or desire to have or control.

To protect their stuff law and legal constructions had to be introduced, made to be law and not only that, by law no one could look behind this "trust" veil under any circumstances. Actually, a rather brilliant idea which did and does protect. But whom does it protect. Today, as then, it protects those with means. If you don't have means it is not likely you will have success dabbling in this racket precisely because you don't have means.

Now with perhaps this brief analysis presented for your consideration, please re-read the definitions above which were all taken on-line from Merriam Webster and are all reasonable for what trust has "eroded" too. Definition 1a) *"assured reliance on the character, ability, strength, or truth of someone or something"* is a very reasonable definition for what one might consider trust to be. Some of the others are logical, but I would like to focus on 3b) *a combination of firms or corporations formed by a legal agreement, especially one that reduces or threatens to reduce competition*. It is this definition that is proof that, if I am correct, "trust law" because man cannot be trusted has become an institution, and industry, a protection for those with means to "reduce" or "threaten to reduce" anyone that interferes with their stuff or the stuff they may wish to acquire, or precisely defined, a cabal.

Lastly for your consideration please consider the "intransitive verb" definition of trust. ***1a)*** *to place confidence, depend, trust in God, trust to luck*. The key here is to place "trust in God." Now notice the definition of "intransitive": *characterized by not having or containing a direct object.* Could it be that "God" in this definition cannot be an object by the definition of intransitive, i.e., to trust in God would be to trust in an intangible entity like luck?

The above definitions were obtained from the Merriam-Webster website. Knowing that Noah Webster was very much a Christ follower, the intransitive verb definition inference to God as *not* being considered a direct object gave me pause especially having just added Noah's dying words as a postscript to "The Hope that is Easter" in Chapter 13. I went home and pulled out a 1972 Merriam Webster dictionary inherited from my dad. What I found was a bit disturbing, but a corroboration of the title of this section, i.e., "The Erosion of Trust."

> **1972 Merriam Webster --- trust: 1a)** *confidence; a reliance or resting of the mind on the integrity, veracity, justice, friendship, or other sound principle of another person or thing. Example – Whoso putteth his trust in the Lord shall be safe. Proverbs 18.10* **2)** *one who or that which is trusted. Example – O Lord God, thou art my trust from my youth. Psalm 71.5*

> **2023 Merriam Webster ---** ***1a)*** *assured reliance on the character, ability, strength, or truth of someone or something;*

This unplanned disclosure although disturbing is not surprising. I'm not sure when the revision was made, but it doesn't matter, nor is it a surprise. Anyone in America knows that God, and especially Christianity has been systematically attacked for many years. In fifty years the great work of Noah Webster, an accomplished man devoted to the gospel of Christ Jesus, whose reliance on the truth and the "trust" in the God of the Bible to make clear the meaning of this word "trust" has been stripped of the true meaning by removing God to an intransitive consideration of a verb.

Now please consider the biblical definition of trust. The scriptures are replete with "trust in God." America at its inception once believed this, so much so that the coin of the realm says "One nation under God," and "In God We Trust." Now it seems that "trust" has been eroded so much that God is a fiction and used as an example of an intransitive verb form of trust in something that is a non-entity like luck.

> **betrayal**! --- *the act or fact of violating the "trust" or confidence of another*

Interesting! The act and the fact that whomever has taken the reins of the Merriam-Webster dynasty violated the "trust" that with all reason was entrusted to them and in this instance eroded not only the definition of "trust," but have with intent, deceit, and fraud, making claim that God cannot be a direct object. This "erosion" in the case of the intellectual property of Noah Webster while most egregious, the "erosion" of God to a no thing condemns all parties involved to one of two judgments.

> **NKJV --- Matthew 12:31-32** -- *31 "Therefore I say to you, every sin and blasphemy will be forgiven men, but the blasphemy against the Spirit will not be forgiven men. 32 Anyone who speaks a word against the Son of Man, it will be forgiven him; but whoever speaks against the Holy Spirit, it will not be forgiven him, either in this age or in the age to come.*

I confess ignorance here, and am not sure if this blasphemy is against the "Son of Man" or His Spirit. In other words to relegate God, and therefore His Son, and therefore His spirit to an intransitive consideration of a verb and to make God on par with luck it seems is most certainly a blasphemy. God only knows, but whatever kind of blasphemy it is it cannot be good.

Just a thought!

An afterthought – My original intent for the "Erosion of Trust" section was to point out that as if on cue man thinks he can do better than God. If man would live by the moral law and love God with all of his heart, soul, and mind then man's perversions of "trust" into "trust law" would not be necessary at all. The "trust" constructions of legalese contracts are because men and women cannot be trusted to *not* covet, to *not* steal, and *not* encroach on another's person, property, papers, and the all-encompassing "effects." If man could be "trusted" at his word, then the "erosion of trust" from a man's word to this highest form of man's law called "trust law" would be moot.

Just another thought!

~ TWO INDUSTRIES OF MALFEASANCE ~ U.S. CORP & MAIN STREAM MEDIA

industry: *manufacturing activity as a whole; a distinct group of productive or profit-making enterprises; systematic labor especially for some useful purpose or the creation of something of value*

malfeasance: *the performance by a public official of an act that is legally unjustified, harmful, or contrary to law; wrongdoing (used **especially of an act in violation of a public trust**).*

misfeasance: *the performance of a lawful action in an illegal or improper manner*

inexorably: *in a way that is impossible to stop or prevent:*

Industry as defined and generally considered would be to create something useful and of value. Fair enough, but useful to whom and of value to whom and of what value, or what purpose? If not for the public or a portion thereof and for the good of humanity, industries easily corrupt themselves to consider value only as profit rather than what is "good." Most consumer goods provide a value in usefulness, and if not useful the consumer will cease to consider that product as good. Simple supply and demand!

Other things like drugs and alcohol are commodities that are reasonably not "good" for humanity, but do provide tremendous value in profits for the industries engaged in that market. It would be hard to argue that drugs and alcohol "generally" are for the "public good," to the contrary, if there was a "public bad" category of industries these two commodities would reasonable occupy positions #1 and #2 on the list of "public bad" commodities and with reason could never be considered a "public good." And to be fair I think very highly of Jon Taffer and how he changes lives. Different topic involving moderation perhaps.

That aside, U.S. Corp and the MSM are industries of words. U.S. Corp. should *not* be an industry for profit but it has become only that and therefore is now an industry for profit, producing billions in profit for the words they produce that ingratiate others while also ingratiating themselves. If it were not thus, none of them would seek lifelong appointments to whatever chair they occupy. If they had talent to produce something of real value they would move on to the private sector after one term as the servants they are supposed to be.

Not possessing skills to produce anything of real tangible value and generally lacking in virtue the cottage industry of politics turns out to be an excellent alternative career choice. Groomed by certain industries of schooling that teaches the constructions of words that arm the politician with the skills necessary to make malfeasance and misfeasance an art form. Once so groomed and or inclined to non-virtue, Washington D.C., aka, "the swamp" is perfect destination for what has come to be known as a swamp rat. Sad certainly for at one time congressmen, senators, and judges were considered with high regard, but by their fruit you will know them. In 2023 one is hard pressed to find an average American that would trust a politician to be left alone with their children. If their fruit was righteous they would not have lost the public trust and have a nickname like "swamp rat."

The swamp is a perverted industry that feeds its perversions from the public teat. Why not? Power, booze, parties, junkets, insider trading, real estate, sexual perversions, travel, etc., and all of those perks sometimes while "on the clock" and sometimes "off the clock" and all while drawing a salary. There is even an insurance policy or bucket of money for suits against sexually related improprieties of members. Awesome gig!

MSM should be for profit and it is. Once upon a time what is now known as MSM was referred to as the "press" which had and still does have protections in the republic of America's "Constitution" to criticize, question, ridicule, make fun of, and perhaps most importantly make sure that the servants of the people are not making a profit from the words they produce. Any words produced by U.S. Corp should with reason protect the rights of the people to engage in industry and any profits derived from righteous "public good" commodities so created.

For over a hundred years "bankers" and "lawyers" have molded both of these "industries of words" to the benefit of the "bankers" and by graft and corruption have tied these two industries inexorably together for the benefit and profit of the "money masters." While there should be a clear distinction between these two industries of "words," one for profit keeping in check the other which should not be for profit. Now they scratch each other's greedy itches.

If this logic makes a case that these two industries of words, once distinct and separate, are now two sides of the same coin, then malfeasance and misfeasance as defined above, is the game of words they play to protect their masters, which with discernment in 2023 and for over a century is not the people they are supposed to serve. All they do, while veiled and cleverly hidden, are industries of words for the same beast. If all that we hear and see are clearly violations of righteousness, then it follows that the master of these "industries of words" is not the master of the universe.

Does it not make sense that every act by U.S. Corp. and MSM, since they are scratching each other's greedy itches are tentacles of the same beast and hence not acting for the public good? Would not both industries with a small measure of discernment be an abomination to righteousness and therefore God's requirements for good?

Just a thought!

~ THE EXCEPTION TO THE RULE ~

An odd turn of phrase to be sure, but a phrase perhaps glossed over in its utility to consider, find, understand and know the truth. Rather than consider the rule which is generally revealed to all and should, one would think, be the go to common sense conclusion of the category being contemplated. Often it is, but more and more in this world of subjective truth the exceptions and the rules may seem blurry and unclear. But are they?

When man meddles in the world and notices rules he also stumbles on exceptions. Or does he? For example, all men for all of time possessing a mature mind can walk into a room and tell who the men are and who the women are. Likewise, all women for all of time possessing a mature mind can walk into a room and tell who the men are and who the women are. No exceptions, not ever, not even once. Now, enter in deception, in other words, costumes. "Costumes of visual" or "costumes of mind." Now, it may appear there is an exception. But, strip away the "costume of visual" and the "costume of mind" and the associated acting, and the truth finds us back at the rule.

Relative to all of recorded time a very new deception can reasonably be labeled "costume of mind." A certain deception or "costume of mind" giving rise to "perceived" exceptions to the rule has been labeled dysphoria.

> **dysphoria defined:** *A state of feeling unhappy, dissatisfaction or frustration.*

Feeling "unhappy," "dissatisfaction," or "frustration" about the rule, i.e., the truth about whom God has created as a boy or girl, does not change the rule nor does it create an exception. It does however "create" a lie, which is a rule without exceptions, i.e., to purport that an obvious truth is another thing is a lie and as it turns out is one of the Big Ten. God's ninth commandment is the rule and states, "Thou shall not bear false witness against thy neighbor." This is truth, which we know at the very core of our being and is a "rule" without exception.

For an individual to feel "unhappy," "dissatisfaction," or "frustration" about his or her biological sex and lie to God, lie to himself or herself, and "demand" that the entire world lie on his or her behalf supports the rule of what a lie is, but in no way changes the rule of God's created order. For that part of the world that adjoins itself with the lie, rather than call it out, only supports the rule of liars. The rule of what boys and girls are has therefore not been changed by a "perceived" or "costume of mind" exception. The truth of biology is still intact and the truth of what liars are is still intact.

Just a thought!

Afterthought – In the above thoughts I spoke of men and women possessing a mature mind walking in a room and being able to decipher who is a man and who is a woman. It occurs to me that I may have slighted God's little ones. My granddaughter is four years old. I asked her once how she knows that her Poppy is a boy. She touched my face and said because you have a mustache Poppy. I thought awesome, that's good enough for now. As I think on her mental capacities I feel 100% confident that she could go to her little preschool and if asked to sort the room by boys and girls she could do so with 100% accuracy and so could every one of God's little image bearers at the tender age of four and probably at three. I must repent for this error!!!

Just another thought!

~ WASTED TIME ~

A curious consideration of life --- In the sixteen, plus or minus hours the brain is on in a day, how much time is frivolous, i.e., not having any serious purpose or value? When a mind pursues knowledge, wisdom "might" follow. It seems reasonable that the type of knowledge "may" or "may not" be fruitful for wisdom. To be aware of the tripe that passes for knowledge is foundational for wisdom also, for to understand up, down must be known. Discernment then, is an element of knowledge which is a must for which fruit will nourish the mind and which fruit is rotten.

Sadly with newly found discernment discovered way too late in this old man's life a particular discipline of knowledge that would have helped me not waste so much time is philosophy. While schooled well in true, plumb, and square, i.e., some of the physical sciences, never was a philosophy class to ever cross my path. When I stumbled on Jordan Peterson it was clear that I missed out. Then other philosophers like R.C. Sproul, Voddie Bachman, Frank Turek, John Lennox, and many others made me realize, however it happened, I had been cheated. While the true, plumb, and square disciplines of mathematics were useful they never made me consider the why of things. Things like being. R.C. Sproul's lecture on the philosophical considerations of being, and once so considered the logical extensions to yet another proof of the existence of God are as wondrous to me as listening to Michael Behe and Steven Meyer teach about the cell which with reason and rational thought are all proofs of the glory of God.

Providence I suppose is why philosophy would not be introduced to me until I was discovering the Word of God. Would I have been tempted had I been introduced to philosophy at a young age to not know God? Perhaps. Weighty considerations and ironically a waste of time to waste too much time dwelling on the "what ifs" of God's providence for the trajectory of my life. In any event I can say that now I enjoy philosophy and listening to philosophers like Jordan Peterson.

As it concerns wasted time it was Jordan that convicted me to not waste time as it pertains to learning. I knew I could find one hour a day to listen to someone, anyone talk or teach in a variety of disciplines for one hour a day. At first it took some discipline to get the one hour a day. What happen after about three months I discovered that there was so much to know and interesting stuff at that. TV became boring realizing I could learn something. The one hour turned in to 2 hours/day which on the weekends turned into 4 hours/day most of which could be done simultaneously while working on other projects around the house and listening to many disciplines of knowledge on my magic rectangle.

For a real look at "wasted time" in my life the following is perhaps a reasonable math equation to consider how much time I wasted. If I analyze my grown up years from say 20 years old till 60 just for a simple math consideration:

(40 years) x (2 hrs/day) x (365 days/yr) = 29,200 hours of wasted time. This assumes that I might have been watching TV or otherwise not acquiring useful knowledge which is in fact a correct assumption. If ½ of that time, or 1 hour/day was spent reading the Bible that would be 14,600 hours spent that with reason might have made me a better fisher of men. Anyway, do some math in your life especially if you are young and don't

let knowledge slip away into "wasted time." If you are older, consider this math: 1/hr x 365 days = 365 hours. 2/hr x 365 days = 730. The point is what might you learn for shutting off the TV and or other distractions. What could you learn in 365 or 730 hours this year????

Just a thought!

~ APPEALING TO AUTHORITY ~

presupposition: *a thing tacitly assumed beforehand at the beginning of a line of argument or course of action.*

supposition: *something that is generally assumed or believed to be the case, but not necessarily so:*

academy: *1) a school usually above the elementary level; 2) a body of established opinion widely accepted as authoritative in a particular field.*

academic: *1) of, relating to, or associated with an academy or school especially of higher learning; 2) a person who is academic in background, outlook, or methods.*

expert: *1) one with the special skill or knowledge representing mastery of a particular subject or experience*

appeal: *1) an application (as to a recognized authority) for corroboration, vindication, or decision; 2) an earnest plea; 3) the power to arousing a sympathetic response*

authority: *1) the power or right to give orders, make decisions, and enforce obedience; 2) the power to influence others, especially because of one's commanding manner or one's recognized knowledge about something.*

right: *a moral or legal entitlement to have or obtain something or to act in a certain way*

> **claim**: *n. 1) an assertion of the truth of something, typically one that is disputed or in doubt; 2) state or assert that something is the case, typically without providing evidence or proof*

The world has been brain washed to think experts can only come from academy where theoretical "higher learning" is learned and once so "theoretically learned" creates an expert then considered an authority on this or that. True in many spheres, but not so much in others, teachers for example. Just yesterday a teacher, in this case of "elementary" students not "higher" education students, stood at a podium in Arizona appealing to lawmakers, she stating that parents have "no right" to weigh in much less decide what she teaches "elementary" children. Why, because she has a "masters" degree. This teacher is of the ilk that thinks children should be taught sex related topics of a pornographic nature.

Let's examine her claims:

1. Parents have "no rights" whatsoever for what she decides;
2. Which tacitly implies she does have "rights" to do as she pleases;
3. Her "right" apparently bequeathed to her by a "master's degree" by her exhorting that it is so.

To examine her claims I "appeal" to the definitions of words and in this case the words above. It may not be all that is needed to get to the bottom of her claims, but it is a good start. First it is reasonable to infer that her "presuppositions" are at best "suppositions" without merit because she thinks that her attendance at an "academy" made her an "academic" in this case with a "master's degree" which makes her a supposed "expert" in child pornography for children. Armed with a piece of paper that says "masters" she "appeals" to what she perceives as the "authority," i.e., the government that has the "power" to "enforce obedience" of her "mastery" of sexual perversion for children.

She exhorts that parents have no right, i.e., ***"a moral or legal entitlement to have or obtain something or to act in a certain way,"*** which necessarily implies she does have ***"a moral or legal entitlement to have or obtain something or to act in a certain way."*** Really? Let's break down this definition of "right."

Moral entitlement for the parents seems straightforward. Further, in the academy of parenthood, the ***"body of established opinion widely accepted as authoritative in the field of parenting,"*** is that parents and parents alone are the sole authority in all matters concerning their property, which is their offspring.

If moral entitlement shifts from parent to teacher by a legal entitlement surely there must be an attachment to the "master's degree" that shifts the moral entitlement with a legal notice to the parents that the parents are no longer responsible for the moral considerations of their children. Surely this teacher must have receipts, i.e., this bequeathed "right," if in fact a "right" must have a legal document to back up her claimed right. If so, then she can merely appeal to the local magistrate to serve the parents and strip them of the, let's call them, moral and lawful entitlements bequeathed on them by the highest authority of all. You know, the God of nature that gave mothers the instinct to mother, and fathers the instinct to protect the mothers and the babies from predators such as this theoretical "master" of elementary pornographic curriculum for children.

It is this sort of predator that makes consideration of a comedic definition of "expert" apropos (see definition below), i.e., the waste product that spews forth from a mouth such as hers makes a mockery of "higher learning." Further, it makes "appealing to authority" also a mockery for they listen to this tripe and in some cases support such perversion, which if at all considered is an indictment that certain members of government themselves are lacking in elementary facts of the created order. God help them. Why? It's the millstone thing. Repentance is most certainly required, therefore I pray for all of the souls whose "master's degree" is underwritten by Satan.

It is just such foolishness that is swinging the pendulum and making mothers and fathers make their appeals heard at school boards and state houses since common sense is clearly not a requirement of "higher" learning for government officials. This woman, unbeknownst to her for she obviously is neither gifted nor educated in reason, revealed that more is needed in academy before the degree of "master" is given so frivolously especially to anyone charged with being in the same room as a child. Subjects like, rights and where they come from; morality and where it comes from; common sense and reason and where they come from; and for good measure what is a woman and where did they come from. In other words, when appealing to authority, higher learning is not higher if it does not appeal to the highest authority.

In a great irony children at an elementary level are very much capable of understanding where they come from, the moral law and why the moral law, sin and salvation. If this teacher had been exposed to this elementary level of education she never would have ventured to the state house to make such a misguided, uneducated, blind, and not so "masterful" appeal.

Note: the comedic definition below does not use foul language, but does make an allegorical reference to a waste product. Different than the apostle Paul, who made the following statement,

> **KJV --- Philippians 3:8** -- 8 Yea doubtless, and I count all things but loss for the excellency of the knowledge of Christ Jesus my Lord: for whom I have suffered the loss of all things, and do count them but **dung**, that I may win Christ,

(dung or the Greek word skubala is the Greek word for the English word shit). Paul makes his point in a bold way that all is loss and totally and completely worthless save faith in Christ Jesus.

In certain circumstances man has recognized utterances of a ridiculous nature as "bull ____, or horse ____." It is in this spirit that I, and I dare say others, but not all, will recognize the utility to make bold references as necessary to shine a light on liars and the lies they spew, which is reasonably a waste product of some sort. Please note in this comedic definition of "expert" nary a bad word is used! Let the reader decide which type of expert this "master" teacher is!

> **expert (comedic):** *1) ex is a "has been" and "(s)pert" is a drip under pressure; 2) ex is a "has been" and (s)pert is the last bit of urine expelled by males when urinating - urine being a waste product.*

A very comedic theatrical example that was and is still pure comedy gold is a scene in the movie, "Liar Liar," starring Jim Carrey. Jim plays an attorney who finds himself unable to lie because his son wished that his dad could not lie. In order to delay the court Jim excuses himself to the bathroom to relieve himself as he had nervously downed a pitcher of water in the courtroom. Many a movie have shown the common and ordinary scene of men urinating at a urinal, but only Jim Carrey could make even that scene extraordinarily hilarious. Anyway, if I might suggest as it relates to this comedic consideration of "expert," now that it's in your grey matter, the next time you hear that someone is an "expert" use discernment that he/she may in fact be the normal recognized definition of the word, or if you discern that he/she is not in fact so, perhaps see the humor of an alternate consideration.

I suspect I may be admonished by my church elders for treading in comedic waters of this type and perhaps I deserve it, but in my defense as noted by my daughter when she gifted me with a tee shirt that said, "Sarcasm --- just one of my many talents," such wit seems foundational to gifts bequeathed me from outside myself --- just sayin! And now that it's out there the next time you hear the word "expert" just try to not recall the above definition of "expert" and its usefulness for certain, but not all, persons claiming the title of "expert."

Just a thought!

~ SOCIALLY CONSTRUCTED IDIOTS ~

In the social sciences there is a field of study called "social constructionism." It is reasonable for man once again to consider a category of God's created order and study it, make observations about it, postulate theories, and throw out said theories into the ethos for consideration. Some such theories are obvious and would comport to the natural state of human interaction. Others not so much. While some of the great thinkers of history proposed reasonable postulations some are stupid. Some of the stupid mixed together with salient thoughts in the same sentence. For example:

In the 16th century, Michel de Montaigne wrote that, "*We need to interpret interpretations more than to interpret things.*" This is absurd in that once the definitions of words is considered, written down in dictionaries, reasonably understood to define or explain a truth, used by the masses, i.e., the social beings, then to stand on such a postulation without push back you end up with what may be useful for a weasel. Lawyers and politicians make an art form of such, let's call them doctrines of weasels. Then without remorse much less the needed repentance a man, a highly educated man from both Georgetown University and Yale and recipient of a Rhodes scholarship no less, rising to the most powerful position on the planet, secularly speaking, indoctrinated with such "enlightened" postmodern thinking dodges an inquiry into the truth of using power and position to bang an intern in the White House and using the Montaigne postulation to say, "It depends on what the definition of is is."

In 1886 or 1887, Friedrich Nietzsche put it similarly: "Facts do not exist, only interpretations." Once again an otherwise brilliant man postulating an extremely absurd idea. This type of thinking has caused devolution in the factual binary of men and women into a 21st century subjective reality world in which a growing number of socially constructed idiots "cannot" say the words, "a woman is an adult human female."

Further, such thinking has infected like a metastasizing cancer the minds of boys and girls, men and women to think it's okay for men to claim to be women, crush them in sports, women required to be naked with men in locker rooms, get raped in prisons, claim menstruation, uterus and all that is a girl, female, or woman, suggest that an actual real man should desire to have sex with such a person or said man is a bigot. Further, by the power of the state have the sane of mind put their minds and their will under the boot of stupidity, stupid having been made the legal master. I dare say even Nietzsche would not have envisioned such metastasized lunacy.

In his 1922 book *Public Opinion*, Walter Lippmann said, "*The real environment is altogether too big, too complex, and too fleeting for direct acquaintance*" between people and their environment. This is absurd! The world is big, yes; complex, yes; fleeting, yes; to fleeting for direct acquaintance, insane idea.

Each and every person is "directly acquainted" daily with all or a portion of God's created order. The expanse of the universe in the night sky is not fleeting; the smells that are encountered from food to flowers to fresh cut grass are not fleeting; the touch of a child when they hug your neck is not fleeting; the sounds of birds chirping in the morning is not fleeting; the taste of fresh fruit is not fleeting. Parenting is not fleeting, marriage is not fleeting, school is not fleeting, friendships are not fleeting, and betrayal is not fleeting.

Yes it is true that "in one sense" time for the human can "seem" fleeting, even yesterday has elements that might seem long ago, but consider if you will those things in the list above, i.e., the night sky and its breath taking expanse and wonder; the smell of flowers or fresh cut grass or hay; your child or grandchild's little arms hugging you; birds chirping or hopping along on the lawn; the taste of a fresh banana, pineapple, strawberry, or hot baked potato with butter salt and pepper; friendships from your preteen years; friendships and or even short lived friendships from school classes, team sports, or activities, your first love, your first broken heart, the first time you were deceived or betrayed; insert your own memory here ___________!!!

You may not have experienced some of these things for months, years or decades, but the act of pulling them to the front of the mind by merely reading the suggestive words above your memory can see, hear, smell, feel, and taste them or stated in one word "sense" them. To pull up these experienced past actions especially those long since passed is yet another of Gods gifts and God's grace to mankind. In other words life is in no ways fleeting if you but think to consider your past through your memory.

Curiously certain words uttered by the great thinkers of the past are useful, others not so much. It's not that ideas should not be expressed, they should, but not without at least trying to discern the implications. Make the point, great, but consider the counter point or what might it mean taken to its logical conclusion. Such a thing used to be called "critical thinking." When the "counterpoint" is not considered or discussed in the classroom "critical thinking" morphs into a one sided point we might recognize today as "CRT," or "critical race theory" or other such one-sided conventions. Students today in 2023 are not in an environment where the counterpoint is considered at all, much less allowed to ask a question or discuss where such an idea might take us if it is played out to its logical conclusion.

One sided ideas, like "social justice" and "CRT" are absorbed into a certain type of mind that cannot seem to discern that such words are or should be considered dangerous. I say "certain" type of mind for we do hear of the students that don't buy it, but for the sake of getting a good grade are in every sense of the word "blackmailed" into toeing the line. While those examples of questioning and discerning students are encouraging to many students are lost into the vortex of non-discernment and are then sadly graduated with diplomas underwritten by a lot of stupid.

Sadly such ideas metastasize and evolve and after a time academia teaches all is subjective and objective truth is not true but subjective.

And here we are in 2023 academia turning out academically created mindless rubes not capable of rational thought because of the evolution of irrational ideas morphed into ideologies inconsistent with rational objective truth. These rubes sent into teaching jobs to groom children that God is not real and this world and universe was created by chance from nothing and that if you feel like it you can by emoted feeling ignore your biological God given and created very specific sex and delusionally claim you are not that sex and can by your dysphoric feelings take on the other and hire con men and or women to take your money and butcher what was a gift to you from God.

Lippmann goes further: Each person constructs a pseudo-environment that is a subjective, biased, and necessarily abridged mental image of the world, and to a degree, everyone's pseudo-environment is a fiction. People "*live in the same world, but they think and feel in different ones.*" Someone else noted of Lippmann's statement that "environment" might be called "reality," and his "pseudo-environment" seems equivalent to what today is called "constructed reality."

Walter Lippmann is not wrong here and he did do some great analysis of the world or "constructed realities" or socially constructed ideologies. The thing is if the socially constructed ideas make, as Lippmann says, a "pseudo-environment" it is, as Lippmann also notes, "a fiction" and therefore not true or as recently observed and properly coined "fake news." Any such "constructed reality" that does not comport with reality is a fraud, and a lie.

One internet explanation states:

> ***"A social construct is a concept that exists not in objective reality, but as a result of human interaction. It exists because humans agree that it exists."***

This is useful for malleable minds that latch on to such a definition to use it as a pseudo club to dismiss objective reality itself. For example, and most useful for the secular materialist is to stand on such a statement to say that God is a social construct because humans socially "agree" that God exists. This allows an immature mind to look no further, or not study, since all is socially constructed and therefore manufactured by the whim of the day. Further inquiry need not be done, no study of history, no study of the great minds of the past, no reading of the great literature of the past, no study or consideration of the sciences and especially the recent scientific discoveries that do point directly to God, and most importantly deny that which is written on your heart, i.e., moralities and virtues known intuitively to one's conscience.

Since critical thinking was not taught then it is understandable that uneducated or ignorant minds will never consider the question, "Who created those moralities and virtues?" All such dismissal makes for easy dismissal of any consideration to read the most important book ever to be penned, the Bible.

Institutions of learning, at whatever level, today offer as little as possible in the history of thought, and most importantly the skill of thinking, and more important than that, discerning. Truth over nonsense, right over wrong, good versus evil, etc., are filtered through "social constructions" instead of "foundations of truth" such as "nothing cannot, has not, never will produce something."

Rather than "foundational truths" if it is all constructed then my construction is as good as the last guy and before you know it you have a generation of narcissistic "socially constructed" worshipers of self. Look no further than "social media" platforms, any of them that have, not a "socially constructed," but a "technologically constructed" construct with tools to create "self-worshiping" idolatrous narcissists, whose idols are twofold.

First the idol of the platform, whether it's Facebook, TikTok, Twitter, or whatever "social platform" and also would include the idol of the "smart phone." The second idol is "socially constructed" by the availability of the 1st idols and that idol is "self" complete with worshipers, or "followers" that make the "self" feel significant.

To be fair, these tools can and are used for good or I would not have written this book. It is also true that there are socially constructed ideas that are not good or righteous. In America the idea to have a country that has been called and or considered ***"the great melting pot"*** with a stanza of a poem by Emma Lazarus in 1883, that stanza once referred to as the "conscience of America" enshrined on the base of the "Statue of Liberty" as follows:

> ***Give me your tired, your poor,***
> ***Your huddled masses yearning to breathe free,***
> ***The wretched refuse of your teeming shore.***
> ***Send these, the homeless, tempest-tost to me,***
> ***I lift my lamp beside the golden door!"***

Why!, America itself was "socially constructed" and conceived by those that suffered and "discerned" because of the lessons of historical suffering what would make America great. The "Statue of Liberty" was conceived and ultimately erected about two decades after the civil war by French "Abolitionist," Édouard René de Laboulaye. Discerning and suffering through revolutions in America and France a century earlier in the late 1700s and thinking through the concepts of "freedom" and "liberty" and what "social constructs" would make for the "common good," these men and women thought deeply about such things, as did the Puritans, and the God fearing Christian founding fathers of America.

Through the stains of the despotism of kings and the stains of slavery a created work of art; both statue and words; placed at a main gateway to this great nation so that America might celebrate the end of slavery and consider what it was in the "socially constructed" American experiment that made for such a great nation. Then from time to time Americans might stop to think and even celebrate, consider and not forget why and through what struggles made America a place where even now as we are losing our way and devolving into a despotic nation, people the world over still want to come here because of those original constructions. For goodness sake, that is to say for God's sake America, discern wisely for America as conceived and "socially constructed" is falling apart into another thing.

If it can be ascertained that America itself is a "social construct" then certain "constructions" held it together until now. With discernment those "constructions" that held to God ordained constructions made America great. For example:

- The Words of God in the Bible with particular attention to the 10 commandments and the obvious virtue of 5 through 10 underwritten and understood only by the foundations of 1 through 4
- The New Testament in its entirety which underwrites the Christian church, i.e., the bride of Christ, this construct of God having started the American experiment in the first place
- The "Great Charter" or "Magna Carta"
- The Declaration of Independence
- The Constitution for the united States of America the most important part of which are the first ten Amendments. The "Preamble" to those amendments which are not oft printed but should be,

  i.e., *The conventions of a number of the States having at the time of their adopting the Constitution, expressed a desire, in order to prevent misconstruction or abuse of its powers, that further **declaratory and restrictive** clauses should be added: And as extending the ground of public confidence in the Government, will best insure the beneficent ends of its institution.*

There have been exponential usurpations of these original documents ironically identical to the usurpations listed in the "Declaration of

Independence" that have and are causing the devolution of the "socially constructed" ideas that made America great.

The most recent and new ridiculous "socially constructed" ideas would be things such as:

- social justice
- safe spaces
- micro aggressions
- radical feminism
- theoretical hate speech, hate thought, and hate crime
- the "your speech offends me" doctrine(s)
- cancel culture (not including the power, or "vote" of the purse)
- vacuous 3 or 4 word platitudes and tantrums
- same sex marriage
- subsidized abortion on demand
- subsidized marginalized groups especially single motherhood
- subsidized contraception
- subsidized dependence on drugs
- subsidized anything which should be private
- racists policies such as affirmative action
- CRT or "critical race theory"
- anti-white ism or any other anti-melanin related isms
- trans human and trans humanism
- artificial intelligence
- LGBTQIA and their holier than thou self-constructions of "missing the mark" and that "missing the mark" need be held up by the power of state as virtue
- as yet undefined psychosis {CDEFHJKMNOPRSUVWXY and or Z}
- and the "coup de ignoramus" of ideas and or ideologies constructed from pure stupid is that of not being able to answer the question "What is a woman?"

These silly and stupid constructions which clearly have been successful in "socially constructing" various tribes of the same type of idiot, as evidenced by the ever growing number of "letters" on their "short bus" and the ever growing number of colors on the flag of their "State of Lunacy."

To be fair many are not on the "short bus" or represented by a color on the "Lunacy" flag, but they do "affirm," "support," "agree," or otherwise think these things are in any ways righteous and or okay and not harmful to Gods created order.

The damage and their obvious terrible and evil impacts to women, girls, men, boys, children, the unborn, and society at large are proofs that idiots can and in fact are socially constructed, and sadly these idiots vote.

Just a thought!

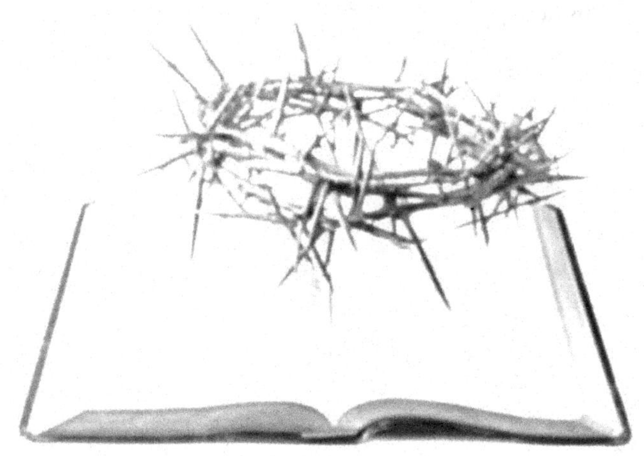

Close Calls are Grace!

Grace from Whom?

Chapter 17

CLOSE CALLS & REDEMPTION

~ FORD HILL & MOUNTAIN LION ~

Where I grew up in the mountains of Colorado there was a two room country school house which I attended in the eighth grade. It's still there. To the east of the school there is a hill the locals call Ford Hill supposedly because in the early days of the automobile only Fords could make it up the hill. Several years ago the janitor at the school used to run up and down that hill. On one occasion he ran up the hill, got to the top and was beginning the jog back down. He heard a noise, a quite noise behind him. When he turned around there was a mountain lion at his heels. He was being stalked by a predator and was presumably almost dinner. Fortunately a car crested the hill behind him, a redeemer if you will and gave the janitor I suspect a new lease on life, literally. The car scared the mountain lion off and the janitor chose to get in the car and get a ride away from the big cat. How close this man was to a silent and horrific death...very! I don't know this man, and don't know his faith, but it seems death was close that day and I would hope he considered that he was thrown a redemptive life line that day. Did it affect him, his decisions, how he looked at life, his consideration of life, of death, of heaven, of hell, a redeemer, salvation? Could it be that the story would only be local lore to be forgotten in a decade? I hope it helped him consider the Cross. Or, is it possible his story would only be resurrected in my memory years later to write down in this book to possibly and hopefully scare the dickens out of someone he nor I will ever know, but may consider how death is closer than we might ever think possible. Providence? Let's hope for the best outcome, i.e., that this fellow, the people in the car, the locals, all those who have heard the story, me, and all whom might read this account years later might consider that death is at your heels.

We don't think on the possibility of death by mountain lion, the thought taken to its horrific conclusion is terrifying. We do, however, know of death by car accident, cancer, old age, and other things that we don't think on much and when we do the thought is fleeting for there is the next meal to consider. We should perhaps think on it sometimes, thank God for this gift of life, consider greatly that God desires that we come home to Heaven and if you haven't done it yet search out that eternal home and how to get there.

Other thoughts as I consider the mountain lion – The janitor as he starts his run up the hill is like us as we drive to church every Sunday morning. What he sees is an incline in front of him, the same view he sees time after time on his way up the mountain. In a similar way we see the same view time after time on our way to church. The runner runs often and we go to church often to move to a goal. The runner for temporal highs, the church goer for eternal highs. When the runner gets to the top of Ford hill and turns around he will see a valley below and in the far distance to the west there is a view of snowcapped glorious mountains, heaven on earth if you will. I have been on the top of Ford hill many times and have seen that view and can attest to its beauty. I took that view for granted and it is reasonable that the janitor also took for granted the bliss of such closeness to the best of God's handiwork.

Now that I have found a true church I think of it in a similar way as the journey up Ford hill. I very much enjoy going to church. On a typical Sunday at this church I feel blessed by the Pastor, who like a trainer or coach, is concerned for the souls of all and that we win the race and cross the finish line through the narrow gate. Each Sunday after the team stretches and warms up by worshiping the Lord in song, the Pastor not unlike a coach gives us proper motivation for the win, but also how to play the game and like a good coach lets us know the pitfalls to be encountered that might cause us to stumble and worst case scenario, not finish the race at all.

~ NAVY SEAL & THE HELICOPTER PILOT ~

1968 Vietnam. Six Navy Seals are up river on a covert mission to do what they are trained to do. Mission completed they make their way down river and into the South China Sea in a small rubber raft to be extracted by a submarine. Something went wrong; the sub was not at the extraction point at the designated time. What to do? Radio silence necessary so that they not be detected by the enemy, they spent the next several hours bobbing around the ocean. Unsure for a time about their fate the whop, whop, whop of a helicopter was heard in the distance. Salvation appeared and sent the lifesaving cable down to each Seal. One by one each Seal extracted from the perils of the ocean.

The sailor in the helicopter responsible for operation of the cable hoist looked down into the face of six different men that day as they looked up at him as he plucked them from the clutches of Davy Jones locker.

Fast forward to 2015 in a coffee shop in Phoenix, Arizona. One of the Navy Seals now an old man is enjoying coffee with friends at their local haunt. A stranger comes in orders a coffee and notices a face he is certain he recognizes from 43 years earlier.

The stranger says to the Navy Seal, "I know you."

The Navy Seal suggests he is mistaken. The stranger emphatically states, "No, I know you. Were you in Vietnam in 1968?"

The Navy Seal affirmed that he was. The stranger asked the Navy Seal, "Were you ever picked up by a helicopter in the South China Sea."

Incredulous, the Navy Seal realizes this stranger knows something he could only know were he there. They talk for a while. The stranger was the cable hoist operator on the helicopter.

The Navy Seal is my friend Jim that I mentioned in Chapter 7. When Jim recounted the story to me I expressed to him what I surmised was an excellent story of redemption. What are the odds that a man in the fog of war extracts six men from the ocean with the roar of the rotors, the mist of the ocean spray, looking down into the faces of six men, each for only 60 to 90 seconds, each reasonably not staring directly into the eyes of the other for the entire hoist, these six men only six of countless others, would remember almost half century later this particular Seal. Why?

Previously Jim had noted that back in his time as a Seal and afterward he was not a standup guy, he had his own journey which years later would lead him to the Cross. I suggested to Jim that in a most unusual way providence was reaching down from the skies that day to save him. For whatever reason that same hand that reached down to him from above, would four decades later reach out to him again. Did or does Jim need a salvific hand again? I don't know, but it is hard, at least for this brain to not consider that this most unusual encounter could or would be for naught. If nothing else that encounter is now in memoriam for the consideration of others.

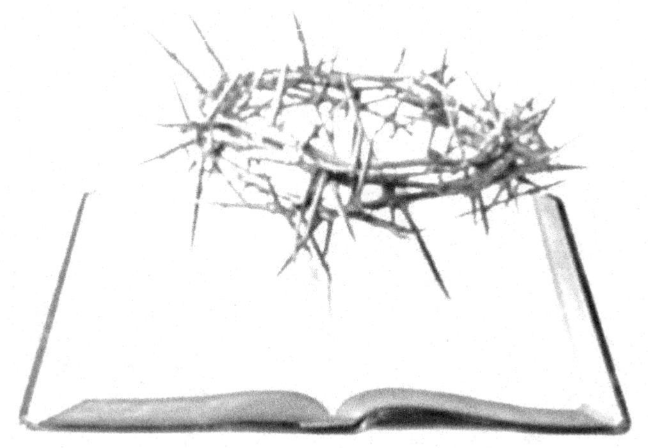

Thinking

Lots of Thinking

I think I'll Take a Nap

Chapter 18

WRAP IT UP

I have been writing for over a year now so it's time to wrap this endeavor up. The process has been illuminating, thought provoking, challenging, and I dare say had a spiritual element, or phrased differently, the process and its elements considered pursuant to my new found knowledge of a philosophical consideration called the metaphysical. Considering, ruminating, discerning, and putting to pen what I hope are realities rightly thought through.

This journey like it, or perhaps not, did come from a place that cannot be explained adequately without the word metaphysical attached. Some of the thoughts that fell out of my brain, most clearly were connected to a mind, in this case mine. In other words for the first time in my life I was confronted with mind vs. brain. Those chemical and electrical discharges in the fleshy mass called the brain coming out in reason, logic, math, love, hate, etc., none of which can be picked from a tree or dug from the ground, or physically extracted from the fleshy brain, but all of which exist.

The summary considerations of this mind is that the chemical and electrical discharges in the brain that connect the eyes, ears, nose, tongue, and touch, to the tangible world are not random and with reason could not happen by chance. Reason about what creation means, i.e., nothing "cannot" create something, it takes a mind….. so you know --- GOD.

The complexity of the human organism above all other organisms makes it clear that man as a creation is unique. History shows that the mind is malleable and can be easily deceived and as noted long ago the greatest deception of Satan was to convince man that he could be like God and or that God does not exist. But, reason it out, starting with the "nothing cannot create something" paradigm.

It strikes me as I finished the above paragraph that most of the reasoning that produced this work while certainly influenced by the sum total of what has entered my brain through the senses, many hours spent alone thinking, contemplating, and reasoning produced the conclusions herein. I say this to make the distinction between a hive mind or mob mentality. I had to think and reason through many never before considered things and I did it alone. All of that to say we are not bees, although we can act like it, for instance the hive mentalities of feminists, gangs, politicians, democrats, republicans, sports fans, BLM, etc.

However, if you sit alone and contemplate why you are here at all, why the perfect balance of gases that allow you to breath, why water and how it works and so abundant to sustain all life, why day and night, why you need sleep, why is music pleasing, why do you see beauty, why do you see ugly, and on and on. The point is you are an individual and you should get away from whatever distraction keeps you from being alone to think on such things. Whether that distraction is a mob, a culture, a group, the internet, social media, and on and on and on. Please find time to be alone and think, reason, and consider that you, in fact, were created and if so reason will tell you that you are created in the likeness of someone who is personal. That my friend is God. The rest of the story is in the Bible. You were born and you can be born again. God, your creator wants and desires for you to know the truth of things and the finality of truth is death. So, then what?

So as not to be misunderstood, being alone to think and contemplate should not be misconstrued to becoming a loner. We are, after all, social creatures, but do stop long enough to think about things by yourself, first you will find there is more to it all than just you, second you will come to use your senses to know your senses and the tangibles they were designed to interact with, and third you will learn to think and consider the intangibles of your mind and in so doing you will come to know God.

Once you get that far you will find you want to know more, especially what God has in mind for mankind and you. Then at some point you will desire to pick up a Bible and know the rest of the story. If you are like me you will then find a church and you will find yourself wanting and desiring to be with believers and sing and worship and study together. That part I cannot explain adequately but it's true.

There is so much to know, for instance, since man's original thoughts on the universe, cells, and atoms, it would take centuries of discovery to find the truth of these spheres of knowledge and we still don't know from all of those advancements in the physical sciences what holds the universe together and what makes the mustard seed, acorn, chicken egg/embryo, fertilized dog egg, fertilized human egg, move in only one direction, and that direction being "specifically" and "only" in the direction of a mustard tree, an oak tree, a chicken, a dog, and the human, respectively.

Notice in the above paragraph it was easy and without proper consideration that I typed the words, "we still don't know." Shame on me, for while man still cannot "explain" electricity, magnetism, or what holds the universe and life together, we do, in fact know. In this instance one need not have a doctorate in philosophy, or PhD. Walk outside anywhere on earth and contemplate that man had nothing to do with what you see in nature and neither did the atheists favorite god, "chance." A piece of paper with a bequeathed title does not negate what is seen, and further a piece of paper with a bequeathed title that requires a denial of what is seen is a lie and therefore not worth the paper it's printed on.

There is sadly one anomaly to the phrase, "we still don't know" that doesn't turn the phrase on its head, although it should, and is quite embarrassing. That would be what the public is led to believe about the rule for atheist scientists verses theist scientists. The greatest minds of all time no matter what discipline of science they pursued have smacked headlong into the existence of God. Some scientists love the quest for knowledge realizing that every new discovery is to know the mind of God just a little better. Sadly, those that kick against the goads we are led to believe are the majority. It cannot be known in the 20th and 21st centuries how many scientists believe in God for the roost of academia is guarded viscously by wolves, so much so that now government legislates by fiat and law that

God and God's intelligence may not be considered nor uttered in the public square and most especially in institutions of learning. Although in the past couple of decades certain scientists are making compelling arguments for "intelligent design." This is thrilling, the arguments are solid and backed up with the very scientific method the secular / atheistic scientist say would disprove an intelligent designer.

A very curious emotionally driven response from the material only crowd rather than a reason driven response is that while some concessions that "intelligent design" may have merit, this intelligence cannot, must not, be given the label God. Awkward in that men or women whom make discoveries of mountains, stars, planets, comets, germs, or do a never before accomplished gymnastic move, skateboard move, etc. are given the honor of naming that new thing on their behalf, when the author of any and all of it is God.

Why then the irrational push back when the obvious intelligent designer is known, and has been known as God since the beginning. The irrationality of the "materialistic crowd" seems to hold sway over the "intelligent designer" crowd to tip toe and tread lightly about boldly saying that these newly discovered proofs are in fact God created. I understand the rational of moving slowly and God is long suffering, but it is sad nevertheless.

I started this project by making a table of contents with topics I thought I might want to cover and for the most part mission accomplished. Chapter 16 – "Just a Thought," clearly were topics ripped from the headlines, some of the crazy not even a thing when I started writing this book, or if it was it was shame that kept it in the closet or at bay. Why, just today I listened to "Louder with Crowder" as they reviewed actual documents from the United Nations purporting that having sex with minors is okay. Well, it's not! Sorry, wrapping it up is hard as the world is burning down around us.

In any event, I have thought for a while now that this work is like a tackle box. Like most people that have felt a call to write about "The Way" for whatever reason all such works are tackle boxes that authors produce as fishers of men. Any consideration in any format whatsoever that can possibly and hopefully have a soul look to Jesus the Rescuer is worth it if only one soul is turned toward Christ.

The thoughts and considerations of "this" and "that" sometimes were related to experience, while others were brand new having never been previously considered. I think most were reasoned, some right, some wrong, and some may get me admonished by my church elders. We'll see! I hope this book causes a conversation or two. I realize some of the thoughts from the brain trust of this ***"Old Man Thinking For the First Time"*** through a lens that found me seeing so very clearly a Man nailed to a Cross, side pierced, blood and water falling to the ground, buried to rise alive, walk among the living and then as attested to by first hand eye witnesses and recorded in affidavit form for all to see in a Book known the world over as the Christian Bible. That attestation is as follows:

> **NKJV --- Acts 1, 9-11** -- *Now when He had spoken these things, while they watched, He was taken up, and a cloud received Him out of their sight. And while they looked steadfastly toward heaven as He went up, behold, two men stood by them in white apparel, who also said, "Men of Galilee, why do you stand gazing up into heaven? This same Jesus, who was taken up from you into heaven, will so come in like manner as you saw Him go into heaven."*

That Man, Jesus, is clearly something greater than man. That Man is God. That Man, that God, that God-Man, Jesus the Rescuer, rescued me. I pray He finds you too and if this work nudges you along, makes you think, then yea!! If so, it hopefully can be said of this work that in some sense it is thought provoking, but if nothing else I hope it might be said of this book that:

THE OLD MAN WAS THINKING

~ THINKING ABOUT THOUGHT ~

I never thought much about thinking,
Never gave it a thought!
But as long as I can remember while I was awake,
My mind would think thoughts whether I liked it or not.

When I lay down my head and drift off to sleep,
The thoughts seem to fade if I think to count sheep.

But as I awake in the morning at the dawn of a new day,
My mind stirs with thoughts conjured up in the night,
That come from a place that doesn't seem right.

As I think about those thoughts,
I am perplexed and at loss.
For my mind seems alive when it should be turned off,
Those thoughts called dreaming are curious for sure.

But it's the thoughts in the day the ones to consider,
Through my senses all I encounter is processed in my brain,
But the noumenon of my mind cannot be explained.

It is this thought that stirred a reaction to act,
To search for meaning in things deemed abstract.
The thought that all this thinking might all be for naught,
Led me to think more, think harder, learn more, and don't stop.

It took most of my life, and now I am old,
But some of that thinking I thought, I thought to write down.
I hope that my thoughts may stir others to think,
And while some of the thoughts that I think, may seem odd,
Were expressed with the first thought...In the beginning God!

JKF 2-20-2024

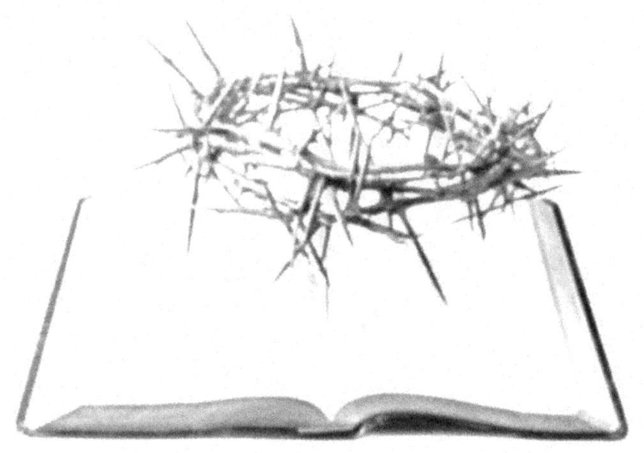

An Advocate for Christ Jesus!

My friend Gary M. Gerrard

EPILOGUE

As has been common and necessary in this journey, many words although in my vocabulary and perhaps understood a little bit by usage, it was very useful for me to look up the definitions of certain words so that I might think on things a little deeper than my normal shallow existence and that I might better articulate this view of the world through these new lenses. I am hopeful that it was helpful for the reader as well.

> **epilogue:** *1) a concluding section that "rounds out" the design of a literary work; 2a) a speech often in verse addressed to the audience by an actor at the end of a play; also: the actor speaking such an epilogue; 2b) the final scene of a play that comments on or summarizes the main action*
>
> **advocate:** *1) one who defends or maintains a cause or proposal; 2) one who supports or promotes the interests of a cause or group; 3) one who pleads the cause of another - specifically : one who pleads the cause of another before a tribunal or judicial court*
>
> **enjoy:** *1) to have for one's use, benefit, or lot; 2) to take pleasure or satisfaction in*

Having never written a book, but knowing that some literary works end with an epilogue I looked up the word. Per the first definition of the word epilogue, it is what might be said that rounds out all of the thoughts that spilled out onto paper of this work, i.e., ***"An Old Man Thinking for the First Time."***

I just stared at the "table of contents" for a while to think on: "Why did I do it?" "What have I done?" And "What do I hope to accomplish?" And now, how do I write an epilogue that "rounds out" what I did?

1. Why did I do it? As noted in the prologue I felt compelled to write that I might go fishing.
2. What have I done? I fashioned a tackle box complete with lures.
3. What do I hope to accomplish? I pray that this work might be seen as a "tackle box" with a "variety of compartments" with a "variety of lures" to fish in the many "variety of lakes" of man to "catch the attention" of men and women to swim to the "surface of reality" and "see the light."

I direct the reader's attention to the definition of "epilogue" above. The definition provides clarity and direction for what this section is. The problem in the definition is the word "actor" that addresses the audience at the end of a play or in this case this literary work. Actor while appropriate and adequate to a play is inappropriate and inadequate to a work that fishes for men.

Wanting to conform to the literary conventions of our time, but realizing that actor doesn't cut it is why I added the definition of "advocate." In other words, if this work is to be summarized by someone other than the author, an "advocate" not an "actor" is necessary. In this case the third definition of advocate, or, ***3) one who pleads the cause of another - specifically: one who pleads the cause of another before a tribunal or judicial court.*** It is this definition that seems appropriate. I need an advocate that might know this work and plead my case and not be ashamed to plead it before a tribunal or judicial court or the church and or the court of God. It turns out I have such an advocate whom is also a true friend. Although my friend may not agree with every point, generally my friend understands and supports the intent.

I introduced the reader to my friend Gary in Chapter 7 – Baptism. Gary and I have been friends since 1967 and he has been a great and true friend. I am grateful to Gary for his consul and his patience as he listened to me read portions of this book back to him for his feedback. (Like he had a choice!)

Gary sent me the poem "Proof of Grace" included in Chapter 7 which was an inspiration for me to dabble into the world of poetry now sprinkled here and there in this book. However, it dawned on me that Gary has a tackle box of poems that could be useful to the cause of fishing for men. One of Gary's poems he shared with me in this journey is titled "The Gift" and advocates nicely I think for this work.

I called my friend and pleaded the case to consider one or more of his poems as an epilogue to this tackle box. We reasoned together and per my good friends' counsel "The Gift," which is not from an actor, but a true advocate of Christ Jesus, The Redeemer of mankind is, I dare say, an excellent advocate epilogue for ***"An Old Man Thinking for the First Time."***

I am truly honored that my friend Gary let me share "The Gift" and that Gary's poem "is" the epilogue. Enjoy!!

~ THE GIFT ~

The thought of someone giving me a gift that had great price;
To take a treasure offered free without my own device.
Questioned my self-worthiness and power to repay;
As though I were but penniless, a beggar in the way.

Then I beheld the merchandise cherished more than gold;
Or anything this world could prize, more than hand could hold.
What is the value of a soul, what could this pauper give;
To mollify the righteous wrath of God that I might live?

Money could not satisfy, the debt that I've incurred;
Works, no matter how I've tried, were worthless and absurd.
Then a thought came quite abrupt, flesh-withering in scope;
Not only was I found bankrupt, but dead and without hope.

The payment then of greatest price I now could clearly see;
I'd never satisfy though twice, I died eternally.
Then I looked beyond myself to Jesus in my stead;
Whose blood became imputed wealth, once risen from the dead.

Now with praise my voice I lift by faith and not of me;
I see salvation's perfect gift; Unspeakable.....and free.

Amen
Gary Michael Gerrard

Printed in the United States
by Baker & Taylor Publisher Services

Printed in the United States
by Baker & Taylor Publisher Services